Renata Enghels, Bart Defrancq, Marlies Jansegers (Eds.)
New Approaches to Contrastive Linguistics

Trends in Linguistics
Studies and Monographs

Editors
Chiara Gianollo
Daniël Van Olmen

Editorial Board
Walter Bisang
Tine Breban
Volker Gast
Hans Henrich Hock
Karen Lahousse
Natalia Levshina
Caterina Mauri
Heiko Narrog
Salvador Pons
Niina Ning Zhang
Amir Zeldes

Editor responsible for this volume
Daniël Van Olmen

Volume 336

New Approaches to Contrastive Linguistics

Empirical and Methodological Challenges

Edtited by
Renata Enghels
Bart Defrancq
Marlies Jansegers

ISBN 978-3-11-099498-8
e-ISBN (PDF) 978-3-11-068258-8
e-ISBN (EPUB) 978-3-11-068267-0

Library of Congress Control Number: 2020934820

Bibliographic information published by the Deutsche Nationalbibliothek
The Deutsche Nationalbibliothek lists this publication in the Deutsche Nationalbibliografie;
detailed bibliographic data are available on the Internet at http://dnb.dnb.de.

© 2022 Walter de Gruyter GmbH, Berlin/Boston
This volume is text- and page-identical with the hardback published in 2020.
Typesetting: Integra Software Services Pvt. Ltd.
Printing and binding: CPI books GmbH, Leck

www.degruyter.com

Contents

Renata Enghels, Bart Defrancq, and Marlies Jansegers
Reflections on the use of data and methods in contrastive linguistics —— 1

Hans C. Boas
A roadmap towards determining the universal status of semantic frames —— 21

Stefan Th. Gries, Marlies Jansegers, and Viola G. Miglio
Quantitative methods for corpus-based contrastive linguistics —— 53

Pauline De Baets, Lore Vandevoorde, and Gert De Sutter
On the usefulness of comparable and parallel corpora for contrastive linguistics. Testing the semantic stability hypothesis —— 85

Stella Neumann
Is German more nominal than English? Evidence from a translation corpus —— 127

Bart Defrancq and Camille Collard
Using data from simultaneous interpreting in contrastive linguistics —— 159

Tom Bossuyt and Torsten Leuschner
WH-*ever* in German, Dutch and English: a contrastive study showcasing the *ConverGENTiecorpus* —— 183

Olli O. Silvennoinen
Comparing corrective constructions: Contrastive negation in parallel and monolingual data —— 221

Åke Viberg
Contrasting semantic fields across languages —— 265

adopting a broader typological spectrum (Silvennoinen). The papers also touch upon a wide variety of phenomena situated at different linguistic levels: cross-linguistic lexical near-synonyms (perception verbs in Gries, Jansegers, and Miglio; inchoative lexemes in De Baets, Vandevoorde, and De Sutter; verbs of cutting and breaking in Viberg; irrelevance particles by Bossuyt and Leuschner; cognitive verbs in Defrancq and Collard), near-synonymous constructions and frames (cf. contrastive negation constructions by Silvennoinen; questioning frames by Boas; verbal and nominal constructions by Neumann).

2 Contrastive linguistics and nature of the data

2.1 In search of the *tertium comparationis*

The practice of comparing languages inevitably leads to the use of notions such as *equivalence* or *correspondence* which are far from undisputed in the literature. In order to compare linguistic structures, items or meanings across languages, the common ground on which to compare, or *tertium comparationis* (Lewandowska-Tomaszczyk 1999), needs to be settled, because "it is only against a background of sameness that differences are significant" (James 1980: 169). This common platform of comparison (Connor and Moreno 2005) needs to be kept constant, and the contrastive linguist's task is to analyze whether in different languages the same linguistic devices are used. Taking such an approach determines several aspects of the research: it determines (i) what types of corpora are useful to build and to exploit, (ii) which concepts the cross-linguistic research can focus on, and (iii) what linguistic strategies used cross-linguistically to instantiate those concepts can be investigated.

With respect to the first aspect, the lack of full comparability across texts in different languages constitutes a major stumbling block in the composition of comparable corpora. As an example, the paper of Bossuyt and Leuschner (this volume) showcases the *ConVerGENTie corpus*, a multilingual comparable corpus including seven subcorpora in English, Dutch, German, French, Spanish, Portuguese and Italian (of each approximately 1.5 million words), collected through identical sampling strategies. It is shown by the authors that the downside of the rigorous corpus design is the limited extension of the database as a whole and, hence, the difficulty to find a representative sample of a particular phenomenon one wants to study in different languages. A solution for this data problem may consist in the reference to additional individual monolingual corpora, and as such, abandon the maximum comparability requirement.

and the compilation of data drawn from social media, like Twitter (e.g. Argüelles Álvarez and Muñoz Muñoz 2012). The use of these resources is not yet widespread among linguists, but, more importantly, the question as to whether and to what extent particular types of data can help answer research questions in the area of contrastive linguistics is still open.

A second challenge relates to the methodological branch of corpus-based contrastive linguistics, which, according to Gast (2015: 5), "is still tender". Advanced methods and procedures (such as logistic and mixed-effects regression techniques, clustering analyses, cf. among others Gries 2013; Levshina 2015), are becoming common ground in linguistics, but are still underrepresented in contrastive linguistics.

The above-mentioned challenges were addressed during the workshop *New Approaches to Contrastive Linguistics: Empirical and Methodological Challenges* organized in September 2017 in Zürich, in the framework of the SLE conference. This volume is a selection of the papers presented in Zürich collected with an aim to reflect on the value and applicability of theories, types of empirical data and advanced research methods in contrastive linguistics. The contributions present contrastive (case) studies and make use of (more) rigorous empirically-based contrastive analyses and/or new data types. As such, some of the main research questions guiding the papers throughout the volume are:

– What (new) types of data are the most useful for what kind of contrastive questions and which data pose risks?
– How can we most efficiently make use of translation corpora for contrastive linguistics, while taking into account linguistic interferences and translation universals?
– Is it mandatory to complement translation data with comparable corpus data, or does this depend on the level of linguistic analysis (e.g. studies on lexical cognates vs. syntactic cognates vs. pragmatic phenomena)?
– How can we go beyond a mere comparison of frequency tables between different comparable corpora?
– Which (advanced) statistical techniques are most suited to deal with the multidimensionality of contrastive research questions?
– How can we compare multifactoriality behind specific linguistic phenomena in two or more languages?

Answers to these questions are provided through the contrastive analysis of many different languages: Romance (Spanish/French/Italian in Gries, Jansegers, and Miglio), Germanic (English/German in Boas, and in Neumann; English/Dutch in Defrancq and Collard, and in De Baets, Vandevoorde, and De Sutter; English/Dutch/German in Bossuyt and Leuschner; English/Swedish in Viberg), or by

The synchronic orientation is shared with linguistic typology studies. However, both disciplines focus on different kinds of research questions and methodologies. Whereas typology "analyzes a few parameters of variation across a wide variety of languages", contrastive linguistics "analyze[s] many different parameters of variation in only two (or three) languages" (König 2012: 10). Thus, whereas typology seeks to classify languages on the basis of a set of well-described properties (or language universals), contrastive linguistics may be concerned with fine-grained analyses of often less-known or incompletely described phenomena. This difference in descriptive granularity is mainly due to the fact that there are far more resources available for doing contrastive linguistics than for typological research. Still, the difference in focus does not prevent the two disciplines from informing each other: a contrastive analysis of just a few languages can spark a broader typological approach of the observed similarities and dissimilarities.[1] Conversely, as a discipline, contrastive linguistics could benefit greatly from the generalization strategies characteristic of typological studies to go beyond the merely descriptive. Moreover, recent typological studies incorporate different types of distributional graphs (e.g. Verkerk 2014) which, from a methodological viewpoint, could inspire more graph-based language comparisons.

Still, until today there are many different challenges to the field of contrastive linguistics that have not yet been fully addressed. First, while a decade ago it was still possible to claim that the focus has mainly been on European (Germanic and Romance) languages (Gast 2012), the contrastive study of Slavic languages and of Chinese has gained ground. But, more languages and language groups should be included in future contrastive studies. Contrastive approaches also struggle with the question what kind of empirical data (translation data, comparable data, etc.) is best suited to reach valid conclusions. A first challenge of contrastive linguistics thus relates to the nature of the empirical data it resorts to. Traditionally contrastive linguists have turned to corpora of translations as a means of establishing cross-linguistic relationships (Granger 2003; Granger, Lerot, and Petch-Tyson 2003; Johansson 2007). However, the use of translations as a source of contrastive data is not undisputed. While the research community is still determining whether translations can be relied upon, new types of parallel data are emerging, such as subtitle corpora (e.g. Levshina 2016) or the Wikipedia Parallel Titles Corpora. In parallel, more and better resources become available to build comparable corpora. The amount of data has increased exponentially with the creation of huge web-based corpora, such as WebCorp and Sketch Engine,

---

[1] This leads van der Auwera (2012) to conclude that contrastive linguistic studies can be viewed as pilot studies in typology, and that three-way studies are better than two-way ones.

Renata Enghels, Bart Defrancq, and Marlies Jansegers
Reflections on the use of data and methods in contrastive linguistics

1 Introduction

The practice of comparing languages has a long tradition characterized by a cyclic pattern of interest (Granger 2003; Schmied 2009). This is due to the fact that contrastive linguistics as a discipline in its own right has been struggling with defining its relationships and limits with respect to adjacent domains such as historical linguistics, typology, intercultural communication and translation studies. The importance of language comparison was indeed already recognized in the historical-philological tradition in the 19th century, and was emphasized again from a purely applied perspective mainly for foreign language teaching (as formulated in the "Contrastive Hypothesis" by Lado (1957)) during a short boom in the 1960s and 1970s. In the 1970s and 1980s, contrastive studies were conducted mainly from a generative (Krzeszowski 1978) or typological viewpoint (König 1996), and small-scaled but highly detailed language comparisons were used as a means to discover correlations between various properties of different grammatical systems or languages (for an example, see Hawkins 1986).

Still, it is not until quite recently that contrastive linguistics has risen to the fore again in linguistic scholarship, and this mainly under the influence of cognitive and functional theories. In the 1990s contrastive linguistics underwent a significant revival, which mainly originated from its meeting with corpus linguistics. This has led to a new wave of corpus-based contrastive studies, gradually extending from morpho-syntactically and phonologically related topics towards new domains, including discourse studies and pragmatics (e.g. House and Blum-Kulka 1986). Ever since this last "revival", contrastive linguistics has been able to gradually define its own agenda with respect to related disciplines (König 2012).

As opposed to historical comparative linguistics, contrastive linguistics has a purely synchronic orientation, and is not necessarily concerned with describing genetic relationships (although a historical description may contribute to a more adequate contrastive one, and allows situating languages on a historical cline).

Renata Enghels, Ghent University, Linguistics Department, GLiMS research group, Gent, Belgium
Bart Defrancq, Ghent University, EQTIS, Ghent, Belgium
Marlies Jansegers, Erasmushogeschool Brussel, Departement Management, Media & Maatschappij, Brussel, Belgium

https://doi.org/10.1515/9783110682588-001

With respect to the level of comparability of concepts and linguistic strategies, Haspelmath (2010) argues for a careful distinction between descriptive categories, which are language specific (e.g. cases, word classes, grammatical relations), and true comparative concepts (e.g. tense, expression of property, irrealis) which are most suited to conduct cross-linguistic and typological studies. Only comparative concepts allow the formulation of generalizations across languages. However, most authors adopt a more moderate position, arguing that complete cross-linguistic correspondence between categories is very rare in natural language (e.g. Altenberg and Granger 2002; Divjak 2010). It would therefore not be realistic to try to proceed from a *tertium comparationis* requiring uniform cross-linguistic categories, but, rather, contrastive studies should start from an assumed maximum similarity.

The collection of papers in this volume shows that the problem of maximum comparability is intrinsically related to any kind of contrastive research. The paper by Boas looks into the universal status of semantic frames. According to this model developed by Charles Fillmore, the comparability across languages (and thus the comparative concepts, in Haspelmath's terms) can be guaranteed by turning to a set of semantic roles. These semantic frames also constitute the starting point for Viberg's contrastive analysis of cutting and breaking verbs in English and Swedish. Most papers, however, including the study of Viberg, face the comparability problem by carefully choosing the input data.

Indeed, ever since the empirical turn reached contrastive linguistics, the assumption of comparability has been sought by resorting to particular types of data such as translations and other kinds of bilingual information. In general terms, the data can be defined as "bilingual output". Gast (2012: 7) distinguishes between "balanced bilingual output" or "data sets which instantiate each of the linguistic systems in ways that do not differ substantially from output produced by native speakers of the relevant languages" and "unbalanced bilingual output" or "data sets which are characterized by deviance from relevant output produced by native speakers in one of the languages involved". The latter type of data can be typically found in learner corpora, in which speakers of different languages produce a particular second language (cf. the *International Corpus of Learner English*, ICLE at UCLouvain). The analysis of the "interlanguage" is said to reveal particular features in which L1 and L2 differ (for an overview on contrastive interlanguage studies, see for instance Granger 2015). However, most of the papers collected in this volume are concerned with the first type of data, namely "balanced bilingual output" as represented by parallel corpora based on translations.

Translation corpora have been said to be of great value regarding the problem of the *tertium comparationis*. As parallel texts are supposed to express the same meaning, some contrastive linguists feel entitled to outsource the search for a *tertium comparationis* to the translators of the texts included in the corpus they use. The additional advantage of such an approach is that cross-linguistic semantic equivalence is established independently from the individual researcher, enhancing objectiveness. Caveats against such an approach are however numerous and are treated in detail in the next section.

2.2 Contrastive linguistics featuring translation data

With its focus on detailed investigation of contrast between a limited range of languages, contrastive linguistics has benefited enormously from the increasing availability of corpus data, and first and foremost of parallel corpus data. The first parallel corpora were set up with language comparison in mind. As Johansson, Ebeling, and Hofland (1996: 87) put it: "[T]he aim of the English-Norwegian Parallel Corpus (ENPC) project is to produce a computer corpus for use in contrastive analysis and translation studies." Numerous parallel databases have been created and exploited, many of which have been assembled in OPUS, the Open Parallel CorpUS, http://opus.nlpl.eu/. Considering that it is the most widespread translated text in human history, the Bible has a special place in the parallel corpus-compilation effort (e.g. the Multilingual Bible Parallel Corpus). Another popular parallel corpus is the Europarl Parallel Corpus, compiled from the proceedings of the European Parliament in all 24 official languages of the European Union and used by one of the studies in this volume (Silvennoinen's analysis of contrastive negation). Many more parallel corpora have been compiled across the globe, some of which are used by contributors to this volume: the Dutch Parallel Corpus in De Baets, Vandevoorde, and De Sutter's study; the English Swedish Parallel Corpus used by Viberg; and the CroCo corpus cited by Neumann. The former corpora are similar in genre distribution, containing both fictional and non-fictional genres, while the CroCo corpus is restricted to essays, speeches and tourism brochures.

With the emergence of corpora in general and the use of large bodies of parallel texts in particular, the last three decades have witnessed an increasing cross-fertilization between contrastive linguistics and translation studies as two converging disciplines (Johansson 2007).

However, the mere fact of working with translated texts poses some significant challenges, precisely because of the specific nature of translation itself.

First, a large part of the agenda for corpus-based translation studies aims at identifying "translation universals", i.e. "features which typically occur in translated text rather than original utterances and which are not the result of interference from specific linguistic systems" (Baker 1993: 243). These characteristics include "explicitation", "simplification", "normalization", "shining through", etc. (cf. among others Laviosa 1998; Olohan and Baker 2000). Such potential systemic differences between translations and non-mediated texts in the same language pose a significant challenge to the use of translations in contrastive linguistics as translation-related phenomena threaten to obscure the systemic properties contrastive linguistics seek to describe. The papers by De Baets, Vandevoorde, and De Sutter as well as Defrancq and Collard in this volume even argue that translation and its spoken variant, interpreting, affect the semantic properties of individual lexical items. Semantic equivalence of parallel texts at the micro-level of lexical items should therefore not be taken for granted. The most frequently cited problem related to using parallel data is so-called "translationese", i.e. the possible interference from the source language during the translation process (cf. among others Gellerstam 1986; Van Hoecke and Goyens 1990). This is especially the case for sister languages within particular language groups (which are also often the elected pairs of contrastive studies). Therefore, some linguists explicitly warn against the use of translation corpora in contrastive linguistics, because they "cannot but give a distorted picture of the language they present" (Teubert 1996: 247) and advocate thus the exclusive use of comparable original texts (Lauridsen 1996).

On the other hand, the existence of translation universals remains highly controversial. For instance, it has been increasingly recognized that the difference between translated and non-translated texts cannot be captured on the basis of the alleged universals alone, but that text type, source language and other factors may be relevant as well (cf. House 2008; Becher 2010). More rigorous and multidimensional corpus-based translation studies are necessary (e.g. De Sutter et al. 2012).

More empirical research is also needed on other issues. For instance: can it be empirically demonstrated that research based on translation corpora vs. comparable data yields different results for the same object of study? Are there certain restrictions in the use of translation or comparable corpora according to the linguistic level of analysis (lexical, (morpho)syntactic, discursive)? Johansson (2007), for instance, argues that discourse-related phenomena such as tag questions are highly sensitive to the problem of translationese, more than other syntactic phenomena (see also Schmied 2009 for more examples).

Taking into account the (dis)advantages of both translation and comparable corpora, linguists (e.g. among others Altenberg and Granger 2002; Viberg 2005; Gilquin 2008; McEnery and Xiao 2008; Mortier and Degand 2009; Vanderschueren 2010; Enghels and Jansegers 2013; Jansegers 2017) have argued in favor of a combination of parallel and comparable corpora, where these two are considered as complementary sources of cross-linguistic data. The majority of the papers in this volume (Bossuyt and Leuschner; De Baets, Vandevoorde, and De Sutter; Gries, Jansegers, and Miglio; Neumann; Silvennoinen; Viberg) further exploit the potential of this combined corpus method.

2.3 Contrastive linguistics featuring new data sources

While more research is needed on the suitability of translations for contrastive linguistics, new types of parallel data also need to be explored. A particular case in point are linguistic phenomena related to spoken rather than written language which, over the last decades, have gained increasing attention among linguists. Spontaneously produced informal language is indeed strongly under-represented in the linguistic data available to a contrastive linguist (and typologist). Two kinds of corpora, used in several papers of this volume, may offer a way out of this practical impasse, namely multilingual parallel corpora of film subtitles and multilingual interpretation corpora.

First, multilingual subtitle corpora are built by downloading subtitles in different languages (through www.opensubtitles.be or www.subscene.com for instance). The advantages of these corpora over traditional parallel written corpora include: (1) the fact that they are freely downloadable, (2) they are closer to spoken language than other parallel corpora mostly including texts, (3) they are said to be a reliable source for lexical norms, and (4) represent many different genres (a.o. Quaglio 2008; Keuleers, Brysbaert, and New 2010; Levshina 2016, 2017). Parallel subtitling corpora have recently even been included in foreign language learning programs through the development of specific applications such as LLN (*Language Learning with Netflix*). However, film or series subtitles also present a number of peculiarities and concerns. In general, it is difficult to guarantee the quality of the subtitling, and the lexical and constructional choices that a professional subtitle translator makes may be influenced by rules of subtitling (e.g. the maximum length of a line).

An important question relates to whether or not subtitles compare to natural conversation. Some important differences have been observed when comparing both genres. TV series and film dialogues contain more greetings and polite formula than natural conversations,[2] and their language may be more dramatic and emotional than in normal conversations (Bednarek 2011). Typical narrative elements (such as discourse markers, disfluency or corrective markers, hedges,

---

[2] Given that they represent more dynamic social situations in which the interlocutors (thus, characters) come and go more often than in normal conversations (Freddi 2012).

tag questions etc.) are underrepresented in film and TV dialogues compared to natural conversations (because of planned discourse and/or space limits). Series' and films' discourse is also less narrative than natural conversations, which may have an impact on the use of particular verbal forms. Finally, vague language forms and constructions are also under-represented in series and films subtitles compared to natural dialogue (Quaglio 2008). These characteristics have been called "filmese" or "serialese" (Levshina 2017: 330). Although many of those differences are mostly a matter of degree (Levshina 2017: 327), they must be taken into account whenever one wants to (contrastively) study phenomena such as address terms or discourse markers, resp. over- and under-represented in subtitles.

A second important issue relates to a possible effect of the aforementioned translationese. It could be even more manifest than in the case of translated texts, because it is often difficult to know the source language of series or movies subtitles (e.g. an English movie can be translated to Spanish directly or through French). However, it appears that the translationese effects are rather moderate and are mostly found in language expressions related to the domain of (in) formality and interactivity. Original subtitles are said to be closer to spontaneous informal language as they include a larger number of discourse markers, greetings, terms of address, and vague expressions. In contrast, the language of translated subtitles is more narrative than that of original subtitles. According to Levshina (2017) this may be due to cultural differences associated with particular languages. A solution to all issues mentioned above would be to compare the outcomes of the analysis of multilingual subtitle corpora with the results coming from comparable original corpora of natural conversations, both in terms of the relative frequencies and the distributional features of a particular phenomenon. This strategy is to some extent applied in the paper by Viberg (this volume).

Parallel corpora of spoken language are another source of under-exploited data in contrastive linguistics. Some contrastive scholars even explicitly warn against using them (Mikhailov and Cooper 2016). However, they have the potential to complement written parallel data in the investigation of systemic properties of languages. Currently, contrastive linguistics is excessively biased in favor of written language. Findings are therefore only poorly generalizable. Research into the properties of mediated spoken language in itself is scarce for lack of suitable data. Only since fifteen years or so are researchers compiling corpora of interpreting (Bendazzoli and Sandrelli 2005) and the amounts of data are still very modest, limiting severely the potential for linguistic exploitation. With the rapid development of automatic speech recognition software, the available data is expected to increase spectacularly over the coming years. Preliminary research results show potential for contrastive studies, with the same caveats as for the written parallel data: interpreting data are potentially affected by the mediation process between languages. However, recent studies have shown that linguistic properties related to translation universals tend to be less manifest in interpreting (Ferraresi and Miličević 2017).

3 Contrastive linguistics and quantitative methods of analysis

Traditional contrastive approaches are based on fine-grained qualitative analyses. However, the last two decades have witnessed a "quantitative turn" in linguistics (and the social sciences) in general. As a consequence, in order to describe particular language phenomena, their occurrence and characteristics are measured and accounted for by statistical methods (amongst others Janda 2013). Glynn (2010) argues that quantification permits verification and therefore also the testing of hypotheses. In other words, quantitative methods facilitate the empirical cycle of proposing hypotheses and testing them. Against this background, contrastive linguists – as well as typologists (Stoll and Bickel 2009) and dialectologist (Szmrecsanyi 2011) – have become increasingly aware of the need to use more advanced quantitative methods and procedures also in multilingual studies. However, the application of statistical tools to this object of study is not always straightforward. The current volume also aims at contributing to the quantitative contrastive toolkit.

The general aim is to disclose quantitative and statistically significant differences in grammatically, lexically or semantically defined areas between two or more languages. It is therefore necessary to go beyond a mere comparison of frequency tables between comparable corpora and look for advanced statistical techniques which are most suited to deal with the multidimensionality of contrastive research questions. The methodological tools suited for the linguistic phenomena within one language cannot be directly transferred to contrastive data without a consideration, given the increased complexity of the latter. Language comparison indeed involves an additional crucial factor to take into account in the models that are developed.

An inherent problem to contrastive research is that it is hard to identify a priori which dimensions related to a particular phenomenon will be interesting and which will not. However, it has repeatedly been stated that, if data are selected that are too heterogeneous and complex, this could lead to invalid conclusions (cf. Weichmann 2011: 199 for more detailed information on those risks). Therefore, the quantitative contrastive procedure should consist of different phases: (1) collect maximally comparable samples of a particular phenomenon in two or more languages; (2) annotate a high number of linguistic properties in the different samples; (3) look for relevant dimensions of contrast through exploratory techniques of bivariate or multivariate nature; (4) the most discriminating variables constitute the input of more detailed quantitative (and qualitative) analyses, which will measure, model and try to explain the impact of observed contrasts.

It is thus important to distinguish between exploratory techniques which identify relevant contrasts in a bottom-up fashion (in this respect the importance of visualization techniques should not be overlooked, see also Gries, Jansegers, and Miglio, this volume), and analytical techniques which may provide explanations for the observed tendencies. With respect to the former, constructional information (including syntactic patterns and lexical neighbors or collocations) allows to quantitatively operationalize semantic (e.g. Divjak 2010 on interlinguistic near-synonymy; see also Gries, Jansegers, and Miglio; and De Baets, Vandevoorde, and De Sutter, this volume) and grammatical differences (Defrancq and Collard, this volume) between languages and constitutes the input of exploratory statistical techniques. These include (1) hierarchical clustering models and tree models (e.g. Random Forests and Conditional Inference trees which group together items based on their degree of similarity and difference, cf. Wiechmann 2011; cf. also Gries, Jansegers, and Miglio, this volume), including (2) Behavioral Profile Analysis (e.g. Divjak and Gries 2006; Gries, Jansegers, and Miglio; De Baets, Vandevoorde, and De Sutter; Defrancq and Collard, this volume), (3) Multidimensional Scaling (providing token-based probabilistic maps which take into account distances between tokens in different languages, cf. Levshina 2016), or (4) Principal Component Analysis (which identifies factor loadings of various linguistic features on the dimension of language variation, cf. Van Wettere 2018). In this volume Silvennoinen and De Baets, Vandevoorde, and De Sutter apply respectively Multiple Correspondence Analysis and Correspondence Regression as exploratory dimensionality reduction techniques.

A subsequent step of the quantitative analysis consists in applying multivariate analytical techniques to measure "the distance" between different languages. Multivariable regression models are among the most cited techniques, including Poisson Regression Analysis (Neumann, this volume), Multinomial Linear Regression (Defrancq and Collard, this volume), Binomial Multivariable Logistic Regression (Wiechmann 2011). However interesting and innovative these approaches are, more methodological consideration should be given to questions regarding the level at which the language parameter operates. For instance, can LANGUAGE simply be taken as a response variable in regression models in order to compare different sensitivities to certain variables in the choice for particular linguistic expressions (as suggested for instance by Wiechmann 2011 in his study on relative clause constructions in English and German)? Another question that should be addressed in future studies is the question of whether there is a difference between the (quantitative) comparison of genetically related and unrelated languages.

4 Overview of the chapters in this volume

Boas' paper offers a succinct introduction to the concept of Fillmorean semantic frames in order to demonstrate their great potential for contrastive research. One of the central questions is whether semantic frames can be used as a *tertium comparationis* and to what degree they might be considered universal or language-specific. The case study used for this demonstration, which involves the QUESTIONING frame in English and German, offers a first step towards establishing a methodology for investigating the potential "universal" inventory of meaning structures useful for research in contrastive linguistics. Coupling this theoretical focus with a methodological focus, Boas proposes three different levels of equivalence that can be used to identify universal frames: translation equivalence, valence equivalence and cultural equivalence. The case study shows how these criteria can be applied not only to frames that occur across languages, but also how they can be used to identify culture-specific frames that do not have equivalents in other languages.

The issue of how advanced empirical methods and statistical techniques mainly developed for monolingual studies can be applied to comparative (and typological) research questions constitutes the central topic of the paper by **Gries, Jansegers, and Miglio**. It is argued that classical monofactorial designs (based on observed (relative) frequencies) can best be complemented by multifactorial ones, given the high complexity and multidimensionality of most linguistic phenomena. The paper offers an impressive overview of different kinds of analyses that can be performed with both comparable or parallel corpus data, paying special attention to advanced visualization techniques. Besides adding to the toolbox of contrastive linguistics, the paper aims at theoretical advancements: high levels of analytical empirical detail may provide usage-based evidence for (cognitive) linguistics statements, and may further uncover the source of cross-linguistic (dis)similarities. The paper puts special emphasis on semantic research questions, and focuses on a series of challenging concepts for the analysis of cross-linguistic near-synonymy: polysemy and sense distinctiveness, prototypicality and identification of discriminatory variables. The concrete case of near-synonymy relates to the verb *sentir(e)* in Spanish, French and Italian and focuses on two kinds of data, namely annotated concordance data and Behavioral Profile vectors based on these annotated data. With respect to the problem of polysemy and sense distinctiveness, the article showcases the results of hierarchical agglomerative cluster analysis, fuzzy clustering approaches and the use of network analysis. The questions related to prototypicality and the identification of discriminatory variables is tackled by analyzing the cue validity (identifying which levels have the highest degree of predictive power), by applying the random forest methodology and association rules, and by looking into different markedness considerations (based on the principle that the most prototypical elements will be least formally constrained).

The purpose of the paper by **De Baets, Vandevoorde and De Sutter** is to investigate semantic differences for four inchoative lexemes between translated (from English) and non-translated Dutch in an attempt to test the usability of parallel corpus data in contrastive research. The authors follow a rigorous methodological path combining (1) the semantic mirroring technique (Dyvik 2010) to select the relevant items, and (2) Behavioral Profile analysis and Correspondence Analysis on parallel and comparable corpus data to analyze and visualize semantic similarities and differences between the lexical items. Their conclusion is that the frequency patterns of the items differ significantly between the translated and non-translated corpus and that, therefore, the internal semantic structure of the field of inchoativity is different. The dominant item in terms of frequency becomes even more dominant in translation, prompting the conclusion that translators seem to overuse the most typical structures in the target language, a tendency called "levelling-out" or "normalization" (Baker 1993). These findings are important for contrastive linguists in that they support the view that parallel (i.e. translated) data are to be handled with care. Contrastive linguists tend to take semantic equivalence for granted when using parallel data, but this study shows that subtle semantic differences occur in translation.

The traditional claim that German has a more nominal character than English has been around for a considerable amount of time. However, up to the present, little systematic empirical evaluation of this claim has been realized and the evidence remains inconclusive. **Neumann**'s paper aims at re-examining this question of the respective quantitative role of nouns in English and German on the basis of the CroCo Corpus, a corpus containing originals and matching translations in eight comparable registers in the language pair. Since the CroCo Corpus includes alignment of matching translations, translation equivalents are used as a *tertium comparationis* to analyze the contrastive nominal structures in more detail. In order to address this question, Neumann carries out a Poisson Regression for count data with mixed effects. The results challenge traditional assumptions about the nominal character of German as well as previous corpus-based claims because they indicate that there is no statistically significant difference in the overall number of nouns per sentence between the two languages. Moreover, it turns out that including translations in the analysis distorts results rather than providing useful information, suggesting that syntactic studies – more than lexical-semantic topics – are more susceptible to the influence of translation-specific features.

Studies of contrastive research based data from parallel corpora are mostly based on written data. This observation constitutes the starting point of **Defrancq and Collard's** paper, which examines to what extent interpreting data are a reliable source of information for linguists interested in contrastive research on features of spoken language. The authors carefully present the various arguments which have been raised in the literature to define interpreting data as useful or not for contrastive research. However, all previous studies share one mayor drawback: the lack of empirical verification of the claims they make with respect to the highly particular nature of "parallel spoken data". Before solving this issue, the article provides further insight into the complex nature of the interpretation process itself, and concretizes some of the linguistic consequences (such as disfluencies) of the high cognitive load typically associated with interpretation. The authors conclude that interpreting data are not less or more suited for contrastive research than translation data, given that both contain the same type of inaccuracies (such as omissions), although possibly to a different degree.

The empirical part of the paper compares verbs that govern embedded *wh*-interrogatives and *that*-complements in Dutch and English. The analysis is built upon the Behavioral Profile Method according to which relative frequencies of different complementation types are assumed to be determined by the semantic properties of the verbs they combine with. The Behavioral Profiles are used to compare identical verb pairs (*know/weten, say/zeggen*) in interpreted and non-interpreted data, and to check whether semantic properties of verbs in mediated versus non-mediated contexts stay constant or are liable to an interpreting effect. The verbs' profiles are collected in three types of corpora: (1) a corpus of non-mediated spoken language drawn from national parliaments (British and Flemish/Dutch), (2) a corpus of non-mediated spoken language drawn from the European Parliament, (3) a corpus of simultaneous interpreting as carried out at the European Parliament. These data serve as the input for a Multinomial Linear Regression which allows to determine the effects of three independent variables (meaning of the verb, mediated or non-mediated nature of the data and the context in which they were produced) on the dependent variable, which is the type of selected complement. The statistical analysis leads to a number of interesting results. First, it shows that equivalent verbs across languages have similar complementation profiles whereas non-equivalent pairs are significantly different. Second, for both languages, Dutch and English, there is a significant effect of the meaning of the verb and the mediatedness of the data; whereas the factor related to the context appeared to be non-significant. As a main cause for the observed interpreting effect, the authors resort to the "normalization hypothesis" according to which, in interpretation, less frequent structures (such as particular *Wh*-complements) tend to be replaced by more frequent ones, in the concrete case the *that*-complement. However, the authors demonstrate that the interpreting effect is real but does not compromise cross-linguistic equivalence relations. As a consequence, interpreting data are defined as not unreliable *per se* for contrastive analysis.

Bossuyt and Leuschner investigate irrelevance particles in English, German and Dutch, i.e. combinations of a *wh*-item and conjoined or disjoint morphemes such as *-ever* (English), *immer/auch* (German) and *(dan) ook* (Dutch), both as primary and secondary particles. The latter are derived from the former undergoing a grammaticalization process that makes them useable for particular discourse functions. Irrelevance particles are collected in two sets of monolingual data: (1) a comparable multilingual corpus set up according to all standards applying to comparable data, and (2) massive collections of online data for the three languages involved. To avoid information overflow, the involvement of the massive online corpora was limited to providing data for combinations of *wh*-items expressing person (*who*) and object (*what*). Systematic comparisons are drawn between the two data collections in terms of frequencies of distributional patterns, showing on the one hand that grammaticalization patterns diverge in the three languages considered, and, on the other, that combined work on small, comparable and large, non-comparable corpora provides an excellent framework for contrastive research: massive non-comparable corpora churn out barely manageable amounts of data. To get a complete, representative picture of the use and distributional pattern of irrelevance patterns, the use of a small comparable corpus offers a suitable controlled environment. Searches in massive online corpora can then be used to complement specific patterns whose absence in the small corpus is likely to be due to the size of the corpus.

Silvennoinen presents a vast parallel corpus study, including eleven European languages, combined with a more limited comparable corpus study on contrastive negation, i.e. sequences of affirmation and negation in which the focus of affirmation replaces the focus of negation. At first sight, a study based on parallel corpora does not seem promising in this context as European languages offer very similar means to express such sequences. A very detailed correspondence analysis of the different linguistic realizations of the sequence, and the functional features that may explain the variation offers interesting tendencies that cannot be fully accounted for neither in genealogical nor in areal terms. Silvennoinen's study is innovative in that it applies quantitative corpus-based contrastive linguistics to a large array of languages, whereas contrastive studies focus mostly on two or three languages only. To deal with the known shortcomings of the use of parallel corpora, Silvennoinen also includes comparable corpus data for Finnish in the analysis, showing that, overall, parallel data are useful and fairly reliable in contrastive linguistics. One considerable translation effect is found, though, in the scope of contrastive negation.

Viberg's paper pays close attention to the search of the most relevant data. It discusses three basic problems related to contrastive research: (1) "equivalence", or the problem of identifying corresponding elements across languages, (2) "authenticity", or the problem of using data that present ordinary language use, and (3) "representativeness", meaning that the researcher needs to look for data that are representative for the languages as a whole, and which are not restricted to a specific type of text. These issues are further examined through a detailed comparison of cutting and breaking verbs in Swedish and English. First, the author argues that contrastive semantics should best be based on the comparison of semantic fields rather than individual lexical items. The concrete analysis is based on the model of Frame Semantics (FrameNet), whose main advantages consist in the fact that (1) it provides a clear picture of the most basic relationships between conceptual structure and syntactic realizations, and (2) it relates cross-linguistically valid frames to the overall structure of language-specific lexicons (see also Boas, this volume). In order to meet the authenticity and representativeness problems, the author proposes to combine different kinds of data. For his study, he compares a large translation corpus consisting of subtitles with monolingual (fictional and press) data and word sketches obtained through Sketch Engine. The subtitle corpus is characterized as representing a special register and is argued to be relatively close to spoken informal language. The empirical corpus study not only provides a more detailed picture of the semantics of cutting and breaking verbs in Swedish and English, it also refines the conclusions of previous typological work. An interesting outcome of the comparison of the different data sources is that there seems to be some dependence between the use of certain verbs, their meanings, and particular registers (that is, informal spoken vs. fictional vs. press texts). Subtitles, for instance, turn out to favor certain types of meanings.

References

Altenberg, Bent & Sylviane Granger. 2002. Recent trends in cross-linguistic lexical studies. In Bent Altenberg & Sylviana Granger (eds.), *Lexis in Contrast. Corpus-based approaches*, 3–48. Amsterdam: John Benjamins.

Argüelles Álvarez Irina & Alfonso Muñoz Muñoz. 2012. An insight into Twitter: A corpus based contrastive study in English and Spanish. *Revista de Lingüística y Lenguas aplicadas* 7. 37–50.

Baker, Mona. 1993. Corpus linguistics and translation studies. Implications and applications. In Mona Baker, Gill Francis & Elena Tognini-Bonelli (eds.), *Text and technology. In honour of John Sinclair*, 233–250. Amsterdam: John Benjamins.

Becher, Viktor. 2010. Abandoning the notion of "translation-inherent" explicitation: Against a dogma of translation studies. *Across languages and cultures* 11. 1–28.

Bednarek, Monika. 2011. The language of fictional television: a case study of the "dramedy" Gilmore Girls. *English Text Construction* 4 (1). 54–84.

Bendazzoli, Claudio & Annalisa Sandrelli. 2005. An approach to corpus-based interpreting studies: developing EPIC (European Parliament Interpreting Corpus). In *Proceedings of the EU-High-Level Scientific Conference Series MuTra 2005. Challenges of Multidimensional Translation.*

Connor, Ulla M. & Ana Moreno. 2005. Tertium Comparationis: A vital component in contrastive research methodology. In Paul Bruthiaux, Dwight Atkinson, William Eggington, William Grabe & Vaidehi Ramanathan (eds.), *Directions in Applied Linguistics: Essays in Honor of Robert B. Kaplan*, 153–164. Clevedon: Multilingual Matters.

De Sutter, Gert, Patrick Goethals, Torsten Leuschner & Sonia Vandepitte. 2012. Towards methodologically more rigorous corpus-based translation studies. *Across languages and cultures* 13. 137–143.

Divjak, Dagmar. 2010. *Structuring the lexicon. A clustered model for near-synonymy*. Berlin & New York: Mouton de Gruyter.

Divjak, Dagmar & Stefan Th. Gries. 2006. Ways of trying in Russian: clustering behavioral profiles. *Corpus Linguistics and Linguistic Theory* 2. 23–60.

Enghels, Renata & Marlies Jansegers. 2013. On the cross-linguistic equivalence of *sentir(e)* in Romance languages: a contrastive study in semantics. *Linguistics* 51 (5). 957–991.

Ferraresi, Adriano & Maja Miličević. 2017. Phraseological patterns in translation and interpreting. Similar or different? In Gert De Sutter, Marie-Aude Lefer & Isabel Delaere (eds.), *Empirical Translation Studies. New Methodological and Theoretical Traditions*, 157–182. Berlin: De Gruyter

Freddi, Maria. 2012. What AVT can make of corpora: some findings from the Pavia Corpus of Film Dialogue. In Aline Remael, Pilar Orero and Mary Carroll (eds.), *Audiovisual Translation and Media Accessibility at the Crossroads*, 381–407. Amsterdam: Rodopi.

Gast, Volker. 2012. Contrastive linguistics: Theories and methods. In *Dictionaries of linguistics and communication science: Linguistic theory and methodology*. Berlin: Mouton de Gruyter.

Gast, Volker. 2015. On the use of translation corpora in contrastive linguistics. A case study of impersonalization in English and German. *Languages in Contrast* 15 (1). 4–33.

Gellerstam, Martin. 1986. Translationese in Swedish novels translated from English. *Translation studies in Scandinavia* 1. 88–95.

Gilquin, Gaëtanelle 2008. Causative *make* and *faire*: A case of mismatch. In María de los Ángeles Gómez González, J. Lachlan Mackenzie & Elsa M. González Álvarez (eds.), *Current trends in contrastive linguistics: Functional and cognitive perspectives*, 177–201. Amsterdam: John Benjamins.

Glynn, Dylan. 2010. Synonymy, lexical fields, and grammatical constructions. A study in usage-based cognitive semantics. In Hans-Jörg Schmid & Susanne Handle (eds.), *Cognitive foundations of linguistic usage patterns*, 89–118. Berlin & New York: Mouton De Gruyter.

Granger, Sylviane. 2003. The corpus approach: a common way forward for Contrastive Linguistics and Translation Studies? In Sylviane Granger, Jacques Lerot & Stephanie Petch-Tyson (eds.), *Corpus-based Approaches to Contrastive Linguistics and Translation Studies*, 17–29. Amsterdam: Rodopi.

Granger, Sylviane. 2015. Contrastive interlanguage analysis: A reappraisal. *International Journal of Learner Corpus Research* 1 (1). 7–24.

Granger, Sylviane, Jacques Lerot & Stephanie Petch-Tyson (eds.). 2003. *Corpus-based approaches to contrastive linguistics and translation studies*. Amsterdam: Rodopi.

Gries, Stefan Th. 2013. *Statistics for linguistics with R. A practical introduction*. Berlin: Mouton De Gruyter.

Haspelmath, Martin. 2010. Comparative concepts and descriptive categories in crosslinguistic studies. *Language* 86. 663–687.

Hawkins, John. 1986. *A comparative typology of English and German. Unifying the contrasts.* London: Croom Helm.

House, Juliane. 2008. Beyond intervention: Universals in translation. *Trans-kom* 1 (1). 6–19.

House, Juliane & Shoshana Blum-Kulka. 1986. *Interlingual and intercultural communication: Discourse and cognition in translation and second language acquisition studies*. Tübingen: Gunter Narr.

James, Carl. 1980. *Contrastive analysis*. Harlow: Longman.

Janda Laura A. (ed.). 2013. *Cognitive Linguistics: The quantitative turn. The essential reader.* Berlin: Mouton de Gruyter.

Jansegers, Marlies. 2017. *Hacia un enfoque múltiple de la polisemia. Un estudio empírico del verbo multimodal* sentir *desde una perspectiva sincrónica y diacrónica*. Berlin: Mouton De Gruyter.

Johansson, Stig. 2007. *Seeing through multilingual corpora. On the use of corpora in contrastive studies*. Amsterdam: John Benjamins.

Johansson, Stig, Jarle Ebeling & Knut Hofland. 1996. Coding and aligning the English-Norwegian Parallel Corpus. In Karin Aijmer, Bengt Altenberg & Mats Johansson (eds.), *Languages in contrast. Papers from a symposium on text-based cross-linguistic studies in Lund, 4–5 March 1994*, 87–112. Lund: Lund University Press.

Keuleers, Emmanuel, Marc Brysbaert & Boris New. 2010. SUBTLEX-NL: A new frequency measure for Dutch words based on film subtitles. *Behavior Research Methods* 42. 643–650.

König, Ekkehard. 1996. Kontrastive Grammatik und Typologie. In Ewald Lang & Gisela Zifonun (eds.), *Deutsch typologisch*, 31–54. Berlin: Mouton de Gruyter.

König, Ekkehard. 2012. Contrastive linguistics and language comparison. *Languages in Contrast* 12 (1). 3–26.

Krzeszowski, Tomasz P. 1978. English reference grammar for Polish learners. *Studies in second language acquisition* 1 (1), 85–94.

Lado, Robert. 1957. *Linguistics across cultures: Applied linguistics for language teachers*. Michigan: University of Michigan Press.

Lauridsen, Karen. 1996. Text corpora and contrastive linguistics: Which type of corpus for which type of analysis?. *Lund studies in English* 88. 63–72.

Laviosa-Braithwaite, Sara. 1998. Universals of translation. In Mona Baker & Kirsten Malmkjær (eds.), *Routledge encyclopedia of translation studies*, 288–291. London: Routledge.

Levshina, Natalia. 2015. *How to do linguistics with R. Data exploration and statistical analysis*. Amsterdam: John Benjamins.

Levshina, Natalia. 2016. Verbs of letting in Germanic and Romance languages: A quantitative investigation based on a parallel corpus of film subtitles. *Languages in contrast* 16 (1). 84–117.

Levshina, Natalia. 2017. Online film subtitles as a corpus: an n-gram approach. *Corpora* 12. 311–338.

Lewandowska-Tomaszczyk, Barbara. 1999. A Cognitive-interactional model of cross-linguistic analysis: New perspectives on *tertium comparationis* and the concept of equivalence. In Barbara Lewandowska-Tomaszczyk (ed.), *Cognitive perspectives on language*, 53–76. Frankfurt am Main: Peter Lang.

McEnery, Tony & Richard Xiao. 2008. Parallel and comparable corpora: What is happening? In Gunilla M. Anderman & Margaret Rogers (eds.), *Incorporating corpora. The linguist and the translator*, 18–31. Clevedon: Multilingual Matters Ltd.

Mikhailov, Mikhail & Robert Cooper. 2016. *Corpus linguistics for contrastive and translation studies*. Oxon: Routledge

Mortier, Liesbeth & Liesbeth Degand, L. 2009. Adversative discourse markers in contrast. The need for a combined corpus approach. *International journal of corpus linguistics* 14 (3). 301–329.

Olohan, Maeve & Mona Baker 2000. Reporting that in translated English. Evidence for subconscious processes of explicitation?. *Across languages and cultures* 1. 141–158.

Quaglio, Paulo. 2008. Television dialogue and natural conversation: Linguistic similarities and functional differences. In Annelie Ädel and Randi Reppen (eds.), *Corpora and discourse: The challenges of different settings*, 189–210. Amsterdam: John Benjamins.

Schmied, Josef 2009. Contrastive corpus studies. In Anke Lüdeling & Merja Kytö (eds.), *Corpus linguistics: An international handbook*, 1140–1159. Berlin: Mouton De Gruyter.

Stoll, Sabine & Balthasar Bickel. 2009. How deep are differences in referential density? In Jiansheng Guo, Elena Lieven, Nancy Budwig, Susan Ervin-Tripp, Keiko Nakamura & Seyda Ozcaliskan (eds.), *Crosslinguistic approaches to the psychology of language: Research in the traditions of Dan Slobin*, 543–555. London: Psychology Press.

Szmrecsanyi, Benedikt. 2011. Corpus-based dialectometry: A methodological sketch. *Corpora* 6 (1). 45–76.

Teubert, Wolfgang. 1996. Comparable or parallel corpora?. *International journal of lexicography* 9. 238–264.

Van der Auwera, Johan. 2012. From contrastive linguistics to linguistic typology. *Languages in contrast* 12 (1). 69–86.

Vanderschueren, Clara. 2010. The use of translations in linguistic argumentation. A case study on Spanish and Portuguese subordinate clauses introduced by *para*. *Languages in contrast* 10 (1). 76–101.

Van Hoecke, Willy & Michèle Goyens. 1990. Translation as a witness to semantic change. *Belgian journal of linguistics* 5. 109–131.

Van Wettere, Niek. 2018. *Copularité et productivité. Une analyse contrastive des verbes attributifs issus de verbes de mouvement en français et en néerlandais*. PhD, Ghent University.

Verkerk, Annemarie. 2014. *The evolutionary dynamics of motion event encoding*. PhD, Max Planck Institute for Psycholinguistics.

Viberg, Åke. 2005. The lexical typological profile of Swedish mental verbs. *Languages in contrast* 5 (1). 121–157.

Wiechmann, Daniel. 2011. Exploring probabilistic differences between genetically related languages. *Languages in contrast* 11 (2). 193–215.

Hans C. Boas
A roadmap towards determining the universal status of semantic frames

Abstract: The Berkeley FrameNet project, founded in 1997, organizes the lexicon of English by semantic frames (Fillmore 1982), with valence information derived from attested, manually annotated corpus examples. The resulting FrameNet database contains more than one thousand frames, together with more than twelve thousand lexical unites and close to 200,000 annotated example sentences. FrameNet data have been used to answer a variety of empirical research questions on the mapping from semantics to syntax and they have been employed in a number of NLP tasks such as role labeling and text summarization. Since the early 2000s, several projects have re-used the semantic frames based on English for constructing FrameNets for other languages, most notably Spanish, Japanese, German, and Swedish, among others. While the tools, corpora, and databases differ from each other, the main organizing principle, the semantic frame, used for structuring the lexicon remains similar across all the FrameNets for different languages. The motivation for re-using semantic frames from English for other languages is the idea that frames are universal, similar to Fillmore's original case roles. However, there has not yet been any empirical investigation into what constitutes "universal" frames or how one can possibly determine the universal status of semantic frames. This paper proposes a systematic method for identifying semantic frames that could be labeled "universal" (based only on data from languages under investigation). We specifically address the question of how semantic frames can be used for contrastive analysis.

Keywords: Frame Semantics, Contrastive Linguistics, FrameNet, Semantic Frames

1 Introduction

This paper investigates the nature of semantic frames as developed by Charles Fillmore during the 1970s and 1980s in order to determine their usability for contrastive linguistics. More specifically, this paper discusses how semantic frames can be used to establish cross-linguistic relationships in the context of what Granger (2003) calls the corpus approach for contrastive linguistics and

---

Hans C. Boas, The University of Texas at Austin, Department of Germanic Studies, Austin, U.S.A

translation studies (see also Gast 2015; Hasegawa et al. 2016; Hansen-Schirra et al. 2017). One of the central questions to be investigated is whether semantic frames can be used as a *tertium comparationis* (see Connor and Moreno 2005; Boas 2010a; Boas 2010b) and to what degree they might be considered universal or language-specific. In doing so, this paper also addresses the question of how semantic frames can be employed to establish comparability between languages, specifically in the context of different types of data. Because of space limitations, this paper focuses primarily on determining how semantic frames based on English can be applied to another language, specifically German. While the insights based on this comparison are potentially limited, they nevertheless provide insights into the question of whether semantic frames could potentially be considered as providing a (limited) "universal" inventory of meaning structures useful for research in Contrastive Linguistics.

The paper is structured as follows. Section 2 provides (1) an introduction to the notion of semantic frame in the Berkeley FrameNet project, and (2) an in-depth look at how FrameNet frames are used to structure and analyze the lexicon of English. Section 3 discusses how semantic frames of English have been re-used for the analysis of lexicons of other languages, most notably Spanish, Japanese, German, and Swedish. Based on ideas proposed by Heid (1996), Fontenelle (1997), and Boas (2002), Section 4 then develops systematic criteria that can be used to identify universal frames such as Motion, Communication, and Ingestion. I propose three sets of criteria: (1) translation equivalence; (2) valence equivalence; and (3) cultural equivalence. Section 5 shows how these criteria can be applied not only to frames that re-occur across languages, but also how they can be used to identify culture-specific frames that do not have equivalents in other languages, such as Personal_relationship. Finally, Section 6 summarizes the paper and provides suggestions for further research.

2 Semantic frames and the Berkeley FrameNet project

This section sets the stage for our discussion of the potentially universal status of semantic frames in the remainder of this paper. More specifically, it discusses the notion of semantic frame and how it has been implemented in the Berkeley FrameNet Project for English. The next section discusses how semantic frames derived on the basis of English have been applied to the analysis of words in other languages.

We begin with the concept of semantic frame, which can be traced back to Fillmore's (1968) seminal paper *The Case for Case*. In this paper, Fillmore proposed a limited set of semantic roles (also known as deep cases) such as Agentive, Instrumental, Dative, Locative, and Objective that were thought to be organized in a hierarchy for realizing grammatical functions. Fillmore's proposals were different from previous approaches, because they explicitly called for the identification of a restricted set of (universal) semantic roles that would be applicable to any argument of any verb. In addition, semantic roles were defined independently of verb meaning, they were regarded as unanalyzable, and each semantic role was supposed to be realized by only one argument. At the same time, each syntactic argument should bear only one semantic role and semantic roles were thought to be universal and applicable across languages. As such they were thought to be capable of capturing the lexical semantics of verbs at a level at which they could be compared across languages, while also providing language-specific hierarchies and linking rules. Fillmore's (1968) concept of semantic roles seemed initially attractive to many researchers, but during the 1970s multiple problems concerning the granularity of semantic roles and their systematic mapping properties led the research community to abandon the original concept of Fillmore's semantic roles (see Fillmore 1977; Levin and Rappaport Hovav 2005; and Boas and Dux 2017 for an overview).

In a series of publications throughout the 1970s, Fillmore revised and extended his original theory of case, eventually leading him to propose a theory called Frame Semantics. His new approach to meaning was driven by the insight that cultural and world knowledge motivate much of what we regard as "meaning" and that such knowledge is embedded in linguistic expressions. The theory of Frame Semantics (Fillmore 1982, 1985), originally developed on the basis of data from English, emphasized that solely truth-conditional semantic approaches cannot account for these aspects of word meaning, necessitating a "semantics of understanding" (see also Fillmore 1975). The core ideas underlying research in Frame Semantics are summarized in the following quote:

> A word's meaning can be understood only with reference to a structured background of experience, beliefs, or practices, constituting a kind of conceptual prerequisite for understanding the meaning. Speakers can be said to know the meaning of the word only by first understanding the background frames that motivate the concept that the word encodes.
> (Fillmore and Atkins 1992: 76–77)

While the main concepts of Frame Semantics were originally developed by Fillmore on the basis of English during the 1970s and 1980s, several other studies during the 1980s explored the application of semantic frames to languages other than English, including German (Lambrecht 1984) and Hebrew (Petruck 1986).

Fillmore and Atkins' (1992) detailed study of *to risk* focused on lexicographic and grammatical issues regarding the syntactic realization of (semantic) participants (a.k.a. roles). Their seminal research offered a detailed investigation of how the concept of 'risk' is realized linguistically by (1) identifying all participants in the risk scenario, (2) documenting how participants are formally realized in concrete linguistic expressions, and finally (3) summarizing the various ways in which the concept can be realized syntactically. They show, for instance, that 'risk' can be construed in (at least) two ways and therefore evokes two different frames, with expressions such as *take a risk* perspectivizing the risky activity carried out by the risk-taker and *put at risk* perspectivizing the entity endangered by the risky activity (see also Ohara 2009 and Boas and Dux 2017). Fillmore and Atkins' (1992) laid the groundwork for the development of FrameNet (http://framenet.icsi.berkeley.edu), which started at the International Computer Science Institute in Berkeley, California, in 1997.

FrameNet (FN) organizes the lexicon of English by semantic frames, with valence information derived from attested, manually annotated corpus examples (Fillmore and Baker 2010, Ruppenhofer et al. 2013, 2017). FrameNet's workflow involves a number of stages starting with the selection of a target word (including multi-word expressions) and determining the frame it evokes by "characterizing schematically the kind of entity or situation represented by the frame" (Fillmore/Petruck/Ruppenhofer/Wright 2003: 297). To achieve this goal, FN researchers use a combination of corpus data and intuition to determine what features are necessary for the understanding of the word and assign mnemonic labels to each of the Frame Elements (FEs) defining the frame. Next, a thorough corpus search is conducted for expressions deemed semantically similar to the target word in order to determine whether they have the same frame semantics and Frame Elements, thereby arriving at a full list of lexical units for the frame (a lexical unit (LU) is a word in one of its senses).[1] For each of these lexical units, a number of representative corpus sentences are extracted and manually annotated for both syntactic and (frame-)semantic information. Specifically, the grammatical function and phrase type for each Frame Element occurring in the sentence is documented, resulting in layered annotations. The resulting FN database contains more than 1,300 frames, together with more than 13,000 lexical units and more than 200,000 annotated example sentences (see Baker, Fillmore and Cronin 2003 for an overview of the FN database).

---

[1] FrameNet takes a splitting approach to determining the multiple senses of a word. Whenever there is enough corpus evidence available that supports the characterization of a particular use (sense) of a word as evoking a separate semantic frame, then FrameNet creates an extra entry for another LU (a word in one of its senses).

To illustrate the end-result of this workflow, consider the information about the LU *to crawl* evoking the Self_motion frame in the FN database. Typing *to crawl* into the search form on the FrameNet website yields three different links relevant to *crawl* in the Self_motion frame.[2] Clicking on the first link provides the user with detailed information about the Self_motion frame, as in Figures 1–3 below. The top of the frame definition in Figure 1 provides a prose description of the Self_motion frame, in which the target-evoking LUs are marked in black, while the Frame Elements (FEs) are marked in color.[3] The definition of the frame includes example sentences taken from the British National Corpus to illustrate how the prototypical meaning of LUs evoking the frame is realized in context. Each colored FE in the definition is a situation-specific semantic role that is defined more precisely in the remainder of the frame description, as shown in Figures 2 and 3 below.

Self_motion

Lexical Unit Index

Definition:

The Self_mover, a living being, moves under its own direction along a Path. Alternatively or in addition to Path, an Area, Direction, Source, or Goal for the movement may be mentioned.

She WALKED along the road for a while.

Many of the lexical units in this frame can also describe the motion of vehicles (e.g., as external arguments). We treat these as belonging in this frame.

The cars SCOOTED slowly towards the intersection.

Self_motion most prototypically involves individuals moving under their own power by means of their bodies. Many words also specify the manner of motion (*swim, walk*). This frame contains mostly words that fit this prototypical scenario, but the frame itself does not specify whether a separate vehicle is impossible, necessary, or unspecified. Lexical units that involve separate vehicles are associated with FEs that are not appropriate for the more general case of motion, so they are placed in the Operate_vehicle or Ride_vehicle frames (e.g., *He drove across the country, She flew to Europe*).

Figure 1: Definition of Self_motion frame.

Following the definition of the Self_motion frame, there are three more parts that make up the description of the frame. First, the definitions of so-called core FEs in Figure 2. Core FEs are those FEs which are central to a semantic frame (see Ruppenhofer et al. 2017).

Non-core Frame Elements, as in Figure 3, are FEs that are grammatically less prominent than core FEs. They can also be thought of as less semantically central to a semantic frame. For example, the non-core FE Duration (The amount of time for

---

[2] Other results include the noun *crawl* (which also evokes the Self_motion frame) and a different LU *to crawl*, which evokes the Abounding_with frame (e.g. *The table is crawling with ants.*)
[3] In this paper, names of Frame Elements and annotated sentences including Frame Elements appear in different shades of grey. The color representation refers to the online lexical entries of FrameNet.

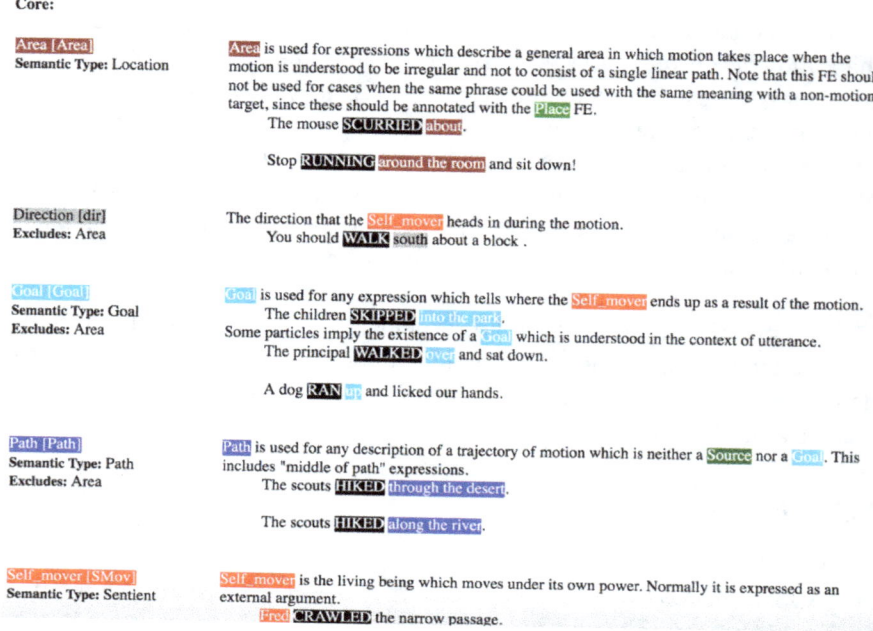

Figure 2: Core frame elements of the Self_motion frame.

which a state holds or a process is ongoing) in Figure 3 is a non-core FE of the Self_motion frame. In contrast, the FE Self_mover (The living being that moves under its own power. Normally, it is expressed as an external argument) in Figure 2 is a core FE of the Self_motion frame. Other information provided for each frame description includes a list of frame-to-frame relations and a table of LUs that evoke the frame (see Petruck et al. 2004; Ruppenhofer et al. 2013; Boas 2017a; Boas and Dux 2017).

Recall that frame descriptions, including the definition of the frame and its FEs, are the end-result of a workflow involving several lexicographers relying on their intuitions and coming to an agreement about frame definitions that are supported by corpus evidence. As we will see in Section 3 below, these frame descriptions derived on the basis of English can be reused for the description and analysis of LUs in other languages, too. This means that frame descriptions can be thought of as a type of cross-linguistic (and possibly universal) metalanguage for lexical analysis.

Returning to our discussion of *to crawl* evoking the Self_motion frame, users can access two different types of reports about each LU. The Annotation Report provides the corpus sentences together with their frame-semantic annotations, the result of the manual annotation by FN annotators. These sentences form the

Non-Core:

Concessive []
An event or circumstance that would not be expected given the nature of the particular Self_motion event.

Coordinated_event [coo]
The label Coordinated_event is to be used for phrases denoting an event-it does not allow states-that the Traversing is rhythmically aligned with. The Coordinated_event is conceived of as independent: it would occur regardless of the event expressed by the target, which is not even an incidental or optional sub-part of the Coordinated_event.

Cotheme [Thm_c]
Semantic Type: Physical_object
An entity whose motion is correlated with that of the Self_mover, following and tracking the Self_mover, being followed and tracked, or with both parties mutually matching Paths.
We CLOMPED down to the shore with a whole troop of younglings.
I had little hope of catching up, but I CRAWLED after her as fast as I could.
The troops MARCHING in front of him paid no attention to the beggar by the roadside.

Depictive [Dep]
Semantic Type: State
Depictive phrase describing the actor of an action
We WANDERED around naked.

Distance [Dist]
Semantic Type: Quantity
Any expression which characterizes the extent of motion expresses the frame element Distance.
I barely HOBBLED six feet before collapsing.
We HIKED a short distance into the forest and sat down.

Duration [Dur]
Semantic Type: Duration
The amount of time for which a state holds or a process is ongoing.

Figure 3: Non-core frame elements of the Self_motion frame.

Purpose	(8)	VPto.Dep (7) Sfin.Dep (1)
Result	(2)	VPing.Dep (2)
Self_mover	(144)	NP.Ext (143) CNI.-- (1)
Source	(25)	PP[off].Dep (6) PP[out].Dep (11) PP[from].Dep (6) AVP.Dep (6)
Speed	(2)	AVP.Dep (1) PP[at].Dep (1)

Figure 4: First part of the lexical entry report of *to crawl* in the Self_motion frame: Summary of FEs and their syntactic realizations (excerpt).

basis for the Lexical Entry Report, which consists of two parts. It first offers a list of how individual FEs are realized syntactically in the sentences annotated by the FN team. Figure 4 shows the different ways in which some of the FEs of the Self_motion frame are realized syntactically with *to crawl* (not all FEs are shown because of space limitations).

Figure 4 shows how FEs differ in their syntactic realizations in terms of phrase type (e.g. NP or PP) and grammatical function (e.g. Dep(endent)). While the FE Result has only one syntactic realization with *to crawl*, namely as a dependent VPing, other FEs exhibit a greater range of syntactic realizations: The FEs Purpose, Self_mover, and Speed each exhibit two different types of syntactic realizations while the FE Source shows four different types of syntactic realizations.

Note that FN captures not only overt syntactic realizations of FEs, but also cases in which FEs are not explicitly realized. Such cases are known as null instantiation, of which there are three different types. In Figure 4, the FE Self_mover may be null instantiated in terms of a Constructional Null Instantiation (CNI) such as the passive construction.[4] The two other types of null instantiation happen through the idiosyncratic licensing of a LU and cannot be captured in terms of higher-level generalizations such as grammatical constructions. In the partial valence pattern table for *to crawl* in the Self_motion frame in Figure 5 below we find one case of Indefinite Null Instantiation (INI), where the FE Path is null instantiated. INIs are instances in which FEs are merely existentially bound. In contrast, Definite Null Instantiation (DNI) are instances in which FEs are unrealized but which have to be recoverable from context (there is no example of DNI in the FN entry of *to crawl*). For more information on the different types of null instantiation, see Fillmore (1986), Lyngfelt (2012), Boas (2017b), and Ruppenhofer (2018).

Let us now turn to the second part of a LU's Lexical Entry Report, the valence pattern report, which is based on corpus examples that have been annotated by hand by FN annotators. It provides a summary of the many different ways in which combinations of FEs in sentences (so-called Frame Element Configurations (FECs)) are realized syntactically. For example, at the top of Figure 5 we find the FEC [Goal, Manner, Self_mover, Time], which is realized syntactically as [PP[to].Dep, PP[on].Dep, NP.Ext, PP[at].Dep]. While some FECs have only one particular syntactic realization, others may have multiple syntactic realizations as the third FEC [Goal, Path, Self_mover] from the top in Figure 5 shows. It has two syntactic realizations. Because of space limitations, only 6 FECs of the valence table for *to crawl* are shown in Figure 5. Overall, the valence table for *to crawl* has a total of 60 FECs with a total of 112 different syntactic realizations.

This brief overview illustrating the level of detail in FN lexical entries is important for our discussion of potential frame universality, because it shows three

---

[4] For an overview of the so-called Constructicon, an online database of corpus-based construction entries, parallel to the FrameNet lexical database, see Fillmore (2008), Boas (2017a), and Ziem and Boas (2017).

1 TOTAL	Goal	Manner	Self_mover	Time
(1)	PP[to] Dep	PP[on] Dep	NP Ext	PP[at] Dep
1 TOTAL	Goal	Path	Purpose	Self_mover
(1)	PP[to] Dep	PP[along] Dep	Sfin Dep	NP Ext
2 TOTAL	Goal	Path	Self_mover	
(1)	PP[into] Dep	PP[up] Dep	NP Ext	
(1)	PP[to] Dep	PP[around] Dep	NP Ext	
1 TOTAL	Goal	Path	Self_mover	Time
(1)	PP[into] Dep	AVP Dep	NP Ext	PPing[before] Dep
1 TOTAL	Goal	Purpose	Self_mover	
(1)	AVP Dep	VPto Dep	NP Ext	
1 TOTAL	Goal	Purpose	Self_mover	Source
(1)	AVP Dep	VPto Dep	NP Ext	AVP Dep

Figure 5: Second part of the lexical entry report of *to crawl* in the Self_motion frame: Summary of valence patterns showing how FEs are realized syntactically (excerpt).

things. First, each FN entry captures, among other things, the different semantic configurations of FEs and their various syntactic realizations. This idiosyncratic information differs from LU to LU evoking the same semantic frame in English. While there is some overlap in how LUs evoking the same semantic frame realize their FEs syntactically, the majority of cases of how LUs realize their FEs syntactically is idiosyncratic and cannot be captured at a more general or abstract level (see Boas 2010c; Dux 2016). Second, at the lexical level there appears to be very little predictability as to how the semantics of a frame is realized syntactically. Unlike research claiming that verbs closely related in meaning also exhibit the same patterns of syntactic distribution (Levin 1993), research on English verbs in Frame Semantics by Baker and Ruppenhofer (2002), Boas (2003b), Boas (2011b), and Dux (2018) shows that most aspects of a verb's syntactic distribution appear to be idiosyncratic (when compared to other verbs closely related in meaning). Third, even though the LUs differ so drastically in how they realize the FEs of the same frame differently, their meanings can still be captured at a somewhat general level that goes beyond the individual LU, namely the semantic frame. As I will show in Sections 3 and 4 below, this level of description and generalization does not only hold for English, but also for other languages, which means that the concept of semantic frame should be considered as a basis for contrastive (and potentially cross-linguistic) analyses.[5]

FrameNet data have been used to answer a variety of empirical research questions on the mapping from semantics to syntax, they have been employed in a number of NLP tasks such as role labeling and text summarization, and they have been used for supporting foreign language teaching (for an overview, see Boas and Dux 2017). The next section discusses how semantic frames derived on the basis of English have been used to explore the lexicons of other languages, thereby establishing FrameNet databases for these languages. In this context it is important to keep in mind that the primary nature of these efforts is lexicographic in nature.[6] We begin by looking at some preliminary case studies that laid the theoretical groundwork for the architecture of multilingual FrameNets.

3 Semantic frames for multilingual lexicography

3.1 Exploring contrastive lexicon fragments

Exploratory studies such as Heid (1996) and Fontenelle (1997) show how English semantic frames could be applied to the analysis of the lexicons of other languages, such as French and German. The motivation for re-using semantic frames from English for other languages was the idea that frames could be universal (similar to Fillmore's 1968 original case roles) and that they could be used to create parallel lexicon fragments. Subsequent research demonstrates in greater detail how English-based semantic frames derived on the basis of English data could be employed for the analysis of polysemy structures of English verbs and their translation equivalents in other languages. One of the main goals of this research is to determine whether semantic frames could be used as a *tertium comparationis*, or what Connor and Moreno (2005: 157) call "a platform for comparison".

---

[5] FrameNet differs from other lexical databases such as WordNet (Fellbaum 1998) in that it does not primarily rely on lexical relations such as synonymy, meronomy, etc. to structure the lexicon. Instead, it makes use of independent organizational units that are larger than words, i.e. semantic frames (see Boas 2005b). As such, FrameNet facilitates a comparison of the comprehensive lexical descriptions and their manually annotated corpus-based example sentences with those of other LUs (also of other parts of speech) (see Boas 2009b).
[6] For different approaches of how semantic frames can be employed for translation studies, see Boas (2013) and Czulo (2013).

For example, following Fillmore and Atkins (2000), Boas (2001) employs semantic frames to investigate the polysemy structures of English and German motion verbs to find out whether a contrastive analysis of their polysemy structures allows for systematic predictions about translation equivalence or not. Based on examples such as those in (1) and (2), Boas (2001: 64) notes that some usages of the verbs *to run* and *to walk* evoke the same semantic frame, while other usages evoke different semantic frames: the semantics of *run* in (1a) is similar to the semantics of *walk* in (2a) in that both LUs evoke the Self_motion frame, in which a Self_mover moves on its own volition form a Source along a Path to a Goal.

(1) a. *Julie ran to the store.*[7]
    b. *Julie ran Pat off the street.*

(2) a. *Rod walked to the door.*
    b. *Rod walked Melissa to the door.* (Boas 2001: 64)

In contrast, *walk* differs from *run* in at least two respects, according to Boas. First, the manner of motion of *walk* is different from *run* in that the speed is slower, but this difference appears to have no direct influence on the type(s) of frame(s) evoked by the two verbs. Second, there is a difference in the types of semantic frames evoked by the two verbs. While both evoke the Self_motion frame, *run* also evokes the Cause_motion frame (i.e. the usage of *run* in (1b) constitutes a separate LU from the usage of *run* in (1a)), involving contact with force.[8] Note that the usage of *walk* in (2b) does not evoke the Cause_motion frame (there is

---

[7] Note that the examples in (1) and (2) are representative of only one syntactic realization of a Frame Element Configuration (see above) of the verbs *to run* and *to walk* evoking the Self_motion and Cause_motion frames. The valence tables of the LUs exhibit significant differences. For example, the valence table of *to walk* in the Self_motion frame lists many more FECs and syntactic realizations than the valence table of the LU *to run* in the Self_motion frame, which lists different FECs and syntactic realizations.

[8] FN definition of the Cause_motion frame: An Agent causes a Theme to move from a Source, along a Path, to a Goal. Different members of the frame emphasize the trajectory to different degrees, and a given instance of the frame will usually leave some of the Source, Path and/or Goal implicit. The completion of motion is not required (unlike the Placing frame, see below), although individual sentences annotated with this frame may emphasize the Goal. This frame is very broad and contains several different kinds of words that refer to causing motion. Some words in this frame do not emphasize the Manner/Means of causing the motion (transfer.v, move.v). For many of the others (cast.v, throw.v, chuck.v, etc.), the Agent has control of the Theme only at the Source of motion, and does not experience overall motion. For others (e.g. drag.v, push.v, shove.v, etc.) the Agent has control of the Theme throughout the motion; for these words, the Theme is resistant to motion due to some friction with the surface along which they move.

no contact with force), but rather the Cotheme_motion frame, in which a Theme moves together with the Cotheme in a Direction (along a Source, Path, and Goal).⁹ In other words, the four LUs in (1)-(2) above evoke a total of three different semantic frames: Self_motion, Cause_motion, and Cotheme_motion. Note that this is not only relevant to these two verbs, but applies to a broader variety of verbs, too, as Table 1 shows.

Table 1: Different verbs / LUs evoking different semantic frames.

	Self_motion	Cause_motion	Cotheme_motion
run	X	X	
walk	X		X
crawl	X		
hike	X		
scoot	X	X	
trail			X
slam		X	

The distribution of LUs and semantic frames evoked by them is only a small snapshot from the FN lists of LUs evoking the the three frames. But they illustrate an important point, namely that there is no direct way of predicting which LUs will evoke which frames. In other words, just because a particular LU evokes the Self_motion frame does not automatically mean that it also evokes the Cause_motion or the Cotheme_motion frames. The data thus suggest that the types of meanings cannot be systematically predicted based on frame membership alone, but that they need to be catalogued manually.¹⁰

---

9 FN definition of the Cotheme frame: This frame contains words that necessarily indicate the motion of two distinct objects. The Theme is typically animate and is expressed the same way a Self-mover is expressed in the Self_motion frame--i.e. as the subject of a target verb. The Cotheme may or may not be animate and is typically expressed as a direct object or an oblique. Source, Path, Goal, and the other frame elements common to motion words also regularly occur with the words in this frame. For more details, please see [https://framenet2.icsi.berkeley.edu/fnReports/data/frameIndex.xml?frame=Cotheme].

10 Fillmore and Atkins (2000: 103) provide a much more detailed corpus study of *to crawl*, employing corpus data to show that the different senses of motion verbs can be represented in terms of a semantic network diagram. In such a systematic representation of a verb's various meanings (in terms of frames), there is one central sense and sense extensions are represented by lines connecting the central sense and more extended senses. Fillmore and Atkins' comparison of English

Looking at the distribution of English LUs and the frames they evoke one might ask: How is this distinction relevant to a paper on contrastive linguistics? It is relevant because semantic frames are important not only for determining and modeling sense distinctions and polysemy networks in one language, but also across languages, thereby serving as a helpful structuring device for identifying, linking, and investigating word senses across languages. Part of this research asks the question of whether the semantic frames derived on the basis of English are also applicable for the description and analysis of other languages and whether semantic frames could be regarded as potentially universal linguistic concepts applicable across the languages of the world.

But before examining the question of how "universal" semantic frames are, let us first take a more straightforward bottom-up approach by determining how semantic frames derived on the basis of English can be applied to just one other languages. Consider, for example, the German counterparts of (1) and (2) above. Boas (2001) shows that while the basic types of situations described by *run* and *walk* in (1a) and (2a) are typically expressed by *rennen* 'run' and *gehen* 'go' (both evoking the Self_motion frame), thereby showing considerable syntactic and semantic overlap, there is no such overlap between *run* in (1b) above and *rennen* in (3b).

(3) a. *Tina rannte zum   Geschäft.*
    Tina ran   to-the store
    'Tina ran to the store.'
  b. **Tina rannte Enno von   der Strasse ab.*
    Tina ran.   Enno from the street   off
  c. *Tina drängte Enno (beim Rennen) von   der Strasse ab.* (Boas 2001: 65)
    Tina pushed. Enno while running from the street   off
    'Tina ran Enno off the street.'

The data in (3b) show that there is no LU of *rennen* that evokes the Cause_motion frame in parallel to run in (1b). This is a case of diverging polysemy (Altenberg and Granger 2002; Viberg 2002), in which items in two languages have different types and networks of meaning extensions. In the case of German *rennen* and English *to run*, this means that the translation equivalent of the Cause_motion sense evoked by *run* in (1b) is expressed by a completely different type of verb,

---

crawl with its French counterpart *ramper* demonstrates that even though the basic senses of the two verbs can be regarded as translation equivalents of each other, the semantic network of *ramper* with its sense extensions is very different from the semantic network of *crawl*.

namely *abdrängen* 'push aside' in (3c). Note that *abdrängen* itself does still not provide an adequate translation equivalent of the Cause_motion sense of *to run*, because it does not encode the manner in which the Theme (i.e. *Enno* in (3c)) has been caused to move to its end location. Information about the manner in which the caused motion took place has to be provided by a separate phrase *beim Rennen* ('by means of running'), because German *abdrängen* conforms to a different type of lexicalization pattern than English *to run*. Without this information it is not clear how the caused motion took place.

Similar observations can be made about the German translation equivalents of *walk* in (2) above: Boas (2001: 65) shows that the German translation equivalent of *walk* in (2a) evoking the Self_motion frame, the verb *gehen* in (4a), cannot be used as a translation equivalent for the Cotheme sense of *walk* in (2b). Instead, the different lexicalization in German requires that a different verb be used to express the Cotheme semantics, in this case *begleiten* ('to accompany').

(4) a. *Bernd ging zur Tür.*
    b. **Bernd ging Anna zur Tür.*
    c. *Bernd begleitete Anna zur Tür.* (Boas 2001: 65)

Observations such as these lead Boas (2001) to the conclusion that semantic frames are a useful tool for conducting a contrastive analysis of English motion verbs and their German translation equivalents. In a series of other papers, Boas presents further case studies employing semantic frames as contrastive structuring devices to create and link parallel lexicon fragments for communication verbs in English and German (Boas 2002), English and German verbs describing operating a vehicle, affecting a person's mental state, and transportation (Boas 2003a), and communication verbs in English, German and Spanish (Boas 2005a).

What unifies these case studies are three important insights. First, semantic frames derived on the basis of English can also be employed for the description and analysis of verbs in other languages, laying the foundation for creating parallel lexicon fragments. Second, semantic frames serve as a useful tool for linking parallel lexicon fragments between English, German, and other language pairs. Third, as the examples with *run* and *rennen* above have demonstrated, it is very difficult to predict the exact types of sense extensions (and the frames evoked by them) of a translation equivalent of an English verb. Just because the basic sense of an English motion verb evokes the Self_motion frame does not automatically mean that another sense of the same verb evokes the Cause_motion or the Cotheme frame (see Table 1 above). This means that in most cases parallel lexicon fragments cannot be predicted on the basic sense of a verb (i.e. one LU) evoking a particular frame, but the sense extensions (other LUs) and the frames evoked by them (the other LUs) need to be identified and catalogued by hand and linked to their parallel lexicon fragment. We now turn to a discussion of how the idea of using English semantic frames for the description and analysis of other languages has been implemented in FrameNet-type projects for other languages.

3.2 Multilingual FrameNets: How universal are semantic frames?

Over the past 15 years, the Berkeley FrameNet database for English has served as inspiration for FrameNets for other languages. Building on insights by Heid (1996), Fontenelle (1997), Fillmore and Atkins (2000), and Boas (2001, 2002, 2005a), these other FrameNet projects differ in the types of corpora, tools, databases, workflows, and methodologies they employ (for a discussion, see Boas 2009b), but they are all similar in that they seek to create lexical entries employing semantic frames from the Berkeley FrameNet database for English.[11] In 2002, Spanish FrameNet started as the first large-scale FrameNet for a language other than English (Subirats and Petruck 2003; Subirats 2009). Since then, FrameNets for other languages, including Japanese (Ohara et al. 2004; Ohara 2009), German (Burchardt et al. 2009), Swedish (Borin et al. 2010), Brazilian Portuguese (Salomão et al. 2013), and French (Candito et al. 2014) have been applying semantic frames derived on the basis of English to the description and analysis of the lexicons of their languages.[12]

Due in large part to funding constraints, none of these FrameNets offer the same amount of coverage or continuity as the Berkeley FrameNet for English, which has been in operation since 1997. For example, the SALSA project for

---

11 Parallel efforts are under way to create parallel repositories of construction entries, so-called constructicons for a variety of languages. See Fillmore (2008), Boas (2017), Ziem and Boas (2017), Boas et al. (2019), and the contributions in Lyngfelt et al. (2018) for details.
12 This does not necessarily imply that all FrameNets for other languages started out only with the semantic frames for English. Instead, each FrameNet has been using their own linguistic data in order to create their frames for their languages, while at the same time keeping an eye to how those frames compare with frames created for English by the Berkeley FrameNet project. Note that besides general-domain multilingual FrameNets, there are also domain-specific FrameNet-type projects and databases dealing with specific aspects of the lexicon, such as the Kicktionary for soccer terminology in English, French, and German (Schmidt 2009), BioFrameNet covering biomedical terminology (Dolbey et al. 2016), Bertoldi and Chishman (2012) for legal terminology, and the German Frame-based Online Dictionary, a learner's dictionary for English speakers learning German (Boas and Dux 2013; Boas et al. 2016).

German (2002–2010) explored methods for large-scale manual frame-semantic annotation of the German TIGER Treebank (Brants et al. 2002), and multilingual approaches to inducing and verifying frame semantic annotations. The SALSA team also used the English FN frames where possible, but instead of starting with English frames and LUs and identifying equivalent German ones, they conducted full text annotation. When they ran into words for which there was no corresponding LU in the English FN database, they created so-called proto-frames, i.e. provisional frames for a single lexeme, without grouping them into larger frames. The eight years of SALSA funding resulted in roughly 20,000 annotations for verbs and 17,000 for nouns. In contrast, Spanish FrameNet (from 2002–2015) put together their own 940-million-word Spanish corpus and created their own tagging system in order to directly use the frames and frame elements from the English FN database for the vast majority of their LUs, resulting in a total of 10,334 manually annotated lexicographic examples as the basis for 1,124 LUs in 325 frames.

Since the 1980s, one of the questions asked by research in Frame Semantics has been whether frames should be regarded as "universals" of human language or whether they are language specific. Over the past 15 years, the process of employing semantic frames developed on the basis of English to develop FrameNets for other languages strongly suggest that many frames can be regarded as applicable across different languages, especially those relating to basic human experience such as eating, drinking, sleeping, and walking (see the contributions in Boas 2009a). Even some cultural practices appear to be comparable across many languages, such as commercial transaction: in many cultures, we find a specific type of exchange that can be characterized as a type of commercial transaction involving the FEs Buyer, Seller, Money, and Goods. However, to date there has been no empirical study determining the universal applicability of semantic frames across languages. This is due to at least three problems.

The first problem concerns coverage of the lexicon. English FrameNet, which so far has the largest inventory of more than 1,200 frames together with entries for more than 13,600 lexical units, does not yet provide a large coverage of the English lexicon. Recall that unlike traditional dictionaries, which are organized alphabetically, FrameNet describes and analyzes the English lexicon frame by frame. While with traditional dictionaries we can estimate their coverage by looking at how many words they have covered under each letter of the alphabet, this is somewhat more difficult with FrameNet because we do not have a clear understanding of how extensive FrameNet's coverage of the English lexicon really is. Researchers estimate that average speakers of English have an average active knowledge of about 20,000 words (and a passive knowledge of about 40,000 words) (cf. Na &

Nation 1985).¹³ But even this estimate is somewhat unreliable because the notion of "word" itself is problematic. More specifically, lexicographers do not always agree on how many senses a word has, depending on whether they are lumpers or splitters (see Kilgarriff 1997). Our short discussion nevertheless suggests that currently English FrameNet does not adequately cover the average active vocabulary of a speaker of English. This, in turn, means that if we employ the current inventory of semantic frames based on English to explore their universal applicability to the description and analysis of other languages, we have to keep in mind that there are large gaps.¹⁴ As such, getting closer to answering the question of how universal semantic frames really are will first require a more elaborate coverage of English FrameNet or a FrameNet for another language.¹⁵

The second problem concerns the methodology: Which frames should we select for our investigation? To date, we have no solid empirical criteria to measure how universal a frame is, let alone how to go about identifying which frames we should investigate. More specifically: Should we employ the Swadesh list of 207 basic concepts that are intended to cover those areas central to human life, and if we find corresponding frames based on empirical evidence in all the world's languages, should we then speak of a set of "universal" frames? What role should the concept of frequency play? These are all open questions (besides others) that will need to be

---

13 Note that there is no single agreed-upon list of criteria of what constitutes the basic vocabulary of a language. This point alone makes it difficult to evaluate the potential "universal" applicability of semantic frames. Some researchers argue that the core of the lexicon consists of those words that are most useful for the speaker and hearer depending on whether (1) they are most frequent in texts of different genres, (2) they designate concepts that are central to human life, or (3) they suffice to paraphrase and explain all the other words in the lexicon. See Goddard (2001) and Lehmann (2018) for a discussion of the so-called Swadesh list of 207 basic concepts and Ogden's (1930) Basic English list containing 850 items.
14 Note that other approaches, such as the Natural Semantic Metalanguage (Wierzbicka 2005), claiming to have found a universal inventory of semantic descriptors, face similar issues related to coverage.
15 Despite the perceived lack of coverage, FrameNet has come a long way during its more than 20 years of analyzing the English lexicon. The FrameNet database is so far unmatched in terms of level of detail of how the meanings of semantically related words are expressed syntactically (see Boas 2005b, 2017a). Its corpus-based methodology, resulting in more than 200,000 manually annotated example sentences, is time and labor-intensive, but the proof of concept and its underlying methodology are well-established. The current lack in coverage by FrameNet is due in large part to funding constraints. This situation can be compared with a traditional dictionary losing its funding after having completed entries covering only the relevant words starting with the letters A-N. With the remaining words starting with O-Z not being covered, such a traditional dictionary would also be regarded as lacking coverage. This means that if there were enough funding available for FrameNet, it would be relatively easy to solve the perceived lack of coverage.

addressed. Another related issue in trying to establish whether semantic frames are universal or not, is that we need to keep in mind that there might be many different types of frames and while some might be considered "universal", others might not, while others might only be considered partially universal (as is the case when typological restrictions in a language preclude the explicit morpho-syntactic coding of certain semantic categories). Consider, for example, the importance of culture-specific words, frames, and ways of thinking that are deeply embedded in the beliefs, customs, and practices of particular cultures, but not other cultures. As the Modern Language Association ad Hoc Committee on Foreign Languages (2007: 2) points out:

> Expressions such as the 'pursuit of happiness', 'liberté, egalité, fraternité' and 'la Raza' connote cultural dimensions that extend well beyond their immediate translation. [...] deep cultural knowledge and linguistic competence are equally necessary if one wishes to understand people and their communities.
> (MLA ad Hoc Committee on Foreign Languages 2007: 2)

The third problem concerns the idea of universality itself. Much linguistic research, in particular in the generative and typological paradigms of the second half of the 20th century, focused on establishing universal categories, patterns, or generalizations to arrive at a "universal" theory about language (for a critique see Croft 2001). But the empirical basis for many of the claims about universality are difficult to prove or to falsify because of a lack of data. Most claims about a particular universal aspect of language rests on a limited set of data from a limited set of languages, whether they are 5, 10, or 100 languages.[16] But even with larger numbers of languages being covered, the claim about a supposedly "universal" aspect of language cannot be upheld until we have solid descriptions of all of the world's 6,000 or so languages (many of which are endangered to various degrees, see Crystal 2000). Thus, when using the term "universal" throughout the remainder of this paper it should be interpreted as "potentially" universal.

More specifically, in what follows I will focus on investigating different ways of establishing criteria for re-using semantic frames derived on the basis of English that can be employed to describe and analyze words and concepts in other languages. For the most part, this will involve contrastive comparisons only, thereby laying the foundation for further comparisons down the road. This bottom-up approach is only a very tiny first step towards establishing a methodology for investigating the potential "universal" status of semantic frames.

---

16 See the Leipzig Valency Classes Project, which aims at arriving at cross-linguistic generalizations about how valency is expressed in the world's languages: https://www.eva.mpg.de/lingua/valency/files/project.php

4 Towards a methodology for identifying "universal" frames

To illustrate how frames can be identified as potential candidates for "universal" frame-hood, let us consider the Berkeley FrameNet Questioning frame. The words in this frame have to do with a Speaker asking an Addressee a question which calls for a reply (as opposed to making a request which calls for an action on the part of the Addressee). LUs evoking the Questioning frame include *to ask, to inquire, to question, inquiry, question*, etc. In order to determine whether the same frame can be applied to the description and analysis of other languages it does not suffice to just take the frame description from English and apply it to other languages.

Instead, we need to determine whether we find in the other language, in this case German, translation equivalents or near-translation equivalents corresponding to the English LUs of the "original" Questioning frame. Because of a lack of space, I will not be able to discuss possible translation equivalents of all LUs evoking the Questioning frame, let alone translation equivalents for all FECs found in the valence table of a single English LU. Instead, I will focus here for illustrative purposes only on discussing a single straightforward case of a German translation equivalent of one English LU, namely the verb *to ask* evoking the Questioning frame. After discussing this one example, I will address the issues surrounding finding translation equivalents for other frame element configurations, and other LUs evoking the same frame.[17]

The valence information in the FrameNet entry of the LU *to ask* in the Questioning frame contains a total of 15 FECs with a total of 69 syntactic realizations (the various syntactic realizations of frame elements, also known as miniconstructions; Boas 2003a). Because of a lack of space, Figure 6 only illustrates a subset, namely 8 FE configurations with 16 valence realizations. Of these 16 syntactic realizations, let us take a look at only one syntactic realization, namely the one in which *to ask* appears with an external NP, an object NP, and a PP headed by *about* (marked by an arrow in Figure 6 below) as in the sentence *The immigration authorities asked her about her profession* (based on Boas 2011b).

Using the information in this one syntactic realization, we are able to map the form information [NP.Ext, *ask*.V, NP.Obj, PP_*about*.Comp] to the frame-semantic meaning of the Questioning frame, so that the external NP is identified as the Speaker FE, the object NP as the Addressee FE, and the PP headed by *about* as

---

[17] Because of space limitations, we cannot discuss other translation equivalents for other languages. As such, the current paper is intended to serve only as a case study.

	Addressee	Speaker	Time	
2 TOTAL				
(1)	DNI --	NP Ext	AVP Dep	
(1)	NP Obj	NP Ext	AVP Dep	
1 TOTAL	Addressee	Speaker	Time	Topic
(1)	NP Obj	NP Ext	AVP Dep	PP[about] Dep
16 TOTAL	Addressee	Speaker	Topic	
(4)	DNI --	NP Ext	NP Obj	
(1)	DNI --	NP Ext	PP[about] Dep	
(1)	DNI --	NP Ext	PPing[about] Dep	
(1)	DNI --	NP Ext	Sfin Dep	
(1)	DNI --	NP Obj	PP[about] Dep	
(1)	NP Ext	CNI --	PP[about] Dep	
(2)	NP Obj	CNI --	PP[about] Dep	
(1)	NP Obj	CNI --	PPing[about] Dep	
(1)	NP Obj	NP Ext	NP Dep	
→ (1)	NP Obj	NP Ext	PP[about] Dep	
(2)	NP Obj	NP Ext	PPing[about] Dep	

Figure 6: Valence table of *to ask* in the Questioning frame (excerpt).

the Topic FE. With this mapping of the English form of the sentence *The immigration authorities asked her about her profession* we now have an approximate frame-semantic representation of its meaning based on our knowledge of the Questioning frame including its definition. Recall that the Questioning frame under discussion is derived on the basis of English corpus data. We are now interested in determining how this very same frame can be reused for analyzing other languages in order to determine to what degree semantic frames are useful for contrastive analysis, and, more broadly, to cross-linguistic analysis.

To show how this can be achieved, we focus here on just one syntactic realization of the FEC [Speaker, Addressee, Topic] to just one corresponding syntactic realization of one corresponding FEC in another language, in this case German. Figure 7 illustrates how this parallel mapping of syntactic realizations of FECs

Speaker	TARGET	Addressee	Topic
NP.Ext	ask.V	NP.Obj	PP_about.Comp

↕

Speaker	TARGET	Addressee	Topic
NP.Ext	fragen.V	NP.Obj	PP_nach.Comp

Figure 7: Parallel lexicon fragment: Cross-linguistic identification of *to ask* and *fragen* based on valence realizations of the same semantic frame (see Boas 2011b).

can be implemented using semantic frames derived on the basis of English. The relevant German counterpart of English *to ask* is German *fragen* 'to ask'.

The result is a correspondence between the FEs Speaker, Addressee, and Topic between English and German, representing the English sentence *The immigration authorities asked her about her profession* and its German counterpart *Die Einwanderungsbehörde fragte sie nach ihrem Beruf*. This example shows that employing semantic frames for mapping between an English syntactic realization of an FEC contained in a verb's valence table and its German counterpart is feasible (see also Boas 2002, 2011b). It also demonstrates that the Questioning frame derived on the basis of English is applicable to German in a straightforward way.

In this paper, I call cases such as illustrated in Figure 7, in which there is one clear match between the syntactic realization of one LU in one language and a corresponding LU in another language evoking the same frame, "surface translation equivalence". The term "surface" is not to be understood as in the generative transformational paradigm, but rather as denoting a situation in which there is a clear match between two syntactic realizations of the two valence tables, such that it appears at the "surface" as if they are translation equivalents. As such, "surface translation equivalence" is a much weaker version of what Viberg (2002) calls translation equivalence.[18]

---

[18] Because of space limitations I leave aside here a discussion of differences in lexicalization patterns, which are relevant when dealing with typologically different languages and how they realize the semantics of a frame. For example, Subirats (2009) discusses lexicalization differences in Spanish and English for emotion predicates, and Subirats and Sato (2004) report on constructional differences between English and Spanish motion verbs. These differences need to be addressed within a broader context of typological differences such as expressional differences in motion events between Germanic and Romance languages (Slobin 1996). However, it is important to remember that such typological differences do not put in question the usability of semantic frames (see also Ohara 2009 on differences between English *to risk* and Japanese *kakeru*). Schmidt (2009) provides an insightful discussion of some typological differences in football language in English, German, and French.

Our example also suggests that semantic frames can be useful tools for establishing (1) translation equivalence (the English and German sentences convey the same meanings) and (2) valence equivalence (there is a one-to-one mapping between FEs, phrase types, and grammatical functions), but only at a low level. A systematic comparison of cultural equivalence would require a larger in-depth study involving parallel corpus data to determine to what degree the English LU *to ask* and the German LU *fragen* evoking the Questioning frame can be considered to be equivalent at a cultural level (more on that issue below). Our discussion so far suggests that semantic frames derived on the basis of English are useful for comparing and contrasting the lexicons of other languages. As such, semantic frames could be considered as possible candidates for translation universals.

However, a number of disclaimers are in place. Note, first, that our example of a corresponding parallel English-German lexicon fragment in Figure 7 represents only one syntactic realization of one of 15 FECs with a total of 69 syntactic realizations of English *to ask* evoking the Questioning frame.[19] We have not addressed the 5 other syntactic realizations of the same FEC, let alone the 63 other syntactic realizations of the 14 other FECs. This is why I tentatively labeled the situation depicted in Figure 7 "surface translation equivalence." In order to establish the degree to which *to ask* and *fragen* really evoke the same semantic frame and the degree to which there is more of a correspondence between the syntactic realizations in the valence tables of the two LUs we need to repeat the same procedure for each syntactic realization.

Cases in which there is a high degree of correspondence between the syntactic realizations of FEs of the semantic frame in one language with the syntactic realizations of FEs in another language are called "valence equivalence." Whenever we find more cases in which the syntactic realizations found in the valence tables of two LUs thought to evoke the same frame are equivalents of each other, the higher the degree of valence equivalence. Put differently, "surface translation equivalence" like the one depicted in Figure 7 above is the lowest degree of "valence equivalence", because we have so far only one clear case of two matching syntactic realizations across languages. Note that most likely there are no cases in which there is complete "valence equivalence" between the valence tables of two LUs from different languages and that as such the notion

---

19 Dux (2016, 2018) points out the importance of paying close attention to verb valence patterns across languages to formulate frame-semantic classes. He shows that the types of verb classes resulting from a frame-semantic classification do not always present an exact overlap between different languages. This insight leads him to propose a more fine-grained approach that uses verbal valency for the formulation of verb-valency classes together with semantic frames.

of valence equivalence is one of degree. In other words, the greater the number of corresponding syntactic realizations in the valence tables of two LUs from different languages that evoke the same frame is, the larger the degree of "valence equivalence."

Unfortunately, we cannot establish whether there is a high degree of valence correspondence between *to ask* and *fragen* evoking the Questioning frame because of limited space in this paper. This would require us to do an in-depth investigation to determine possible valence equivalents of each of the remaining 68 syntactic realizations of *to ask*. Note, however, that there are a few important points we can briefly review here, which may serve as the starting point for a future paper investigating the degree of cross-linguistic correspondence between two LUs from different languages evoking the same semantic frame.

5 Culture-specific semantic frames

So far, we have only reviewed the concepts of translation equivalence and valence equivalence to determine the degree to which there is overlap between two LUs in different languages evoking the same frame. The third concept relevant in this context is what I call "cultural equivalence," and this concept may be the most difficult to define, identify, and measure. Cultural equivalence concerns cases in which two LUs from different languages evoking the same semantic frame can be used in the same contexts with the same cultural connotations. One way of going about determining cultural equivalence (or perhaps, to a lesser degree, cultural correspondence) is to adopt insights from Wierzbicka's (2005) theory of cultural scripts, which seeks to systematically account for cultural values in the semantics of words in a given language.

VanNoy (2017) presents a first account of how Wierzbicka's (2005) cultural scripts can be combined with Fillmore's semantic frames in order to highlight and investigate cultural similarities and differences of words in two languages thought to evoke the same frame. For example, VanNoy (2017) provides an analysis of the English noun *friend* and its German counterpart *der Freund/ die Freundin* (male/female). Noting that both nouns have the same Germanic root and that both nouns can be used in many of the same contexts in contemporary English and German denoting friendship as they evoke the Personal_relatioinship frame, VanNoy also points out that there are a number of significant differences (see also Atzler 2011). Following the ideas underlying Fillmore and Atkins' (2000) semantic network analysis, VanNoy uses a combination of data from monolingual dictionaries, bilingual dictionaries, and corpus data to show that the two nouns differ in a number of important aspects. For example, the English and German nouns differ in the types of personal relationships they denote, specifically the intensity of the relationship, the duration of the relationship, and whether the relationship is romantic and/or intimate or not.

Based on collocational information for the English noun *friend* and its German counterpart *der Freund/die Freundin*, VanNoy points out that such important cultural differences are not included in frame-semantic descriptions and that existing semantic frames derived on the basis of English should be augmented by more fine-grained cultural information. These observations lead her to propose two related frames for German that are more specific than the general Personal_relationship frame derived on the basis of English. More specifically, she proposes for German a Platonic_Personal_Relationship sub-frame (VanNoy 2017: 185)[20] and a Non_Marital_Personal_Relationship sub-frame (VanNoy 2017: 189), augmenting each with German-specific cultural scripts emphasizing the different levels of intensity, duration, and exclusivity of relationships. VanNoy shows that augmenting existing English frames with cultural scripts makes it possible to capture the entirety of cultural connotations using Frame Semantics at different levels of granularity within and across languages.

What have we learned from our short discussion of "cultural equivalence"? First, recall that our motivation for re-using semantic frames from English for other languages is the idea that frames could possibly be universal, similar to what has been claimed about Fillmore's (1968) original case roles. To establish degrees of equivalence or correspondence between two LUs from different languages thought to evoke the same semantic frame, I proposed three different levels of equivalence, namely translation equivalence, valence equivalence, and cultural equivalence. Second, as shown above, it is possible to determine translation equivalence and valence equivalence relatively straightforwardly by comparing and contrasting the valence tables of two LUs from different languages thought to evoke the same frame. Third, there are cases in which semantic frames derived on the basis of English are not fine-grained enough to be re-usable for the analysis of corresponding LUs in other languages. To identify and measure such cases of cultural equivalence I argued for adopting VanNoy's (2017) proposals to combine insights from Fillmore's Frame Semantics with that of Wier-

---

20 An example of VanNoy's (2017: 185) use of semantic scripts, following Wierzbicka (2005), is additional information augmenting the Platonic_Personal_Relationship sub-frame: X is someone like this: X is someone I know; X is someone I have met before. When I think of X I think: I know this person, but I do not know much about this person and I do not feel close to this person. Many people think like this: I have many of X because there are many people I have met I know. Evoking LU: *Bekannter* ('acquaintance').

zbicka's theory of cultural scripts. Note that we discussed only one example from the Personal_relationship frame, but the literature on Wierzbicka's cultural scripts is full of similar cases (e.g. particular words expressing politeness, personal distance, worldview, customer service, etc.) that merit a further in-depth investigation in the context of determining the possibility universality of frames (see Goddard 2001; Wierzbicka 2005).

Returning to our discussion of *to ask* and its German counterpart *fragen* above, it is important to note that there does not seem to be a need for the inclusion of cultural scripts to augment particular sub-frames to the general Communication_questioning frame derived on the basis of English. But as our example of the Personal_relationship frame has shown, there are differences between frames when it comes to cultural equivalence. How many semantic frames derived on the basis of English will require the explicit formulation of sub-frames with corresponding cultural scripts is open to further empirical investigation. This will depend on the number and types of semantic frames as well as the number and types of LUs and languages under investigation. Combining the insights of Fillmore's Frame Semantics with Wierzbicka's theory of cultural scripts may bring us one step closer to determining what types of frames are truly applicable cross-linguistically to the degree that we might eventually call them universal and what types of frames require fine-tuning depending on individual languages and cultures.

One final point worth mentioning concerns the important roles of paraphrase relations, polysemy, and translational equivalence. When determining translation, valence, and cultural equivalencies we have so far only focused on finding correspondences within single sentences and not across broader contexts. Thus, in finding an adequate equivalent for *to ask* in *The immigration authorities asked her about her profession* above we used the default German translation equivalent of *fragen* for *to ask*. While this may work in most default contexts, it is important to note that English *to ask* has multiple German translation equivalents, each of which evoke the Questioning frame, depending on context.[21] The difference in translations is typically triggered by specific background information provided by the sentence or the broader context in which the sentence containing *to ask* occurs: *ausfragen* 'to quiz somebody about something' highlights a particular aspect of the Questioning frame by focusing on a detailed, intense, or curious manner of questioning; *befragen* 'to interrogate someone' highlights

---

[21] To determine the extent to which German translation equivalents of *to ask* differ from each other it will be necessary to conduct a detailed corpus-based investigation into how each syntactic realization in the valence table of *to ask* is realized by potentially different German LUs.

a particularly intense or authoritative manner of questioning; *bezweifeln* 'to challenge something' highlights the attitude of the Speaker of the Questioning frame, who does not believe the Addressee; *prüfen* 'to investigate' focuses on an investigative aspect of the Questioning frame, which the Speaker puts to the test whether something that the Addressee is claiming is true or not.

6 Conclusions and outlook

The procedures and proposals for identifying potentially universal semantic frames presented in this paper are only of a very preliminary nature and need to be significantly refined by future research. In this paper I have outlined how cross-linguistic correspondences between two LUs from different languages evoking the same semantic frame can be established. But note that this step alone, which itself appears to be quite labor intensive, addresses only two corresponding LUs evoking the same semantic frame. Above we discussed this procedure in the context of *to ask* and *fragen* evoking the Questioning frame. To determine the degree to which the Questioning frame could be considered a possible candidate for a universal frame would first require repeating the same procedure for the remaining 11 English LUs evoking the Questioning frame. Once we know which English LUs have German counterparts we can propose a common Questioning frame evoked and shared by both English and German LUs. Note, however, that this frame would only cover English and German, not any other languages. In other words, we would need to repeat the same procedure for all other known languages, i.e. identifying corresponding LUs with equivalent meanings, in order to see whether the same frame is evoked by LUs across the board.

If we were indeed to find corresponding LUs with roughly equivalent meanings evoking the same Questioning frame across all languages (with expected minor typological differences), then it should be possible to claim that the Questioning frame can be considered a type of "universal" frame in the sense that it is evoked by LUs from all languages. Other likely candidates that could be considered universal include the Motion, Communication, Ingestion, and Bodyparts frames. Of course, the question of universality might turn out to be a gradual notion in the case of semantic frames, because more likely than not we will find that a strict one-to-one correspondence between pairs of LUs from two language or across languages will be the exception. This means that future research needs to address in more detail the complex relationship between translation equivalence, valence equivalence, and cultural equivalence.

Note that the procedures outlined above do not rely on translation studies as a means of establishing cross-linguistic relationships, as is described in Granger (2003) and Johansson (2007). Instead, I proposed to begin with established semantic frames from the Berkeley FrameNet for English and to then use a combination of corpus-driven techniques and linguistic intuition to find and identify possible translation equivalents in monolingual corpora in other languages. While this procedure avoids some of the problems that arise from working with parallel corpora (e.g. interference between the language of the source-text and the translated text, see McEnery and Xiao 2008), it, too, is not free of problems. For example, the use of English frames based on English data to identify LUs in languages other than English raises the question of whether such frames might be too Anglo centric.

In this paper, I proposed a first step towards identifying possible universal semantic frames based on existing frames in English FrameNet. To achieve this goal I argued for a particular systematic procedure that begins with picking a specific English FrameNet frame such as Questioning and to pick a language other than English. The second step involves taking all LUs evoking the semantic frame in English and find translation equivalents in the other language. This step requires that we use a mix of corpus data and linguistic intuition to find for each LU corresponding valence equivalents and culture equivalents. Based on annotated corresponding corpus examples we are then in a position to create parallel lexicon fragments for English and the other language. Establishing these correspondences is a first step towards establishing a potentially universal frame. The same procedure should then be repeated for all other known languages.

Our discussion of culture and language specific words has shown that not all semantic frames derived on the basis of English are good candidates for universal frame-hood. The case of German *Freund/Freundin* has shown that there are cases in which it is necessary to define more fine-grained semantic sub-frames and augment these with more specific cultural information using Wierzbicka's theory of cultural scripts. Culture-specific words evoking particular semantic frames are likely the most difficult cases to investigate as they require a great deal of linguistic intuition and corpus data illustrating collocational restrictions and contextual requirements on the proper use of such words. While this paper has only outlined a roadmap for determining potential candidates for universal frame-hood, it has shown how this can be done in a systematic way using semantic frames based on English. Clearly, much research remains to be done in order to further explore the roadmap laid out in this paper.

References

Altenberg, Bengt & Sylviane Granger. 2002. Introduction. In B. Altenberg & S. Granger (eds.), *Lexis in Contrast*, 3–50. Amsterdam/Philadelphia: John Benjamins.

Atzler, Judith. 2011. *Twist in the list: Frame Semantics as Vocabulary Teaching and Learning Tool*. Unpublished Ph.D. dissertation, University of Texas at Austin.

Baker, Collin & Josef Ruppenhofer. 2002. FrameNet's Frames vs. Levin's Verb Classes. In J. Larson and M. Paster (eds.), *Proceedings of the 28th Annual Meeting of the Berkeley Linguistics Society*, 27–38. UC Berkeley: Berkeley Linguistics Department.

Bertoldi, Anderson & Rove Chishman. 2012. Frame Semantics and legal corpora annotation: Theoretical and applied challenges. *Linguistic Issues in Language Technology*, 7(1).

Boas, Hans C. 2001. Frame Semantics as a framework for describing polysemy and syntactic structures of English and German motion verbs in contrastive computational lexicography. In P. Rayson, A. Wilson, T. McEnery, A. Hardie & S. Khoja (eds.), *Proceedings of Corpus Linguistics 2001*. 64–73.

Boas, Hans C. 2002. Bilingual FrameNet dictionaries for machine translation. In M. González Rodríguez & C. Paz Suárez Araujo (eds.), *Proceedings of the Third International Conference on Language Resources and Evaluation*, Vol. IV, 1364–1371. Las Palmas, Spain.

Boas, Hans C. 2003a. *A constructional approach to resultatives*. Stanford: CSLI Publications.

Boas, Hans C. 2003b. A lexical-constructional account of the locative alternation. In L. Carmichael, C.-H. Huang, & V. Samiian (eds.), *Proceedings of the 2001 Western Conference in Linguistics*. Vol. 13, 27–42.

Boas, Hans C. 2005a. From theory to practice: Frame Semantics and the design of FrameNet. In S. Langer & D. Schnorbusch (eds.), *Semantik im Lexikon*, 129–160. Tübingen: Narr.

Boas, Hans C. 2005b. Semantic frames as interlingual representations for multilingual lexical databases. *International Journal of Lexicography* 18(4). 445–478.

Boas, Hans C. (ed.). 2009a. *Multilingual FrameNets in Computational Lexicography*. Berlin/New York: Mouton de Gruyter.

Boas, Hans C. 2009b. Recent trends in multilingual lexicography. In Boas, Hans C. (ed.), *Multilingual FrameNets in Computational Lexicography*, 1–26. Berlin/New York: Mouton de Gruyter.

Boas, Hans C. (ed.). 2010a. *Contrastive Studies in Construction Grammar*. Amsterdam/Philadelphia: Benjamins.

Boas, Hans C. 2010b. Comparing constructions across languages. In H.C. Boas (ed.), *Contrastive Studies in Construction Grammar*, 1–20. Amsterdam/Philadelphia: Benjamins.

Boas, Hans C. 2010c. Linguistically relevant meaning elements of English communication verbs. *Belgian Journal of Linguistics* 24. 54–82.

Boas, Hans C. 2011a. A frame-semantic approach to syntactic alternations with *build*-verbs. In P. Guerrero Medina (ed.), *Morphosyntactic alternations in English*, 207–234. London: Equinox.

Boas, Hans C. 2011b. Constructing parallel lexicon fragments based on English FrameNet entries: Semantic and syntactic issues. In H. Hedeland, T. Schmidt, & K. Woerner (eds.), *Multilingual Resources and Multilingual Applications. Proceedings of the German Society for Computational Linguistics and Language Technology (GSCL) 2011, Hamburg*. University of Hamburg: Center for Language Corpora. 9–18.

Boas, Hans C. 2013. Frame Semantics and translation. In A. Rojo & I. Ibarretxte-Antunano (eds.), *Cognitive Linguistics and Translation*, 125–158. Berlin/New York: Mouton de Gruyter.

Boas, Hans C. 2017a. Computational Resources: FrameNet and Constructicon. In B. Dancygier (ed.), *The Cambridge Handbook of Cognitive Linguistics*, 549–573. Cambridge: Cambridge University Press.

Boas, Hans C. 2017b. What you see is not what you get: Capturing the meaning of missing words with Frame Semantics. In *Proceedings of the Chicago Linguistics Society* 52. 53–70.

Boas, Hans C. & Ryan Dux. 2013. Semantic frames for foreign language education: Towards a German frame-based dictionary. *Veridas On-line. Special Issue on Frame Semantics and its Technological Applications*. 82–100. http://www.ufjf.br/revistaveredas/edicoes- 2013

Boas, Hans C. & Ryan Dux. 2017. From the past into the present: From case frames to semantic frames. In *Linguistics Vanguard* 2017. 1–14. DOI: 10.1515/lingvan-2016-0003.

Boas, Hans C., Ryan Dux, & Alexander Ziem. 2016. Frames and constructions in an online learner's dictionary of German. In S. De Knop & G. Gilquin (eds.), *Applied Construction Grammar*, 303–326. Berlin: de Gruyter.

Boas, Hans C., Lyngfelt, Benjamin, & Tiago Timponi Torrent. 2019. Framing Constructicography. In *Lexicographica* 35. 41–95.

Borin, Lars, Dana Dannells, Markus Forsberg, Maria Toporowska Gronostaj & Dimitros Kokkinakis. 2010. The past meets the present in Swedish FrameNet++. *Proceedings of EURALEX 2010*. 269–281.

Brants, S., Dipper, S., Hansen, S., Lezius, W., & Smith, G. 2002. The TIGER treebank. In *Proceedings of the workshop on treebanks and linguistic theories* (Vol. 168).

Burchhardt, Aljoscha, Katrin Erk, Anette Frank, Andrea Kowalski, Sebastian Padó, & Manfred Pinkal. 2009. Using FrameNet for the semantic analysis of German: annotation, representation, and automation. In H.C. Boas (ed.), *Multilingual FrameNets: Methods and Applications*, 209–244. Berlin/New York: Mouton de Gruyter.

Candito, M., Amsili, P., Barque, L., Benamara, F., De Chalendar, G., Djemaa, M., Haas, P., Huyghe, R., Mathieu, Y.Y., Muller, P. & Sagot, B., 2014, May. Developing a french framenet: Methodology and first results. In *LREC-The 9th edition of the Language Resources and Evaluation Conference*.

Connor, U. M., & Moreno, A. I. 2005. *Tertium comparationis: A vital component in contrastive rhetoric research.*

Croft, William. 2001. *Radical Construction Grammar*. Oxford: Oxford University Press.

Crystal, David. 2000. *Language Death*. Cambridge: Cambridge University Press.

Czulo, Oliver. 2013. Constructions-and-frames analysis of translations: The interplay of syntax and semantics in translations between English and German. *Constructions and Frames* 5(2). 143–167.

Dolbey, Andrew, Ellsworth, Michael, & Jan Scheffczyk. 2006. BioFrameNet: A Domain-Specific FrameNet Extension with Links to Biomedical Ontologies. In *KR-MED* (Vol. 222).

Dux, Ryan. 2016. *A usage-based account of verb classes in English and German*. Unpublished Ph.D. dissertation, The University of Texas at Austin.

Dux, Ryan. 2018. Frames, verbs, and constructions: German constructions with verbs of stealing. In H.C. Boas & A. Ziem (eds.), *Constructional Approaches to Syntactic Structures in German*, 367–406. Berlin/Boston: de Gruyter Mouton.

Fellbaum, Christiane (ed.). 1998. *WordNet*. Boston, MA: MIT Press.

Fillmore, Charles J. 1968. The case for case. In E. Bach & R. Harms (eds.), *Universals in Linguistic Theory*, 1–90. New York: Rinehart & Winston.

Fillmore, Charles J. 1975. An alternative to checklist theories of meaning. *Proceedings of the First Annual Meeting of the Berkeley Linguistic Society (BLS)*. 123–131.

Fillmore, Charles J. 1977. Topics in Lexical Semantics. In P. Cole (ed.), *Current Issues in Linguistic Theory*, 76–136. Bloomington: Indiana University Press.

Fillmore, Charles J. 1982. Frame Semantics. In: *Linguistics in the Morning Calm*, ed. Linguistic Society of Korea, 111–38. Seoul: Hanshin.

Fillmore, Charles J. 1985. Frames and the Semantics of Understanding. *Quaderni di Semantica* 6. 222–254.

Fillmore, Charles J. 1986. Pragmatically controlled zero anaphora. *Proceedings of the Berkeley Linguistics Society*. 95–107.

Fillmore, Charles J. 2008. Border Conflicts: FrameNet meets Construction Grammar. *Proceedings of the XIII EURALEX International Congress* (Barcelona, 15–19 July 2008). 49–68.

Fillmore, Charles J. & Beryl T.S. Atkins. 1992. Toward a Frame-based Lexicon: The Semantics of RISK and its Neighbors. In A. Lehrer & E. Kittay (eds.), *Frames, Fields and Contrasts: New Essays in Semantic and Lexical Organization*, 75–102. Hillsdale: Erlbaum.

Fillmore, Charles J. & Berly T.S. Atkins. 2000. Describing polysemy: The case of crawl. In Y. Ravin & C. Leacock (eds.), *Polysemy: Linguistic and computational approaches*, 91–110. Oxford: Oxford University Press.

Fillmore, Charles J. & Colin Baker. 2010. A frames approach to semantic analysis. In B. Heine & H. Narrog (eds.), *The Oxford Handbook of Linguistic Analysis*, 313–340. Oxford: Oxford University Press.

Fillmore, Charles J., Baker, Collin, & Beau Cronin 2003. The structure of the FrameNet database. *International Journal of Lexicography* 16.3. 281–296.

Fillmore, Charles J., Johnson, Chris, & Miriam Petruck. 2003. Background to FrameNet. *International Journal of Lexicography* 16. 235–251.

Fillmore, Charles J., Petruck, Miriam R.L., Ruppenhofer, Josef & Abby Wright. 2003. FrameNet in Action: The case of Attaching. *International Journal of Lexicography* 16. 297–332.

Fontenelle, Thierry. 1997. Using a bilingual dictionary to create semantic networks. *International Journal of Lexicography* 10.4. 275–303.

Gast, Volker. 2015. On the use of translation corpora in contrastive linguistics: A case study of impersonalization in English and German. *Languages in Contrast*, 15(1). 4–33.

Goddard, Cliff 2001. Lexico-semantic universals: A critical overview. *Linguistic Typology* 5. 1–65.

Goddard, Cliff. 2005. *Semantic Analysis*. Oxford: Oxford University Press.

Granger, Sylviane. 2003. The corpus approach: a common way forward for Contrastive Linguistics and Translation Studies. *Corpus-based approaches to contrastive linguistics and translation studies*, 20. 17.

Hansen-Schirra, Silvia, Nitzke, Jean, & Katharina Oster. 2017. Predicting cognate translation. In S. Hansen-Schirra, O. Czulo, & S. Hoffmann (ed.), *Empirical modelling of translation and interpreting*, 3–23. Berlin: Language Science Press.

Hasegawa, Yoko, Lee-Goldman, Russell, & Charles J. Fillmore. 2016. On the universality of semantic frames. In M. Hilpert & J.-O. Oestman (eds.), *Constructions across grammars*, 34–66. Amsterdam/Philadelphia: John Benjamins.

Heid, Ulrich. 1996. Creating a multilingual data collection for bilingual lexicography from parallel monolingual lexicons. In *Proceedings of the VIIth EURALEX International Congress*, Gothenburg 1996. 573–559.

Johansson, Stig. 2007. *Seeing through multilingual corpora*. Amsterdam/Philadelphia: John Benjamins.

Kilgarriff, Adam. 1997. I don't believe in Word Senses. *Computers and the Humanities* 31.2. 91–113.

Lambrecht, Knud. 1984. Formulaicity, frame semantics, and pragmatics in German binomial expressions. *Language*. 753–796.

Lehmann, Christian. 2018. Basic Vocabulary. [https://www.christianlehmann.eu/ling/ling_meth/ling_description/lexicography/basic_vocabulary.html]. Last accessed April 26, 2018.

Levin, Beth. 1993. *English verb class and alternations*. Chicago: Chicago University Press.

Levin, Beth & Malka Rappaport Hovav. 2005. *Argument Realization*. Cambridge: Cambridge University Press.

Lyngfelt, Benjamin. 2012. Re-thinking FNI. On null instantiation and control in Construction Grammar. *Constructions and Frames* 4.1. 1–23.

Lyngfelt, Benjamin, Bori, Lars, Ohara, Kyoko & Torrent, Tiago. (eds.). 2018. *Constructiography: Constructicon development across languages*. Amsterdam/Philadelphia: John Benjamins.

McEnery, Tony & Xiao, Richard. 2008. Parallel and comparable corpora: what is happening? In G. Anderman & M. Rogers (eds.), *Incorporating corpora: The linguist and the translator*, 18–31. Clevedon: Multilingual Matters Ltd.

Modern Language Ad Hoc Committee on Foreign Languages. 2007. Foreign Languages and Higher Education: New Structures for a Changing World. *Profession* 12, 234–245.

Na, Liu & I.S.P. Nation. 1985. Factors affecting guessing vocabulary in context. *RELC journal*, 16(1). 33–42.

Ohara, Kyoko. 2009. Frame-based contrastive lexical semantics in Japanese FrameNet: The case of risk and kakeru. In H.C. Boas (ed.), *Multilingual FrameNets: Methods and Applications*, 163–182. Berlin/New York: Mouton de Gruyter.

Ohara, Kyoko, Fujii, Seiko, Ohori, Toshio, Suzuki, Ryoko, Saito, Hiroaki, & Shun Ishizaki. 2004. The Japanese FrameNet Project: An introduction. In: *Fourth International Conference on Language Resources and Evaluation (LREC 2004). Proceedings of the Satellite Workshop "Building Lexical Resources from Semantically Annotated Corpora"*, 9–11.

Ogden, Charles K. 1930, *Basic English. A general introduction with rules and grammar*. London: Paul Treber (2nd impr. 1940). Cf.: http://ogden.basic-english.org/basiceng.html

Petruck, Miriam. 1986. Body part terminology in Hebrew: A study in lexical semantics. Ph.D. dissertation, University of California, Berkeley.

Petruck, Miriam R. L., Charles J. Fillmore, Collin Baker, Michael Ellsworth, & Josef Ruppenhofer. 2004. Reframing FrameNet data. In *Proceedings of the 11th EURALEX International Congress*, Lorient, France. 405–416.

Ruppenhofer, Josef. 2018. Argument omission in multiple German corpora. In H.C. Boas & A. Ziem (eds.), *Constructional Approaches to Syntactic Structures in German*, 204–244. Berlin/Boston: de Gruyter Mouton.

Ruppenhofer, Josef, Boas, Hans C., & Collin Baker. 2013. The FrameNet approach to relating syntax and semantics. In R.H. Gouws, U. Heid, W. Schweickhard & H.E. Wiegand (eds.), *Dictionaries. An International Encyclopedia of Lexicography*, 1320–1329. Berlin/New York: Mouton.

Ruppenhofer, Josef, Hans C. Boas, and Collin F. Baker. 2017. FrameNet. In P. A. Fuertes-Olivera (ed.), *The Routledge Handbook of Lexicography*, 383–398. New York: Routledge.

Salomão, Maria Margarida Martins, Tiago Timponi Torrent & Thais Fernandes Sampaio. 2013. A Linguística de Corpus Encontra a Linguística Computacional: Notícias do Projeto FrameNet Brasil. *Cadernos de Estudos Linguísticos*, 55(1),7–34.

Schmidt, Thomas. 2009. The Kicktionary – A multilingual lexical resource of football language. In H.C. Boas (ed.), *Multilingual FrameNets: Methods and Applications*, 101–134. Berlin/New York: Mouton de Gruyter.

Slobin, Dan. 1996. Two ways to travel: Verbs of motion in English and Spanish. In M. Shibatani and S. Thompson (eds.), *Grammatical constructions: Their form and meaning*, 195–217. Oxford: Oxford University Press.
Subirats, Carlos. 2009. Spanish FrameNet: A frame-semantic analysis of the Spanish lexicon. In: H.C. Boas (ed.), *Multilingual FrameNets: Methods and Applications*, 135–162. Berlin/New York: Mouton de Gruyter.
Subirats, Carlos & Miriam Petruck. 2003. Surprise: Spanish FrameNet! *Proceedings of CIL 17*. CD-ROM. Prague: Matfyzpress.
Subirats, Carlos & Hiroaki Sato. 2004. Spanish FrameNet and FrameSQL. In *Proceedings of {LREC} 2004. Workshop on Building Lexical Resources from Semantically Annotated Corpora*, Lisbon, Portugal.
VanNoy, Annika. 2017. *Culture specific aspects of semantic frames in multilingual frame descriptions*. Unpublished Ph.D. dissertation, The University of Texas at Austin.
Viberg, Åke. 2002. Polysemy and disambiguation cues across languages. In B. Altenberg & S. Granger (eds.), Lexis in Contrast, 119–150. Amsterdam/Philadelphia: John Benjamins.
Wierzbicka, Anna. 2005. *English. Meaning and Culture*. Oxford: Oxford University Press.
Ziem, Alexander & Hans C. Boas 2017. Towards a Constructicon for German. In *Proceedings of the AAAI 2017 Spring Symposium on Computational Construction Grammar and Natural Language Understanding*. Technical Report SS-17-02, Stanford University. 274–277.

Stefan Th. Gries, Marlies Jansegers, and Viola G. Miglio
Quantitative methods for corpus-based contrastive linguistics

Abstract: The present paper makes a methodological contribution to the field of corpus-based contrastive linguistics. Contrary to the large majority of studies in contrastive linguistics that are mainly based on observed (relative) frequencies of (translation) data and are essentially monofactorial in nature, our study leverages more complex contrastive data that do justice to the complexity and multifactorial nature of cross-linguistic phenomena. Specifically, we focus on four challenging notions for the study of cross-linguistic near-synonymy: polysemy, degree of sense distinctiveness, prototypicality and identification of discriminatory variables. Each of these phenomena is tackled by means of a variety of statistical analyses based on two different kinds of input data that offer different kinds of resolutions on the data: (i) annotated concordance data and (ii) Behavorial Profile vectors. In an attempt to add to the toolbox of contrastive linguistics, we pay special attention to visualization techniques for cross-linguistic (dis)similarities such as hierarchical agglomerative cluster analysis, fuzzy clustering, and network analysis. These statistical methods will be illustrated on the basis of a case of cross-linguistic near-synonymy, namely the verb *sentir(e)* in Romance Languages.

Keywords: cross-linguistic near-synonymy, Behavioral Profile, data visualization (fuzzy clustering, network analysis), Romance perception verbs

1 Introduction

1.1 General introduction

Over the last few decades, linguistics has experienced a strong empirical and quantitative turn towards both experimental and observational, esp. corpus, data. Much of corpus linguistics was originally centered on monolingual corpora, but

---

Stefan Th. Gries, Department of Linguistics, University of California, Santa Barbara, United States of America; Justus Liebig University Giessen, Germany
Marlies Jansegers, Erasmus University College Brussels, Zespenningenstraat, Brussels
Viola G. Miglio, Department of Spanish and Portuguese, University of California, Santa Barbara, United States of America

https://doi.org/10.1515/9783110682588-003

over time corpus methods also became more widespread in contrastive-linguistic studies. However, although much of the revival of Contrastive Linguistics in the 1990s is due to its meeting with corpus linguistics, cross-fertilization between both disciplines is still rather limited as there are two main challenges that have not yet been fully addressed, namely (i) an empirical assessment of the nature of the data which are commonly used in cross-linguistic studies (namely translation data vs. comparable data), and (ii) the development of advanced methods and statistical techniques suitably adapted to the methodological challenges that are raised by contrastive research questions. Contrary to the other contributions in this volume, which largely focus on the nature of the data, the present paper focuses on this second challenge and focuses on making a methodological contribution to the field of contrastive linguistics (even though it should go without saying that improved methodology also has huge implications for what is possible in the areas of theory development and testing).

Even anno 2015, Gast (2015: 6) states that "the methodological branch of corpus-based contrastive linguistics is still tender", an inconvenient truth that becomes particularly evident when considering for example the specific field of contrastive semantics. Indeed, a closer look at the recent bibliography in contrastive corpus-based semantics shows that, with the notable exception of studies such as Levshina (2016), many analyses are based exclusively on frequency counts of translation equivalents (among others Viberg 1999, 2002, 2005; Altenberg 2002; Schmied 2008). Other studies make use of comparable corpora instead of translations or a combination of both, but are again largely based on mere (relative) frequencies (among others Enghels and Jansegers 2013; Comer and Enghels 2016; Rozumko 2016; Lansari 2017; Molino 2017).

With the objective of making the methodological branch of corpus linguistics less tender, the present paper is both programmatic and methodological in nature in that we aim to showcase the use of different statistical methods that can be applied to contrastive corpus-based semantics, which will be illustrated on the basis of a data set on cross-linguistic near-synonymy. Specifically, we are following up on Enghels and Jansegers (2013), a study of the semantics of the cognate verbs *SENTIR(E)* in the three Romance languages (French, Spanish, and Italian) combining parallel and comparable corpora.[1] The two main findings of this study were the following:

---

[1] The definition of these kinds of data and the difference between parallel and comparable corpora has been discussed elsewhere in this volume, see especially the papers from De Baets et al. and Viberg.

(i) It showed that the *tertium comparationis* at its most basic level can be defined as "general physical perception without any modality of perception being specified", as exemplified by the translation equivalents in (1):

(1) a. *Harry **sentit** la chaleur se répandre autour de lui comme s'il venait de plonger dans un bain tiède.* (French)
 b. *Harry **sintió** que el calor lo cubría como si estuviera metido en un baño caliente.* (Spanish)
 c. *Harry **sentì** il calore inondarlo come se si fosse immerso in un bagno caldo.* (Italian)
 'Harry felt the warmth wash over him as though he'd sunk into a hot bath.' (Harry Potter and the Philosopher's stone)

In other words, this translation equivalence shows that *SENTIR(E)* has been defined as a general physical perception verb in all three languages and it is this classification that constitutes the *tertium comparationis* at its most basic level. Therefore, *tertium comparationis* or "common ground" of comparison (Altenberg and Granger 2002: 15) for this study does not only refer to formal identity but also this basic semantic similarity between the three verbs.

(ii) However, apart from this small common core of perfect lexical correspondence, there seem to be some important language specific features: French *sentir* most dominantly covers the field of cognitive (but often intuitive) perception (see (2)). Italian seems to be the language where *sentire* most clearly belongs to the category of perception verbs, referring in the vast majority of the cases to auditory perception (see (3)). Spanish, on the other hand, has strongly developed the emotional sense of the verb and related to this, refers to the emotional meaning "regret, deplore" in a unique way (see (4)):

(2) a. *Il l'avait **senti** plus **qu'entendu**: quelque chose ou quelqu'un se trouvait dans l'espace étroit entre le muret et le garage de la maison devant laquelle il s'était arrêté.* (French)
 b. *Más que **oírlo**, lo **intuyó**: había alguien detrás de él, en el estrecho hueco que se abría entre el garaje y la valla.* (Spanish)
 c. *Lo **avvertiva**, più che **sentirlo** con le orecchie: c'era qualcuno o qualcosa lì nello stretto passaggio tra il garage e la staccionata alle sue spalle.* (Italian)
 'He had **sensed** rather than **heard** it: someone or something was standing in the narrow gap between the garage and the fence behind him.' (Harry Potter and the prisoner of Azkaban)

(3) a. *Elle **entendit** soudain battre son propre cœur. Ma famille?* (French)
   b. *De pronto Sophie se **oía** los latidos de su corazón. ¿Mi familia?* (Spanish)
   c. *Sophie aveva **sentito** che il cuore accelerava i battiti. La mia famiglia?* (Italian)
   'Sophie suddenly could **hear** her own heart. My family?' (Da Vinci Code)

(4) a. ***Je suis désolée**, Potter, reprit-elle, mais c'est mon dernier mot.* (French)
   b. ***Lo siento**, Potter; pero es mi última palabra.* (Spanish)
   c. ***Mi dispiace**, Potter, ma è la mia ultima parola.* (Italian)
   '**I'm sorry**, Potter, but that's my final word.' (Harry Potter and the prisoner of Azkaban)

In the present study, we take these observations as a starting point but we would like to make several suggestions for how it can be extended, both from a methodological and a more qualitative perspective:

- While the study by Enghels and Jansegers (2013) mainly addresses the issue of the comparability / compatibility between translation and comparable corpus data, it is based on observed (relative) frequencies, and is essentially monofactorial in nature. Our study, by contrast, focuses on the methodological challenge for the field of Contrastive Linguistics. It leverages more complex contrastive data derived from Behavioral Profiles (BPs) that are based on the similarities of vectors in order to explore the question of how this degree of cross-linguistic near-synonymy can be operationalized and investigated on an empirical and quantitative basis. That is, how can we compare multifactoriality behind this case of near-synonymy between sister languages? In an attempt to add to the toolbox of contrastive linguistics, we also extend this method for better visualization of cross-linguistic differences.

- On a more qualitative level, the study by Enghels and Jansegers focuses largely on the semantics of the verbs, and adopts moreover a coarse-grained perspective by focusing on three general semantic categories such as physical perception, emotional perception and cognitive perception. Since the BP method starts from the distributional hypothesis, namely the idea that differences in function/meaning are reflected in differences in distribution, we performed a very fine-grained manual annotation of dozens of features that include not only semantic, but also morphological, syntactic, and other characteristics. In this way, we hope to answer the question to what extent do these semantic differences correlate with syntactic diverging patterns.

In what follows, we will briefly describe the outline and of this chapter as well as the kinds of phenomena we discuss.

1.2 Overview of the present paper

As mentioned above, this paper is intended to be two things: (i) programmatic in nature and (ii) methodological. Specifically, we wish to discuss how a variety of research questions that are common in contrastive linguistics (with a special emphasis on semantic questions) can be studied on the basis of corpus data and their differently sophisticated statistical analyses. Given constraints of space, the proposed methodologies can only be exemplified briefly, which makes it even more necessary than generally to structure this overview well. Two issues need to be covered in particular: the range of phenomena we will cover and the kinds of input data whose statistical analysis will be discussed.

With regard to the former – the phenomena – we will focus on the following concepts, each of which will be briefly addressed in a separate section below:

- *degree of sense distinctiveness*: How many different senses of an expression are there in each language separately and how do these senses relate to each other within and across languages?
- *polysemy*: To the extent that senses can be delineated/operationalized, which senses are there and how do they differ especially across languages?
- *prototypicality*: To what degree are prototypical meanings of cognate words similar or different across languages? Is it possible to identify one cross-linguistic prototype?
- *identification of discriminatory variables*: What are the (morphosyntactic and semantic) variables correlating with a specific sense that most strongly discriminate between languages?

With regard to the latter – the input data – there are two kinds of data we will consider, since they offer different levels of resolution and of usefulness for further analysis. In particular, we will focus on the following kinds of data:

- *Annotated concordance data*: where the input will consist of, typically, a spreadsheet kind of structure in which each row represents one line of a concordance output (i.e., one match) and in which each column represents one variable with regard to which the match has been annotated (for what follows, such variables will also be referred to as ID tags, see Atkins 1987) and the different values that each variable/ID tag can assume will be referred to as ID Tag levels; for example, each subject of a verb could be annotated for the variable/ID tag *subject animacy* using one of, say, four, ID tag levels

(e.g. *human, animate, concrete inanimate, abstract*). This format is commonly referred to as the case-by-variable format (e.g. Maindonald and Braun 2010 or Fox and Weisberg 2011) or "the long format".
- *Behavioral Profile vectors* (based on annotated concordance data): this format is based on percentages. Behavioral Profiles is a statistical method to analyze semantic and syntactic aspects of corpus/concordance data with regard to semantic questions such as (near) synonymy, polysemy, and others. It was developed by Gries (2006) and Divjak (2006). If one created the above kind of annotated concordance data for – say – a set *x* of near-synonymous verbs in one language, then Behavioral Profile (BP) vectors are generated from it by computing for each of the *x* verbs, the percentage that each ID tag level makes up each ID tag. This is the technical way for saying something statistically quite easy: It means that, to use the above example of *subject animacy*, for each verb, we compute how many instances in % of the subjects are *human*, are *animate*, are *concrete inanimate*, and are *abstract*; these percentages will add up to 1 (100%), and we do the same for each verb and for each other ID tag. That way, each verb's overall behavior will be characterized by a concatenation of ID tag percentages (each adding up to 1), which can then be analyzed in various ways; for applications, see Divjak and Gries (2009); Gries (2010a); Gries and Otani (2010).

In the next section, we discuss the data we use in this paper to exemplify our analyses, first the annotated concordance data (Section 1.3.1), then the BP vectors (Section 1.3.2).

1.3 The current data

1.3.1 The annotated concordance data

In order to study *SENTIR(E)* from a cross-linguistic perspective, we compiled a comparable corpus consisting of authentic texts in each language that match as far as possible in terms of text type, subject matter and communicative function (Altenberg and Granger 2002: 8), but are not translations of each other. From this corpus, 1,500 occurrences of the verb *sentir(e)* were retrieved – 500 per language – half of which were drawn from literature (fiction) and the other half from press texts.[2] From these comparable data we generated and annotated

---

[2] The availability of representative corpora differs considerably from one language to another. The Spanish database CREA contains both fiction and journalistic data, but for French the literary

pseudo-randomly sampled concordance lines of *SENTIR(E)* in all three languages for a large variety of morphosyntactic and semantic properties, called ID tags (Atkins 1987). A wide range of objectively verifiable (observable) parameters were distinguished according to four general levels of analysis, that is (i) the properties of the verb itself, (ii) the argument structure of the verb, (iii) the characteristics of other adjuncts, and (iv) discourse phenomena. Table 1 presents an example of such ID tags and their levels:

Table 1: Examples of ID tags and their levels.

General level	Type of ID tag	ID tag	ID tag level
Verb	morphosyntactic properties	Tense	present, past, future, infinitive
		Person	1, 2, 3
		number	singular, plural
	semantic properties	semantic category	general physical, specific physical, emotional, cognitive, ambiguous
		fine-grained sense (40)	emotional experience, to hear, general physical experience, to realize, to consider/judge, to intuit, tactile experience, to regret, ... (=70%)
Argument structure	properties of subject form	lexical S	with S, without S
	properties of object form	lexical DO	with DO, without DO
	semantics of DO	referent DO	person, concrete entity, abstract entity, situation, ambiguous
Adjunct	properties of adverbial adjuncts	presence of adverbial adjunct	w/ adverbial adjunct, w/out adverbial adjunct
		form of adverbial adjunct	adverb, prepositional phrase, nominal phrase, etc.
Discourse	scope	predicational autonomy	no, yes

---

database FRANTEXT was complemented by data retrieved from the newspaper Le Monde. The Italian journalistic database *Il Corriere della Sera* (CdS) was supplemented with data drawn from two novels: *La luna di carta* (A. Camilleri) and *L'intreccio di universi paralleli* (A. Lo Gatto).

As an essential part of the analysis, the sense annotation merits some additional comments. As indicated in Table 1, the semantic analysis of the verb itself was done in two different resolutions. First, we resorted to a very fine-grained annotation of the different possible senses that were minimally different. Second, this fine-grained analysis then led to a more coarse-grained classification into four general semantic categories, namely (i) general physical perception, (ii) specific modality of physical perception, (iii) emotional perception and (iv) cognitive perception. This was done manually and mainly on the basis of the Romance comparative study of *SENTIR(E)* by Enghels and Jansegers (2013) where a lexicographic analysis was complemented with the results of a parallel corpus, based on translation data.[3]

The output of this first step then is a spreadsheet with one row for every concordance match of *SENTIR(E)*, some columns describing the language and maybe corpus of each match, and minimally one additional column for every ID tag that has been annotated, as exemplified in Table 2.

Table 2: Snippet of a concordance spreadsheet with annotation.

Preceding	Match	Subsequent	X	Y	Z	...
a b c	sentir	d e f	k	l	m	...
o p q	sentir	r s t	w	x	y	...
...	...	...	...	...	...	...

1.3.2 The BP vectors

After the retrieval and manual annotation of all the occurrences, we converted these data into a co-occurrence percentage table that provides the relative frequency of co-occurrence of each sense of the verb *sentir* (in the columns) with each ID tag level (in the rows). This procedure was performed with Gries's (2010b)

---

[3] The consulted Spanish dictionaries are: the *Diccionario de la Lengua Española* (DRAE), the *Diccionario de Uso del Español* (DUE), the *Diccionario del Español Actual* (DEA) and the *Gran Diccionario de la Lengua Española* (GDLE) for the synchronic data. For French, the lexicographic study is based on *Le Nouveau Petit Robert: Dictionnaire alphabétique et analogique de la langue française* and for Italian the *Grande dizionario Italiano dell'uso*. The translation corpus (approx. 2,5 million words) contains source texts written in a non-Romance language and their translations in Spanish, French, and Italian. Ideally, all of the annotation could have been double-checked by additional annotators, a practice not yet very widespread in corpus linguistics.

BehavioralProfiles 1.01 script using the R statistical software package. As exemplified in Table 3, the percentages of ID tag levels add up to 1 within each ID tag so that each column represents a set of co-occurrence percentages for one sense of the verb. It is precisely these vector of co-occurrence percentages – i.e. 0.3, 0.35, 0.01, 0.34, 0.18, 0.82, ... for "experience: physical perception" – that are called "Behavioral Profiles".

Table 3: Examples of BP vectors.

ID tag	ID tag level	experience: physical perception	experience: emotional perception	auditory perception	consider, judge	...
tense	present	0.30	0.36	0.29	0.55	...
	past	0.35	0.40	0.53	0.30	...
	future	0.01	0.01	0.00	0.02	...
	infinitive	0.34	0.23	0.18	0.13	...
lexical S	with S	0.18	0.41	0.24	0.41	...
	without S	0.82	0.59	0.76	0.59	...
...	...	...	...	...	...	...

This BP method has proven useful for the analysis of different phenomena in lexical semantics such as near-synonymy (Divjak and Gries 2006; Divjak 2010), antonymy (Gries and Otani 2010) and polysemy (Gries 2006; Berez and Gries 2009; Jansegers et al. 2015) and has recently also been successfully applied to diachronic data (Jansegers and Gries to appear). However, we will make and exemplify two suggestions for how it can be extended. First, while most existing BP studies focus mainly on monolingual corpora, we will apply the BP approach to contrastive linguistic research questions in lexical semantics. Second, whereas most BP studies used hierarchical agglomerative cluster analysis (HAC) as their main exploratory tool, we will also pay special attention to other visualization techniques for cross-linguistic (dis)similarities.

1.3.3 Final preliminary comments

It should be mentioned that we are not particularly concerned with how this kind of annotation was arrived at. We understand that there is no tried and true mechanistic way of distinguishing between different senses of a polysemous lexeme in general and that any such sense discrimination will need to consider not only the immediate linguistic context of the sentence it appears in, but possibly also the pragmatic context of use (Rozovskaya and Girju 2009). Much like the lexicographic work of sense identification, the annotation leading to BPs is usually an iterative process, where for instance, ID tags are modified, corrected or their number extended as different contexts of usage in the corpus come to light. In other words, we are not considering the question of sense identification/discrimination as theoretically or methodologically unambiguously resolved, just as tractable for practical purposes (again as in lexicographic work)[4] or there would be much fewer problems with lexical semantics and lexical relations within the context of machine learning, where different senses need to be extracted automatically, rather than manually coded (Romeo et al. 2013). In coding the ID tags for this work, we are first of all building on decades of traditional semantic, cognitive-linguistic, and psycholinguistic research attesting to the fact that it is possible to distinguish between senses and meanings of polysemous terms, and we adopted a pragmatic view that linguistically trained coders, who are also speakers of the languages at hand, would be able to disambiguate the senses through the perusal of the term's linguistic context. Secondly, our use of a concordance avoids looking at the term out of context or hand-picking terms occurring in a limited syntactic context or with predetermined senses. We accepted instead the full gamut of natural language usage and its complexity, as found in the corpora we used, and we also allowed for senses being annotated as *ambiguous/unidentifiable*. Thirdly, the methods outlined in this study can actually help in perfecting some of these fine-grained distinctions in meaning, which is what BPs were originally developed for (Gries 2006). Finally, results can of course be made even more robust and replicable by implementing any method requiring inter-annotator agreement.

2 Polysemy and senses' differences/distinctiveness

Assuming one has data of the above kind, the question of the most important and common senses there are across languages and which ones are language-

---

[4] We realize how much this sounds like a cop-out, but such situations abound in linguistics in many domains other than semantic as well; after all, it is not like scholars would agree on the syntactic analysis of constructions, the morphological status of affixes, the status of certain morphemes or words in child language acquisition data, etc. In all these disciplines, researchers adopt solutions that are not perfect but feasible enough for certain analytical or practical purposes.

specific can sometimes be relatively straightforward to answer: The simplest way is cross-tabulation of the annotated concordance data and visualization (which could be followed by significance testing (χ^2 or G^2), if one's data meet the assumption of independence of data points).

This shows minimally that the three languages differ significantly with regard to which senses *SENTIR(E)* expresses (in the coarse resolution of just five senses): In French, the cognitive and the physical.general senses are more frequent than expected, in Italian, the physical.specific sense is, and in Spanish the emotional one is. Also, in French, the emotional sense is very rare (see Figure 1). Obviously, this can be done with more fine-grained sense classifications: Adopting the more fine-grained classification discussed above, Cramer's *V* increases to 0.69.

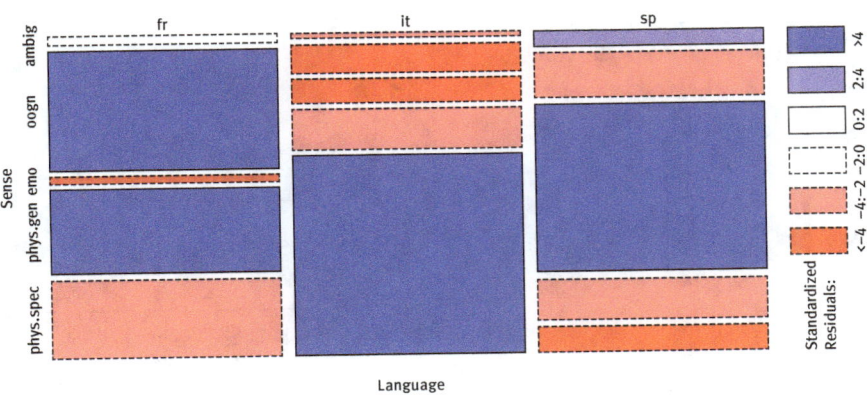

Figure 1: Mosaic plot of Table 4.

In addition, data such as Table 4 also permit us to compare how similar the different languages are in their sense frequencies. One way to do so would involve a hierarchical agglomerative cluster analysis (see Gries 2013: Section 5.6, Moisl 2015), where the languages are clustered on the basis of how similar the senses' frequencies are to each other; the result of such an analysis (based on Euclidean distances and the "complete" amalgamation method) is shown in the left panel of Figure 2. Another way to do so would be a correspondence analysis (see Glynn 2010, Desagulier 2017: Section 10.4–10.5).

The left panel shows that the sense frequencies in French and Italian are much more similar to each other than they are to Spanish. The right panel shows that, too: The three languages are clearly separated along the *x*-axis, with French and Italian being close together and far apart from Spanish; moreover, French and Italian are associated more with cognitive and physical senses, whereas

Table 4: Cross-tabulation ($G^2 = 852.3$, $df = 8$, $p < 10^{-100}$, Cramer's $V = 0.54$).

	French		Italian		Spanish		Totals
ambiguous	13	(2.6%)	7	(1.4%)	26	(5.2%)	46
cognitive	203	(40.6%)	49	(9.8%)	77	(15.4%)	329
emotional	11	(2.2%)	40	(8%)	288	(57.6%)	339
physical.general	144	(28.8%)	68	(13.6%)	69	(13.8%)	281
physical.specific	129	(25.8%)	336	(67.2%)	40	(8%)	505
Totals	500		500		500		1,500

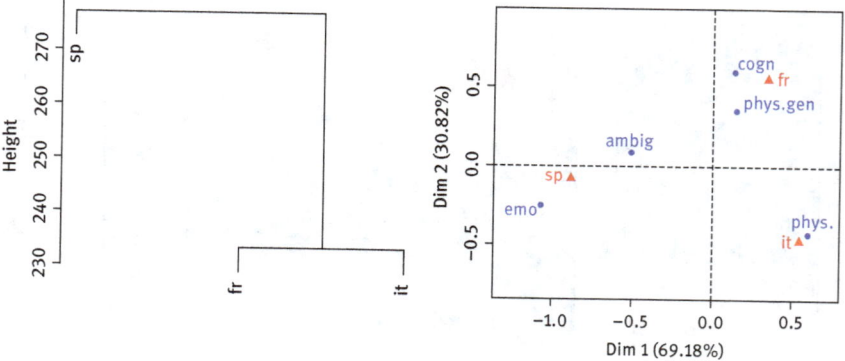

Figure 2: Further analytical plots of Table 4 (left: hierarchical cluster analysis, right: correspondence analysis).

Spanish is more closely associated with the emotional sense; notice also how, in a nicely intuitive way, the ambiguous uses occupy a central position in the plot. In this case, both powerful tools do not offer much beyond the simpler analyses of the mosaic plot above, but that is why these simple data exemplify the kinds of attainable outcomes well. With more complex multivariate data, cluster and correspondence analysis have of course more to offer.

Different analytical possibilities arise when we change the resolution, which we can do in two ways. First, we can switch from the annotated concordance data to the BP vectors; second, we can create a new variable that combines – for each line – its language (i.e. French, Italian, and Spanish) with its sense (in either a coarse or a fine-grained resolution). This can be used to determine which (groups of) senses behave alike across (which) languages. Let us first briefly discuss the result of a cluster analysis of the combination of languages with coarse-grained

senses based on the BP vectors. Before we show the results, it is instructive to consider the range of results one might get:
- one theoretical extreme is that the dendrogram would group together all senses (i.e. their BP vectors) within each language, therefore, we would get three clusters (essentially as in the left panel of Figure 2);
- another theoretical extreme is that the dendrogram would group together all senses (i.e. their BP vectors) across languages, therefore, we would get four clusters (because we are leaving out the ambiguous cases now);
- a complete mess, either because there is no discernible structure in the data or there is, but it makes no sense either way.

The actual results are now shown in Figure 3 below and they are remarkably clear.

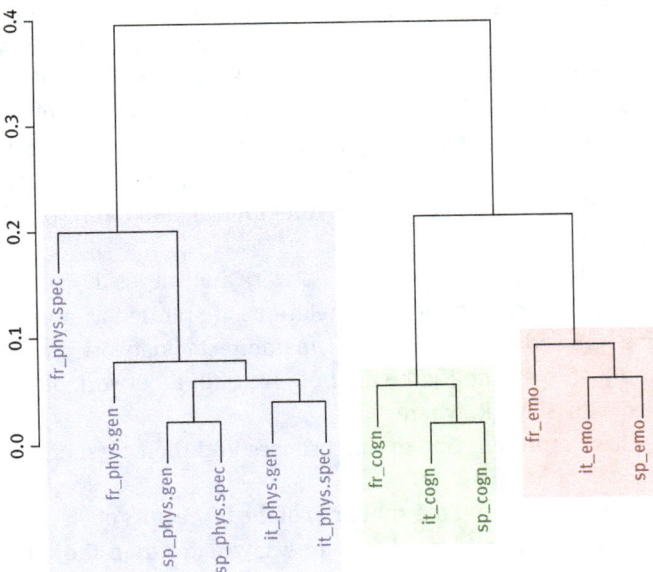

Figure 3: Dendrogram from a hierarchical cluster analysis of combinations of languages and coarse senses.

It makes sense to recognize three clusters as highlighted (based on average silhouette widths), and they are of the second theoretical kind: the obtained clusters point to the fact that senses pattern together *across languages* rather than patterning together *within the same language*. The pink cluster indicates that the emotional uses behave more similarly across the three languages than within each one of them, as it contains all and only all emotional senses; another cluster contains all cognitive senses across the three languages, and the biggest one contains all physical senses with one "outlier sense" (French physical.specific). Follow-up analyses of such dendrograms (along the lines of Divjak and Gries 2006) can then help determine which of the annotated ID tags and their levels drive this particular clustering outcome.

A similar analysis of the fine-grained senses returns many more and more diverse clusters, but it still offers a result that groups senses together more than languages. For instance, all and only all emotional.experience senses are together in one cluster, as are all consider.judge senses, whereas the cognitive. realize, cognitive.think, and cognitive.intuit senses are also together in the same cluster.

Obviously, alternative cluster-analytical approaches are conceivable – for instance, these data can also be analyzed with more cognitively plausible fuzzy clustering approaches, which allow for graded cluster memberships of the clustered elements, towards senses within one language only.[5] For example, Figure 4 is one possible visualization of a fuzzy clustering of the BP vectors of the fine-grained senses in Italian (with 4 desired clusters); this clustering is quite fuzzy (normalized Dunn coefficient = 0.25), but the membership values clearly support, among others, a fairly robust cognitive cluster (red, on the left), a fairly robust cluster of multiple physical.specific senses (green, foreground), and one of physical.general_experience (turquoise, in the center).

A final analytical example involves the use of network analysis as discussed in Ellis et al. (2013), where senses and their interrelations are plotted as nodes/ vertices and connecting links/edges respectively in an undirected network graph. In the present case and just to exemplify the method, we built a network of the French senses observed with SENTIR, where

- vertices and their sizes represent fine-grained senses and their frequencies in the French data;
- edges and their thickness represent the similarity of the BP vectors of all pairs of senses whose similarity (Euclidean distance) was greater than the 40% quantile of all pairwise similarities (this was done to avoid having to plot even edges that reflect low degrees of sense similarity; the cut-off point of 40% is arbitrary and was chosen here on the basis of visual inspection);

---

[5] We are considering these cognitively more plausible for the simple reason that they allow for graded category membership and prototypicality in a way that is extremely compatible with the kind of cognitive-linguistic or usage-based approach we are adopting here as well.

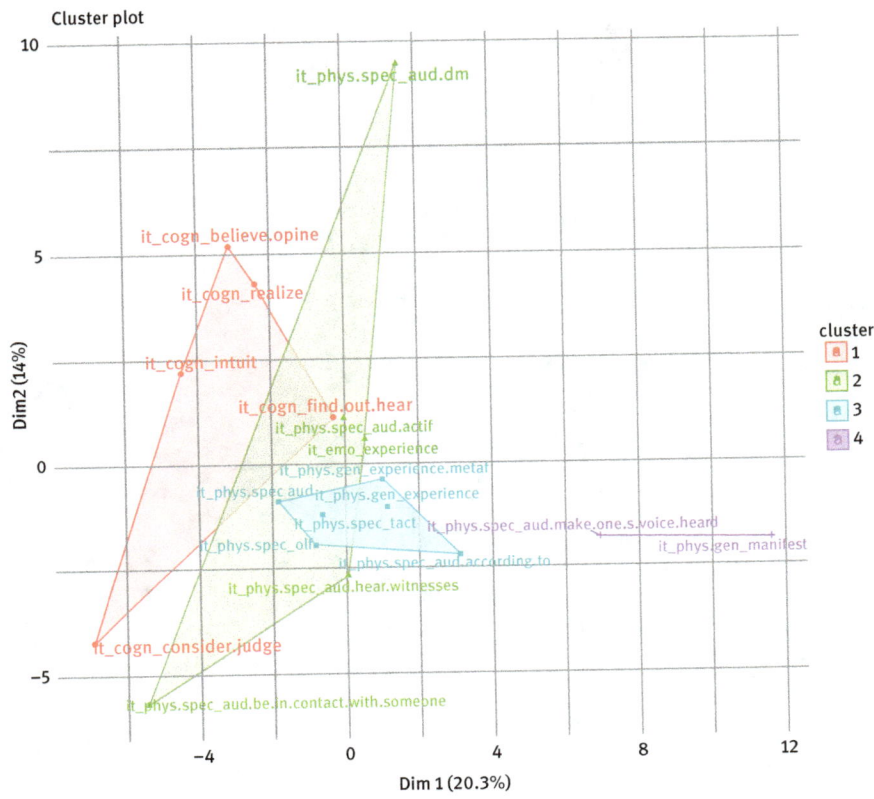

Figure 4: Dendrogram from a fuzzy cluster analysis of the Italian fine-grained senses.

– the vertices' colors represent the three "communities" of senses identified by a multi-level modularity optimization algorithm for finding community structure based in the pairwise similarities mentioned above.[6]

The network algorithm finds three communities whose elements are differently strongly related to each other and which are represented in Figure 5: (i) a red community consisting of all cognitive senses as well as emotional.experience, (ii) a green community consisting of all physical.general senses and one physical.

---

[6] Modularity in graph theory is treated as a quality measure of the amount and "cleanliness" of a cluster structure in a network. Much like in cluster analysis, it refers to the notion of clusters in a network exhibiting (i) high internal connectivity/similarity but (ii) low connectivity/similarity to other clusters.

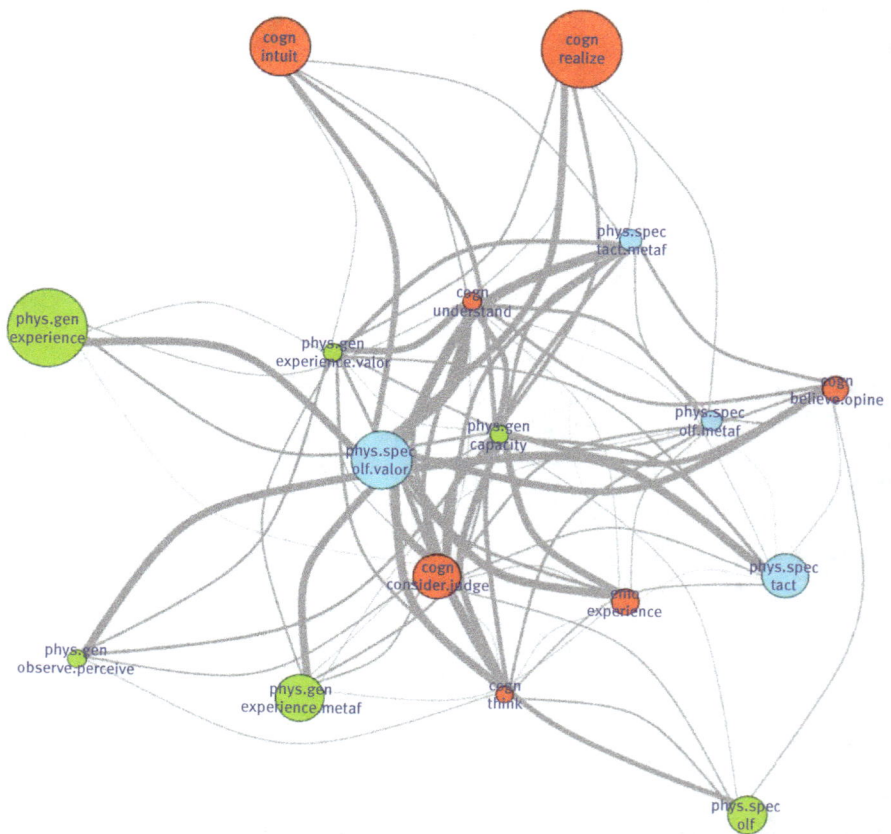

Figure 5: Semantic network analysis plot of the fine-grained French senses of *SENTIR*.

specific sense (bottom right), and (iii) a light blue community consisting of all remaining physical.specific senses. In this case, the result is quite clear and the bottom-up and multivariate method lends strong support to both the method per se, the sense annotation, and, most importantly for contrastive linguists from a cognitive perspective, a grouping of senses that is compatible with cognitive-linguistic theorizing, e.g. the clear distinctions of more mental (cognitive and emotional) senses on the one hand and more physical ones on the other.

We now turn to the questions of how to identify prototypical configurations of ID tag levels and prototypes as well as how to identify which ID tag levels are most discriminatory within and across languages.

3 Prototypicality, markedness, and identifying discriminatory/predictive variables

The question of identifying prototypical senses of *SENTIR(E)* is one that is best approached by, first determining a likely candidate for "the prototype" in each language (or, alternatively, a candidate set), and then compare those prototypes across languages. Gries (2006) discusses a variety of ways in which prototypes of the verb *to run* may be explored. Given the nature of the concept "prototype" itself, it is not surprising that there are few, if any, individual necessary and jointly sufficient conditions/diagnostics; there are, however, different ways to approach the issue.

One is obviously frequency, which is arguably at least somewhat related to prototypicality and can easily be obtained from the annotated data. According to this criterion the prototype for Italian *SENTIR(E)* would be physical.specific (specifically, from the fine-grained data, the sense physical.auditory), whereas for Spanish it would be emotional.experience (especially including the grammaticalization of the construction into the fixed form *lo siento*).[7] For French, however, we immediately recognize the problem of granularity: Table 4 suggests that the cognitive sense (of cognitive.realize) is most frequent, but it is also obvious that the two physical senses *together* would outnumber this one. This might be a case of a radial category with multiple centroids (in the same way that, to use a well-known example, the word *game* might have multiple local prototypes, e.g. one for games involving sports-like physical activity like "playing catch", one for games involving no physical aspects but mental acuity such as card games like Poker, …).

---

[7] The connection between the Spanish emotional meaning of *sentir* and its prototypicality is due to the historical evolution of this sense in the language. While "being affected by something already exists in the Latin meaning of the verb" (Verbeke 2011: 21), Verbeke also shows that the verb in Spanish evolves from denoting physical sensation ('to feel cold'), extends to feeling emotions ('to feel joy, anger, sadness'), among which both dictionaries (for instance Covarrubias in 1611) and corpora start numbering a few examples of feelings of regret or dissatisfaction already in the 15th century. By the 18th century the *Diccionario de Autoridades* marks one of the senses of *sentir* as 'to feel anguish or sorrow' (p. 23) and soon competes with *lamentar* 'to regret'. *Sentir* has become the go-to generic perception verb by the 20th century with 83% of modern uses, among them many with negative and emotional perceptions and 9% more exclusively in the 'to regret' sense according to Verbeke (2011: 47). In this last sense, the subjectivized verb has also undergone grammaticalization along a morphosyntactic cline producing many instances of the fixed form *lo siento* in the 20th century corpus. Its literal meaning is 'I regret it', nowadays used as an interjection with the simple meaning of 'sorry!'. As such it significantly increases the frequency of the emotional sense of *sentir* in modern texts, and contributes to the prototypicality of the emotional sense in Spanish.

Another way of approaching prototypicality is based on the notion of cue validity. Much research on prototypes now argues that prototypes are an abstract entity combining the properties with the highest cue validity for the category in question, where cue validity is essentially the conditional probability p(category membership | property); for instance the property 'having feathers' has a high cue validity for the category BIRD (because most birds have feathers and most non-birds don't) whereas 'having eyes' does not have a high cue validity for BIRD because while most if not all birds have eyes, most other animals do too.

This simple definition is instructive in how it points to the possibility of exploring prototypicality on the basis of classifiers and similar techniques such as regression models, (linear/quadratic) discriminant analysis, classification trees or random forests, and many others. This is because these techniques can all do two things: they can identify which ID tags and levels have the highest degree of predictive power per sense (per language) and they can compute a predicted probability of a sense (per language) for each case in the data. How does that relate to prototypicality? It does along the lines argued first by Gries (2003a, 2003b), who used the probabilities with which a binary constructional choice was predicted to identify the most prototypical instances in the data: the highest predicted probabilities for a constructional choice reflected that these instances combined many features that raised the (conditional) probability for that constructional choice, making them (close to) prototypical. The same logic can be applied here: one can run a classifier on either the senses (across all languages) or the language-sense combinations and then, if the classifier does a good job,
- use measures of variable importance to determine which predictors are most important for predictions;
- determine for each level of the dependent variable, which cases yield the highest and correctly predicted probabilities to abstract away to a prototype.

To briefly exemplify this kind of analysis, we used random forests to try and predict from all annotated ID tags and their levels a variable that consisted of the language and the coarse-grained senses; in other words, the dependent variable had levels such as "fr_emo", "fr_cog", "fr_phys.gen", etc. Random forests are an extension of simple classification (and regression) trees. Classification (and regression) trees are a partitioning approach that consists of successively splitting the data into two groups based on predictors (here ID tags) such that the split maximizes the classification accuracy regarding the dependent variable. This process is recursive, i.e. repeated until no further split would increase the classification accuracy enough anymore. Random forests in turn add two layers of randomness to the analysis, which help (i) recognizing the impact of variables or their combinations that a normal classification tree might not register and (ii) protecting against overfitting.

On the one hand, the algorithm constructs many different trees (we used 500), each of which is fitted to a different bootstrapped sample of the full data. On the other hand, each split in each tree could choose from only a randomly-chosen subset of predictors (we set that parameter to five predictors). The overall result is then based on amalgamating all 500 trees that have been generated by identifying the majority vote of the forest's predictions for each cases.[8]

The baseline for such a classifier is typically computed as the highest probability of any level of the dependent variable, which here is 0.224 (for the most frequent sense of ita_phys.spec). We then ran a random forest (using all default settings of the function party::cforest in R, see Hothorn et al. 2006) on the data and obtained a very good prediction accuracy of 0.656, i.e. nearly three times as good as, and significantly different from, the baseline. The most important ID tags (as determined by variable importance plots) for this excellent result were the semantic role and form of the subject as well as the referent and the form of the direct object; in fact, those four ID tags alone already yield a prediction accuracy of 0.648. We then finally looked at the combinations of ID tag levels for each language-sense combination that were most frequent, had the highest predicted probability, and were correctly predicted, which yielded, among others, the following prototypes:
- French cognitive: a pronominal experiencer SUBJ and a clausal DO referring to a situation/event, which is very similar to the Spanish cognitive: a non-lexical SUBJ (since Spanish is pro-drop, the subject is typically not expressed by a pronoun or a NP) with the same kind of DO. The Italian cognitive uses were hardly ever predicted correctly by the classifier.

(5) *Le militantisme était devenu une contrainte. Je* **sentais** *que le monde était plus complexe que nos discours* (French, Le Monde, 1998).
'Activism had become a constraint. I realized that the world was more complex than our speeches.'

- Italian physical.specific: a non-lexical (since Italian is also pro-drop, the subject is typically not expressed by a pronoun or a NP) perpt (perceptor, i.e. an entity that experiences *physical* perception, visual, auditory, tactile etc.) with a concrete-entity DO NP (6) or infinitive; the corresponding French sense has a stimulus NP as a subject and no DO. The corresponding Spanish sense was hardly ever predicted correctly.

---

[8] Note that random forests do not require the same kind of training vs. test sampling procedure because the predictions that the algorithm returns are OOB (out-of-bag) predictions, i.e. predictions made not for the data points on which a tree was trained, but the ones held out.

(6) Ho **sentito** un boato – racconta Aurora Falcone – è poi sono stata catapultata sulla strada. [Italian, CdS, 2010]
'I heard an explosion – says Aurora Falcone – and then I was catapulted on the road.'

Thus, random forests or any other classifier that returns predicted probabilities can help identify both concrete examples in the data as well as abstract combinations of features with high cue validities that correspond to what in cognitive linguistic approaches are prototypes.

The next method to be briefly mentioned is that of association rules, a much more exploratory and extremely granular machine learning method that looks at potentially quite large data sets of categorical variables. This method is also applied to the annotated concordance data. Association rules are essentially just conditional sentences, consisting of

- an *if*-clause or antecedent, which can contain more than one condition (up to a user-defined number, we used 4); in association-rules terminology, this is referred to as "the left-hand side" (LHS);
- a main clause or consequent, which contains one resultant condition; in association-rules terminology, this is referred to as "the right-hand side" (RHS).

An example of a rule in the present context (using the coarse-grained senses) would be "if Language = "French" and if FormOfDO = "clause" (LHS), then Sense = "cognitive (RHS)". If an analyst wishes to apply this method to a data set (such as the 1,500 concordance lines times 26 ID tag columns of the present data), (s)he usually specifies three parameters that serve to put a cap on the number of such rules that are generated:

- a parameter called *support*: the proportion of data points that contains all conditions/items in the rule (i.e. both LHS and RHS). In the above case, the 1,500 data points contain 106 cases of French uses with the sense "cognitive" where the DO is a clause, i.e. support = $106/1{,}500 \approx 0.071$. Support is used to state the minimum number of cases to which a rule must apply for it to be returned;
- a parameter called *confidence*: the proportion of times the rule is correct. In the above case, there are 16 additional cases of French cases with a clausal DO that do *not* come with the sense "cognitive", which means the rule is right $106/122 \approx 0.869$ of the time;
- a parameter called *maxlen*, which specifies the number of elements in the rule or, since the length of the RHS is set to 1, the number of conditions usable in the LHS. In the above example, the length of the rule is of course 3.

We applied this approach to our data (with min. support = 0.05, min. confidence = 0.6, maxlen = 5) and obtained approximately 1,5 million rules. However, to see which senses are most different between languages, this number was then reduced to only those rules that featured Language in the LHS and Sense in the RHS, which returned 10,3K rules. Obviously, these cannot all be studied so analysts have a wide range of options to narrow down which rules to study. These options include
- specific statistics that quantify the "noteworthiness" of each rule (examples include statistics such as *lift, hyper-lift, hyper-confidence*, and just about any other association measures that can be applied to 2×2 tables, see Hahsler and Hornik 2007; Hahsler et al. 2008). Lift is a measure reflecting how much observed co-occurrence differs from expected co-occurrence; hyper-lift is a more robust variant of that statistic.
- common-sense and phenomenon-specific considerations such as the diverging syntax-semantics interfaces across languages, here, being particularly interested in rules, whose LHS differ only by language and whose RHS differ only by sense (which means that they predict different senses).

Figure 6 shows two plots that would help analysts analyze the data. Both panels plot all 10.3K association rules on the basis of their support (*x*-axis) and their hyper-lift (*y*-axis), with the point size indicating the confidence. The left panel uses RGB coloring to indicate the language to which the rule applies and it is immediately obvious that the rules for Italian are characterized by much less hyper-lift than those of the other languages; the median for Spanish is highest, followed by French, followed by the much smaller Italian. The right panel uses RGB coloring to indicate the coarse-grained sense which the rule involves, and here it is clear that the cognitive sense is characterized by the highest hyper-lift, compared to lower values for emotional, followed by much lower values for the two physical senses.

Sorting all rules by their LHSs and/or by the number of rules in which a certain LHS is embedded is a path towards a more detailed analysis. For instance, we find the following kinds of differences between the languages:
- SEMANTIC_ROLE_S=perpt is correlated with physical.general senses in French and Spanish, but with physical.specific in Italian (see (6) above, esp. when no other adjuncts and complements are present or when the subject is animate/human):

(7) *Mariana se convirtió en una muchacha de aspecto lánguido, con la sonrisa triste de las personas que padecen sin* **sentir** *dolor en el cuerpo* (Spanish, CREA, 1996).
'Mariana became a languid-looking girl, with the sad smile of those people who suffer without feeling pain in their body.'

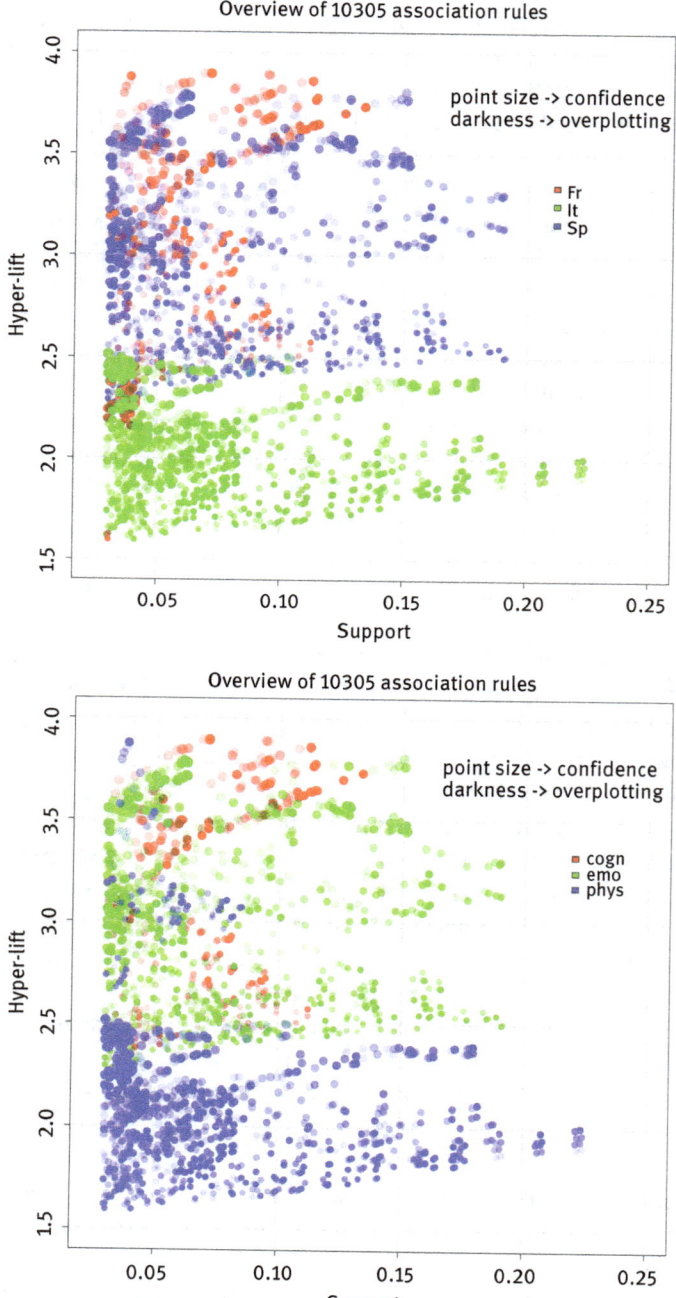

Figure 6: Overview of association rules results.

- infinitive DOs are correlated with physical.general senses in French (see (8)), but with physical.specific in Italian (see (9)):

(8) *Je commençais à suer, à **sentir** sourdre la sueur sous mes aisselles* (French, Frantext, 2006).
'I began to sweat, to feel the sweat well up under my armpits.'

(9) *Come **sentire** squillare un cellulare in sala o vedere un abbigliamento non consono al teatro. Il messaggio è lanciato.* (Italian, CdS, 2017)
'Like hearing a cell phone ring at the cinema or see inappropriate attire at the theater. The message has been sent.'

- BASIC_AS=abs (esp. with no additional adjuncts or complements) are correlated with physical.specific senses in French and Italian, but not in Spanish; etc. These are cases of the absolute use of the verb, without explicit DO. For example, French *sentir* often appears in a copulative construction, expressing a certain valorization of the olfactory process:

(10) *Il n'aimait pas son odeur, ça **sent** le poisson pourri, il ne pouvait pas le faire.* (French, Frantext, 2006)
'He did not like her smell; [lit.] it smells like rotten fish, he could not do it.'

While the technique is highly exploratory, it can help reveal much probabilistic structure in the data, and interactive visualization tools (see Hahsler 2017), which cannot be shown in a printed paper, can serve to highlight patterns in the data that would otherwise remain invisible to the naked eye just studying concordance lines.

Moving on to the BP vectors, another criterion can be derived from markedness considerations, leading to the assumption that the prototypical sense should be (among) the formally least constrained senses. For BP data, this criterion could lead to the question of which senses have the smallest numbers of zeros in their BP vectors, i.e. which senses are attested with the largest variety of ID tags. For the present data, this leads to
- for French: cognitive.consider/judge and physical.general_experience;
- for Italian: physical.specific_auditory and physical.general_experience;
- for Spanish emotional.experience and physical.general_experience.

In other words and maybe unsurprisingly given *SENTIR(E)*'s "general meaning", physical.general_experience is always part of the least restrained senses, but then the languages differ in terms of the other least restrained sense. Virtually the same results are obtained from using a more advanced approach, namely by computing, for each language separately, how much the ID tag level percentages with a specific sense differ from the same ID tag level percentages with *all* senses with the Kullback-Leibler divergence (see Cover and Thomas 2006: 19–20), a directional measure that quantifies how much one probability distribution differs from another. Then one adds up how much each sense's ID tag level distribution is different from those of all senses because the least marked sense(s) should exhibit the smallest difference(s). We obtain the same results as with the simpler approach – the only difference is that this approach returns cognitive.intuit for French rather than cognitive.consider/judge; everything else stays the same. This leads to two interesting findings: First, all three proposed criteria largely converge in each language, which is reassuring. Second, that in turn makes it less straightforward to want to postulate any prototype more specific than physical.general_experience, since all three languages share that meaning component, but not the other.[9]

Finally, possibly the simplest analysis using BP vectors that is still insightful is to determine what the differences are, if any, within a sense (e.g. of physical.general_experience) between the languages by computing pairwise differences between the BP vectors of – say – French and Italian (because they are in one cluster in Figure 2) or of Italian and Spanish (to see what might be behind their big difference in Figure 2). These comparisons show that the differences between French and Italian are mostly form-related: most larger ID tag differences involve morphosyntactic ID tags – the main semantic differences are that the French DOs of SENTIR(E) are much more often situation/events (see (7) above) and much less often have no DO than in Italian, and that the semantic role of the SUBJ is much more often a perceptor (perpt, i.e. an entity that experiences *physical* perception, visual, auditory, tactile etc.) than an experiencer (exp, i.e. an entity that experiences *mental* perception). The differences between Italian and Spanish are various and both morphosyntactic and semantic in nature. With regard to the former, Italian has many more 1st person uses and many fewer 3rd person uses than Spanish; Italian has many more cases without a DO referent or with a concrete one (see (11)), but many fewer abstract-entity DOs and situations/events than Spanish, for instance. Such results, as visualized in Figure 7, can be pointers for subsequent study.

---

[9] See Lester (2018) for a similar approach using the Kullback-Leibler divergence to explore prototypicality.

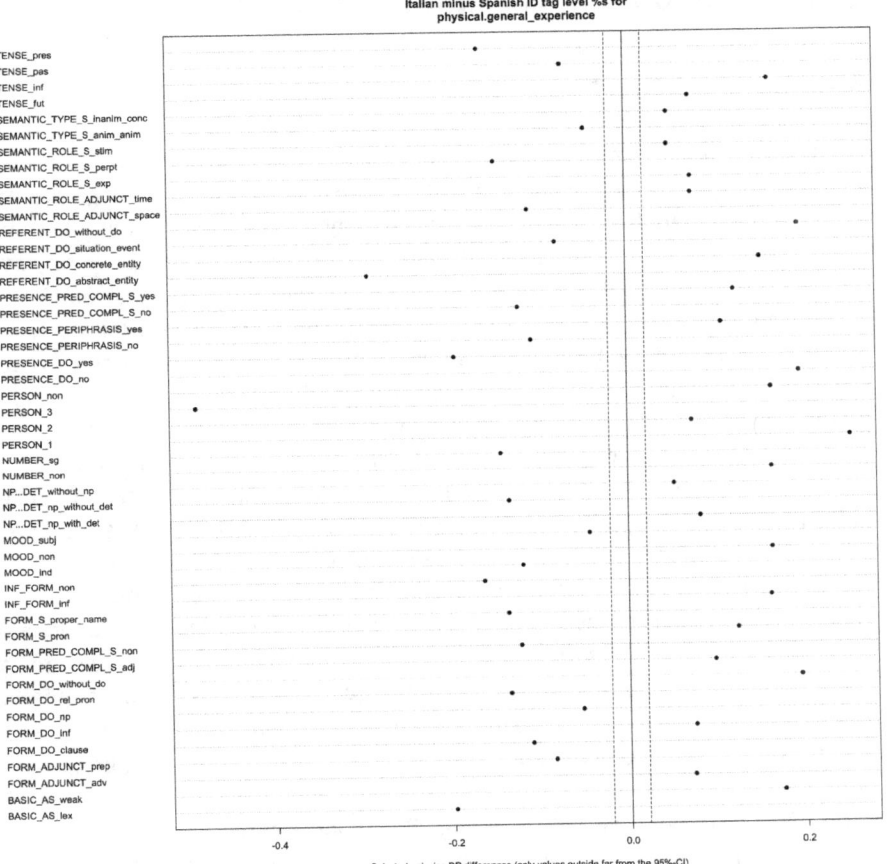

Figure 7: Differences between Italian and Spanish: positive and negative values reflect over- and underrepresentation in Italian (relative to Spanish) respectively.

(11) Ora **sento** l'adrenalina, sono in grado di fare cose che il 90 per cento delle persone non si sogna nemmeno. (Italian, CdS, 2010)
'Now I feel the adrenaline, I can do things that 90% of people do not even dream of.'

4 Discussion and concluding remarks

4.1 Interim summary

In the previous sections, we discussed how a variety of research questions common in contrastive linguistics can be studied on the basis of corpus data and advanced statistical techniques. Specifically, we focused on four (highly) interrelated challenging notions for the study of cross-linguistic near-synonymy, namely: polysemy and degree of sense distinctiveness (Section 2) and prototypicality and identification of discriminatory variables (Section 3). Each of these phenomena was tackled by means of a variety of statistical analyses based on two different kinds of input data that offer different kinds of resolutions on the data: (i) annotated concordance data and (ii) BP vectors.

First, the simplest way to determine the most important and common senses across and within languages, is cross-tabulation of the annotated concordance data. This cross-tabulation can then be visualized in a variety of ways such as a mosaic plot, hierarchical cluster analysis and correspondence analysis. These visualizations, in turn, allow for comparing the precise extent to which the languages differ in their senses' frequencies. Although the analysis based on the raw data shows what the most important senses across and within languages are, it is not the most appropriate way to tackle the question of sense distinctiveness. That is, the question of how many different senses there are in each language and how these senses relate to each other can be addressed better by shifting the resolution from the annotated data to the BP vectors. For example, one might want to do a kind of broad clustering covering all languages and all possible senses in order to determine which senses behave alike across which languages. However, a significant downside of a hierarchical agglomerative cluster analysis is that it implies forced binary splits of the data, which will typically not be a cognitively realistic representation of a phenomenon like near-synonymy. Therefore, in order to visualize the senses and their interrelations in a more faithful way, alternative cluster-analytical approaches can be used such as fuzzy clustering and network analysis.

The identification of the prototypical sense can be done on the basis of a variety of criteria. Three ways of approaching prototypicality on the basis of the annotated concordance data were discussed here: (i) frequency, (ii) cue validity, and (iii) association rules. The notion of cue validity allows exploring prototypicality on the basis of classifiers such as random forests. Changing again the resolution from the raw, annotated data to the BP vectors adds other analytical possibilities. Another way of handling prototypicality is based on markedness considerations: More prototypical elements are taken to be less formally constrained and thus could appear in a wider variety of (formally and/or lexically defined) contexts. Using BP vectors, this can be done by taking into account the smallest numbers of zeros in the BP vectors or by computing how much the ID tag level percentages with a specific sense differ from the same ID tag level percentages with all senses. The latter can be done with the Kullback-Leibler divergence. Finally, we also illustrated how one can compute pairwise differences between the BP vectors in order to determine and visualize which variables are responsible for the differences between the same senses in different languages.

4.2 Implications

The above overview of different advanced methods and statistical techniques for addressing contrastive linguistic research questions leads to several substantial implications for contrastive linguistic and lexical semantic studies. Although recent research has gradually moved away from comparing individual dictionary definitions or using a philological approach to text analysis towards the use of corpora with examples from actual natural language use, the methodology applied has by and large impeded substantial advances in the field. The problems this chapter aimed at raising, if not solving, are essentially of a dual nature: one aspect of the question concerns the more basic nature of data visualization, and the other, a more theoretical one, concerns the impossibility of finding the existing structure in larger data sets without the help of different statistical approaches. Without them it is impossible to highlight the connections between forms and functions, between different senses of the same word, diverging evolutions of the same etymon in sister languages, or different translations of a term in parallel corpora.

Visualization is a fundamental tool for exploratory analyses, and yet even accurate and detailed analyses in the contrastive linguistic and lexical typology tradition, often use tables comparing raw data or percentages to describe the frequencies of senses of a lexeme or near-synonymous terms (verbs of emotion, mental verbs etc.), or side-by-side comparison of constructions used in the parallel corpora of translated texts (see for instance Viberg's (2008) contrastive analysis of Swedish verbs of perception as an example: p. 129, 132 for tables, and 131, 133 for side-by-side comparisons). Side-by-side examples may be useful to elucidate members of a specific category, but tables of raw data or percentages can never allow the analyst (or the reader) to construct a mental overview of the results: we simply cannot analyze large amounts of data without statistics and we miss the generalizations obtained by graphing them in colors and patterns that highlight the most relevant variables causing some specific distribution.

The more theoretical point is related to the need for improved data analysis. The large majority of studies in contrastive linguistics are mainly based on observed (relative) frequencies of (translation) data and are essentially monofactorial in nature. However, most linguistic problems are intrinsically multifactorial, as is the case of near-synonymy between sister languages analyzed in this chapter. We have shown that different statistical analyses can provide more or less granularity (the sense frequencies from the mosaic plot in Figure 1 *vs.* BP vectors or cluster analysis based on BP vectors in Figure 3 or fuzzy clustering in Figure 4).

More specifically, this chapter also presents some improvements with regard to previous applications of the BP approach. First, while most existing BP studies mainly focus on monolingual corpora (Divjak and Gries 2009 being an exception), our study presents an application of the approach to contrastive linguistic data. Second, whereas most BP studies use hierarchical agglomerative cluster analysis as their main exploratory tool, we paid special attention to other visualization techniques for cross-linguistic (dis)similarities such as network analysis and fuzzy clustering. While it is true that Behavioral Profiles require a lot of largely manual annotation and are still exploratory in nature, what we gain is a very high level of analytical detail, which allows for a wide range of exploratory possibilities of the data. It not only facilitates comparability within and across languages, but also allows comparing specific senses within and across languages both in general and with regard to their structural manifestations.

The use of advanced statistical techniques also has implications on a more qualitative, theoretical level. For example, the application of methods such as network analysis and fuzzy clustering offers usage-based evidence for cognitive linguistic theorizing concerning polysemous networks: As mentioned above, HAC results can arguably overemphasize discreteness and mutual exclusivity of (elements within) meaning clusters, whereas the use of fuzzy clustering exemplified here allows for a clearer identification of graded cluster memberships of the clustered elements in the semantic space both within and across languages. From a cross-linguistic perspective, then, the present paper offers some powerful tools for the analysis and visualization of cross-linguistic (dis)similarities. As illustrated by the big cluster analysis in Figure 3, the BP method allows for comparing multiple languages not on the basis of their mere senses' frequencies, but on the basis of a very fine-grained annotation that includes semantic, morphological, syntactic, and other characteristics shared across languages, thus uncovering the source of the cross-linguistic (dis)similarity.

Finally, the proposed analyses also highlight features in the data that would otherwise remain concealed, such as language-specific structural reflexes of grammaticalized/ constructionalized senses (see e.g. Hilpert 2013; Traugott and

Trousale 2013). A clear example is the extreme position of the "it_phys.spec_aud. dm" sense (graphed in purple) in the Italian data visualized in the dendrogram from the fuzzy cluster analysis of the Italian fine-grained senses (Figure 4). This sense underlines the different behavior of a discourse marker derived from the verb *sentire* in Italian, which does not exist in the corresponding verbs of its sister languages French or Spanish. In other words, the proposed methods in this paper are an excellent way to display diverging grammaticalization/constructionalization patterns in cognate languages, confirming Viberg's (1999) conclusion that grammaticalization can drive cognates apart semantically.

4.3 Where to go from here

Considering the possibilities for further analysis mentioned at the end of Section 3 above, it would be interesting to compute pairwise differences between the BP vectors of French and Italian to see why they are in one cluster in Figure 2, or those of Italian and Spanish to see what might cause the big difference between the two languages in the same figure. These comparisons show that the differences between French and Italian are mostly form-related, whereas there are several morphosyntactic and semantic differences separating Italian and Spanish. A detailed study looking at these differences could uncover their causes, and supply a more thorough linguistic analysis of the data that this chapter, because of its methodological nature, did not provide.

The techniques suggested in this chapter have wide potential applications both for lexical semantic analyses within and across languages, and potentially also for the diachronic evolution of the senses of polysemous terms, possibly revealing phenomena of subjectification and grammaticalization. In this sense, further work on new or previously published data applying these statistical methods is bound to uncover extremely interesting tendencies and generalizations.

References

Altenberg, Bengt. 2002. Causative constructions in English and Swedish A corpus-based contrastive study. In Bengt Altenberg & Sylviane Granger (eds.), Recent trends in cross-linguistic lexical studies, 97–116. Amsterdam/Philadelphia: John Benjamins.
Altenberg, Bengt & Sylviane Granger. 2002. Recent trends in cross-linguistic lexical studies. In Bengt Altenberg & Sylviane Granger (eds.), *Lexis in contrast: corpus-based approaches*, 3–48. Amsterdam & Philadelphia: John Benjamins.

Atkins, Beryl. T. Sue. 1987. Semantic ID tags: Corpus evidence for dictionary senses. In *Proceedings of the Third Annual Conference of the UW Centre for the New Oxford English Dictionary*, 17–36.

Berez, Andrea L. & Stefan Th. Gries. 2009. In defense of corpus-based methods: a behavioral profile analysis of polysemous *get* in English. In Steven Moran, Darren S. Tanner, & Michael Scanlon (eds.), *Proceedings of the 24th Northwest Linguistics Conference*, 157–166. Seattle, WA: Department of Linguistics.

Comer, Marie & Renata Enghels. 2016. La polisemia de los verbos de colocación. Descripción sincrónica y evolución diacrónica de los cuasi-sinónimos *poner/meter* y *poser/mettre*. *Revue Romane* 51 (1). 70–94.

Cover, Thomas M. & Joy A. Thomas. 2006. *Elements of information theory*. 2nd ed. Hoboken, NJ: John Wiley & Sons.

Desagulier, Guillaume. 2017. *Corpus linguistics and statistics with R: introduction to quantitative methods in linguistics*. Berlin & New York: Springer.

Divjak, Dagmar. 2006. Ways of intending: delinieating and structuring near synonyms. In Stefan Th. Gries & Anatol Stefanowitsch (eds.), *Corpora in cognitive linguistics: corpus-based approaches to syntax and lexis*, 19–56. Berlin & New York: Mouton de Gruyter.

Divjak, Dagmar. 2010. *Structuring the lexicon. A clustered model for near-synonymy*. Berlin & New York: Mouton de Gruyter.

Divjak, Dagmar & Stefan Th. Gries. 2006. Ways of trying in Russian: Clustering behavioral profiles. *Corpus Linguistics and Linguistic Theory* 2 (1). 23–60.

Divjak, Dagmar & Stefan Th. Gries. 2009. Corpus-based cognitive semantics: A contrastive study of phasal verbs in English and Russian. In Katarzyna Dziwirek & Barbara Lewandowska-Tomaszczyk (eds.), *Studies in cognitive corpus linguistics*, 273–296. Frankfurt am Main: Peter Lang.

Ellis, Nick C., Matthew B. O'Donnell & Ute Römer. 2013. Usage-based language: Investigating the latent structures that underpin Acquisition. *Language Learning* 63 (Suppl 1). 25–51.

Enghels, Renata & Marlies Jansegers. 2013. On the cross-linguistic equivalence of *sentir(e)* in Romance languages: a contrastive study in semantics. *Linguistics* 51 (5). 957–991.

Fox, John & Sanford Weisberg 2011. *An R companion to applied regression*. 2nd ed. Thousand Oaks, CA & London: Sage.

Gast, Volker. 2015. On the use of translation corpora in contrastive linguistics. A case study of impersonalization in English and German. *Languages in Contrast* 15 (1). 4–33.

Glynn, Dylan. 2010. Correspondence analysis: exploring data and identifying patterns. In Dylan Glynn & Kerstin Fischer (eds.), *Corpus methods for semantics: quantitative methods in polysemy and synonymy*, 443–485. Amsterdam & Philadelphia: John Benjamins.

Gries, Stefan Th. 2003a. *Multifactorial analysis in corpus linguistics: a study of Particle Placement*. London & New York: Continuum Press.

Gries, Stefan Th. 2003b. Towards a corpus-based identification of prototypical instances of constructions. *Annual Review of Cognitive Linguistics* 1. 1–27.

Gries, Stefan Th. 2006. Corpus-based methods and cognitive semantics: the many meanings of *to run*. In Stefan Th. Gries & Anatol Stefanowitsch (eds.), *Corpora in cognitive linguistics: corpus-based approaches to syntax and lexis*, 57–99. Berlin & New York: Mouton de Gruyter.

Gries, Stefan Th. 2010a. Behavioral Profiles: a fine-grained and quantitative approach in corpus-based lexical semantics. *The Mental Lexicon* 5 (3). 323–346.

Gries, Stefan Th. 2010b. BehavioralProfiles 1.01. A program for R 2.7.1 and higher.

Gries, Stefan Th. 2013. *Statistics for linguistics with R: a practical introduction*. Berlin & Boston: De Gruyter Mouton.
Gries, Stefan Th. & Naoki Otani. 2010. Behavioral profiles: a corpus-based perspective on synonymy and antonymy. *ICAME Journal* 34. 121–150.
Hahsler, Michael. 2017. arulesViz: Visualizing association rules with R. *R Journal* 9 (2). 163–175.
Hahsler, Michael, Christian Buchta, & Kurt Hornik. 2008. Selective association rule generation. *Computational Statistics* 23 (2). 303–315.
Hahsler, Michael & Kurt Hornik. 2007. New probabilistic interest measures for association rules. *Intelligent Data Analysis* 11 (5). 437–455.
Hilpert, Martin. 2013. *Constructional change in English: Developments in Allomorphy, Word Formation, and Syntax*. Cambridge: Cambridge University Press.
Hothorn, Torsten, Peter Buehlmann, Sandrine Dudoit, Annette Molinaro, & Mark Van Der Laan. 2006. Survival Ensembles. *Biostatistics* 7 (3). 355–373.
Jansegers, Marlies, Clara Vanderschueren, & Renata Enghels. 2015. The polysemy of the Spanish verb *sentir*: a Behavioral Profile analysis *Cognitive Linguistics* 26 (3). 381–421.
Jansegers, Marlies & Stefan Th. Gries (to appear). Towards a dynamic behavioral profile: a diachronic study of polysemous *sentir* in Spanish. *Corpus Linguistics and Linguistic Theory*.
Lansari, Laure. 2017. *I was going to say / j'allais dire* as discourse markers in contemporary English and French. *Languages in Contrast* 17 (2). 205–228.
Lester, Nicholas A. 2018. The syntactic bits of nouns: How prior syntactic distributions affect comprehension, production, and acquisition. Unpublished Ph.D. dissertation, University of California, Santa Barbara.
Levshina, Natalia. 2016. Verbs of letting in Germanic and Romance languages. A quantitative investigation based on a parallel corpus of film subtitles. *Languages in Contrast* 16 (1). 84–117.
Maindonald, John & W. John Braun. 2010. *Data analysis and graphics using R: an example-based approach*. 3rd ed. Cambridge: Cambridge University Press.
Molino, Alessandra. 2017. A contrastive analysis of reporting clauses in comparable and translated academic texts in English and Italian. *Languages in Contrast* 17 (1). 18–42.
Moisl, Hermann. 2015. *Cluster analysis for corpus linguistics*. Berlin, Munich, & Boston: Mouton de Gruyter.
Romeo, Lauren, Sara Mendes & Núria Bel. 2013. Using qualia information to identify lexical semantic classes in an unsupervised clustering task. *Proceedings of COLING 2012: Posters*, 1029–1038.
Rozovskaya, Alla & Roxana Girju. 2009. Identifying semantic relations in context: near-misses and overlaps. *International Conference RANLP 2009 Recent Advances in Natural Language Processing, Borovets, Bulgaria*, 381–387.
Rozumko, Agata. 2016. Adverbs of certainty in a cross-linguistic and cross-cultural perspective English-Polish. *Languages in Contrast* 16(2). 239–263.
Schmied, Josef. 2008. Contrastive Corpus Studies. In Anke Lüdeling & Merja Kytö (eds.), *Corpus Linguistics: An international handbook*, 1140–1159. Berlin & New York: Mouton de Gruyter.
Traugott, Elizabeth C. & Graeme Trousdale. 2013. *Constructionalization and Constructional Changes*. Oxford: Oxford University Press.
Verbeke, Charlotte. 2011. *Sentir: ¿un verbo de percepción o un verbo de emoción?* Ghent: Ghent University MA thesis.
Viberg, Åke. 1999. The polysemous cognates Swedish *gå* and English *go*: universal and language-specific characteristics. *Languages in Contrast* 2 (1). 87–113.

Viberg, Åke. 2002. Polysemy and disambiguation cues across languages. The case of Swedish *få* and English *get*. In Bengt Altenberg and Sylviane Granger (eds.), *Lexis in contrast: corpus-based approaches*, 119–150. Amsterdam & Philadelphia: John Benjamins.

Viberg, Åke. 2005. The lexical typological profile of Swedish mental verbs. *Languages in Contrast* 5 (1). 121–157.

Viberg, Åke. 2008. Swedish verbs of perception from a typological and contrastive perspective. In María de los Ángeles Gómez González, J. Lachlan Mackenzie, & Elsa M. González Álvarez (eds.). *Languages and cultures in contrast and comparison*, 123–172. Amsterdam & Philadelphia: John Benjamins.

Pauline De Baets, Lore Vandevoorde, and Gert De Sutter
On the usefulness of comparable and parallel corpora for contrastive linguistics. Testing the semantic stability hypothesis

Abstract: The last two decades, empirical evidence has shown that different types of translational effects are likely to occur in translated texts, thereby potentially reducing the representativeness of translations for contrastive-linguistic research. Yet, a question that has rarely been asked is whether translational effects can also be found on the semantic level. Consequently, the main objective of this paper is to investigate whether the (sub-)meanings associated with near-synonyms change during translation, or – put differently – whether the hypothesis that there is semantic stability between translated and non-translated language can be confirmed. We first applied Johansson's procedure to tease apart contrastive relations and translation effects in a case study on the frequency distribution of Dutch and English verbs of inchoativity and found that in translations the most frequent expressions were overused when compared to non-translated data. Secondly, we tested the semantic stability hypothesis by comparing the meaning structure of the field of inchoativity in a parallel corpus of English-to-Dutch translations to that of the same field in a comparable corpus of authentic Dutch texts. The lexemes were selected via the semantic mirroring procedure and were submitted to the behavioral profile method, which allows us to operationalize semantic (dis)similarity by annotating the linguistic context of each lexeme for a variety of ID-tags. Via correspondence regression we explored the structure of the semantic field. The results of our analyses show that the positions of the lexemes do not remain stable among the different corpus components, running counter to the semantic stability hypothesis. Consequently, the assumption of semantic stability between source and target text, which is one of the motivations to use parallel corpora in contrastive linguistics, seems not completely tenable.

Keywords: corpus-based translation studies, behavioral profile, semantic stability, correspondence regression, inchoativity

---

Pauline De Baets, Lore Vandevoorde, Gert De Sutter, Department of Translation, Interpreting and Communication, Research unit EQTIS, Ghent University, Groot-Brittanniëlaan 45, Belgium

https://doi.org/10.1515/9783110682588-004

1 Introduction

Over the last two or three decades, scholars within corpus-based translation studies (CBTS) have been investigating if and how translated texts differ from original, non-translated texts. A great number of studies have been focusing on different types of translational effects that are likely to occur in translated texts (see Kruger and Rooy 2012 for an overview), with the lion's share of these studies focusing on validating or refuting hypotheses on the lexical, morphosyntactic and pragmatic level (e.g. Laviosa 1998; Olohan & Baker 2000). It appears that, compared to non-translated texts, translated texts are more norm-adherent (see e.g. Delaere et al. 2012), more explicit (see e.g. Olohan and Baker 2000), more levelled-out (Laviosa 1998) and are sometimes subject to source language interference (also called shining through, see e.g. Teich 2003; Evert and Neumann 2017). In addition, it has been found that those differences can be related to social and cognitive causes that are typical of the context of direct language mediation: translators need to transfer the source language message to a new target audience, thereby directly mediating between different languages and cultures. Such an act of mediation inevitably influences the way translators use the linguistic repertoire in the target language. Kruger and De Sutter (2018), for instance, argue that all writers, including translators, are subject to processing constraints (illustrated by the observation that more demanding cognitive environments incite more explicit linguistic choices) and conventionalization (the urge to use the more "standard" form) in choosing between explicit and implicit *that* in English complementizer constructions, albeit translators experience those constraints and conventionalizations to a much larger extent, which results in them making their linguistic output identifiably different compared to South-African and British monolingual writers. The researchers hypothesize that this can be traced back to an intensified cognitive pressure during translation and social risk aversion (cf. Pym 2005).

The observation that the specific circumstances in which translators operate have an effect on their linguistic output has obvious consequences for the usability of translated texts in the field of contrastive linguistics (CL), an issue that was already addressed by Johansson (1998: 6): "To what extent can we then make generalizations based on translated texts? And can we really be sure that the same meanings are expressed in the source and the target text? ... In using translation corpora in contrastive studies, it is therefore important to be able to control for translation effects." The procedure suggested by Johansson for disentangling contrastive relations and translational effects compares frequency distributions in a parallel corpus (including source texts and their respective translations) and a comparable corpus (including non-translations in two or more languages). Johansson (1998) tested the procedure in three case studies (involving a modal particle, a noun and a verb), where he investigated translations and cross-linguistic relations. In the three case studies, he found contrastive differences as well as a marked difference in the distribution between non-translated and translated language. In the first case study Johansson found that the modal particle *nok* was underused in translated Norwegian, compared to non-translated Norwegian, and the English particle *probably* was overused in translated English. The results of the second and third case study on the verb and the noun turned out to be similar, with overuse of certain constructions in one corpus component and underuse in the other corpus component. The three case studies confirm Johansson's idea that in contrastive studies, it is important to be able to control for translation effects by including translations in both directions (in his case: English to Norwegian and Norwegian to English) so that the translated variety of a language can be compared directly to the non-translated variety of the same language.

What we will call the "Johansson procedure" is an important tool for contrastive linguists who use parallel corpora. The procedure seems to be effective for the identification of differences in frequency distribution of the use of formally identifiable linguistic units, such as morphemes, lexemes, constructions and so on, but less so for semantic differences. Paradoxically, the question uttered by Johansson himself – can we really be sure that the same meanings are expressed in the source and target text? – cannot be answered using his procedure. The semantic-pragmatic stability of linguistic units when using translated texts in contrastive-linguistic research is however a crucial assumption, as "translation corpora are an ideal resource for establishing equivalence between languages since they convey the same semantic content" (Granger 2003: 19). Within contrastive linguistics and translation studies, researchers often start from the assumption of semantic stability, i.e. they consider meaning as the invariant of translation (Klaudy 2010), although it is under-researched whether this assumption really holds. In Section 2, we will present a number of investigations which have been dealing with semantic issues within translation studies.

The present paper has two interrelated objectives. First, Johansson's procedure is tested and second, the tenability of the so-called semantic stability hypothesis is investigated or, to put it somewhat differently, we investigate the extent to which semantic differences occur in translations. More particularly, the semantic properties of four verbal lexemes belonging to the semantic field of inchoativity in Dutch are determined on the basis of well-established corpus-based methods in the field of cognitive and variational linguistics, viz. behavioral profiling (Gries and Divjak 2009). The results of the behavioral profiling analysis are then submitted to correspondence regression, a multivariate technique based on correspondence analysis (Plevoets 2015), which measures and visualizes the main semantic similarities and differences of the inchoative lexemes in translations and non-translations.

This paper is structured as follows. Section 2 gives a brief state-of-the-art overview; in Section 3, we present the data and methodology underlying our research; and in Section 4 we present and discuss the results. In the final section, we summarize the main findings and indicate some interesting possibilities for further research.

2 Semantic differences in translation

Despite the large amount of empirical studies evidencing specific morphological, lexical, syntactic and pragmatic features of translated language compared to source texts and comparable non-translated texts, very few studies have addressed the issue of specific translational features on the semantic level. Indeed, the study of meaning and meaning relations within the field of CBTS is still largely unexplored. Questions such as whether the prototypical meanings of a lexical item in non-translated language are prototypical in translated language too, or whether polysemous words are more or less polysemous in translated texts are rarely asked. As a consequence, little is known about the impact of translation on the lexico-semantic level of a target language. Vandevoorde (2016, 2018) sees different reasons for this research gap. First of all, Baker's (1993) seminal paper, which introduced a research program for CBTS, focused predominantly on validating or refuting so-called translation universals on the lexical and grammatical level, thereby ignoring studies of meaning. Second, and somewhat paradoxically, meaning itself is often considered the very core of what translation is. Klaudy (2010: 82) states that "it seems to be firmly embedded in public opinion that in translation it is the meaning that has to remain unchanged". As meaning is considered as the "invariant of translation also by some translation scholars" (Klaudy 2010: 82), it is rarely the subject of linguistic research. Finally, meaning is an abstract notion, which makes it difficult to empirically capture meaning and to operationalize semantic differences in natural language (Noël 2003; Jansegers et al. 2015; Vandevoorde 2016).

Nevertheless, a handful of researchers has focused on semantic matters within CBTS. For instance, Halverson (1996, 2003, 2007, 2010) adopts psycholinguistic models of bilingual semantic representation to explain translational phenomena and Malmkjaer (2011) offers an overview of linguistic-philosophical theories focusing on meaning and translation. Interestingly, Szymor (2015) is among the first researchers to apply behavioral profiling for the study of lexical semantics in translation. However, her comparison of two near-synonymous deontic modal verbs in translated and non-translated Polish mainly focuses on the application of behavioral profiling in translation studies, rather than analyzing the specific semantic field of those modal verbs. She does, nevertheless, observe significant differences between translated and non-translated verbs with the aspectual difference as the most remarkable one. Szymor's (2015) study shows that there are opposite aspectual preferences in translated and non-translated texts. Another notable study that addressed semantic issues using empirical research methods in the field of CBTS is the work of Vandevoorde (2016, 2018). By implementing and extending methodological tools from terminology studies (semantic mirroring) and variational linguistics (correspondence analysis and hierarchical cluster analysis) in translation studies, Vandevoorde (2016, 2018) was able to detect subtle lexical-semantic differences between translations and non-translations in the field of inchoativity in Dutch. She observed, for instance, that translated language displays less meaning differentiation, although the general structure of the semantic field of inchoativity is similar in both translated and non-translated Dutch. She also found more deviations in the semantic field based on translations from a form-similar source language (English) than from a source language that exhibits less formal similarities (French). The present paper continues this line of research by using other methodological tools to explore semantic differences in translation. Although Vandevoorde's (2016, 2018) research tackled the under-researched question of meaning in translation, the study was primarily exploratory in nature, both on the conceptual and on the methodological level and was not able to determine the factors that cause the attested semantic differences.

The observation that the translational activity introduces subtle semantic differences has obvious implications for empirical contrastive linguistics, which uses among other tools parallel corpora to investigate systemic cross-linguistic differences as well as usage differences. Since the early 1990s (with the development of large corpora), both contrastive linguistics and translation studies have access to large sets of multilingual data containing translations, although the use of translational data for contrastive studies is to some extent still controversial. On the one hand, parallel corpora contain texts with allegedly the same semantic content and the same discourse functions in two (or more) languages (Johansson 1998), since it is presumed that translators aim to achieve a perfect match between source and target language (Aerts 1998), making translations eminently suited for contrastive research. The same line of reasoning can be found in Ebeling (1998) and Gast (2015), who consider translation equivalence the common ground on which languages can be compared, while at the same time allowing the comparison of individual pairs of sentences. Noël (2003) emphasizes a more conceptual advantage of parallel corpora, as translation can be considered as a performative task that makes meaning observable:

> the texts produced by translators can be treated as a collection of informants' judgments about the meaning of the linguistic forms in the source texts, with the added advantage that they are readily available to the linguist [...]. Translation corpora can therefore be considered to be a means of empirically testing one's intuitions (or hypotheses) about the semantics of linguistic forms that is complementary to the systematic exploitation of the circumstantial evidence provided by monolingual corpora. (Noël 2003:759)

The main underlying assumption of this argument is that between the source-language unit and the target-language unit, the meaning selected by the translator is invariant. This immediately shows one of the risks of using translations in contrastive-linguistic research: it presumes that translation conveys invariant meaning. Noël (2003) himself also warns of the risk that using a parallel corpus is a way of testing the performance of the translator instead of comparing languages on a more general level, and that detected differences can be due to the specific regularities of translated language.

Contrastive linguists are becoming increasingly aware of the growing body of evidence of differences between translated and non-translated language, whereby the translation activity is seen as an intrusive factor for the use of parallel corpora as a research tool to compare different languages (e.g. Johansson 1998, 2007; Noël 2003). Because of the possible presence of translational effects, Johansson (1998) emphasizes the importance of mechanisms that control for those features, for instance by checking observations based on a parallel corpus against a comparable corpus. If the patterns are dissimilar, the features found in the parallel corpus may reflect the process of translation instead of laying bare contrastive differences. The use of parallel corpora within corpus-based contrastive linguistics, however, remains vivid, as can be seen in the last three volumes of the Benjamins journal *Languages in Contrast: International Journal for Contrastive Linguistics* (2015, 2016, 2017): of 24 corpus-based contrastive studies, 14 relied on comparable corpora only, while 10 other studies chose to use parallel corpora. This again confirms the importance of testing the semantic stability hypothesis, both for research within the field of CBTS and CL.

3 Data and methodology

In order to apply Johansson's procedure and to find out whether there are any differences in the semantic field of inchoativity in Dutch translated texts compared to non-translated texts, we use the Dutch Parallel Corpus (Macken et al. 2011), which is the largest available parallel and comparable corpus of written Dutch, containing ten million words. It is also balanced with respect to five text types (journalistic texts, instructive texts, administrative texts, external communication and literature) and four translation directions (English to Dutch, Dutch to English, French to Dutch and Dutch to French), as illustrated in Figure 1:

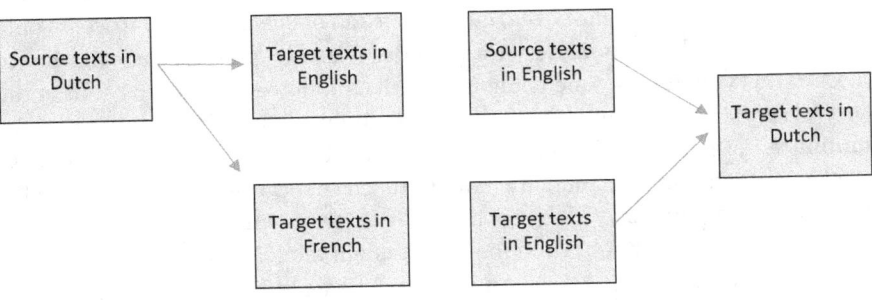

Figure 1: Structure of the Dutch Parallel Corpus.

Finally, it is a sentence-aligned and POS-tagged corpus, which facilitates corpus querying.

In Section 3.1 we present the method that was used to select candidate lexemes for the semantic field of inchoativity. In Section 3.2 we explain the application of the behavioral profile method on our data sets. This usage-based method is a fine-grained and objective method to retrieve contextual information from the lexemes under study. Via the contextual information, we can analyze the meaning of the selected verbs. Section 3.3 then covers the application of Johansson's procedure to the Dutch Parallel Corpus.

3.1 Selecting inchoative verbs using semantic mirroring

In order to decide in a non-intuitive manner which verbs belong to the semantic field of inchoativity, we take a two-step approach. In the first step, we select the most prototypical verbs of the semantic field using lexicographical information and frequency information, the second step then uses these prototypical verbs in a semantic mirroring approach to detect what the largest homogeneous set of verbs in the semantic field is. In the remainder of this section we discuss each of these two steps.

In the first step, we look up all translational equivalents of the verb *beginnen* 'to begin' in a Dutch-to-English (Van Dale 2006a) and Dutch-to-French (Van Dale 2006b) translational dictionary. We consider the verb *beginnen* to be the most prototypical verb expressing inchoativity. *Beginnen* is the most frequently used verb of inchoativity (see the frequencies in Table 1) in Dutch and is acquired in a rather early stage of the language acquisition (according to Brysbaert et al. 2014, at the age of 6.22 years). We then look up all resulting verbal lexemes in English (*to begin, to start, to commence*) and French (*commencer*) in an English-to-Dutch (Van Dale 2006c) and French-to-Dutch dictionary (Van Dale 2006d). This yields the Dutch verbs *beginnen, starten, aanvangen* and *openen*. As *openen* occurs only once in one of the dictionaries, we consider it as not prototypical, and hence discard this verb for the time being (this verb can, however, pop up again in the second step). The idea underlying the lexicographical part of this step is that the mutual set of back-translations of *beginnen* constitutes the prototypical core of the semantic field of inchoativity,[1] an approach first put forward by Ivir (1987). Next, we extract the token frequencies of the three remaining verbs (see Table 1) in the Dutch Parallel Corpus and the independent monolingual reference corpus SONAR (Oostdijk et al. 2013); as *aanvangen* is rather infrequent (DPC: n = 29), it is decided to only take into account the most frequent verbs *beginnen* and *starten* as the basis for the second step. The fact that *aanvangen* is infrequent is not in line with what is expected from a prototypical lexeme, as it is believed that prototypicality is – among other factors – based on the frequency of an expression (Geeraerts 2006; Gilquin 2006).

Table 1: Frequency distribution of the prototypical verbs.

Lexeme	Corpus	Frequency
Beginnen	SONAR (500,000,000 words)	291,320 attestations
	DPC (3,667,606 Dutch words)	1,867 attestations
Starten	SONAR (500,000,000 words)	63,528 attestations
	DPC (3,667,606 Dutch words)	1,037 attestations
Aanvangen	SONAR (500,000,000 words)	1,974 attestations
	DPC (3,667,606 Dutch words)	29 attestations

---

[1] Research conducted by Vandevoorde et al. (2017) resulted in a broader semantic field of inchoativity, with adverbs such as *eerst,* nouns such as *start, begin,* ... and verbs such as *gaan, worden,* ...

Beginnen and *starten* are then submitted to the semantic mirroring procedure, a corpus-based method based on back-and-forth translational equivalence in a parallel corpus. The advantage of this method is that it enables us to look beyond the lexemes found in a dictionary so that we can retrieve candidate lexemes to build a data-driven, bottom-up semantic field of inchoativity. The semantic mirroring procedure (see Figure 2) was originally developed by Dyvik (1998, 2004) and extended by Vandevoorde (Vandevoorde 2016, 2018; Vandevoorde et al. 2017). It is based on the idea that "semantically closely related words ought to have strongly overlapping sets of translations" (Dyvik 2004: 311). Dyvik (2004) starts from an initial *lexeme a* in language A and extracts all its translations in language B from a parallel and sentence-aligned corpus (viz. The English-Norwegian Parallel Corpus) to arrive at a first set of translations that is called the first T-image of *a* in language B. For the next step, the back-translations of that first T-image are looked up to obtain the Inverse T-image of *a* in language A. Finally, the translations in language B of the inverse T-image are queried again, resulting in the Second T-image. The aim of this last step is to uncover the exact semantic relationships between the lexemes in both language A and language B: the more recurring translations a lexeme in language A holds in the Second T-image, the higher it will rank in the structured hierarchy of lexemes.

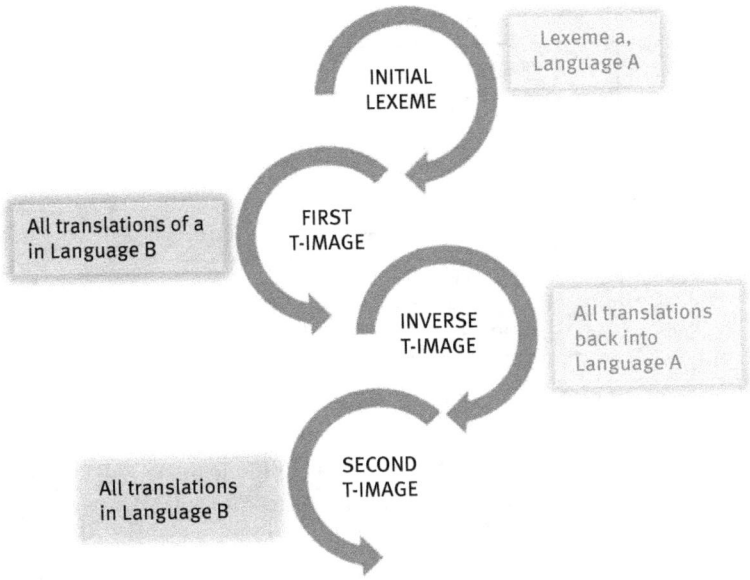

Figure 2: Semantic Mirroring Method (Vandevoorde 2016: 76).

As we only use the method to select relevant lexemes in the semantic field of inchoativity (see, however, Vandevoorde et al. 2017, for the full procedure), we only applied the first two steps of the semantic mirroring method, thus creating only the first and inverse T-image. When doing so, we use an additional overlap criterion: every lexeme in the first-T-image and inverse T-image had to be a translation of at least 2 different source language lexemes. This extension to the semantic mirroring method was first introduced by Vandevoorde (2016, 2018) and aims at excluding lexemes that belong to a different semantic field than the field under investigation. We also choose a cumulative frequency threshold of 75% to exclude less frequent translations, which are often (quasi-)idiosyncratic: only the most frequent lexemes which represent 75% of all the attestations are selected. One final restriction we impose is that the procedure should only yield verbal lexemes,[2] although the procedure in principle yields lexemes from different word classes (see Vandevoorde et al. 2017). We add this third restriction because it is believed that verbs have a greater breadth of meaning than nouns and because their meaning is more dependent on their linguistic context (Van Hell and De Groot 1998), which makes verbal lexemes more suited to be used in behavioral profile-based research. A third reason to limit ourselves to only one word class, is the fact that the behavioral profile method requires all the corpus occurrences to be coded for the same set of variables (Jansegers et al. 2015). The results of the first T-image are shown in Figures 3 and 4.

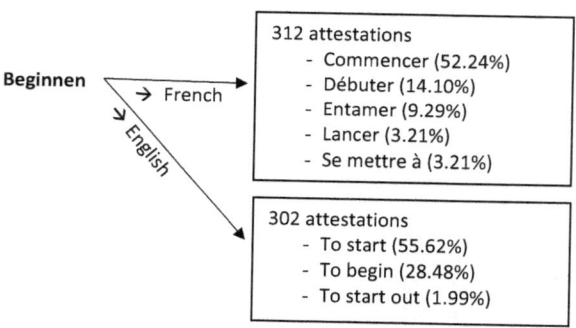

Figure 3: First T-image 'beginnen'.

As mentioned above, we use *beginnen* and *starten* as initial lexemes. All the sentences in the Dutch Parallel Corpus containing one of these lexemes are extracted

---

2 Non-verbal lexemes, however, did not represent a big portion of the data: on average 90% of the translations were verbal lexemes. An example of an inchoative expression that was ruled out by the verb criterion is *the start-up* (n = 11) as translation of *starten* (n = 181).

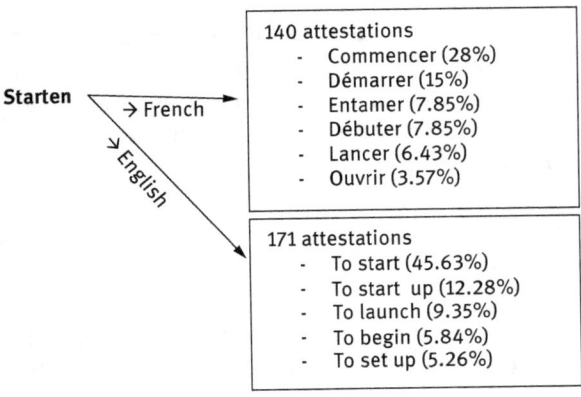

Figure 4: First T-image 'starten'.

from the corpus and for each instance of a lexeme under study, the translation equivalent in the English or French part of the corpus is annotated. By taking into account the cumulative frequency threshold and the overlap criterion, five translational equivalents remain: *commencer, débuter, entamer* (in French) and *to start* and *to begin* (in English). These are used in a new corpus query, to create the inverse T-image (see Figure 5).

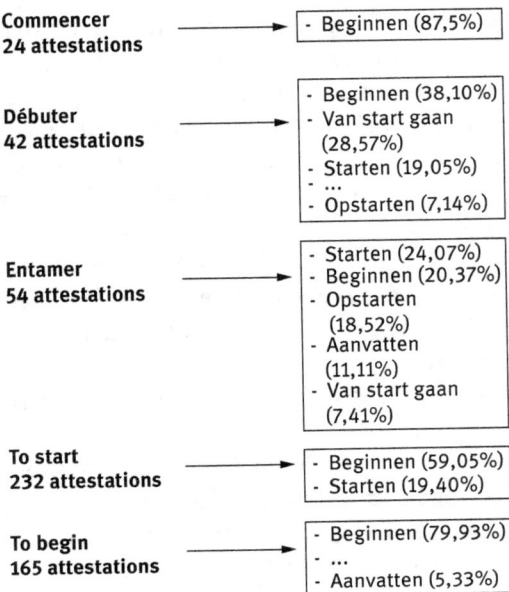

Figure 5: Inverse T-image.

We again implement a cumulative frequency threshold to exclude more peripheral and idiosyncratic translations, and by doing so, we obtain a final set of five lexemes of inchoativity (a literal back-translation is given within parentheses), namely *beginnen* 'to begin', *starten* 'to start', *aanvatten* 'to commence', *opstarten* 'to start up' and *van start gaan* 'to take off'.

3.2 Behavioral profiles

In order to test the semantic stability hypothesis, we had to find a method that is able to retrieve word meaning and meaning differences in a non-intuitive way. Obviously, one of the problems of empirically analyzing semantics is that "meaning is a non-observable relation in our mind and is therefore beyond the reach of absolute objectivity" (Jansegers et al. 2015: 4). As a result, researchers have been struggling with the question as how meaning can be defined in an objective and measurable way. One of the possible answers to that question, is the idea that the meaning of a word can be deduced "from the company it keeps" (Harris 1954; Firth 1957): words occurring in similar linguistic contexts, tend to be semantically similar (Lin 1998; Curran 2004; Lenci 2008) and vice versa. If, for instance, one wants to understand the meaning of the (non-existing) word *tezgüno*, one can look at the words it frequently co-occurs with: "(1) There is a bottle of *tezgüno* on the table. (2) Yesterday, he drank too much *tezgüno*. (3) *Tezgüno* is made of grapes." (Lin 1998: 768). The idea that the meaning of a word can be deduced from its context is the central assumption in distributional semantics: semantic (dis)similarities between words are measured by analyzing the amount of shared words in their contexts; the more often two words share similar co-occurring words, the more likely it is that they are semantically similar. This idea is widespread in lexical semantics and has led to the advent of (semi-)automatic retrieval methods of semantically similar words such as latent semantic analysis (Landauer and Dumais 1997) and first and second order bag-of-words models (Manning and Schütze 1999). These models are generally characterized as distributional, which means that they capture word meaning in relation to their context in large corpora.

Despite the widespread use of distributional semantics as a way of empirically investigating semantic issues, there are some considerable downsides to the method. A first disadvantage is that the contextual information that emerges from a distributional analysis is often not linguistically enriched, because it consists of nothing more than the contiguous words of a lexeme under study, without any further syntactic or semantic information thus complicating the interpretation of obtained results. Moreover, distributional analyses often adopt "a very coarse-grained perspective both in terms of the number of distinctions made and in terms how little the two kinds of information are combined" (Gries 2010: 325) as previous (distributional) studies tend to focus only on collocations *or* colligations instead of combining the two. Many studies in lexical semantics only include all collocates in a user-defined window, without further investigating other distributional characteristics. More specifically, in a distributional analysis a researcher often sets a certain window (e.g. 5 words to the left and 5 words to the right of the lexeme under study) and only includes context words within that window without considering other distributional characteristics such as the syntactic or semantic properties of those context words. Consequently, they often restrict themselves to observed frequencies of co-occurrences only, instead of analyzing the data in more elaborate ways (Gries 2010). To gain more insight in the mechanisms that play a role in the meaning differentiation between near-synonyms, we decided to apply the usage-based behavioral profile (BP) approach (Divjak and Gries 2006, 2009), a method that builds on the idea that corpus data provide distributional frequencies and that distributional similarity reflects functional and semantic similarity (Jansegers et al. 2015: 5). As we want to investigate semantic similarity between translated and non-translated lexemes, the BP is an ideal method because of its objective and fine-grained approach. Furthermore, it has the advantage that it offers more linguistically enriched data than a "normal" distributional analysis does. Instead of retrieving only the context words of a lexeme under study, the researcher obtains more generalized lexicogrammatical and semantic information about the context of the lexeme. The investigated features do not only target the specific shape of each verb token but also the morphosyntactic and semantic context it appears in. Moreover, since these features are not based on traditional minimal pair acceptability tests, the use of subjective and introspective knowledge is minimized (Jansegers et al. 2015). Indeed, the BP method is considered as an objective, precise corpus-based method that proves to be suitable to capture the complexity of word meaning and that allows for bottom-up identification of distinctive features (Szymor 2015).

The BP approach involves four steps (Gries and Divjak 2009, 2010; Gries 2010; Gries & Otani 2010; Janseghers et al. 2015; Szymor 2015): firstly, all the instances of the lexeme under study and its context are retrieved from a corpus. Secondly, a large set of (lexical, morphosyntactic, pragmatic ...) properties are manually annotated for each corpus observation of the selected lexemes; these properties are called *ID-tags*. Thirdly, a co-occurrence table is generated and, finally, that table is explored and evaluated by using statistical techniques. For the present study, we drew a random sample of 665 instances and annotated these for 29 different lexicogrammatical, contextual and semantic ID-tags (see Table 2), that were largely based on the work by Gries & Divjak (2009), Gries (2010) and Szymor (2015). By doing so, a behavioral profile was compiled for each verb lemma.

Table 2: Overview of the ID-tags and their levels.

ID-tags		Levels of the ID-tags
Subject-related ID tags	animacy	animate – inanimate
	concreteness	abstract – concrete
	concreteness level	high – medium – low
	concreteness rating	score 1 – 5
	countability	countable – uncountable
	number	singular – plural – uncountable
	proper/common name	common name – proper name
	semantics	action – animate – artefact – concrother – dynamic – human – institute – non-dynamic – place – time – undetermined
Verb-related ID tags	aspect	imperative – infinitive – imperfect – perfect
	mode	imperative – indicative – infinitive
	number	infinitive – singular – plural
	tense	future – imperative – infinitive – past – present– future
	voice	active – passive
Object-related ID-tags	animacy	animate – inanimate – no object
	concreteness	abstract – concrete – no object
	concreteness level	high – medium – low – no object
	concreteness rating	score 1 – 5
	constituent	adverbial constituent – nominal constituent – sentence – no object
	countability	countable – uncountable – no object
	number	singular – plural – no object
	semantics	action – animate – artefact – concrother – dynamic – human – institute – non-dynamic – place – substance – time – undetermined – no object
	type	agent – direct object – indirect object – predicative adjunct – prepositional object – no object
	object2 type	indirect object – predicative adjunct – prepositional object – no object
Contextual ID-tags	temporal indication	duration – starting point – no temporal indication
	modified verb	modified verb – no modified verb
	modifying verb	modifying verb – no modifying verb
	clause type	main sentence – subordinate
Extra-linguistic ID-tags	genre	broad – fiction – instructive – journalistic – legal – political – special – tourism
	domain	communication – consumption – culture – economy – education – environment – finance – foreign affairs – history – home affaires – institutions – justice – leisure – science – transport – welfare state

We based the ID-tags concerning the concreteness level of the subject and object on research conducted by Brysbaert et al. (2014), who validated the concreteness rating of 30,000 Dutch words. Those ratings were used to determine the level of concreteness of a subject or object. The scholars attributed a score between 1 and 5 to each word, with 5 being very concrete and 1 being very abstract. For instance, *aardappel* [potato] gets a rating of 4.97 and is thus a very concrete word whereas *conformisme* [conformism] is assigned a rating of 1.07 and is therefore considered an abstract word. All the lemmas with a concreteness rating lower than 2.5 were tagged 'low' for the ID-tag concreteness_level, lemmas with a concreteness rating between 2.5 and 3.5 were tagged as 'medium' and lemmas with a concreteness rating higher than 3.5 were annotated as 'high'. If we consider the same examples as mentioned above, *aardappel* would be annotated as 'concreteness_level_high', while *conformisme* would receive the tag 'concreteness_level_low'. Regarding the ID-tag Main Clause – Subordinate, we chose not to discriminate between the different types of subordinates. To determine the semantic class of the subject and object, we used the Cornetto Database, a lexical resource for Dutch (Vossen et al. 2013). We included *genre* and *domain* because it is believed that 'social meaning' (i.e. "which a piece of language conveys about the social circumstances of its use", Leech 1990: 14) is an important factor when decoding language. According to Leech (1990), both the style dimension and the illocutionary force of an expression provides information about the meaning of that expression. A second rationale to include *genre* and *domain* is the conclusion drawn by Grondelaers and Geeraerts (2003: 79) that "[...] all the types of semantic variation are [...] also – and to a large extent – influenced by contextual factors". *Genre* concerns the text type (for instance 'journalistic'), and *domain* refers to the subject of the text (for instance 'culture').

As mentioned above, the fourth step of the BP approach involves the statistical exploration of the data matrix. As we want to find out whether the semantics of the verbs remains constant in translated and non-translated Dutch, the data matrix was split according to translation status, separating all instances that were originally written in Dutch from those that were translated into Dutch from another language (i.c. English). The statistical analyses are carried out with the open source statistical software *R* (R Core Team 2014). Via the corregp-package (Plevoets 2015), we were able to transform and analyze our table with the annotations. The resulting table was analyzed with Correspondence Analysis (Lebart et al. 1998; Greenacre 2007). Correspondence Analysis (CA) arrives at a lower-dimensional representation of the row and column categories, analogous to a Semantic Vector Space. At the same time, it enables us to visually explore the data. The output of the CA is a scatterplot, where data points are represented as points in a two-dimensional space. The distance between the data points is related to the degree of similarity between those points. In other words: the closer two points are to one another, the more similar they are. In our case, the CA enabled us to map out the semantic field of inchoativity. The anova-test from the corregp-package (Plevoets 2015) helped us to decide which ID-tags were significant (the full table is included as an appendix). We calculated the confidence interval of every tag and found four ID-tags to be non-significant (viz. subject_number, subject_concreteness, MainClause_Subordinate and Object2_Type). Furthermore, we decided to omit *aanvatten* from our data, because there were not enough attestations of that verb in our data sets (only 15 attestations in non-translated Dutch, and 6 in translated Dutch).

3.3 Johansson's procedure

As mentioned above, Johansson (1998) was well aware of the possible presence of translation effects in parallel corpora and therefore, he suggested to check observations extracted from a parallel corpus against a control corpus, consisting of comparable non-translated texts. If the observations from the parallel corpus deviate from the patterns in the control corpus with non-translated texts, the contrastive study is not validated, and the observed differences between two different languages may be due to translational effects. More precisely, this means that there should be as little divergence between translated texts in a given language and comparable, non-translated texts in that language. Johansson believes that this procedure is a necessary step when working with parallel corpora, but he also emphasizes that it could provide the researcher with new insights into both translation and cross-linguistic relations (Johansson 1998).

For the present case study, we used the Dutch Parallel Corpus as it can be used as a parallel (translation) and comparable corpus. It contains original and translated texts in three languages (French, Dutch and English). As can be seen in Figure 6 below, this case study focused on three components in Dutch and English: viz. English source texts, Dutch target texts and comparable original texts in Dutch.

Following Johansson's procedure, target texts and comparable non-translated texts need to be compared. In this case: Dutch target texts (component B in the figure above) and comparable non-translated texts in Dutch (component C in the figure above) need to be compared if a researcher wants to carry out a contrastive comparison between two languages (in this case: Dutch and English). If minimal differences between component B and component C are observed, the found var-

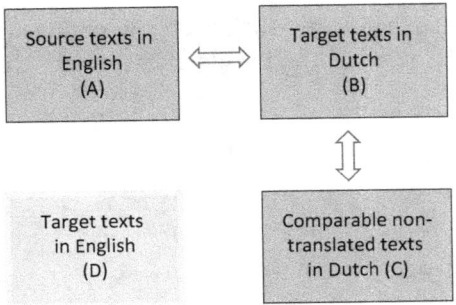

Figure 6: Johansson's procedure.

iation between component A and component B can be further analyzed in a contrastive study. We entered a corpus query for each of the verbs of inchoativity that were selected by the semantic mirroring method (see section 3.1) and compared the resulting frequency distributions.

4 Results

4.1 Johansson's procedure

Before testing the semantic stability hypothesis, we first verify whether Johansson's procedure provides an indication of an asymmetrical relationship between the translated part and the non-translated, comparable part of the corpus, thus teasing apart contrastive relations and translation effects. Our case study focuses on inchoative verbal lexemes in the DPC. We therefore check the frequency distributions of the 5 selected lexemes of inchoativity in the component of the corpus containing translated data and in the component containing non-translated data.[3] As a first step, we conduct a small contrastive

---

[3] Note that we do not consider the Dutch and English lexemes in this table as being each other's best translation equivalents, but that the main aim here is to compare the frequency distribution of the lexemes in each variety.

study on inchoativity in Dutch (translated and non-translated texts combined: 3,667,606 words) and English (1,254,225 words). The results of that study are presented in Table 3:

Table 3: Cross-linguistic frequency distribution of verbs of inchoativity, ordered according to frequency.

English	Dutch
To start	*Beginnen*
535 =63.54%	1778 =66.32%
To begin	*Starten*
266 =31.59%	582 =21.71%
To commence	*Opstarten*
19 =2.26%	215 =8.02%
To start up	*Van start gaan*
15 =1.78%	73 =1.41%
To take off	*Aanvatten*
7 =0.83%	33 =0.96%
Total	
842	2681

First of all, we notice that the verb *beginnen* (the formal equivalent of *to begin*) is the most frequent expression of inchoativity in Dutch (66.32%), whereas in English it is *to start* that is the most frequently used verb of inchoativity (63.54%). In Dutch, *starten* (the formal equivalent of *to start*) is the second most frequent lexeme (21.71%), while in English *to begin* is the second most frequent expression of inchoativity (31.59%). In Dutch, *aanvatten* is only found in 0.96% of the corpus attestations, the least frequent lexeme in English is *to take off* (only found in 0.83% of the attestations). The results of this small-scale contrastive study point in the direction of onomasiological differences between Dutch and English. Not only do Dutch and English have different prototypical lexemes of inchoativity (*beginnen* versus *to start*), they also have different peripheral lexemes (*aanvatten* versus *to take off*). We also see that English shows somewhat less differentiation in the used lexemes than in Dutch: the two most frequent lexemes (*to begin* and *to start*) already represent 95.13% of the corpus attestations, whereas the two most frequent lexemes in Dutch represent "only" 88.03% of the corpus attestations.

Next, we separate the frequency distribution of the lexemes of inchoativity in translated Dutch and original Dutch (Table 4). We mainly focus on the differences between translated and original, non-translated Dutch to test the procedure introduced by Johansson (1998).

Table 4: Intralinguistic frequency distribution of verbs of inchoativity.

	Dutch (translation)	Dutch (original)
Beginnen	958 =71.02%	820 =61.56%
Starten	241 =17.87%	341 =25.60%
Opstarten	118 =8.75%	97 =7.28%
Van start gaan	19 =1.41%	54 =4.05%
Aanvatten	13 =0.96%	20 =1.50%
Total	1349	1332

The table above shows that the frequency distribution of translated Dutch is similar to that of original Dutch, but that there are nevertheless considerable differences between the two varieties. The difference in frequency distribution between translated Dutch and original Dutch is significant, with a p-value <0.00001 ($X^2_{(4)}$ = 48.104). Despite the fact that in both translated and non-translated Dutch *beginnen* is the most frequent verbal expression of inchoativity, it is remarkably more frequent in translated Dutch than in original Dutch. Consequently, if only translational data were taken into account (e.g. in a contrastive analysis based on a translational corpus), the frequency of *beginnen* would be overestimated. In non-translated Dutch, *beginnen* represents 61.56% of the attested inchoative verbs, in contrast to translated Dutch where *beginnen* is used in 71.02% of the total number of corpus attestations containing an inchoative verb. This indicates that in translated Dutch, the most frequent verb of inchoativity (namely *beginnen*) is overused. A similar observation can be made for *van start gaan*: the pattern of original Dutch is exaggerated in translated language with *van start gaan* – despite being low frequent in translated and original Dutch– being underused in translated Dutch (1.41%, compared to 4.05% in original Dutch). The same goes for *starten:* compared to original Dutch (25.60%) it is underused in translated Dutch (17.87%) and for *aanvatten* (original: 1.50% and translated: 0.96%).

The overuse of *beginnen* in translated language and the underuse of *aanvatten, van start gaan* and *starten* confirm the findings of Johansson's corpus studies (1998): lexical features tend to be over- and underused in translated texts compared to non-translated texts. A mechanism which can possibly explain those exaggerated patterns can be found within the usage-based cognitive paradigm. Entrenchment is a general cognitive mechanism that has been shown to underlie all cognitive systems, including the linguistic system (Langacker 1988; Bybee 2010;). We deem it likely that the translator's preference for the more frequent expression is influenced by its entrenchment. An entrenched construction is one that is more frequently used and through this higher frequency of use, it becomes more firmly anchored in the language user's knowledge of that language (Bybee 2010; Geeraerts 2017). Geeraerts (1994, 2017) and Grondelaers and Geeraerts (2003) adopted an onomasiological perspective on entrenchment and salience. Onomasiology "takes its starting-point in a concept and investigates by which different expressions the concept can be [...] named" (Grondelaers and Geeraerts 2003: 69). The different expressions to name a concept have various degrees of entrenchment (Geeraerts et al. 1994), as some expressions are more frequently used and more easily encoded than others. Consequently, onomasiological salience can be considered as the increased frequency of an expression to designate a concept with regard to alternative, competing expressions. As *beginnen* is the most frequent expression of inchoativity in non-translated Dutch, we can assume that it is cognitively more salient than its competing expressions (*starten, aanvatten, opstarten, van start gaan*). If the pattern is exaggerated in translated language, this could mean that the cognitive mechanisms of onomasiological salience and entrenchment play an even bigger role in the translation process. The more demanding cognitive environment in which translators operate (see Kruger and De Sutter 2018) may incite them to opt for the lexeme that is expressed more readily and that is considered the "safe" option (Pym 2005). A second explanatory mechanism that could be at stake is (over-)normalization (Teich 2003), which states that translators conform to patterns typical of the target language. This could explain the overuse of frequent expressions, and the underuse of less-frequent expressions of inchoativity in our case-study. The results from our small corpus study confirm once more that translated language differs from non-translated language and show that Johansson's procedure as applied in his 1998 paper is not only useful in controlling frequency differences in translated and non-translated language, it is also a crucial procedure, and an inevitable step for contrastive-linguistic researchers who want to use data from parallel corpora for a contrastive study.

4.2 Behavioral profile analysis

The results of the Johansson's procedure indicated that there are differences to be found between the frequency distribution of translated and non-translated Dutch, but the procedure did not enable us to further explore those differences. In this section, we verify to what extent the four verbal lexemes (as mentioned above, we decided to omit the low-frequent lexeme *aanvatten* for this analysis) are used in different contexts in translated texts compared to non-translated texts, thus verifying potential semantic differences. On the basis of the 31 ID-tags presented in Section 3.2, which should be understood as a 31-dimensional space, we use correspondence analysis for dimension reduction, yielding a highly interpretable two-dimensional visualization of the original variation in the dataset (Greenacre 2007). In these visualizations (or plots), the distance between two data points can be related to their degree of similarity: more precisely, the positions of the lexemes and the distances between them can be thought to represent the prototypicality of the lexemes and the degree of similarity and difference (Vandevoorde 2016).

We start our discussion with a plot containing the four Dutch verbs of inchoativity as a function of their translation status (translated: 'Tra': *tra_starten*, *tra_beginnen*, *tra_van_start_gaan* and *tra_opstarten* vs. non-translated 'Ori': *ori_starten*, *ori_beginnen*, *ori_van_start_gaan* and *ori_opstarten*) in order to verify the semantic stability hypothesis. The plot represents the semantic field of (verbal) inchoativity and allows us to measure semantic distances between lexemes. The more identical the position of the translated and original variant of a lexeme are, the smaller the semantic distance between the verbs and hence, the smaller the meaning difference between the same verb in translated and in non-translated texts. An identical position of a lexeme and its translated equivalent (or in other words, a complete overlap of the two points in the plot) would imply semantic identity and by consequence would confirm the semantic stability hypothesis. In section 4.2.2, we will zoom in on the ID-tags which cause the largest semantic differences.

4.2.1 General analysis

Figure 7 represents the semantic field of inchoativity in translated and non-translated Dutch.

When looking at the plot, the most striking observation is that the positions of the four verb lemmas in original Dutch are different from the positions of the translated verb lemmas: none of the ellipses encircling the lemmas of a lexeme in original Dutch (ori_lexeme) overlap with their translated counterpart (tra_lexeme). The

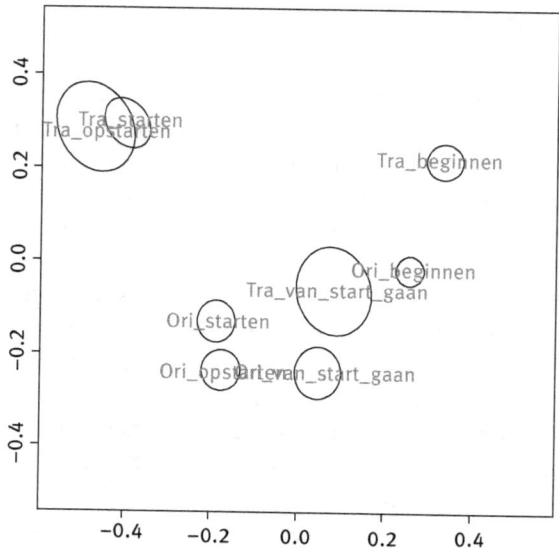

Figure 7: Visualization of the semantic field of inchoativity.

ellipses encircling the lemmas are the two-dimensional variant of the 95% confidence intervals. If an ellipse were to cross the ellipse of another lexeme, this would mean that the difference between the lemmas, based on the 30+ ID-tags, is not significant, and hence there would be no semantic difference between the lemmas. This is not the case for our lemmas: none of the ellipses of an original lemma overlaps with the ellipse of its translated counterpart, which indicates that the meaning of all translated verbs differs significantly from the non-translated variants, hence refuting the semantic stability hypothesis. Moreover, not only is there a considerable distance between the two varieties (translated vs. non-translated), it is also remarkable that the verbs in non-translated Dutch tend to cluster together near the center of the plot, whereas the verbs in translated Dutch are more dispersed over the upper half of the plot. For instance, *ori_beginnen* is located very close to the origin (the zero-point, i.e. the point where the two zero-axes intersect, and which we consider as the center of the semantic space of which the plot is thought to be a representation) and is near to *ori_starten*, whereas *tra_beginnen* finds itself higher and more to the right, much further away from *tra_starten* (on the left). We assume that lexemes near the origin of the plot (i.e. close to the zero-point on the X and Y axis) are prototypical, as lexemes that are associated with many different ID-tag levels are plotted there. In other words, lexemes that have a less specific behavioral profile and that can occur in many different contexts can rightly be considered as prototypical. Close to the plot's origin are *ori_beginnen* and *ori_starten*, which are consequently considered to be prototypical (these are also the most frequent verbs in the DPC and the reference corpus SONAR). By consequence, we can state that *tra_beginnen* takes a less prototypical place in the plot as it is located further away from the prototypical position in the plot.

When we take a look at the distances between the translated verbs, we notice that in general, they are lying further apart from each other (with the exception of *tra_starten* and *tra_opstarten*), which shows that the meaning differences between the lexemes are more clearly expressed than in original Dutch. This means that they have a more specific behavioral profile than the non-translated verbs; this will be further elaborated on in the next section. Another noticeable result is that, according to this plot, the only two verbs that do not have significantly different meanings are *tra_starten* and *tra_opstarten*. This could point in the direction of meaning fusion in translated language, with *starten* and *opstarten* merging their meaning and becoming more synonymous.

In sum, all four lexemes have a meaning that is significantly different in translated Dutch than in non-translated Dutch. For this reason, the semantic stability hypothesis seems not completely tenable, as there are minor differences in the semantic structure. Next, we noticed that non-translated verbs tend to be located closer to the origin of the biplot. This means that their behavioral profile is broader, whereas translated verbs seem to have a more specific behavioral profile.

4.2.2 Detailed analysis of the ID-tags

Although the analysis in the previous section already unveiled significant semantic differences between inchoative verbs in translated and non-translated Dutch, two questions remain unanswered: (1) which of the underlying ID-tags cause these differences and (2) what is the unique behavioral profile of each of the lexemes in translated and non-translated Dutch, i.e. what is the unique combination of ID-tag levels for each of the lexemes? In order to answer the first question, we calculated the size of the contribution for each ID-tag by means of an anova test (Cuevas et al. 2004, Plevoets 2017), which yields X^2 values. Table 5 shows the X^2-values for the significant ID-tags, ranked according to their influence on the position of the lexemes in Figure 7. The higher the X^2-value of an ID-tag, the more variance it covers and the more influence it has on the position of each lexeme. What emerges from this table is that the two most significant factors are language-external in nature (viz. *genre* and *domain*) and that the ID-tags concerning the object (viz. *concreteness level, type, semantics*) seem to affect the position of the verbs of inchoativity in Figure 7 more than ID-tags related to the subject or the main verb.

Table 5: X^2-values of the ID-tags, yielded by the anova-test.

ID-tag	X^2
Domain	308.757
Genre	253.282
Object concreteness level	238.966
Modified verb	197.358
Verb voice	194.887
Object type	164.804
Object semantics	154.659
subject semantics	148.179
Verb tense	136.846
Subject common/proper name	109.130
Temporal indication	74.384
Verb perfectness	71.046
Object concreteness	70.498
Object constituent	69.855
Subject animacy	65.368
Object countability	61.151
Subject concreteness level	57.601
Object number	54.845
Verb mode	50.041
Verb number	48.912
Object animacy	46.176
Modifying verb	33.566
Subject countability	32.045

In the remainder of this section, we will present and discuss the exact influence of the 10 most significant ID tags by adding the position of each of the ID tag levels to the plot with the 8 lexemes from Figure 7. This will allow us to find out what the behavioral profile of each of the lexemes in non-translated and translated Dutch is, and consequently, to answer the question as to what underlies the semantic differences shown in Figure 7.

Figure 8 contains 10 biplots that are all based on the same correspondence regression analysis. Each biplot highlights the levels of one of the 10 most influential ID-tags within the general plot while the positions of the lexemes remain stable

On the usefulness of comparable and parallel corpora for contrastive linguistics — 109

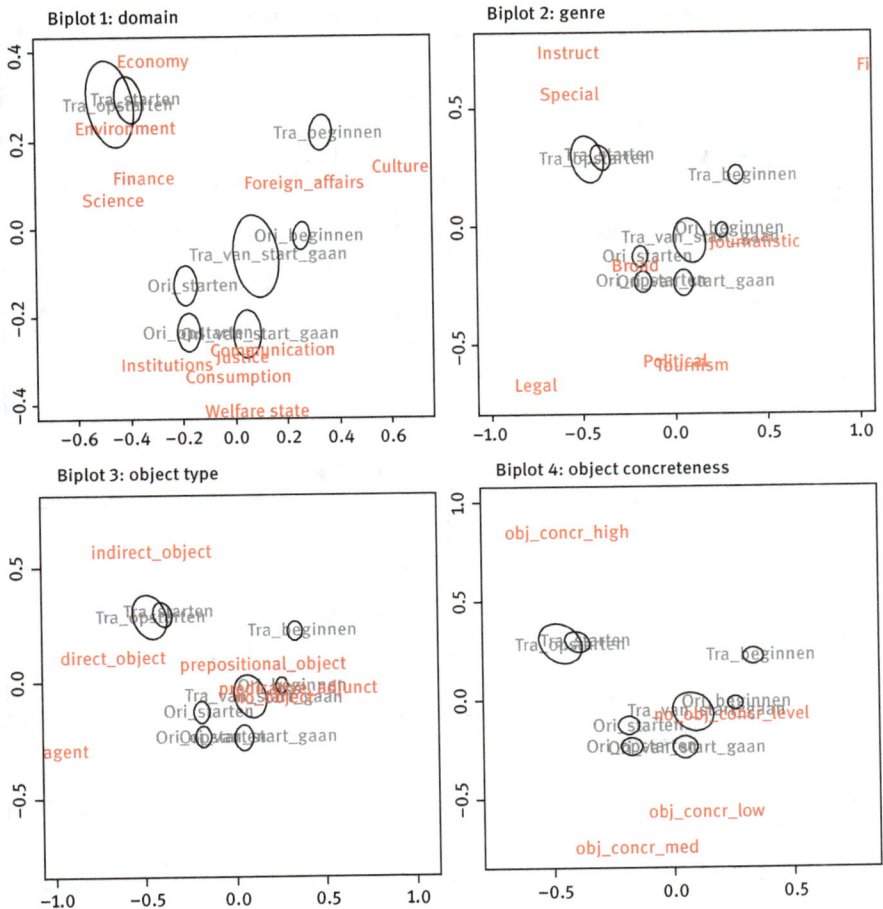

Figure 8: Detailed analysis of the behavioral profile.

in all 10 biplots (and identical to their positions in Figure 7): domain in biplot 1, genre in biplot 2, object type in biplot 3, concreteness of the object in biplot 4, object semantics in biplot 5, tense of the verb in biplot 6, voice of the verb[4] in biplot

---

[4] Note that we considered the proportion of the passive and active voice in original and translated Dutch: in non-translated Dutch, 23% of the corpus occurrences is used in the passive voice. In translated Dutch, 15% of the occurrences is in the active voice. This ratio is slightly higher than the active-passive ratio that was found by Vandenbosch (1992), who investigated the frequency of the active and passive voice in Dutch and noted an overall passive frequency in written discourse of 8.0%, and 13.4% in 'argumentative-scientific' prose.

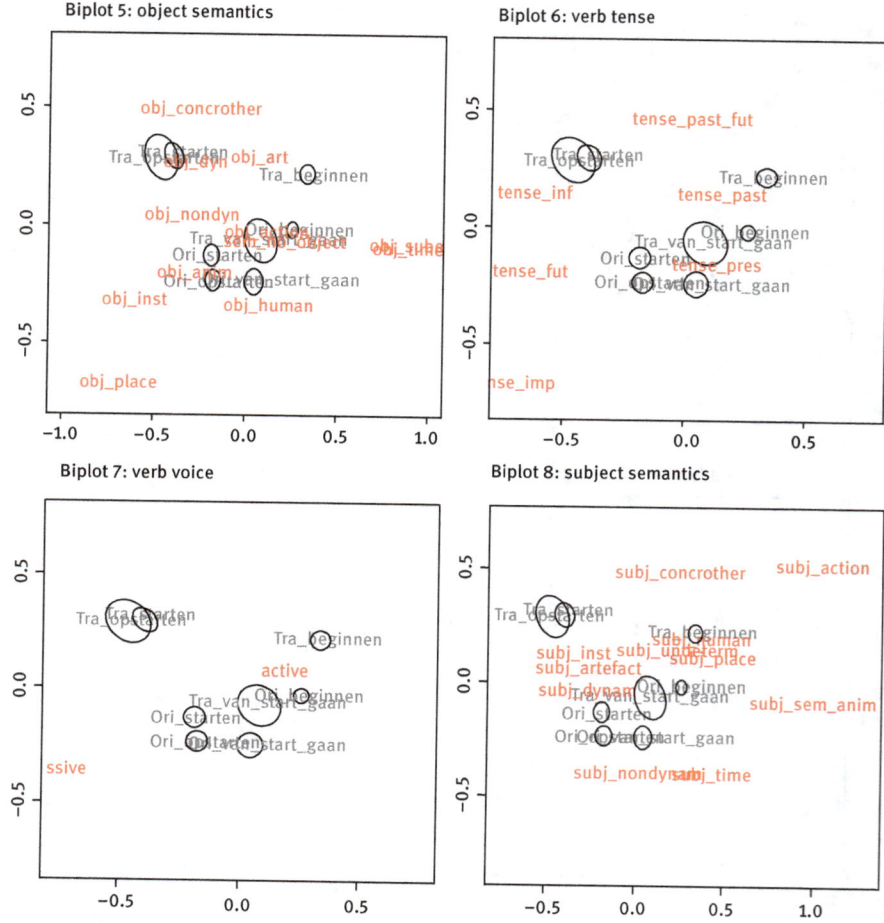

Figure 8 (continued)

7, semantics of the object in biplot 8, common noun or proper name in biplot 9 and the presence of a modified verb in biplot 10). These visualizations allow us to tentatively explain the specific position of each lexeme within that space.

4.2.2.1 *Beginnen* 'to begin'

We start our exploration of the unique behavioral profile of each lexeme with *beginnen* 'to begin'. The general plot in the previous section revealed that there is a considerable distance between the position of *ori_beginnen* and *tra_beginnen*. With regard to the most significant ID-tag *domain* (biplot 1), we observe few

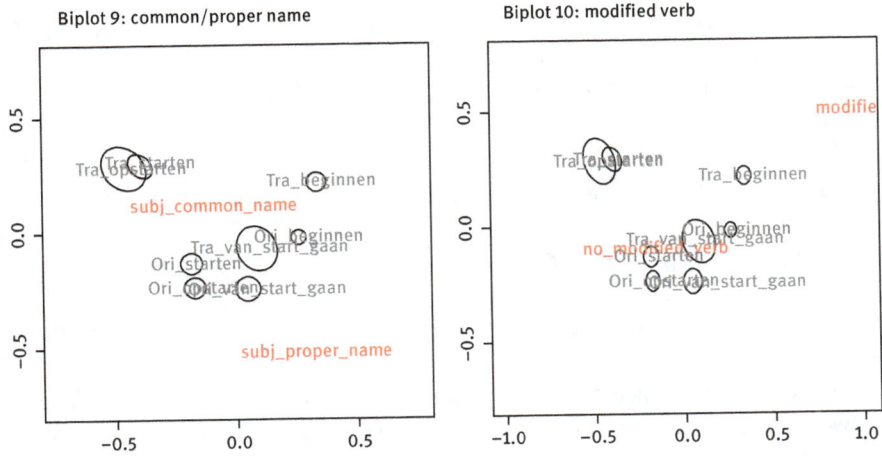

Figure 8 (continued)

differences between original and translated *beginnen:* both are associated with texts about foreign affairs, culture, and – to a lesser extent – with financial and scientific texts. As for the ID-tag *genre* (biplot 2), we see that in originally written journalistic texts and broad communicative texts, *beginnen* is more prominently used than in translated texts of the same genre. *Ori_beginnen* and *tra_beginnen*, also differ in the types of objects they take (biplot 3). *Ori_beginnen* is associated with predicative adjuncts or is used in a monovalent context, whereas *tra_beginnen*, exhibits a slightly stronger preference for indirect objects. Both translated and non-translated *beginnen* are often used with a prepositional object. Biplot 4 concerns the concreteness of the object and shows that non-translated *beginnen*, is more closely associated with objects that are medium concrete or abstract, whereas *tra_beginnen* is closer to highly concrete objects. When focusing on the semantics of the objects (biplot 5), we notice that *tra_beginnen* is located more closely to objects that refer to dynamic concepts (=abstract concept involving change or internal stages), artefacts (=physical entities constructed by man) and "concrother" concepts (according to Vossen et al. 2013, these are concepts which are concrete, but do not refer to substances or artefacts, for instance "finger"), as opposed to *ori_beginnen*, which tends to take an object that expresses an action or does not take an object at all. Biplot 6 informs us about the tense of *beginnen*. We observe that in translated texts, *beginnen* is more often used in the past tense, whereas in original texts, *beginnen* is more strongly associated with present tenses. The following sentence is a clear example of that preference, as the verb *beginnen* is used in the present tense even though it is about an event in the past:

(1) Ori_Dutch197: *"De eigenlijke werken **beginnen** in 1911, maar het oorlogsgeweld zorgt twee keer voor vertraging."*
[The actual works *begin* in 1911, but the war violence caused some delay twice.]

(2) Trans_Dutch3: *"Beide vorsten **begonnen** heel eenvoudige vestingen op te trekken."*
[Both kings *began* to build rudimentary fortresses.]

In translated Dutch, the past tense is used to talk about events in the past (see example 2).

Concerning the voice of *beginnen* (biplot 7), we do not discern any difference between translated and original texts: in both modes, *beginnen* is more used in active voice. The next two biplots visualize the properties of the subjects of *beginnen*. Regarding the semantics of the subject (biplot 8), we notice that *ori_beginnen* is associated with dynamic subjects or artefacts, whereas *tra_beginnen* tends to have a human or undetermined subject or a subject that refers to a place. In biplot 9, we observe few differences: both in translated and in non-translated texts, *beginnen* is inclined to take a subject that refers to common nouns. Finally, biplot 10 depicts the presence of verbs that are modified by *beginnen*, so-called modified verbs. For instance in the sentence 'we start *dancing*', dancing is considered as the modified verb. We conclude that *ori_beginnen* seldomly modifies another verb, while *tra_beginnen* is more often combined with a modified verb. For instance, consider the following examples:

(3) Ori_Dutch168: *"Dat is geen toeval: [...], nergens **begint** het verval van het ambachtswezen zo laat."*
[That is no coincidence: [...] nowhere does the decline of the crafts begin that late]
Subject: *Het verval* ('the decline') is dynamic (it is an abstract concept involving change or internal stages) and inanimate.
Tense: *begint* ('begins') is indicative present and imperfect.
Object: there is no object present
Modified verb: *begint* does not modify any other verb in the sentence.

(4) Trans_Dutch20: *"Later **begon** Khaled te zingen over seks en alcohol [...]"*
[Later, Khaled **began** singing about sex and alcohol [...]]
Subject: *Khaled* is human
Tense: *begon* ('began') is indicative past and imperfect.
Object: there is no object.
Modified verb: *begon* modifies the verb *zingen* ('singing').

4.2.2.2 *Starten* 'to start'

The general analysis again shows an important distance between *ori_starten* and *tra_starten*. Biplot 1 (domain) shows that *tra_starten* is used very often in texts about economy or the environment, while *ori_starten* is situated more closely to the center of the biplot and is more strongly associated with a broad scale of domains. We see a similar pattern considering *genre* (biplot 2), with *starten* having a stronger inclination towards specific genres in translated texts. It is more often used in instructive and specialized genres, whereas in original texts, *starten* is more prominently used in broader texts genres (broad commercial texts and journalistic texts). Biplot 3 displays the types of objects that are associated with *starten*. In translated texts, *starten* more often takes an indirect or direct object than *ori_starten*; the latter is more inclined to agentive objects, prepositional objects or does not take any object at all (see example 5). If *ori_starten* evokes an object, it refers more often to an abstract ("low-concrete") or medium concrete concept (see biplot 4). In contrast, translated *starten* tends to take a very concrete object that is dynamic or refers to an artefact or concrother concept (biplot 5). In original texts *starten* is more strongly associated with human, animate and institutional objects. When we focus on the syntactic properties of *starten*, we see that in translated texts, *starten* is more prominently used in the infinitive (see example 6) or in the past-future tense, while *ori_starten* more often takes the present or the future tense (biplot 6):

(5) Ori_Dutch193: *"De ADCLT-studie **startte** in 1999 onder leiding van Dr. Sparks (Sun Health Research Institute, Sun City, Arizona)"*
[The ADCLT-study **started** in 1999 under supervision of DR. Sparks (Sun Health Research Institute, Sun City, Arizona)]
Subject: *ADCLT-studie* is concrete.
Object: there is no object.
Tense: past.
Voice: active.

(6) Trans_Dutch18: *"Dankzij de opvallende winst- en cashgenerering kon Melexis de voorbije 4 jaar tegelijk interessante dividenden uitkeren en programma's voor terugkoop van eigen aandelen **starten**."*
[Thanks to considerable profit and cash generation Melexis was able to both pay out high dividends and **to start** share buy back programs over the last 4 years.]
Object: *programma's* is direct object.
Tense: *starten* is used in the infinitive.
Voice: active.

With regard to *voice* we see that *starten* is associated with the active voice in both modes. The next two biplots visualize the properties of the subjects of *starten*. Biplot 8 focuses on the semantics of the subject. We notice that *ori_starten* tends to have a dynamic subject or a subject that refers to artefacts or institutions. That preference for artefacts and institutions also applies to *tra_starten*, but, contrary to *ori_starten*, the subject of *tra_starten* can also be a concrother concept. Biplot 9 shows that both in translated and in non-translated texts, the subject of *starten* is likely a common noun. In addition, we see that *ori_starten* seldomly modifies another verb, whereas *tra_starten* is more often combined with another verb (biplot 10).

4.2.2.3 *Opstarten* 'to start up'

The general plot in the previous section revealed that *ori_opstarten* and *tra_opstarten* are the two lexemes that are the furthest removed from each other. This large distance reflects the divergent behavioral profiles of *ori_opstarten* and *tra_opstarten*. In biplot 1, we see that *tra_opstarten* is often used in texts about environment and economy and is also prominent in texts about finances and science, whereas non-translated *opstarten* tends to appear in texts about communication, justice, institutions, consumption and the welfare state. Next, we observe that *tra_opstarten* has the strongest inclination towards (biplot 2) instructive and specialized genres, while *ori_opstarten* is more prominent in political, legal and touristic texts. The next four biplots (biplot 3–6) depict the syntactic pattern of *opstarten*. First, biplot 3 shows us that *tra_opstarten* more often takes an indirect or direct object than *ori_opstarten*. In texts originally written in Dutch, *opstarten* is more strongly associated with an agentive object. From biplot 4, we learn that *tra_opstarten* is more closely located to *object_concreteness_high*, indicating that in translated texts, *opstarten* more often takes an object that is very concrete (see example 8). In texts originally written in Dutch, *opstarten* is more inclined to take abstract or medium concrete objects. When focusing on the association of *opstarten* and the semantics of its objects (biplot 5), we can deduce that in non-translated texts, *opstarten* has a significant tendency for human, animate and institutional objects or for objects that refer to a place or a substance. In translated texts, *opstarten* takes dynamic or concrother objects or is associated with objects that refer to artefacts. When we look at the tenses of *opstarten* (biplot 6), we see that *tra_opstarten* again behaves differently from its original counterpart: in translated texts, *opstarten* is more often used as an infinitive or in the past future tense, whereas in original texts, *opstarten* takes the present or future tense. With regard to its voice (biplot 7), *opstarten* behaves similarly to *van start gaan*: in translated texts, *opstarten* is used in the active voice, while in non-translated texts *opstarten* is more inclined to the passive voice. This also corresponds with the observations concerning the object: as *ori_opstarten* is more often used in the passive voice, it is more strongly linked to an agentive object (see example 7):

(7) Ori_Dutch132: "*Borstelproducent PDC Brush (www.pdcbrush.be)* **werd opgestart** *in Izegem in 1946 door Palmer Decoopman en kende sinds de start een continue groei.*"
[Brush manufacturer PDC Brush (www.pdcbrush.be) **was started up** in Izegem in 1946 by Palmer Decoopman and has experienced continual growth from the beginning.]
Subject: *PDC Brush* is a proper name.
Object: *door Palmer Decoopman* is a human object, and expresses the agent.
Voice: *werd opgestart* is used in the passive voice.

(8) Trans_Dutch56: "*In Thailand schreef Caritas kleine leningen uit aan mensen die hun bedrijf weer wilden* **opstarten**."
[In Thailand, Caritas gave out small loans to people who wanted **to start up** their company again.]
Subject: *Caritas* is a proper name.
Object: *hun bedrijf* is direct object and it is a concrete object
Voice: *opstarten* is active
Tense: *opstarten* is used in the infinitive, and it takes a modifying verb (*wilden*)

The inclination towards the passive voice of *opstarten* and *van start gaan* is remarkable, as the overall difference in voice between translated and non-translated language is not that distinct: for original Dutch, 77% of the corpus occurrences is used in the active voice and in translated Dutch, 85% of the occurrences is in the active voice. The tendency to slightly overuse the active voice in translated language, can point in the direction of translators showing risk-aversion as according to prescriptive handbooks, the passive voice should not be used too often in professional writing (Verhagen 1992 in Cornelis 1996: 252). When looking at the semantic categories of the subject (biplot 8), *ori_opstarten* has a strong tendency to take a non-dynamic subject or a subject that refers to time, while *tra_opstarten* is more strongly associated with subjects that refer to concrother concepts, institutions or artefacts. In addition, we see that *ori_opstarten* is strongly associated with subjects that refer to a proper name (biplot 9), thus referring to a person, a specific company or a brand. In contrast, *tra_opstarten* tends to take a subject that refers to common nouns. Finally, we observe that in both modes, *opstarten* seldomly modifies another verb (biplot 10).

4.2.2.4 *Van start gaan* 'to take off'

From the general plot, we learned that *tra_van_start_gaan* is situated close to the center of the biplot, which indicates that it is highly prototypical, in contrast with original texts, where *van start gaan* is a less prototypical expression of inchoativity. When looking at biplot 1, we notice that *ori_van_start_gaan* is prominent in texts about communication, justice, institutions, consumption and the welfare state, whereas *tra_van_start_gaan* is more often used in texts about foreign affairs, finance and science. We see a similar pattern considering the genres (biplot 2), with tra_*van_start_gaan* being more prominent in broad commercial texts and journalistic texts. In originally written Dutch, *van start gaan* is more associated with legal, political and touristic texts. When we analyze the argument structure of *van start gaan* (biplot 3), we see that *tra_van_start_gaan* behaves as a central lexeme and has a broader profile. It typically takes a predicative adjunct or prepositional object or is used in a monovalent context, in contrast to *ori_van_start_gaan* that tends to take an agentive object. Biplot 4 informs us about the concreteness level of the objects of *van start gaan*. We see that in both varieties, *van start gaan* is associated with an abstract or medium concrete object. When looking at the semantics of the objects (biplot 5) it can be noticed that *tra_van_start_gaan* tends to take an object that expresses an action or does not take an object at all, while *ori_van start gaan* is more associated with human, animate and institutional objects or with objects that refer to a place. In both varieties, *van start gaan* typically occurs in the present tense (biplot 6). Biplot 7 shows that *ori_van_start_gaan* is closely associated with the passive voice, which is in line with our previous observations about the tendency of *ori_van_start_gaan* to take an agentive object. In translated language, *van start gaan* is significantly more often used in the active voice. Biplot 8 and 9 inform us about the properties of the subjects of inchoative verbs. In non-translated texts, *van start gaan* is typically combined with non-dynamic subjects or subjects that refer to time, whereas in translated texts, there is a broader variety of subjects. *Tra_van_start_gaan* is associated with dynamic subjects, animate subjects, artefacts and with subjects that refer to institutions (biplot 8). In biplot 9, then, we see that *ori_van_start_gaan* is associated with subjects that refer to proper names, while *tra_van_start_gaan* more often has a common noun as subject:

(9) Ori_Dutch151: *"Cobar **ging van start** met de industriële diversificaties [...]"*
 [Cabor **took off** with industrial diversification [...]]
 Subject: *Cobar* is a proper name.

Table 6: summarizing table BP-analysis.

ID-tags	Beginnen		Starten		Opstarten		Van start gaan	
	original	transl.	original	transl.	original	transl.	original	transl.
Domain	foreign affairs, culture, finance, science		broad profile	economy environment	comm. justice, institutions, consumpt. welfare state	economy, environment, finances, science	comm., justice, institutions, consumpt welfare state	foreign affairs, finance, science
Genre	Journalistic commercial	broad profile	commercial, journalistic	instructive, specialized	legal, political, touristic	instructive, specialized	legal, political, touristic	commercial journalistic
Object type	predicative adjunct, no object, prep. obj.	indirect obj prep. objb	agent, prep. object	indirect obj; direct obj	agent	indirect obj, direct obj	agent	predicative adjunct, no object prep. obj.
Obj. concreteness	medium concrete, abstract	highly concrete	medium concrete, abstract	highly concrete	medium concrete, abstract	highly concrete	medium concrete, abstract	
Obj. semant.	action, no object	dynamic, artefacts, concrother	human, animate, institution	artefact, concrother	human, animate, institution, place, substance	dynamic, artefact, concrother	human, animate, institution, place	action, no object
Verb tense	present	past	present, future	infinitive, past-future	present, future	infinitive, past-future	present	

(continued)

Table 6 (continued)

ID-tags	Beginnen		Starten		Opstarten		Van start gaan	
	original	transl.	original	transl.	original	transl.	original	transl.
Verb voice	active	active	active	active	passive	active	passive	active
Subj. semant.	dynamic, artefacts	human, undeterm, place	dynamic, artefacts, institution	artefacts	non-dynamic, time	conrother, institutions, artefacts	non-dynamic, time	broad profile
Proper/common noun	common noun	common noun	common noun	common noun	proper name	common noun	proper name	common noun
Modified verb	no	yes	no	yes	no		no	

(10) Trans_Dutch217: Het verkoopsproces van Carling Brewers is van start gegaan.
[The auction process for the sale of Carling brewers took off]
Subject: *verkoopsproces* is a common noun.

Finally, biplot 10 depicts the presence of verbs that are modified by the inchoative verb, so-called modified verbs. We see that neither in non-translated nor in translated texts, the inchoative verb modifies another verb often.

In sum, we noticed that the most significant ID-tags are language-external features (*domain* and *genre*). Furthermore, the 10 biplots above clearly show that the behavioral profile of translated verbs significantly differs from the profile of non-translated verbs. Table 6 underlies the biplots that were discussed supra and aims to summarize the previous discussion. We notice that inchoative verbs in translated texts quite often appear in different contexts than in non-translated texts. Again, as the table is a result of the correspondence analysis that was applied to our data, all the presented ID-tags and their different levels are significant (see section 3.2).

5 Conclusion

With this paper, we aimed to make a contribution to the under-researched field of semantics in translation studies by providing an answer to two interrelated goals. First, we applied Johansson's procedure (Johansson 1998), which aims at teasing apart contrastive and translation-based effects when using parallel corpora and second, we tackled the question of translation effects on the semantic level, causing semantic deviations in translation. In order to detect semantic differences, we started out from the semantic stability hypothesis, which states that meaning is the invariant of translation (Klaudy 2010) and that the (sub-)meanings of lexemes do not change during translation. To empirically verify the semantic stability hypothesis, we had to find a method that succeeds in visualizing possible semantic differences between translated and non-translated language. As mentioned in Section 2, meaning is an abstract notion, and as a result, it is difficult to operationalize semantic differences. As a way to overcome the notorious intangibility of meaning differences, we opted for the behavioral profile approach (BP), a quantitative and corpus-based method that builds further on the distributional idea that you can deduce the meaning of a word from the company it keeps. The BP is based on the assumption that words occurring in different contexts have different meanings. Consequently, if our near-synonyms of inchoativity are used in different contexts, that means that the verbs must have different meanings. The advantage of the BP when compared to more traditional distributional approaches is that it uses linguistically enriched data, which allows for a more fine-grained analysis of the context of a lexeme under study. We focused on the semantic field of inchoativity and opted to zoom in on the structuration of four prototypical verbal lexemes expressing inchoativity. If our verbs under study are used in different contexts in translated texts, the semantic structure of our verbs will show deviances in translated texts and that would mean that the semantic stability hypothesis is not completely tenable.

From our small pilot study, it becomes clear that the application of Johansson's procedure (1998) to rule out translational effects seems inevitable. The frequency patterns from original Dutch were exaggerated in translated Dutch, which means that translators overuse the most frequent lexeme, *beginnen* and underuse the less frequent lexemes *aanvatten, van start gaan* and *opstarten*. This confirms the earlier findings of Johansson (1998), and is in line with the ideas of onomasiological salience (Geeraerts 2017) and over-normalization (Hansen-Schirra and Steiner 2012), namely that a translator over-uses typical patterns of the target language (Teich 2003; Van Oost et al. 2015). Both principles can be connected to the concept of risk-aversion (Pym 2005).

For our second question, we selected four candidate lexemes for the semantic field of inchoativity. We used the semantic mirroring method, a corpus-based and translation-driven method that enables us to include more peripheral lexemes of inchoativity. We then applied the behavioral profile approach to our data sets. Given the results from the conducted research, we noticed that the combination of the semantic mirroring method and the behavioral profile approach yields new and interesting findings, that go beyond what traditional corpus studies (viz. distributional studies) are usually able to reveal. Indeed, the behavioral profile approach succeeds in efficiently charting the context in which the lexemes under study appear. Thanks to the corregp-package, we can visualize and analyze those patterns. It appears from this study that behavioral profiles based on translational data differ from those based on original data, hence pointing at subtle semantic differences. From the visualizations that were yielded via the corregp-package (Figures 7 and 8), we noticed that all four lexemes have a meaning profile that is significantly different in translated Dutch than in non-translated Dutch. For this reason, the semantic stability hypothesis was refuted. The behavioral profile from the non-translated verbs appeared to be broader than the profile of their translated counterparts, which indicates that translated verbs seem to have a more specific and limited meaning.

These conclusions are important for contrastive linguistics, because the results from our study demonstrate that the assumption of semantic stability between source and target text, which is one of the main motivations to use translational corpora in contrastive linguistics, does not seem tenable as there are multiple semantic differences noticeable between the translated and the non-translated verbs of inchoativity. Since it is exactly this assumption of semantic-pragmatic stability of linguistic units that underlies the use of parallel corpora in contrastive linguistics, one needs to be cautious when arriving at contrastive-linguistic conclusions based on translational data only. In addition we found that there are not only morphosyntactic differences between translated and non-translated language, but also subtle semantic differences. However, the analyses presented here should be further corroborated by analyzing more data, by investigating more semantic fields and by using other multivariate techniques.

Appendix

Anova-table, containing confidence intervals:

ANOVA Table (Type III Tests)	Lower	Upper
genre	119.631582	204.68757
Domain	131.416434	224.15403
subject_number	−1.332897	13.99338
subject_animateness	30.960813	84.65939
subject_semantics	89.243244	173.72607
subject_concreteness_level	18.393091	66.59152
subject_concreteness	−2.273940	17.58264
subj_proper_name	0.1521698	27.52696
subject_countable	10.297109	50.257610
verb_voice	140.404893	235.69591
verb_mode	21.225644	70.090444
verb_tense	45.89931	105.87950
verb_aspect	33.1783424	91.62560
verb_collocation	263.2446526	346.18003
verb_number	26.241698	75.03539

MainClause_Subord	−1.9916609	15.93627
object_type	106.464245	176.97454
object_semantics	65.705907	135.87591
object_constituent	27.4805502	78.73030
object_number	20.000707	69.17632
object_animateness	17.247413	63.08603
object_concreteness_level	26.139989	77.42685
object_concreteness	19.194072	67.20477
object_countable	23.349759	75.79760
object2_type	−14,115860	99,125900
modified_verb	152.415242	220.359372
modifying_verb	7.576064	42.60245
temporal	35.773724	97.28820

References

Aerts, Jan. 1998. Introduction. In Stig Johansson & Signe Oksefjell (eds.), *Corpora and cross-linguistic research: Theory, method and case studies*, IX–XIV. Amsterdam & Atlanta: Rodopi.

Baker, Mona. 1993. Corpus Linguistics and Translation Studies. Implications and Applications. In Mona Baker, Gill Francis and Elena Tognini-Bonelli (eds.), *Text and Technology. In Honour of John Sinclair*, 17–45. Philadelphia & Amsterdam: John Benjamins.

Barkhudarov, Stephan. 1975. Language and translation. *International relations*. Moscow.

Brysbaert, Marc, Michaël Stevens, Simon De Deyne, Wouter Voorspoels & Gert Storms. 2014. Norms of age of acquisition and concreteness for 30,000 Dutch words. *Acta psychologica* 150. 80–84.

Bybee, Joan. 2010. *Language, Usage and Cognition*. Cambridge: Cambridge University Press.

Cornelis, Louise. 1996. English and Dutch: The passive difference. *Language Sciences* 18(1–2). 247–264.

Cuevas, Antonio, Manuel Febrero & Ricardo Fraiman. 2004. An anova test for functional data. *Computational statistics & data analysis* 47 (1). 111–122.

Curran, James Richard. 2004. From distributional to semantic similarity. Edinburgh, Scotland: University of Edinburgh dissertation.

Delaere, Isabelle, Gert De Sutter & Koen Plevoets. 2012. Is translated language more standardized than non-translated language? Using profile-based correspondence analysis for measuring linguistic distances between language varieties. *Target* 24 (2). 203–224.

Divjak, Dagmar & Stefan Gries. 2006. Ways of Trying in Russian. Clustering Behavioral Profiles. *Corpus Linguistics and Linguistic Theory* 2 (1). 23–60.

Divjak, Dagmar & Stefan Gries. 2009. Corpus-based cognitive semantics: A contrastive study of phasal verbs in English and Russian. *Studies in cognitive corpus linguistics*, 273–296.

Dyvik, Helge. 1998. A Translational Basis for Semantics. In Stig Johansson & Signe Oksefjell (eds.), *Corpora and cross-linguistic research*, 51–86. Amsterdam & Atlanta: Rodopi.

Dyvik, Helge. 2004. Translations as Semantic Mirrors. From Parallel Corpus to Wordnet. In Karin Aijmer & Bengt Altenberg (eds.), *Language and Computers, Advances in Corpus Linguistics. Papers from the 23rd International Conference on English Language Research on Computerized Corpora (ICAME 23)*, 311–26. Göteborg: Brill Rodopi.

Ebeling, Jarle. 1998. Contrastive Linguistics, Translation, and Parallel Corpora. *Meta: Journal des traducteurs* 43(4). 602–615.

Evert, Stefan & Stella Neumann. 2017. The impact of translation direction on characteristics of translated texts: A multivariate analysis for English and German. *Empirical Translation Studies: New Methodological and Theoretical Traditions* 300. 47–80.

Firth, John Rupert. 1957. A Synopsis of Linguistic Theory 1930–1955. In John R. Firth (ed.), *Studies in Linguistic Analysis*, 1–32. Oxford: Philological Society.

Gast, Volker. 2015. On the use of translation corpora in contrastive linguistics: A case study of impersonalization in english and german. *Languages in Contrast* 15 (1). 4–33.

Geeraerts, Dirk. 2006 [1988]. Where Does Prototypicality Come From? In Dirk Geeraerts, René Dirven & John Taylor (eds.), *Words and Other Wonders*, 27–47. Berlin & New York: Mouton de Gruyter.

Geeraerts, Dirk. 2017. Entrenchment as onomasiological salience. In Hans-Jörg Schmid (ed.), *Entrenchment and the psychology of language learning. How we reorganize and adapt linguistic knowledge*, 153–174. Berlin & Washington: Mouton de Gruyter.

Geeraerts, Dirk, Peter Bakema & Stefan Grondelaers. 1994. *The Structure of Lexical Variation: Meaning, Naming, and Context*. Berlin: Mouton de Gruyter.

Gilquin, Gaëtanelle. 2006. The Place of Prototypicality in Corpus Linguistics. Causation in the Hot Seat. In Stefan Gries & Anatol Stefanowitsch (eds.), *Corpora in Cognitive Linguistics: Corpus-Based Approaches to Syntax and Lexis*, 159–91. Berlin, Heidelberg & New York: Mouton de Gruyter.

Granger, Sylviane. 2003. The corpus approach: a common way forward for Contrastive Linguistics and Translation Studies. In Sylviane Granger, Jacques Lerot, and Stephanie Petch-Tyson (eds.), *Corpus-based approaches to contrastive linguistics and translation studies*, 17–30. Amsterdam & New York: Rodopi.

Greenacre, Michael. 2007. *Correspondence Analysis in Practice, Second Edition*. Boca Raton: Chapman & Hall/CRC.

Gries, Stefan. 2010. Behavioral profiles: A fine-grained and quantitative approach in corpus-based lexical semantics. *The Mental Lexicon* 5 (3). 323–346.

Gries, Stefan & Dagmar Divjak. 2009. Behavioral Profiles. A Corpus-Based Approach to Cognitive Semantic Analysis. In Vyvyan Evans & Stephanie S. Pourcel (eds.), *New Directions in Cognitive Linguistics*, 57–75. Amsterdam & Philadelphia: John Benjamins.

Gries, Stefan & Dagmar Divjak. 2010. Quantitative approaches in usage-based cognitive semantics: myths, erroneous assumptions, and a proposal. In Dylan Glynn & Kerstin Fischer (eds.), *Quantitative methods in cognitive semantics: Corpus-driven approaches*, 333–353. Berlin & New York: Walter de Gruyter.

Gries, Stefan & Otani Naoki. 2010. Behavioral Profiles. A Corpus-Based Perspective on Synonymy and Antonymy. *ICAME Journal* 34. 121–50.

Grondelaers, Stefan & Dirk Geeraerts. 2003. Towards a pragmatic model of cognitive onomasiology. In Hubert Cuyckens, René Dirven & John R. Taylor (eds.), *Cognitive approaches to lexical semantics*. 67–92. Berlin & New York: Walter de Gruyter.

Halverson, Sandra. 1996. Norwegian-English Translation and the Role of Certain Connectors. In Marcel Thelen and Barbara Lewandowska-Tomasczyk (eds.), *Translation and Meaning, Part 3*, 129–139. Maastricht: Hogeschool Maastricht.

Halverson, Sandra. 2003. The cognitive basis of translation universals. *Target. International Journal of Translation Studies* 15 (2). 197–241.

Halverson, Sandra. 2007. A cognitive linguistic approach to translation shifts. *Belgian Journal of Linguistics* 21 (1). 105–121.

Halverson, Sandra. 2010. Cognitive Translation Studies: Developments in Theory and Method. In Gregory Shreve & Erik Angelone (eds.), *Translation and Cognition*, 349–369. Amsterdam: John Benjamins.

Hansen-Schirra, Silvia & Erich Steiner. 2012. Towards a typology of translation properties. In Silvia Hansen-Schirra, Stella Neumann & Erich Steiner (eds.), *Cross-Linguistic Corpora for the Study of Translations: Insights from the Language Pair English-German* 11, 255–280. Berlin & Boston: De Gruyter Mouton.

Harris, Zellig Sabbatai. 1954. Distributional Structure. *Word. Journal of the linguistic circle of New York* 10 (2–3). 146–162.

Ivir, Vladimir. 1987. Functionalism in Contrastive Analysis and Translation Studies. In René Dirven & Vilém Fried (eds.), *Functionalism in Linguistics*, 471–81. Amsterdam & Philadelphia: John Benjamins.

Jansegers, Marlies, Clara Vanderschueren & Renata Enghels. 2015. The polysemy of the Spanish verb *sentir*: A behavioral profile analysis. *Cognitive Linguistics* 26 (3). 381–421.

Johansson, Stig. 1998. On the role of corpora in cross-linguistic research. In Stig Johansson & Signe Oksefjell (eds.), *Corpora and cross-linguistic research: Theory, method and case studies*, 3–24. Amsterdam & Atlanta: Rodopi.

Johansson, Stig. 2007. *Seeing through multilingual corpora: on the use of corpora in contrastive studies* (Vol. 26). Amsterdam & Philadelphia: John Benjamins Publishing.

Klaudy, Kinga. 2010. Specification and Generalisation of Meaning in Translation. In Barbara Lewandowska-Tomasczyk and Marcel Thelen (eds.), *Meaning in Translation*, 81–103. Frankfurt a.M: Peter Lang.

Kruger, Haidee. 2012. A corpus-based study of the mediation effect in translated and edited language. *Target. International Journal of Translation Studies* 24 (2). 355–388.

Kruger, Haidee & Gert De Sutter. 2018. Alternations in contact and non-contact varieties: Reconceptualising *that*-omission in translated and non-translated English using the MuPDAR approach. *Translation, Cognition and Behavior* 1 (2). 251–290.

Kruger, Haidee & Bertus Rooy. 2012. Register and the features of translated language. *Across Languages and Cultures* 13 (1). 33–65.

Landauer, Thomas & Susan Dumais. 1997. A solution to Plato's problem: The latent semantic analysis theory of acquisition, induction, and representation of knowledge. *Psychological review* 104 (2). 211–240.

Langacker, Ronald. 1988. A Usage-Based Model. In Brygida Rudzka-Ostyn (ed.), *Topics in Cognitive Linguistics*, 127–161. Amsterdam: John Benjamins.

Larson, Mildred. 1984. *Meaning-Based Translation: A Guide to Cross-Language Equivalence*. Lanham, New York and London: University Press of America.

Laviosa, Sara. 1998. The Corpus-based Approach: A New Paradigm in Translation Studies. *Meta: Journal des traducteurs* 43(4). 474–479.

Lebart, Ludovic, André Salem & Lisette Berry. 1998. *Exploring Textual Data*. Dordrecht: Kluwer Academic Publishers.

Leech, Geoffrey. 1990. *Semantics: The study of Meaning*. London: Penguin Books.
Lenci, Alessandro. 2008. Distributional semantics in linguistic and cognitive research. *Italian journal of linguistics* 20 (1). 1–31.
Lin, Dekang. 1998. Automatic retrieval and clustering of similar words. *COLING 1998 (2): The 17th International Conference on Computational Linguistics*. 768–774.
Macken, Lieve, Orphée De Clercq & Hans Paulussen. 2011. Dutch Parallel Corpus: A Balanced Copyright-Cleared Parallel Corpus. *Meta: Journal Des Traducteurs* 56 (2). 374–390.
Manning, Christopher & Hinrich Schütze. 1999. *Foundations of Statistical Natural Language Processing*. Massachusetts: MIT Press.
Noël, Dirk. 2003. Translations as evidence for semantics: an illustration. *Linguistics* 41 (4). 757–785.
Olohan, Maeve & Mona Baker. 2000. Reporting that in translated English. Evidence for subconscious processes of explicitation? *Across Languages and Cultures* 1 (2). 141–158.
Oostdijk, Nelleke, Martin Reynaert, Veronique Hoste & Ineke Schuurman. 2013. The construction of a 500-million-word reference corpus of contemporary written Dutch. In Peter Spyns & Jan Odijk (eds.), *Essential speech and language technology for Dutch*, 219–247. Berlin & Heidelberg: Springer.
Plevoets, Koen. 2015. corregp: Functions and Methods for Correspondence Regression.
Pym, Anthony. 2005. Explaining explicitation. In Fóris, Ágota & Krisztina Károly (eds.), *New trends in translation studies. In honour of Kinga Klaudy*, 29–34. Budapest: Akadémiai Kiadó.
R Core Team. 2014. *R: A Language and Environment for Statistical Computing*. R Foundation for Statistical Computing. Vienna.
Szymor, Nina. 2015. Behavioral Profiling in Translation Studies. *trans-kom* 8 (2). 483–498.
Teich, Elke. 2003. *Cross-linguistic variation in system and text: A methodology for the investigation of translations and comparable texts*. Berlin & New York: Mouton de Gruyter
Ulrych, Margherita & Amanda Clare Murphy. 2008. Descriptive translation studies and the use of corpora: Investigating mediation universals. In Carol Taylor Torsello, Katherine Ackerley & Erik Castello (eds.), *Corpora for University Language Teachers*, 141–166. Bern: Peter Lang
Van Dale 2006a. *Van Dale vertaalwoordenboek Nederlands-Engels*. Utrecht: Van Dale Lexicografie
Van Dale 2006b. *Van Dale vertaalwoordenboek Nederlands-Frans*. Utrecht: Van Dale Lexicografie
Van Dale 2006c. *Van Dale vertaalwoordenboek Engels-Nederlands*. Utrecht: Van Dale Lexicografie
Van Dale 2006d. *Van Dale vertaalwoordenboek Frans-Nederlands*. Utrecht: Van Dale Lexicografie
Vandenbosch, Luc. 1992. *Aspekten van passiefvorming in het Nederlands. Een kognitief-pragmatische benadering*. [Aspects of the formation of passive in Dutch. A cognitive-pragmatic approach]. Antwerp, Belgium: Universitaire Instelling Antwerpen dissertation.
Vandevoorde, Lore. 2016. *On semantic differences: a multivariate corpus-based study of the semantic field of inchoativity in translated and non-translated Dutch*. Ghent Belgium, Ghent University dissertation.
Vandevoorde, Lore. 2018. *Semantic differences in translation: Exploring the field of inchoativity*. Berlin: Language Science Press.

Vandevoorde, Lore, Els Lefever, Koen Plevoets & Gert De Sutter. 2017. A Corpus-Based Study of Semantic Differences in Translation. The Case of Dutch Inchoativity. *Target. International Journal of Translation Studies* 29 (3). 388–415.

Van Hell, Janet & Annette De Groot. 1998. Conceptual representation in bilingual memory: Effects of concreteness and cognate status in word association. *Bilingualism: Language and cognition* 1 (3). 193–211.

Van Oost, Astrid, Annelore Willems & De Sutter, Gert. 2016. Asymmetric syntactic patterns in German-Dutch translation: a corpus-based study of the interaction between normalisation and shining through. *International Journal of Translation* 28 (1–2). 7–25.

Vinay, Jean-Paul & Darbelnet, Jean (1958). 1995. Comparative stylistics of French and English: A methodology for translation. In P. Kwieciński (ed.), *Disturbing Strangeness. Foreignisation and Domestication in Translation Procedures in the Context of Cultural Assymetry*, 123–126. Toruń: Wydawnictwo Edytor.

Vossen, Piek, Isa Maks, Roxane Segers, Hennie Van Der Vliet, Marie-Francine Moens, Katja Hofmann & Maarten de Rijke. 2013. Cornetto: a combinatorial lexical semantic database for Dutch. In Peter Spyns & Jan Odijk (eds.), *Essential speech and language technology for Dutch*, 165–184. Berlin & Heidelberg: Springer.

Stella Neumann
Is German more nominal than English? Evidence from a translation corpus

Abstract: Recent corpus studies comparing the frequency of nouns in English and German have produced inconclusive evidence. All existing studies have certain methodological limitations in that they rely on automatic part-of-speech tagging, which involves diverging tokenization based on contrastive spelling differences. Alternatively, counting is based on human categorization, thus avoiding the problems of spelling differences, but using a problematic sampling method. This paper aims at determining nominality in English and German while avoiding both types of problems. The distribution of normal nouns is counted in three random samples of 100 sentences from three different registers drawn independently of the word count, thus foregoing spelling-related differences. The sample is taken from a corpus containing originals and translations in the language pair. Since the corpus also includes alignment of matching translations, translation equivalents are taken into consideration as a *tertium comparationis*, thus offering the opportunity to assess the impact of translation-related decisions. In fact, a tendency of translations to deviate from originals can be observed at least in one register. The general results do not reveal any statistically significant difference in the frequency of nouns between the two languages. This rectifies informal claims that nouns are more frequent in German and contributes to a more accurate characterization of English and German. These findings are of relevance for language learners and translators, whose task is often to conform to target language patterns.

Keywords: noun frequency, corpus study, contrastive comparison, English, German

1 Introduction

Understanding not just what the grammatical features of a foreign language are, but also how they are distributed in comparison to a person's L1, is crucial for writing texts adapted to target language conventions in the foreign language and for translating. Nouns are a grammatical feature that is so central to using language that it may go unnoticed and is researched only sparingly in a cross-linguistic perspective, especially in terms of its frequency distribution. It therefore does not

---

Stella Neumann, Department of English, American and Romance Studies, RWTH Aachen University, Kármánstraße, Aachen, Germany

https://doi.org/10.1515/9783110682588-005

come as a surprise that statements about the frequency of nouns in English and German are often informal observations rather than empirical investigations. Such informal claims suggest that there is a difference between English and German as to the frequency of nominal expressions with German said to be more nominal than English, i.e. to draw more on nouns than English (Königs 2011: 129).

Examples such as (1) and (2) show that there seems to be some truth to this claim, although it cannot be known whether translators of these examples chose this particular translation because they are aware of this claim or because of other factors.[1] The number of nouns is higher in the German translations (4 in example (1), 9 in (2)) than in the respective English originals (1 in example (1), 8 in (2)). In (1) the infinitive verb *modernise* is translated by the deverbal nominalization *Modernisierung* ('modernization'). Additionally, this example contains two more nouns which are mentioned in the source sentence preceding the example. These additions are better described as individual decisions by the translator that cannot be immediately linked to the assumed difference between English and German.

(1) *He used it to modernise the castle (…).*
    Er erbeutete das vom   Schiff mitgeführte Gold und benutzte es zur
    He captured the of-the ship   carried   gold and used   it to-the
    Modernisierung des   Schlosses (…). (CroCo, E2G_TOU_001-s16)
    modernization of-the castle
    'he captured the gold carried by the ship and used it for the modernization of the castle'

(2) *But compared to the massive advantages from access to the markets of the new EU member states, the threat from the proverbial Polish plumber is marginal.* (CroCo, EO_ESSAY_012-s55)
    Im   Vergleich   zu den enormen Vorteilen,   die   Europa durch den Zugang
    In-the comparison to the enormous advantages which Europe through the access
    zu den Märkten der   neuen EU-Staaten   gewinnen kann, ist die Bedrohung
    to the markets of-the new   EU-member-states gain   can, is the threat
    durch   den sprichwörtlichen polnischen Klempner jedoch   geringfügig.
    through the proverbial   Polish   plumber however marginal.
    'However, in comparison with the enormous advantages which Europe can gain from access to the markets of the new EU member states, the threat of the proverbial Polish plumber is marginal.'

---

[1] Unless otherwise stated, examples are taken from the CroCo Corpus (Hansen-Schirra, Neumann, and Steiner 2012) and are provided with their aligned published translation.

The non-finite verb at the beginning of example (2) shows a similar process where the verb *compared* is translated by the corresponding noun *Vergleich* ('comparison'), which is part of a prepositional phrase. In comparison to the source sentence, this results in an additional noun and a reduction by one verb. In both languages both constructions are available: the English author could have chosen a prepositional phrase (*by comparison* or *in comparison to/with*) and the German translator could have chosen the participle *verglichen* ('compared'). A search for the noun *comparison* and the verb form *compared* in the English original subcorpus of the CroCo Corpus (Hansen-Schirra, Neumann and Steiner 2012) and its corresponding German counterparts *Vergleich* and *verglichen* in the German original subcorpus corroborates the point illustrated by the example: whereas the English noun occurs altogether 13 times and the verb 25 times, the German noun occurs 32 times and the verb only 3 times. English thus appears to have a preference for a verbal expression of a comparison, while German seems to prefer a nominal one.

Therefore, intuitively, there seems to be some truth to the informal claim that German draws more on nouns than English. Judging from a look at parallel texts this is a fairly typical case: some kind of non-finite clausal construction in English corresponds to some (prepositional) phrase in German. But does this norm, which might be perpetuated by translator trainers, really correspond to the empirical reality? Motivating this by linguistic studies turns out to be difficult: apparently, it is a rumor rather than a claim supported by linguistic studies. König and Gast (2012) only discuss lexical aspects of nouns in their contrastive comparison, but do not examine any potential difference in the distribution of nouns. The few corpus-based studies that have appeared in recent years will be discussed in more detail in Section 2. But before looking at these, statements from the literature characterizing English and/or German as more or less nominal will be reviewed.

Kortmann and Meyer (1992: 165) suggest that English might have a tendency towards verb phrase maximization whereas German tends to expand the nominal phrase and that this could correspond to these languages being primarily verb-oriented and noun-oriented respectively. Likewise, Fabricius-Hansen (2000: 5) refers to the frequency of nominalizations in German which, she claims, can be correlated with the construction of extreme nominal blocks. Indeed, in comparison to corresponding verbal, or rather clausal structures, nominalizations offer more options for compressing information in the form of potentially nested modifiers and for structuring information by thematization (Halliday 2001). Consider example (3) taken from Halliday and Matthiessen (2014: 720), which captures roughly the same portion of meaning.

(3) a. *He regretted that they had departed.*
    b. *his regret at their departure*

In (3b) both verbs of (3a) are nominalized. One (*regret*) serves as the head of the noun phrase, the other (*departure*) is part of a postmodifier of this head. As nouns they can easily take more modifiers (e.g. *his overly tearful regret at their precipitous departure*). Moreover, the phrase can serve various functions in a clause (subject etc.), but also postmodifier as in *the expression of his regret at their departure* resulting in what Fabricius-Hansen calls extreme nominal blocks, which maximize the amount of lexical information per running word, i.e. the lexical density. It is obviously possible – and depending on the register also likely – to express the same meaning with fewer nominalizations leading to an increased number of clauses including verbs (and running words). So, it appears that claims about the nominal character of German are linked to larger nominal units, i.e. noun phrases, rather than individual nouns. It is easy to see how these larger units can have an influence on the perceived nominal character of a language. While the options just described are equally available in English, it is at least conceivable that languages differ in the extent to which they exploit these options.

Moreover, examples like (1) and (2) indicate that there might be some tendency in German to express modifying clauses as prepositional phrases thus involving nominal elements, where English uses constructions involving a non-finite verb and thus rather clausal structures. According to Halliday and Matthiessen (2014: 424-425) there is a close relationship between prepositional phrases and clause structures with an area of overlap between prepositional phrases and non-finite clauses. They refer to the preposition as a "minor verb" and argue that the internal structure in *across the lake* and *crossing the lake* involving a non-finite verb is similar. Potentially, these similarities are realized differently in the two languages. In functionally similar contexts like postmodification, English might have a tendency to opt for the clausal structure, whereas German might tend to use the prepositional counterpart. If anything, this will result in a higher number of verbs in English than in German. Indeed, Steiner (2012: 80) reports 14.90% verbs in the English original texts in the CroCo Corpus, whereas the German originals contain 12.28% verbs.

Recent studies based on corpus analyses (Steiner 2012; Berg 2017) appear to corroborate the claim that nouns are more frequent in German than in English. However, evidence is inconclusive as Berg et al. (2012) come to a different conclusion. It cannot be assumed that Berg (2017) overrules his own previous findings in Berg et al. (2012) as the latter are based on a different (and potentially sounder) empirical methodology. In fact, all three studies have methodological limitations, which will be discussed in more detail in Section 2. Specifically, the difference in compound spelling poses a major methodological challenge for quantitative approaches and is handled differently by the said studies. These challenges make an analysis with an improved methodology appear warranted in order to settle the question. This paper therefore aims at re-examining the question of the respective quantitative role of nouns in English and German with the help of a corpus approach that accounts for the differences in compound spelling. Given these differences, compounding has to be dealt with when comparing the frequency of nouns in English and German. Nevertheless, the aim of this paper is not to understand potential contrastive differences in compounding. The interesting question of the exact distinction between compounds and phrases, which is particularly hard in English (Biber et al. 1999: 589–591), is irrelevant for the purposes of this paper. The paper also does not directly aim to understand the grammatical category of the noun in a better way, but rather to examine one particular contrastive aspect of the two languages, namely their respective share of nouns.

The remainder of the paper is organized as follows. After summarizing representative corpus studies of nominal elements in English and German in Section 2, the corpus method chosen for this study will be introduced in Section 3. Section 4 summarizes the results of the corpus study, according to which there is no significant difference in the number of nouns in the two languages. These are then discussed in Section 5. The paper closes with some concluding remarks and an outlook on future work in Section 6.

2 State of the art

Definitions of the grammatical category noun are surprisingly hard to come by. Grammars often define nouns by referring to noun phrases (e.g. Quirk et al. 1985: 245; Biber et al. 1999: 230), although this creates some circularity as obviously noun phrases can only be analyzed by identifying the head noun. Quirk et al. (1985: 245-246) and Biber et al. (1999: 241) further specify the distinction between common nouns and proper nouns as well as aspects of countability and definiteness. Alternatively, nouns are characterized in terms of their grammatical features (number, case: Huddleston and Pullum 2002: 326; and additionally gender: Koptjevskaja-Tamm 2006: 721). A combined characterization that also includes syntactic function and semantic aspects appears useful. At this fairly general level, a definition should work for both languages. Crystal (1997: 433) provides one that addresses these aspects: "a word class with a naming function, typically showing contrasts of countability and number, and capable of acting as subject or object of a clause". Koptjevskaja-Tamm (2006: 720) further specifies the naming function by describing that "[p]rototypical nouns refer to things, persons, places, and other more or less concrete objects".

Although the question of the nominal character of German in comparison to English is of practical relevance as pointed out in Section 1, it has only recently been subjected to systematic empirical research. Berg et al. (2012) report a quantitative analysis of compound use in journalese and fiction in English and German including a comparison of the number of non-compound nouns given as a proportion in the two languages. In journalese this German/English proportion is 0.8, that is, there are more nouns in English, and in fiction 1.0, whereas compounds are much more frequent in German than in English (German/English proportion 2.2 and 2.0 in journalese and fiction respectively). On this basis, they conclude that there is a genuine difference in compounding, but no general difference in nominal style between the two languages (Berg et al. 2012: 280). However, this conclusion is based on a data set that is compiled in a particular way to balance out differences between the languages introduced by spelling differences that influence the count (see below). Based on a preliminary comparison between an English and a German sample of 1,000 words for each genre, Berg et al. come to the conclusion that due to the spelling differences more English words would be required to yield a comparable number of compounds. They therefore reduce the German data set and obtain a sample adjusted at word level (82,014 tokens in German and 79,364 tokens in English) to yield a comparable number of nominal segments, i.e. either compounds or simple, non-compound nouns. The reported token frequency is, consequently, a proportion of non-compound nouns in the sample of all nominal segments, not the token frequency per running words in the corpus. It is questionable whether claims about a general difference in nominal style are justified on the basis of this method and certainly it will be more reliable to base the investigation on a data set that is generated independently of the unit under investigation, i.e. in this case the noun.

Steiner (2012) reports the distribution of word classes in the English-German CroCo Corpus consisting of roughly 1 million words in 462 original and translated texts by different authors from 8 different registers in both translation directions (Hansen-Schirra, Neumann, and Steiner 2012). According to Steiner's calculations, German is more nominal than English in terms of a composite of nominal word classes consisting of nouns, pronouns, adjectives and adpositions. He reports a percentage of 49.72% nominals in English and 51.58% in German with the number of pronouns making a considerable contribution to the German class. Moreover, he claims that English is more verbal than German. A combination of the verbal word classes of verbs, adverbs and conjunctions yields 24.27% in English and only 21.64% in German. The latter finding suggests that the overall distribution of nouns and verbs differs in the two languages, since it is not very likely that the difference in the number of verbs is balanced out by other, less frequent word classes. Steiner further reports specific proportions of these nominal and verbal word classes across the registers of the CroCo Corpus as represented in Table 1.

Table 1: Proportions of nominal to verbal word classes in the CroCo Corpus (adapted from Steiner 2012).

	English	German	Difference
ESSAY	2.1	2.3	+0.2
FICTION	1.6	1.8	+0.2
INSTR	2.0	2.3	+0.3
POPSCI	1.8	2.0	+0.2
SHARE	2.3	2.7	+0.4
SPEECH	2.0	2.1	+0.1
TOU	2.8	3.1	+0.3
WEB	2.2	2.7	+0.5

Table 1 shows that all German registers have a higher proportion of nominals than the English ones (on average more than 0.2 points). His results therefore appear to corroborate the informal claims about the nominal character of German. However, the difference tilts in the opposite direction when only including nouns (27.21% in English and 24.51% in German). Steiner's analysis is based on counts of the part-of-speech (PoS) annotation of the CroCo Corpus. While PoS tagger accuracy in general is very high, it differs across languages, even if the same tagger is used, in this case the TnT Tagger (Brants 2000) working with the Susanne tagset for English (Sampson 1995) and the Stuttgart-Tübingen Tagset for German (Schiller et al. 1999). Our own sample analysis for the register ESSAY found that in English originals 6.4% of the noun segments were wrongly tagged as nouns (false positives) and 4.2% were not recognized as nouns (false negatives) by the tagger. In German, only 0.2% of the segments were false positives and 2.6% were false negatives. Consequently, adjusting the counts based on tagger accuracy alone would already change the counts (in this case strengthening claims about the nominal character of German). Moreover, Hansen-Schirra, Neumann and Steiner (2012: 51) report diverging tagger accuracy across registers in the CroCo Corpus. Results are therefore subject to some variability. Steiner's PoS-based counts also do not account for spelling differences between the two languages. As the number of compounds spelled as single words in German by far exceeds that in English, an approach not accounting for these differences will understate the noun frequency in German. Serbina et al. (2017) discuss a conservative estimate according to which half of the modifier elements in German compounds are estimated to be nouns. The resulting overall frequency of nouns in German would be slightly higher than in English (see below). Berg (2017: 61) corroborates Steiner's (2012) claims about the nominal character of German, but also does not account for tagger accuracy per language and register as well as for spelling differences.

Before proceeding with the introduction of this approach, the effect of the differences in compound spelling between English and German on noun counts will be explained in more detail. A precondition for automatic part-of-speech tagging is tokenization, i.e. the automatic identification of word boundaries. Usually, this is achieved simply by identifying all characters between two spaces as (orthographic) words with some exceptions accounting for punctuation marks etc. A marginal problem with this is that any errors during tokenization will be inherited by subsequent PoS tagging as the tagger will assign PoS tags to all items classified as a token in the former step. Orthography-based tokenization will also result in differences in word count between corresponding items in aligned text. Table 2, taken from Serbina et al. (2017), illustrates the diverging word counts of aligned word sequences arguably involving compounding at least in one of the two languages.

Table 2: Exemplary German compound nouns and their aligned English translations (adapted from Serbina et al. 2017).

No.	German	Word token count	English translation	Word token count
1	Soziale Marktwirtschaft	2	social market economy	3
2	Systemwechsel	1	system change	2
3	Fremdsprachenkenntnisse	1	knowledge of foreign languages	4
4	Aufzugtür	1	lift door	2
5	Fallhöhe	1	depth of the fall	4
6	Innenstadt	1	city center	2
7	Haarnetz	1	hairnet	1
8	Kaschmirpullover	1	cashmere sweater	2
Total	(7 nouns not counted separately)	9		20

In total, there are 9 orthographic word tokens in German and 20 in English (including two occurrences of *of* and one determiner). The German examples include 7 additional nouns not counted separately because they are part of compounds spelled as single words in German. Serbina et al. (2017) also report a count of all elements coded in the morphology annotation as compound nouns in the original texts in the CroCo Corpus. While for English only 0.13% of all word tokens are identified as compound nouns, 6.33% of the German word tokens are coded as compounds. Note that the morphological analysis with MPRO (Maas 1998) primarily identifies word sequences spelled with a hyphen such as *second-hand* or *north-west* as compounds in English.

A reliable noun count will have to balance out the spelling differences. There are various strategies to this end. Identification of English compounds, or rather multi-word expressions, is one of the major research fields not just in linguistics (see Berg et al. 2012, Schmid 2016 and references therein) but also in computational linguistics (Sag et al. 2002). Distinguishing English compounds from phrases, on the one hand, and from (lexicalized) monomorphemic words, on the other hand, is riddled with problems as most of the criteria discussed in the literature tend to be unreliable (Berg et al. 2012: 277–278, Schmid 2016: 131–136). Moreover, linguists seem to diverge in their assessment of what counts as a compound. The Longman Grammar avoids the problem of distinguishing compounds from phrases by simply using the term noun-noun sequence (Biber et al. 1999: 589–591) for occurrences of more than one noun. A second option for mapping English onto German nouns is compound chunking in German. This has the advantage that it can be done automatically with high accuracy. Still, it does not solve all problems as German also has lexicalized former compounds that should not be chunked. The MPRO chunking appears to be fairly reliable at this task; but it also shows the problem: does the boundary between noun-noun sequences and monomorphemic nouns run along the same lines in both languages? This leaves us with a third option, namely with manual (or computer-assisted) analysis. This is the option Berg et al. (2012) chose and it is also the method chosen in this study under the assumption that it would make the analysis more reliable.[2]

---

[2] The present study is based on single annotations. As with all human analysis of non-trivial linguistic features this is a somewhat naïve assumption as human annotators are rarely consistent in their analyses. Therefore, major annotation projects involve double annotation, inter-annotator consistency analyses and resolving inconsistencies (see, for example, Brants et al. 2002 on the German TIGER treebank).

3 Method

Previous corpus studies analyzed either complete texts in fairly large corpora (e.g. Steiner 2012) or a sample of individual words (Berg et al. 2012). Both approaches come with disadvantages. Manual analysis even of the CroCo Corpus, a comparably small corpus in comparison with state of the art corpora like the British National Corpus and the Corpus of Contemporary American English, is not feasible, leaving the analyst with the option of relying on automatic tokenization and tagging with all of the above-mentioned limitations. Sampling individual words, nouns in particular, from a large corpus makes manual analysis possible, but leaves the analyst with the issues of comparability of corpus size that were identified by Berg et al. (2012). Our approach to circumventing both problems is to draw a random sample of a linguistic unit that is independent of the unit at stake. 100 random sentences per register are extracted with the help of the IMS Corpus Workbench (Evert and Hardie 2011). This approach has the advantage that it is independent of the word count and builds on the assumption that sentences will be comparable as to the potential number of nouns. The targeted sample comprises 1,200 sentences as summarized in Table 3.

Table 3: Overview of the targeted random sample.

Register	English originals	German translations	German originals	English translations
ESSAY	100	100	100	100
SPEECH	100	100	100	100
TOU	100	100	100	100
Total	300	300	300	300

The sample is drawn from the above-mentioned CroCo Corpus, a corpus containing originals and matching translations in the language pair English and German (Hansen-Schirra, Neumann, and Steiner 2012). Drawing a sample of sentences has the major advantage that it allows us to obtain a sample of comparable size in both languages that is not affected by the spelling differences at word level. At the same time, size is manageable so that nouns can be analyzed manually independently of their spelling. This paper reports on the analysis of the three CroCo registers ESSAY (political essays authored by senior government officials), prepared speeches (SPEECH, again by senior government officials) and tourism brochures (TOU; for a comprehensive characterization of the registers, see Neumann 2013).

The fact that the CroCo Corpus also includes translations of the original texts in both languages aligned at sentence level can be exploited in order to test a claim that has been made in connection with the comparison of the nominal character of English and German. Berg (2017: 47) argues that grammatically and stylistically adequate translations can serve as a basis of comparison in his study of compounding. This approach to overcoming the problem of comparability in contrastive analysis is not new. Johansson (2007: 3) argues that translations are fruitful for corpus-based contrastive analysis as they show what elements may be associated across languages. However, as one of the main tasks of the translator is to create a coherent text, this may be an overly optimistic expectation towards translation as ensuring cohesion and coherence of the target text is one of several potential sources of variation with respect to the contrastive correspondence. Alves and Couto-Vale (2011), for example, report a detailed analysis of translators' strategies to applying changes during the translation process in order to harmonize co-referential (or otherwise cohesively linked) items. Usually, such changes will lead to non-literal choices at word level. More generally, translated texts are claimed to exhibit specific features such as normalization and explicitation (see, e.g. Hansen-Schirra, Neumann, and Steiner 2012), which explain the high accuracy with which machine learning approaches are able to classify translated and non-translated texts (e.g. Volansky, Ordan, and Wintner 2015). This suggests that translators have a systematic tendency to deviate from what is in the source text making translation correspondences harder to use for contrastive analysis.[3] In order to assess the informativeness of translations as a basis of comparison for contrastive comparisons, this study therefore also includes noun counts in the translated sentences aligned with the sentences in the sample. More specifically, separate counts will be made for originals and translations in both languages so as to evaluate the distributions of nouns in these different subsets.

After excluding non-clausal material as well as sentences displaying some kind of technical problem, the final sample consisted of 1,086 sentences. Table 4 summarizes the distribution of these sentences across translation directions and registers.

The identification of nouns was based on standard grammatical categories such as number, case and (at least in German) gender following the description

---

[3] Note that this is a more fundamental potential flaw of using translations as a *tertium comparationis* than the "unexpected decisions" made by individual translators Berg (2017: 47) grants as colouring his data. The latter will likely level out in a large enough quantitative analysis, the former represent systematic properties of translation that arise out of the general context in which translation takes place.

Table 4: Summary of the final sentence sample.

Register	English to German	German to English
ESSAY	92 pairs from 28 texts	96 pairs from 23 texts
SPEECH	94 pairs from 14 texts	89 pairs from 18 texts
TOU	93 pairs from 11 texts	85 pairs from 21 texts

in well-known grammars (Biber et al. 1999 for English; Helbig and Buscha 2001 for German). This allowed to identify, for instance, *ups* and *downs* in *the ups-and-downs* as nouns, because they are in the plural. The German equivalents in *das Auf und Ab* ('the up and down') were also identified as nominal because they were preceded by a definite article marked for neuter grammatical gender. Generally, determiners are an important indication of nominals as in *their will on the many*, where *will* is preceded by a possessive determiner and followed by a prepositional phrase serving as a postmodifier. Genitive case may occasionally also serve as an indicator in English as is the case for *people's* in *the American people's support*. Manual analyses were carried out with the UAM CorpusTool (O'Donnell 2008). As compounding is not the main focus of this paper, all nominal components in compounds were counted individually. In *mass graves* two individual nouns were counted, whereas the German equivalent *Massengräber* was identified as a compound noun in which the two nominal elements *Massen* and *-gräber* were counted separately. The analysis task was thus reduced to determining lexicalized compounds such as *household* or *Wohlstand* ('wealth'), which were counted as one item. For this decision, we tested for word stress and for whether synchronically the components can still be used separately (both *hold* and *Stand* ('rank, status') can be found as nouns but their meaning is not equivalent to their contribution to the nouns *household* and *Wohlstand*). Only free morphemes such as the two nouns in *city center* were identified as separate nouns. This also means that neoclassical compounds, i.e. nouns combining with an affix or combining form of Greek or Latin origin such as *bio-, inter-, -logy* etc. which typically cannot be used as free morphemes, were counted as single words.

4 Results

Let us first explore some descriptive statistics. The analysis yielded a total of 9,112 nouns. Table 5 summarizes the proportion of all nouns and common nouns only per sentence in the English original subcorpus (EO), the matching German

Table 5: Proportion of all nouns and common nouns per sentence in the three registers.

	all nouns				common nouns			
	ESSAY	SPEECH	TOU	mean	ESSAY	SPEECH	TOU	mean
EO	7.31	8.11	8.66	8.03	6.29	6.41	5.55	6.08
GT	8.22	9.08	8.84	8.55	7.22	6.07	7.86	7.05
GO	8.04	6.90	10.05	8.33	7.25	6.06	7.51	6.94
ET	7.97	7.03	10.66	8.71	7.14	7.71	5.97	6.94

translations (GT), German originals (GO) and the corresponding English translations (ET). Common nouns, i.e. all nouns excluding proper nouns, are included because it is possible that proper nouns have a confounding influence on the overall distribution of nouns. Proper nouns are more restricted in their grammatical and semantic properties: they do not refer to a class of entity but to an individual entity and they do not have the same potential for modification as common nouns.[4] However, they enter the same functional relationships in the clause as common nouns do and therefore cannot be simply ignored. At least, their distribution can be expected to differ across registers.

Table 5 suggests that there are some differences between the English and German originals. With 8.03, the mean proportion of nouns per sentence is slightly lower in original English than in original German (8.33). There seems to be less variation in the proportion of nouns per sentence between the English registers with a range of 1.35. In German, the range of variation is 3.15. In ESSAY and TOU, the proportion is higher in German than in English, whereas in SPEECH the opposite can be observed. In both languages, tourism brochures have the highest proportion in comparison to the other two registers. Proportions in translations also vary, although in different tendencies. In ESSAY and SPEECH, the German translations contain a higher proportion of nouns than both their source sentences and comparable sentences in the target language. In TOU this is the case for English translations, which consequently seem to display a strong source language interference effect. As to matching source and target texts, translations have a slightly higher share of nouns than their source texts in five out of six combinations. Since proper nouns could influence the registers differently, proportions for common nouns only are also given in Table 5. On average, English originals have a slightly lower proportion of common nouns than German originals. In fact, the mean for EO is the lowest in comparison to the other subcorpora.

---

4 I am grateful to Lise Fontaine and Miriam Taverniers for a discussion of proper nouns.

Like for all nouns, the proportion of common nouns is lower in the German than in the English SPEECH subcorpora, whereas in ESSAY and TOU it is higher in the German subcorpora. Interestingly, the proportion of common nouns is lowest in the English TOU subcorpora in comparison to the other two registers and highest in the two German subcorpora. When comparing originals with translations, there are more similarities within the languages than for source and target registers. In sum, common nouns do not simply reflect the proportions of all nouns at a lower level, but display some specific patterns.

Figure 1 shows a boxplot of the noun count in the four subcorpora, i.e. ignoring register differentiation. The median is virtually identical across all subcorpora, and the English originals and translations show a similar and limited range of variation. The two German subcorpora display slightly more dispersion, but it is hard to draw any conclusions from this marginal variation.

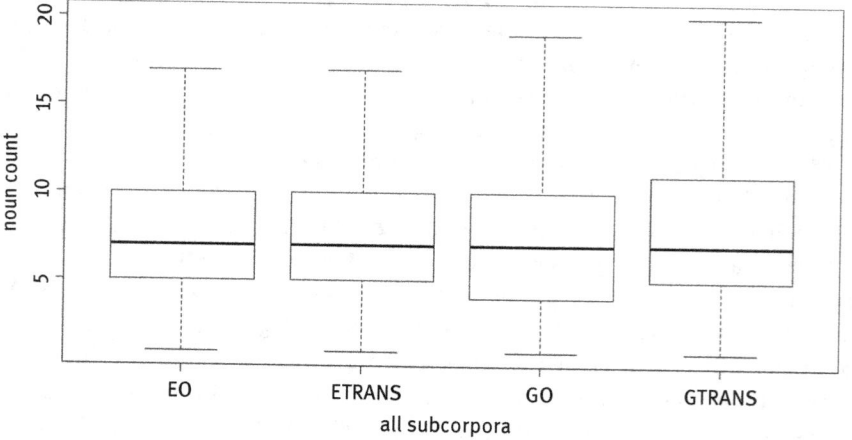

Figure 1: Boxplot of the distribution of nouns in English and German originals and translations.

Inspecting the descriptive statistics by subcorpus allows us to examine the individual registers. Figures 2 and 3 show that both the medians and the ranges of variation display more differences between registers in both languages than the summary by subcorpus in Figure 1 suggests.

As the variation between the medians across registers appears to be brought in mainly by the tourism brochures, especially in German, the increase in the count could be due to a higher number of proper nouns in this register. Therefore boxplots with common nouns only are also included (see Figures 4 and 5).

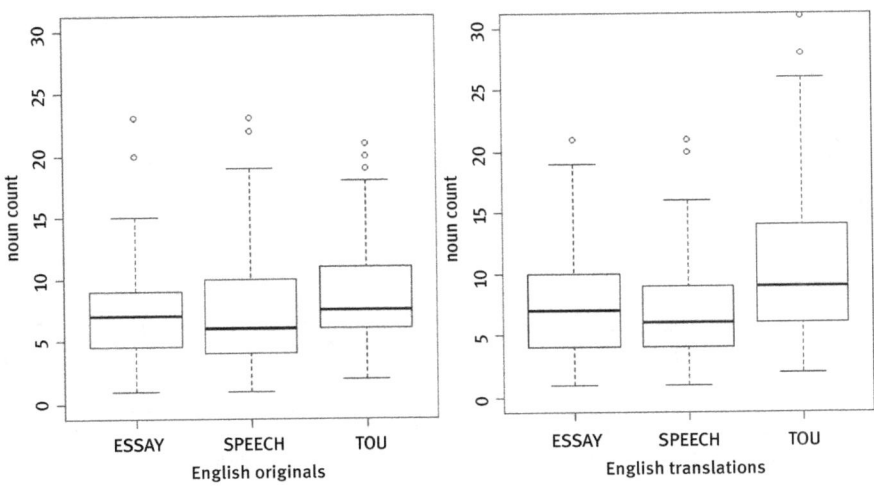

Figure 2: Noun count in English originals (left) and translations (right) by register.

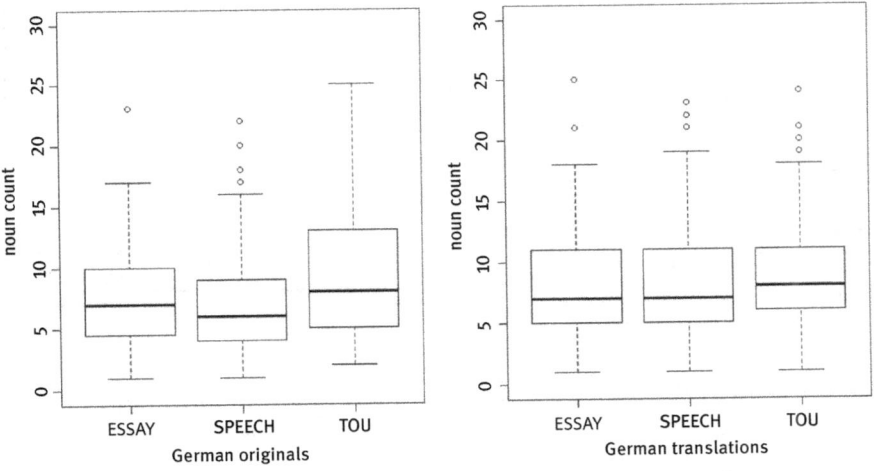

Figure 3: Noun count in German originals (left) and translations (right) by register.

Indeed, some of the register-related differences are levelled out after removing the proper nouns, as shown particularly by the medians in the English originals, which are now almost identical across the three registers. In German, the range of variation in TOU is clearly reduced (23 with proper nouns, 18 with common nouns only, both without outliers). Moreover, as the right panel in Figure 5 shows, the

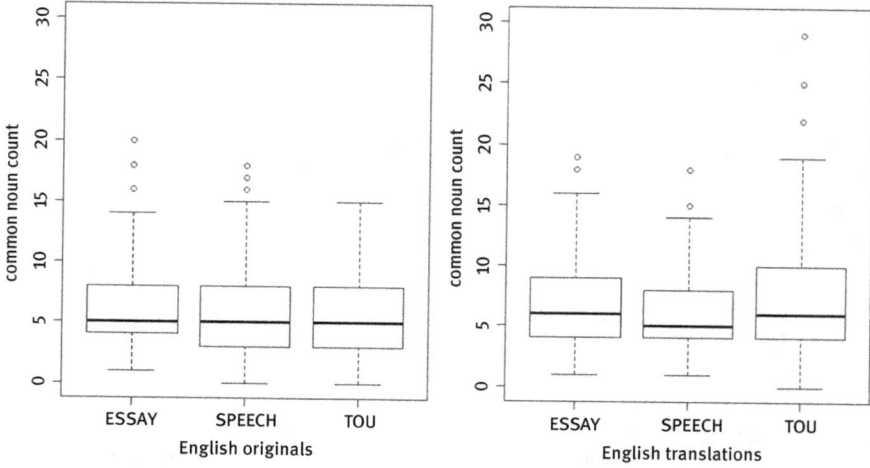

Figure 4: Common nouns in English originals (left) and translations (right).

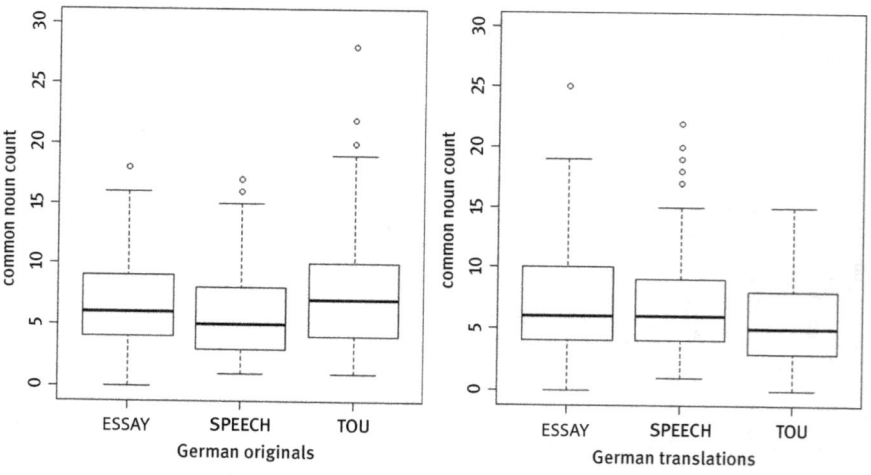

Figure 5: Common nouns in German originals (left) and translations (right).

number of common nouns in German translations is actually lower than in the other two translated registers.

Let us also have a closer look at the contribution of translations to test their usefulness for the contrastive comparison. In this part of the analysis, counts are examined in aligned sentence pairs, whereas before only individual sentences were analyzed. Table 6 specifies the difference in number of nouns per aligned

Table 6: Mean deviation of noun count in translated sentences from aligned source sentences.

Register	English to German	German to English
ESSAY	0.83	−0.03
SPEECH	0.97	0.21
TOU	0.27	0.61

sentence pair given as the mean. A positive value means that there are on average more nouns in the translations than in the originals.

The table shows that there is a general tendency to increase the number of nouns in translation. This tendency is stronger in the translation direction English to German. Only ESSAY in the translation direction German to English displays a marginal tendency to reduce the number of nouns, but not to a level that is lower than the English originals (cf. Table 5).

Descriptive statistics provide a useful impression of the distribution of nouns in the data set. In the next step, the significance of the differences in the distribution of nouns in English and German (including the influence of translation) will be assessed using inferential statistics. To this end, Poisson regression for count data with mixed effects (Winter 2019) was carried out using the lme4 package (Bates et al. 2015) in R (R Core Team 2017). Noun count served as the response variable, language and register and translation status as predicted fixed effects. Since the sample contains more than one sentence from individual texts as shown in Table 4 (see Section 3) text was included as a random effect. It was assumed that both register and translation status could interact with the respective language. Therefore, interaction terms for both were included, however the full model did not converge. A model without the interaction term for language and translation status converges, as does an alternative model without the interaction for language and register. Both models do not retrieve a significant result for an interaction.

Table 7 summarizes the model including the interaction term for register and language. The resulting formula is given below:

$$\text{noun count} \sim \text{language} * \text{register} + \text{translation status} + (1 \mid \text{text})$$

The model summary (see Table 7) shows that only the variable register and specifically TOU in English (used as the intercept) yielded an effect. When relevelling the variable language to German, a marginally significant effect for the difference

Table 7: The full model including terms for language, register, translation status and a random effect for text.

Random effects:

Groups Name	Variance	Std.Dev.
text_id (Intercept)	0.1252	0.3538

Number of obs: 1086, groups: text_id, 230

Fixed effects:

	Estimate	Std. Error	z value	Pr(>|z|)	
(Intercept)	2.18278	0.07719	28.280	<2e-16	***
langG	-0.01022	0.09921	-0.103	0.9180	
registerESSAY	-0.22745	0.09098	-2.500	0.0124	*
registerSPEECH	-0.22850	0.09858	-2.318	0.0205	*
trans_statustrans	0.05655	0.05365	1.054	0.2919	
langG:registerESSAY	0.09065	0.12912	0.702	0.4826	
langG:registerSPEECH	0.06548	0.13955	0.469	0.6389	

between TOU and SPEECH emerges, but not between TOU and ESSAY. Model comparison (see Table 8) was carried out with the afex package (Singmann et al. 2018) for nested mixed models using likelihood ratio tests. It yields a significant effect for register (χ^2 = 10.05, 2 df, p < .01), but not for language, indicating that registers differ significantly in noun counts but not languages. In order to assess the contribution of translations to the variation, the same model is computed without translations. The reduced formula is:

$$\text{noun count} \sim \text{language} * \text{register} + (1 \mid \text{text})$$

Table 8: Model comparison for the full model.

	Effect	df	Chisq	p.value
1	lang	1	0.60	.44
2	register	2	10.05 **	.007
3	trans_status	1	1.11	.29
4	lang:register	2	0.50	.78

The model summarized in Table 9 does not show a significant effect for any of the factors or the interaction. Model comparison does not yield any significant effect either which means that the register effect vanishes.

Table 9: Model without translations.

Random effects:					
GroupsName	Variance	Std.Dev.			
text_id (Intercept)	0.1298	0.3603			
Number of obs: 542, groups: text_id, 115					
Fixed effects:					
	Estimate	Std. Error	z value	Pr(>|z|)	
(Intercept)	1.95988	0.08127	24.114	<2e−16	***
langG	0.06057	0.11828	0.512	0.609	
registerSPEECH	0.05886	0.13220	0.445	0.656	
registerTOU	0.14146	0.14130	1.001	0.317	
langG:registerSPEECH	−0.13069	0.18510	−0.706	0.480	
langG:registerTOU	0.07099	0.18800	0.378	0.706	

To assess the effect of proper nouns, the model summarized in Table 7 was computed again for common nouns only (for the sake of comparability with an interaction term for register and language only). The model did not retrieve any significant effect (Table 10), nor did model comparison. This does indeed suggest that the register-related effect in the full model for all nouns reported above can be linked to the influence of proper nouns as it disappears in the model for common nouns only.

5 Discussion

What can be concluded from the empirical analysis for answering our question whether German is more nominal than English? When using a data sample that is neutral with respect to the unit of analysis and when counting nouns independently of spelling differences, there are no statistically noteworthy differences between English and German. The regression analysis only retrieved an effect of register, meaning that there is no statistically relevant difference between the two languages in the number of nouns in our sample. The comparison to a model with

Table 10: Full model for common nouns only.

Random effects:

Groups Name	Variance	Std.Dev.
text_id (Intercept)	0.1396	0.3736

Number of obs: 1086, groups: text_id, 230

Fixed effects:

	Estimate	Std. Error	z value	Pr(>|z|)	
(Intercept)	1.82603	0.08299	22.002	<2e-16	***
langG	0.01227	0.10683	0.115	0.909	
registerESSAY	−0.01233	0.09737	−0.127	0.899	
registerSPEECH	−0.08035	0.10562	−0.761	0.447	
trans_statustrans	0.07053	0.05716	1.234	0.217	
langG:registerESSAY	0.06149	0.13811	0.445	0.656	
langG:registerSPEECH	0.08443	0.14934	0.565	0.572	

common nouns only shows that the register effect can be explained by a difference in the use of proper nouns. Moreover, the effect is only present in the model that includes translations. As mentioned above, it is implausible to assume that the grammatical and semantic properties of proper nouns differ between English and German. The differential frequency of proper nouns can be explained by the fact that especially in the tourism brochures the class of certain points of interest such as *Kirche/church* is not translated and thus leads to an interpretation as a proper noun. *Schlossberg* ('castle hill') in example (4) is a case in point. The translation *the spectacular view from the castle hill* would be completely adequate and would simply refer to the topology of the place as does the original.

(4) Der faszinierende Blick vom   Schloßberg auf das labyrinthartige Knäuel von
    The fascinating   view from-the castle-hill over the maze-like   tangle of
    engen   Gassen
    narrow lanes
    'the fascinating view from the castle hill down over the maze-like tangle of narrow lanes'
    The spectacular view from the Schlossberg down over the maze of narrow lanes (CroCo, G2E_TOU_003-s68)

For the sample under investigation, this turns out to confirm Berg et al.'s (2012) claim that there is no general difference between English and German in nominal style – and to reject Berg's (2017) claim that German is, in fact, more nominal than English. As to Steiner's (2012) claims summarized in Section 2, the picture is somewhat more intricate. His conclusions from the comparison of the proportion of nouns have to be rejected just like Berg's (2017). Steiner's discussion of the relation between nouns and verbs and specifically of composite nominal and verbal word classes will have to be treated separately. While the methodological limitations of his analysis remain, the combination of word classes addresses an important aspect that goes beyond the scope of this paper. It opens up a perspective on the interaction between larger units in the clause which might actually be more promising for understanding the remaining overall distributional differences between English and German. As our study does not take into consideration the different word classes, future work will have to show whether Steiner's more generalized interpretation can be upheld in a study with a revised methodology.

It is somewhat surprising that there are no differences between the three registers *within* the two languages. Accounts of register variation usually report differences in the frequency of nouns as a clear indicator of register differences (e.g. Biber 1995: 145 on English). Reporting numbers for the complete CroCo Corpus, Neumann (2013: 149) finds significant differences between the eight registers in the corpus based on PoS counts. As to the three registers included in the present study, she reports significantly more nouns in the English original texts in ESSAY and TOU compared to the English reference corpus used as a baseline, whereas SPEECH does not differ in a statistically significant way from the reference corpus. The subsample analyzed in the present study at least corresponds in tendency to these findings (see Figure 2 above). For German originals, Neumann (2013: 202) finds no significant deviations between the German reference corpus and ESSAY and SPEECH, whereas tourism brochures are reported to contain significantly more nouns than the reference corpus (note that PoS-based counting was language-internal and thus not affected by spelling differences). Again these results match the present findings at least in tendency. Arguably, the registers included in this study are more similar to each other than potentially more extreme registers such as literary texts, reported by Neumann (2013) as containing significantly fewer nouns than the reference corpus in both languages. This means that an analysis of a more diverse sample of registers would be likely to show significant differences.

The tendency in translations to add nouns and to do so more in the translation direction English to German is in line with Čulo et al.'s (2008) PoS-tagging based findings for the CroCo register of letters to shareholders (which are subject to the same restrictions as Steiner's 2012 and Berg's 2017 counts). In general terms, they report counts of changes in various parts of speech in both translation directions, which show that changes happen in both directions, even if there is also a tendency to add more nouns in German translations and to add more verbs in English translations. The fact that the register effect disappears in our model without translations suggests that it was only introduced by the translations. This means that including translations in the analysis actually has a detrimental effect as it blurs the data structure in the originals. This was already suggested by the descriptive statistics reported in Section 4, which showed that translators added more nouns than they removed in five out of six combinations of registers and translation directions, i.e. irrespective of the translation direction. Still, this does not necessarily mean that translations should be excluded from all kinds of analysis. Inspection of aligned word pairs should help get a clearer picture of what exactly happens in the language pair. Discussions of the examples below suggest that this is indeed useful. Example (5) from our corpus, for instance, shows an increase by two nouns in the translation.

(5) *Despite continued advances in technology, total U.S. energy consumption is projected to increase from 98 quadrillion British thermal units (Btus) in 2002 to 136 quadrillion Btus in 2025.* (CroCo, EO_ESSAY_001-s8)
Trotz   stetiger   technologischer Fortschritte wird ein Anstieg   des
Despite continued technological   advances   is   an increase of-the
amerikanischen Energieverbrauchs   von   98 Billiarden   britischen Wärmeeinheiten
American   energy-consumption from 98 quadrillion British   thermal-units
(BTUs) im   Jahr 2002 auf 136 Billiarden   BTUs im   Jahr 2025 erwartet.
(BTUs) in-the year 2002 to   136 quadrillion BTUs in-the year 2025 expected.
'Despite continued technological advances, an increase of American energy consumption from 98 quadrillion British thermal units (BTUs) in 2002 to 136 quadrillion BTUs in 2025 is expected.'

In (5), the English sentence contains a total of 10 nouns (*advances, technology, U.S., energy, consumption, quadrillion, units, Btus, quadrillion, Btus*), whereas the aligned translation contains 12 nouns (*Fortschritte, Anstieg, Energie, -verbrauch, Billiarden, Wärme, -einheiten, BTUs, Jahr, Billiarden, BTUs, Jahr*): Two of the English nouns (*technology, U.S.*) are translated with adjectives (*technologisch, amerikanisch*), one English verb (*increase*) is translated with a noun (*Anstieg*, 'increase'), a modifying adjective (*thermal*) is translated with a nominal modifier in a compound (*Wärme*, 'heat') and two nouns are simply added in German (two occurrences of *Jahr*, 'year'). These additions are obligatory as specifications of years usually involve the classifier *Jahr* ('year'; Helbig and Buscha 2001: 296). Example (6) is a similar example in the opposite translation direction.

(6) Gerade   auch nach den jüngsten   Erfahrungen im   Zusammenhang mit dem
    Especially also after the recent-most experiences in-the connection   with the
    Irak-Krieg setzt   sich die Bundesregierung   mit   großem Nachdruck für die
    Iraq-war lobbies REFL the federal-government with great   emphasis for the
    Stärkung   des   Völkerrechts   und für verbindliche Normen, etwa
    strengthening of-the international-law and for binding   norms,   for-example
    für den Welthandel ein.   (CroCo, GO_ESSAY_009-s30)
    for the world-trade PART.
    'Especially also following the most recent experiences in connection with
    the war in Iraq, the federal government lobbies with great emphasis for
    the strengthening of the international law and for binding standards, for
    example, with regard to world trade.'
    *Especially following recent experiences in connection with the war in Iraq, the
    federal government is emphatically supporting the strengthening of international
    law and binding standards, for example, with regard to world trade.*

The German original sentence in (6) contains 13 nouns (*Erfahrungen, Zusammenhang, Irak, Krieg, Bundes, -regierung, Nachdruck, Stärkung, Völker, -rechts, Normen, Welt, -handel*); the translation counts 12 nouns (*experiences, connection, war, Iraq, government, strengthening, law, standards, example, regard, world, trade*) despite the fact that it contains two additional nouns in the fixed expressions *for example* as a translation of the German adverb *etwa* and *with regard to* corresponding to the German preposition *für*. In two cases, a German nominal modifier in a compound (*Bundes, Völker*) corresponds to an adjectival modifier in English (*federal, international*) and in one case the expression *mit Nachdruck* ('with emphasis') is translated by the adverb *emphatically*. The adjectival premodifiers exemplify a phenomenon that is often mentioned when comparing compounding in English and German (Ermlich 2004: 206; Donalies 2008: 312): English appears to draw more on adjectives where, in German, nominal modifiers are used. However, as seen in (5), replacing nouns with adjectives also occurs in translations from English to German. The detailed analysis of aligned sentence pairs shows that there can be a wide range of individual explanations for the specific choices of the translator. For translation studies, this is an interesting finding because it suggests that translator behavior cannot be reduced to the influence of one particular language or register (the specific situation in tourism brochures notwithstanding). For contrastive linguistics, this means that using translations for understanding contrastive differences needs to be treated with particular care.

Does the lack of a difference simply prove those reporting informal observations on perceived differences between English and German wrong? This hardly seems plausible, particularly because there is still a difference in the number of verbs as reported by Steiner (2012) and Berg (2017). This difference is harder to dismiss, as verbs are less prone to compounding, so at least spelling variation will not introduce a large amount of variation.[5] Any remaining differences in the frequency of verbs will still affect the overall proportion of word classes per language resulting, for example, in the reported relevance of nominal blocks mentioned in Section 1.

Indeed, a manual count of verbs in our sample of original sentences shows that there are more verbs in English than in German: the English original sample on average contains 2.04 finite verbs per sentence, whereas German original sentences have a share of 1.71 finite verbs. The proportion of non-finite verbs per finite verbs, i.e. a measure of the number of non-finite verbs per clause, is 0.93 in the English originals and 0.52 in the German originals. To a good deal these non-finites are simply part of analytical verb phrases. If these are excluded and focus is only on non-finite verbs introducing clauses, the differences between English and German originals in the sample become striking: with 0.98, the ratio of non-finite clauses per sentence nears 1 meaning that on average almost every sentence in the English original sample contains a non-finite clause, whereas in German, the proportion is only 0.17. The difference in the frequency of verbs can thus be primarily explained by non-finite clausal structures including those embedded in phrases in English. Consequently, differences can be found mainly on the intermediate grammatical level within the clause, i.e. the phrase or group level. Verbs seem to be explicitly expressed in English capturing both the things/entities and the processes relevant in an event or state with the procedural aspect realized by the verb. In German this does not seem to be the case to the same extent. However, the difference cannot be solely explained in terms of "turning" clausal structures into prepositional phrases (as "shrunken clauses" with the preposition as "a kind of mini-verb", Halliday and Matthiessen 2014: 329) because the German original data set does not contain more prepositions. Alternatively, it could be assumed that in equivalent contexts German simply drops the verbs as illustrated by (7), where the German prepositional phrase *von einem waghalsigen Zeitvertreib einiger Weniger* corresponds to *from the dangerous pastime of a few*, i.e. the English structure just without the non-finite verb *being*. Similarly, the noun phrase *ein Brennpunkt von zweitausend Jahren Geschichte* in (8) corresponds to *hub of a history spanning 2000 years* without the non-finite verb *spanning*.

---

5 Issues of language and register-specific tagger accuracy, of course, remain.

(7) *Then there are areas like the Gower and the Brecon Beacons, where hanggliding developed from being the dangerous pastime of a few, to the much safer but exhilirating [sic] sport that it is today.* (CroCo, EO_TOU_007-s89)
Und Gebiete wie Gower und die Brecon Beacons, in denen sich Drachenfliegen
And areas like Gower and the Brecon Beacons, in which REFL hanggliding
von einem waghalsigen Zeitvertreib einiger Wenigen zu einem mittlerweile
from a daring pastime of-some few to a meanwhile
sicheren und berauschenden Sport entwickelt hat.
safe and exhilarating sport developed has.
'And areas like the Gower and the Brecon Beacons, in which hanggliding developed from a daring pastime of a few to a now safe and exhilarating sport.'

(8) *At the heart of our region, York is one of the medieval cities of Europe, hub of a history spanning 2000 years (...).* (CroCo, EO_TOU_010-s11)
Das Herz dieser Gegend ist York, eine der großen mittelalterlichen Städte
The heart of-this region is York, one of-the great medieval cities
Europas, ein Brennpunkt von zweitausend Jahren Geschichte (...).
Europe-GEN, a focal-point of two-thousand years history
'The heart of the region is York, one of the great medieval cities of Europe, a focal point of history spanning 2000 years.'

In example (9) below, the infinitive *to strengthen* is translated with the corresponding nominalization *Stärkung* as the complement of the preposition *zur*. Moreover, the example contains more related phenomena in the list after the colon: *make flexible* is translated with the nominalization *Flexibilisierung*, the first occurrence of the verb *reduce* becomes the noun *Abbau* ('reduction'), *reform* becomes *Reformierung* and a second occurrence of *reduce* is translated with *Reduzierung*. Consequently, the translation of this sentence sheds altogether five verbs.

(9) *These are areas where the EU has already committed to strengthen competitiveness under the Lisbon Process: make labor markets more flexible, product market reforms, reduce subsidies, reform shop-opening hours, reduce bureaucratic regulation.* (CroCo, EO_SPEECH_005-s20)
Dabei handelt es sich um Bereiche, in denen die EU sich bereits im
Thereby concerns it REFL about areas, in which the EU REFL already in-the
Rahmen des Lissabon-Prozesses zur Stärkung der
framework of-the Lisbon-process to-the strengthening of-the
Wettbewerbsfähigkeit verpflichtet hat: Flexibilisierung der Arbeitsmärkte,
competition-capability committed has: flexibilisation of-the labor-markets,

Produktmarktreformen, Abbau von Subventionen, Reformierung des
product-market-reforms, reduction of subsidies, reformation of-the
Ladenschlusses, Reduzierung bürokratischer Regulierungen.
closing-time, reduction bureaucratic-GEN regulations.
'These are areas in which the EU already committed to the strengthening of the competitiveness in the context of the Lisbon process: flexibilization of the labor markets, reduction of subsidies, reform of the closing times, reduction of bureaucratic regulations.'

To some extent, the differences between the languages can be explained by the transition between nominal and verbal word classes (cf. Sasse 2001). The non-finite verb *preparing* in (10) can be claimed to come close to the boundary of what would be classified as nominal, thus being similar to the German deverbal nominalization *Vorbereitung* ('preparation') with which it is translated. A similar case can be observed in (11) in the opposite translation direction where the German deverbal nominalization *Ausweitung* ('extension') corresponds to the English *extending*.

(10) *Preparing for accession has also been a challenge for current EU members who, to cite one example, have had to reform their Common Agricultural Policy to accommodate new members.* (CroCo, EO_SPEECH_014-s21)
Die Vorbereitung auf den Beitritt ist auch für die derzeitigen EU-Mitglieder eine
The preparation on the accession is also for the current EU-members a
Herausforderung die - um nur ein Beispiel zu nennen - ihre Gemeinsame
challenge who – to only one example to name – their common
Agrarpolitik für die Aufnahme neuer Mitglieder reformieren mußten.
agricultural-policy for the admission new-GEN members reform-INF must-PST.
'The preparation for accession is also a challenge for the current EU members who – to name but one example – had to reform their common agricultural policy for the admission of new members.'

(11) *Dieser Blitzstart der ökonomischen Einigung durch die Ausweitung*
This lightning-start of-the economic unification by the extension
des Geltungsbereichs der DM auf Ostdeutschland mußte wie ein
of-the area-of-application of-the deutschmark on East-Germany must-PST like a
"monetärer Urknall" wirken. (CroCo, GO_ESSAY_003-s10)
'monetary big-bang' act.
'This lightning start of the economic unification by the extension of the area of application of the deutschmark to eastern Germany had to act like a 'monetary big bang'.'

> *The lightning start given to economic union by extending the deutschmark to eastern Germany had the impact of a "monetary big bang".*

Finally, example (12) illustrates a case where the non-finite verb *combined* in the English translation corresponds to the conjunction *und* ('and') in the German original. Cases like this can explain why there may be no significant difference in noun count, but still one in verb count.

(12) *Nur so   und durch eine weitere Liberalisierung in der WTO läßt sich*
     Only this-way and by   a   further liberalization in the WTO lets REFL
     eine fortschreitende soziale Marginalisierung dieser   Länder   verhindern.
     an increasing   social marginalization   of-these countries prevent-INF.
     (CroCo, GO_ESSAY_012-s19)
     'Only in this way and through a further liberalization within the WTO can an increasing social marginalization of these countries be prevented.'
     Only this, combined with further liberalization within the framework of the World Trade Organization (WTO), will prevent the increasing social marginalization of these countries.

Some of the examples discussed here show that the verbs are not necessarily highly informative in the corresponding contexts. As it is not tensed, the English non-finite verb does not provide much grammatical information. If, additionally, it is a copular verb (or a functional equivalent), it will also not be lexically informative. More generally, it can be assumed that German might not make the verb explicit in cases where its meaning contribution is limited and where its role is limited to explicating the procedural character of an event/state. To answer the question posed in the title of this paper: No, German is not more nominal than English, but English may well be more verbal than German.

6 Conclusions and outlook

When using a neutral base unit and counting nouns independently of spelling differences, there are no noteworthy differences between English and German. The register effect found by the regression model was actually introduced by translations and is arguably due to a difference in the use of proper nouns. A limitation of the present study is that this paper only reports findings for three registers. Future work will have to expand the analysis to more diverse registers to test whether there are any registers in which there is a noticeable difference in nominal style.

As to the question of whether translations are useful for working out contrasts between English and German, it turns out that they are – if at all – a confounding factor as they bring in features otherwise unrelated to the contrastive comparison. A comparison of the distribution of verbs using the same approach as this study can determine whether the small reduction in the number of verbs and verbal word classes in English translations in comparison with English originals can further corroborate this finding in a context unlikely to be caused by one specific effect such as proper nouns. This is not to say that translations are altogether useless as a source of information for contrastive linguistics (they are extensively used in this paper to discuss examples), but they appear to be better suited for lexical-semantic studies (where they still require a careful research design such as the one used by Vandevoorde forthc.). In general terms the results provide a clear hint at the importance of rigorous quantitative methodology in contrastive linguistics.

The specific focus on the nominal word class still leaves a wide range of questions open. The interplay between nouns and verbs will have to be investigated in more detail in future work. This also entails the in-depth analysis of larger structural units. Specifically, it will be useful to investigate the role of nominal groups in comparison to clauses in the two languages to test the claim that German draws more on larger nominal blocks (Fabricius-Hansen 2000). This will also have to involve investigating the role of more far-reaching processes like grammatical metaphor (e.g. Taverniers 2006) in the two languages. Lastly, cursory observations during the analysis suggest that the correspondence between German compounds and English phrases (Ermlich 2004) as exemplified by *Rechtsstaat* versus *rule of law*, *Irak-Krieg* versus *war in Iraq* and *Lebensart* versus *way of life* would merit closer investigation in corpus-based analyses. Arguably, the English phrasal structures are similar to the German compounds in terms of level of entrenchment (Langacker 2008). So, although it is to be hoped that this paper allows us to settle a long-standing question about English and German, it raises a range of new questions that will have to be answered in future work.

Acknowledgement: First and foremost, I would like to express my gratitude towards Bianca Schüller who not only did the bulk of the analysis but also researched and discussed the criteria for analysis with me. I am indebted to Jessica Di Napoli for discussions, especially of the regression analysis. I would also like to thank Erich Steiner, Lise Fontaine and Miriam Taverniers for continued discussions about the topic. I gratefully acknowledge the two anonymous reviewers' detailed questions which helped me to clarify the argument of the paper. The research reported here was supported by the German Research Foundation (DFG) in the project TRICKLET (Translation Research in Corpora, Keystroke Logging and Eye Tracking), research grant no. NE1822/2-1.

References

Alves, Fabio & Daniel Couto-Vale. 2011. On drafting and revision in translation: A corpus linguistics oriented analysis of translation process data. *Translation: Computation, Corpora, Cognition* 1 (1). 105–122.
Bates, Douglas, Martin Mächler, Ben Bolker & Steve Walker. 2015. Fitting linear mixed-effects models using lme4. *Journal of Statistical Software* 67 (1). 1–48. https://doi.org/10.18637/jss.v067.i01.
Berg, Thomas. 2017. Compounding in German and English: A quantitative translation study. *Languages in Contrast* 17 (1). 43–66.
Berg, Thomas, Sabine Helmer, Marion Neubauer & Arne Lohmann. 2012. Determinants of the extent of compound use: A contrastive analysis. *Linguistics* 50 (2). 269–303.
Biber, Douglas. 1995. *Dimensions of register variation.* Cambridge: Cambridge University Press.
Biber, Douglas, Stig Johansson, Geoffrey Leech, Susan Conrad & Ed Finegan. 1999. *The Longman grammar of spoken and written English.* London: Longman.
Brants, Thorsten. 2000. TnT: A statistical part-of-speech tagger. In *Proceedings of the sixth conference on applied natural language processing, Seattle, Washington, April 29–May 04, 2000,* 224–231. San Francisco, CA, USA: Morgan Kaufmann Publishers.
Brants, Sabine, Stefanie Dipper, Silvia Hansen, Wolfgang Lezius & George Smith. 2002. The TIGER treebank. In *Proceedings of the workshop on treebanks and linguistic theories,* Sozopol, Bulgaria, 24–41.
Crystal, David. 1997. *The Cambridge encyclopedia of language.* 2nd edn. Cambridge: Cambridge University Press.
Čulo, Oliver, Silvia Hansen-Schirra, Stella Neumann & Mihaela Vela. 2008. Empirical studies on language contrast using the English-German comparable and parallel CroCo corpus. In *Proceedings of the LREC 2008 workshop 'Building and using comparable corpora',* 47–51. Marrakesh, Morocco.
Donalies, Elke. 2008. Komposita, Derivate und Phraseme des Deutschen im europäischen Vergleich. *Deutsche Sprache* 36 (4). 305–323.
Ermlich, Karsten. 2004. Zur Wiedergabe deutscher Substantivkomposita im Englischen. *Deutsch als Fremdsprache* 41 (4). 206–212.
Evert, Stefan & Andrew Hardie. 2011. Twenty-first century corpus workbench: Updating a query architecture for the new millennium. In *Proceedings of the corpus linguistics conference 2011, University of Birmingham, UK, 20–22 July 2011.* Birmingham: University of Birmingham. http://www.birmingham.ac.uk/documents/college-artslaw/corpus/conference-archives/2011/Paper-153.pdf.
Fabricius-Hansen, Cathrine. 2000. Wissenschaftssprache versus Gemeinsprache aus kontrastiver Sicht. *SPRIKreports* 2: 1–22. https://www.hf.uio.no/ilos/forskning/prosjekter/sprik/pdf/cfh/cfhansen1.pdf
Halliday, M. A. K. 2001. Literacy and linguistics: Relationships between spoken and written language. In Anne Burns & Caroline Coffin (eds.), *Analysing English in a global context,* 181–193. London: Routledge.
Halliday, M. A. K. & Christian M. I. M. Matthiessen. 2014. *Halliday's introduction to functional grammar.* 4th rev. edn. Abingdon: Routledge.
Hansen-Schirra, Silvia, Stella Neumann & Erich Steiner. 2012. *Cross-linguistic corpora for the study of translations: Insights from the language pair English-German.* Berlin: Mouton de Gruyter.

Helbig, Gerhard & Joachim Buscha. 2001. *Deutsche Grammatik. Ein Handbuch für den Ausländerunterricht.* Berlin: Langenscheidt.

Huddleston, Rodney D. & Geoffrey K. Pullum. 2002. *The Cambridge grammar of the English language.* Cambridge: Cambridge University Press.

Johansson, Stig. 2007. *Seeing through multilingual corpora.* Amsterdam: John Benjamins.

König, Ekkehard & Volker Gast. 2012. *Understanding English-German contrasts.* 3rd edn. Berlin: Erich Schmidt Verlag.

Königs, Karin. 2011. *Übersetzen Englisch-Deutsch. Lernen mit System.* 3rd edn. München, Wien: Oldenbourg.

Koptjevskaja-Tamm, Maria. 2006. Nouns. In Keith Brown (ed.), *Encyclopedia of language and linguistics*, 2nd edn., 720–724. Oxford: Elsevier.

Kortmann, Bernd & Paul Georg Meyer. 1992. Is English grammar more explicit than German grammar, after all? In Christian Mair & Manfred Markus (eds.), *New departures in contrastive linguistics. Neue Ansätze in der kontrastiven Linguistik: Proceedings of the conference held at the Leopold-Franzens-Universität Innsbruck, Austria, 10–12 May 1991*, volume 1, 155–166. Innsbruck: Verlag des Instituts für Sprachwissenschaft.

Langacker, Ronald W. 2008. *Cognitive grammar: A basic introduction.* Oxford: Oxford University Press.

Maas, Heinz Dieter. 1998. Multilinguale Textproduktion mit MPRO. In Günter Lobin, Heinz Lohse, Siegried Piotrowski & Eva Polakova (eds.), *Europäische Kommunikationskybernetik heute und morgen. Ein wissenschaftlicher Beitrag zur Kommunikationskybernetik.* München: kopaed.

Neumann, Stella. 2013. *Contrastive register variation: A quantitative approach to the comparison of English and German.* Berlin: Mouton de Gruyter.

O'Donnell, Mick. 2008. Demonstration of the UAM CorpusTool for text and image annotation. In *Proceedings of the ACL-08: HLT demo session (Companion Volume)*, 13–16. Columbus, Ohio: Association of Computational Linguistics. http://www.aclweb.org/anthology-new/P/P08/P08-4004.pdf.

Quirk, Randolph, Sidney Greenbaum, Geoffrey Leech & Jan Svartvik. 1985. *A comprehensive grammar of the English language.* Harlow: Longman.

R Core Team. 2017. *R: A language and environment for statistical computing.* Vienna, Austria: R Foundation for Statistical Computing. https://www.R-project.org.

Sag, Ivan, Timothy Baldwin, Francis Bond, Ann Copestake & Dan Flickinger. 2002. Multiword expressions: A pain in the neck for NLP. In *Proceedings of the 3rd international conference on intelligent text processing and computational linguistics (CICLing-2002)*, 1–15. Mexico: CICLing.

Sampson, Geoffrey. 1995. *English for the computer: The Susanne corpus and analytic scheme.* Oxford: Clarendon Press.

Sasse, Hans-Jürgen. 2001. Scales between nouniness and berbiness. In Martin Haspelmath (ed.), *Language Typology and Language Universals*, volume 1, 495–509. Handbücher zur Sprach- und Kommunikationswissenschaft 20. Berlin: Mouton de Gruyter.

Schiller, Anne, Simone Teufel, Christine Stöckert & Christine Thielen. 1999. Guidelines für das Tagging deutscher Textcorpora mit STTS. Stuttgart, Tübingen: Universität Stuttgart, Universität Tübingen. http://www.ims.uni-stuttgart.de/ftp/pub/corpor%tts_guide.ps.gz.

Schmid, Hans-Jörg. 2016. *English morphology and word-formation: An introduction.* 3rd, rev. edn. Berlin: Erich Schmidt Verlag.

Serbina, Tatiana, Sven Hintzen, Paula Niemietz & Stella Neumann. 2017. Changes of word class during translation: Insights from a combined analysis of corpus, keystroke logging and eye-tracking data. In Silvia Hansen-Schirra, Oliver Czulo & Sascha Hofmann (eds.), *Empirical modelling of translation and interpreting*, 177–208. Berlin: Language Science Press.

Singmann, Henrik, Ben Bolker, Jake Westfall & Frederik Aust. 2018. *Afex: Analysis of factorial experiments*. https://CRAN.R-project.org/package=afex.

Steiner, Erich. 2012. A characterization of the resource based on shallow statistics. In Silvia Hansen-Schirra, Stella Neumann & Erich Steiner, *Cross-linguistic corpora for the study of translations: Insights from the language pair English-German*, 71–89. Berlin: Mouton de Gruyter.

Taverniers, Miriam. 2006. Grammatical metaphor and lexical metaphor: Different perspectives on semantic variation. *Neophilologus* 90 (2). 321–32.

Vandevoorde, Lore. forthc. *Semantic differences in translation: Exploring the field of inchoativity*. Berlin: Language Science Press.

Volansky, Vered, Noam Ordan & Shuly Wintner. 2015. On the features of translationese. *Digital Scholarship in the Humanities* 30 (1). 98–118.

Winter, Bodo. 2019. *Statistics for Linguists: An Introduction Using R*. Routledge. https://doi.org/10.4324/9781315165547.

Bart Defrancq and Camille Collard
Using data from simultaneous interpreting in contrastive linguistics

Abstract: This study verifies whether interpreting data are a reliable source of information for contrastive researchers interested in features of spoken language. According to the *communis opinio* in contrastive linguistics and interpreting studies, interpreting corpora are not to be relied upon or should be exploited with extreme caution. However, little empirical evidence supports these views. We therefore analyze possible meaning shifts in the verbal lexicon that could be attributed to interpreting, focusing on Dutch and English verbs that are equivalent in meaning (*know-weten* and *say-zeggen*), can be combined with an embedded interrogative and a subordinate *that*-clause and are frequent enough in the interpreting corpora to afford statistical analysis. Behavioral profiles are defined on the basis of types of *wh*-items and subordinating *that*. Combinations of verbs and *wh*-items or *that* are collected in 3 types of corpora: (i) a corpus of non-mediated spoken language drawn from national parliaments (British and Flemish/Dutch); (ii) a corpus of non-mediated spoken language drawn from the European Parliament; (iii) a corpus of simultaneous interpreting as carried out at the European Parliament. The effects of three predictors are analyzed: the meaning of the verb, the context (European Parliament vs. national parliaments) and the mediated nature of the data (non-mediated data vs. interpreting). Of the three predictors, two turn out to have a significant effect on the frequency distributions: the verb and mediatedness. Verbs are used with slightly different *wh-/that* profiles in interpreting, which can be most plausibly explained by a tendency towards normalisation.

Keywords: simultaneous interpreting, lexical equivalence, contrastive linguistics, *wh-*, embedded interrogatives

1 Introduction

The last 25 years have witnessed an upsurge of corpus-based research in contrastive linguistics. The combination of contrastive research and corpora has proven so successful that it has become difficult to find recent contrastive research that is not based on corpus data, especially also since researchers have become

---

Bart Defrancq, Camille Collard, Ghent University, EQTIS, Groot-Brittanniëlaan, Belgium

https://doi.org/10.1515/9783110682588-006

interested in pragmatic contrasts, for which non-empirical, formal approaches are much less suitable. Warnings have been issued over the years against the uncritical use of corpora, especially parallel corpora: translations are a valuable source of information about language contrasts, but they are also a specific genre within the text production of the target language. They present specific linguistic properties, generically called "translationese" (Gellerstam 1986) or "third code" (Frawley 1984), and that can be traced back to source text influence (the so-called "transfer", "interference", "shining through") and to the linguistic mediation process that translation inherently is (Blum-Kulka 1986). In other words, a corpus of translations is not an entirely reliable source for the analysis of contrasts, as the source and target texts do not arise from the same kind of creative processes. Some scholars therefore advocate the use of comparable corpora as a complement to the analysis of parallel data (Johansson 1998), or more radically as the only source of linguistic data for the analysis of contrasts (Teubert 1996).

One important drawback of parallel corpora which is hardly ever mentioned in the literature, is their exclusive focus on written data. Parallel corpora in use in contrastive linguistics consist exclusively of written source texts and their translations. Inevitably, contrastive research based on such corpora is utterly unrepresentative, especially if conclusions are drawn about languages in general. For the sake of illustration, one quote from a random study on contrastive lexical semantics will suffice:

> The multilingual corpus-based comparison made it possible to show that the extent to which posture verbs are used as translations forms a continuum from German via English to Finnish and French. (Viberg 2013: 166)

Viberg's conclusion is based on data drawn from a corpus called the *Multilingual Pilot Corpus* comprising novels and their translations. Obviously, the claim that it holds for "German", "English", etc. is untenable, as novels only represent one particular genre of the language. There is evidence that, for instance in the area of posture verbs, register and genre differences show quite sharply in corpus data (Newman and Rice 2001). Recent work has also shown that genres determine translation patterns even within the written language (Lapshinova 2017). Including spoken genres in the parallel corpus data would probably yield different results and conclusions.

Parallel spoken data are better known as interpretations. However, the concept of "interpretation" itself is not limited to spoken modalities: sign language interpreting contains a non-spoken component, but is considered interpreting anyway. However, most of the interpreting data available are entirely spoken and they will be the focus of this paper. The question as to whether interpreting data are suited for contrastive research is not entirely new. On some occasions in the past, the possibility seems to have at least been envisaged. In her book on discourse markers, Fischer (2000), for instance, conducts a small-scale pilot study to assess the usefulness of spoken parallel data. Her conclusion is the following:

> To sum up, the analysis of interpreted speech *does not seem to be entirely useful* to get information on the translation equivalents of discourse particles. Discourse particles are not faithfully rendered into the target language, and it may even be argued that those instances of discourse particles that are found in interpreters' speech are not necessarily translations from the source language but may be discourse particles the interpreter needs for herself.
> (Fischer 2000: 202, our emphasis)

It should be noted that Fischer analyzes renditions from only one interpreter in an interpreter-mediated dialogue setting. The empirical basis for dismissing interpreting data is thus extremely narrow, too narrow for a corpus study.

In the same vein, and more recently, Mikhailov and Cooper (2016) claim that:

> [i]*nterpretation corpora do not provide readily usable data for contrastive studies*, because interpreting, unlike translating, is a very flexible process in which a great deal of nonessential information is constantly being transformed, shifted or even omitted. A corpus of interpretation data is therefore not very suitable for drawing up lists of lexical or grammatical correspondences.
> (Mikhailov and Cooper 2016: 210, our emphasis)

Surprisingly, the authors do not adduce any evidence at all for their various claims, as we might expect from corpus linguists. Even more surprising is the fact that the argument is reminiscent of long-held views in Chomskyan strands of linguistic research about the use of corpora: data of language use were long regarded as of no particular interest to linguistics as they are full of performance features (Chomsky 1965). It has since then become clear that performance features need not make linguistic analyses of corpora irrelevant, on the contrary.

This paper is an attempt to assess whether the performance features of interpreting that Mikhailov and Cooper (2016) refer to, pose a real obstacle for the analysis of interpreting data in a contrastive perspective. We will focus on a particular group of verbs in French, Dutch and English, i.e. verbs selecting embedded interrogatives, to determine whether cross-linguistic lexical correspondences that have been found in previous work through profile-based analyses (Defrancq 2005, 2008), are discernible in interpreting data or whether interpretation distorts the semantic profile of those verbs to the extent that interpreting data become irrelevant for contrastive research. We will, however, take a Bakerian perspective (Baker 1993), in that we will not compare source items and their rendition in interpretation, but rather items in interpreting and in non-interpreted spoken varieties in the same language. The main question we will seek to answer is thus whether the semantic properties of verbs in interpreting and non-interpreted spoken language are different.

Section 2 will discuss the status of parallel data in contrastive analysis. In Section 3, we will focus on the definition of interpreting, interpreting modes and the contexts in which interpreting takes place. Section 3 will also provide a general overview of data collections in Interpreting Studies and the status of corpus-based approaches in this field of study, at the end of which the research questions will be formulated. Section 4 will present the verbs used for this study and set out the methodology used to determine their semantic profile. Section 5 presents the results, which are subsequently discussed and interpreted qualitatively in Section 6. Section 7 will provide the concluding remarks.

2 Parallel data in contrastive analysis

Contrastive linguists use parallel data to study contrasts in form-meaning (or form-function) mappings across languages. Meaning is presumed to be kept constant in the translation process. Translations therefore offer an independent empirical basis for the study of formal and structural features of different languages. In a way, by using parallel corpus data, contrastive linguists outsource an important aspect of contrastive methodology: determining a *tertium comparationis*, i.e. a common ground for comparison.

Views on the reliability of parallel data vary considerably in the field. While most scholars use parallel data almost unreservedly, merely pointing out that the assumption that target texts are semantically equivalent with their source is an "idealization" (Gast and Levshina 2014: 400), others, like Teubert (1996), advise linguists to abandon parallel corpora altogether, because they give a "distorted picture of the language they represent" (Teubert 1996: 247). These contradicting views appear to be based on different approaches: parallel corpus enthusiasts privilege an accuracy perspective, comparing target texts and source texts; sceptics are more likely to adopt an acceptability perspective, comparing translated texts with non-translated texts. The latter, supported by corpus researchers working in the area of the translations studies, stress the special nature of translated data: whether it is because they reflect features of the source texts or because the translation process itself shapes them differently, translations are often felt to differ from non-translated texts in the same language. In Translation Studies, the whole paradigm of translation universals (explicitation, leveling out, ...), initiated by Baker (1993), rests on that particular assumption. Consequently, using parallel data to study contrasts between languages is considered methodologically unsound, as one of the datasets (the target text) is partly dependent on features of the other dataset (the source text), or at least influenced by an additional component in the creative process. In other words, the benefits drawn from outsourcing the *tertium comparationis* are outweighed by the loss of representativeness.

However, 25 years of research in corpus-based translation studies have not yielded conclusive evidence that translation universals exist or that their effect is stronger than that of other language-internal determinants of variation, such as genre (Delaere 2015). The evidence for source text influence is relatively strong (Mauranen 2004), but the extent to which this interferes with contrastive findings based on parallel corpora is not known. In this light, the complete rejection of parallel corpora as a source of contrastive data seems exaggerated. In addition, and as said before, the available research exclusively focuses on translated data. Interpreting data may manifest different patterns.

3 Interpreting and interpreting data

Over the years, interpreting has received many definitions. One of the difficulties in defining interpreting is to find a description that fits all the various modes and contexts in which the activity is performed. One of the most adaptable definitions in this respect is the following, proposed in 1968 by Kade:

> Unter Dolmetschen verstehen wir die Translation eines einmalig (in der Regel mündlich) dargebotenen Textes der Ausgangssprache in einen nur bedingt kontrollierbaren und infolge Zeitmangels kaum korrigierbaren Text der Zielsprache. Kade (1968: 35)
>
> 'By interpreting we mean the translation of a uniquely (usually orally) presented text in the source language in a target language text with little control and, due to time constraints, hardly any opportunity to correct.' (our translation)

The crucial point here is uniqueness: interpreters only have one opportunity to render in another language the input they receive on a single occasion. Translators usually have multiple opportunities to consult the input and to revise their output as their time constraints are much more flexible than interpreters'. Interpretation is thus characterized by immediacy: even in consecutive interpreting, where rendition is typically delayed, the delay never exceeds a couple of minutes. This time frame simply does not allow interpreters to consult the input again or to systematically revise and correct their output.

Interpreting comes in various forms. Traditionally, two so-called modes are distinguished: consecutive and simultaneous. In consecutive interpreting, interpreters render their output in a turn which is clearly separated from the input turn. The size of the turns varies considerably. In conference settings, where consecutive interpreting has become extremely rare, turns of several minutes are not uncommon. In dialogue settings, turns are usually not longer than a couple of seconds. For longer turns, interpreters apply a specific kind of note-taking.

In simultaneous interpreting, in contrast, speakers' and interpreters' turns overlap. This implies that they either have to be separated in space, for instance infrastructurally by the presence of interpreting booths, or that the interpreter needs to apply specific techniques so as not to interfere with the source turn. Interpreters will, for instance, "whisper" their output to the ears of one or two listeners.

Interpreters are called in in a variety of contexts: wars, police stations, courts, public services, workers' councils, scientific conferences, political summits, ... Not all forms of interpretation are carried out by professionals. Especially in the public service sector and in the context of conflict, *ad hoc* interpreters are often recruited from the community the service is provided for or the conflict is fought out against.

The variety in interpreting contexts represents the biggest challenge for researchers interested in compiling corpora of interpreting: only in a few contexts do researchers have access to the interpreters and their interpretations. Building corpora that are representative of the whole range of interpreting varieties, as discussed in Section 4, is a herculean task that no researcher or research group has taken on up to this point.

By contrast, researchers around the world have compiled several collections of interpreting data, mostly focusing on one mode and one context. The European Parliament is by far the most popular source of corpus data, due to the access it grants to source speeches and interpretations in 23 languages. With a few exceptions – EPIC (Sandrelli and Bendazzoli 2005); DiK (Bührig et al. 2012) – interpreting corpora are unfortunately not publicly available, prompting Robin Setton to call the discipline of corpus-based interpreting studies a "cottage industry" (Setton 2011: 34). The available corpora are small: EPIC, for instance, contains 170,000 tokens and is one of the largest corpora for European languages. This, of course, seriously compromises the development of corpus-based interpreting studies.

The compilation and use of interpreting corpora are not uncontroversial. Ebru Diriker warns researchers against unconsidered use of corpus data in research:

> The online availability of the speeches and their interpretations at the EP's plenary sessions is certainly an invaluable source for researchers interested in analyzing authentic corpora of interpreting. Caution, however, is necessary, since the online availability of such recordings means they can be used by everyone, including researchers who have never seen the European Parliament in session nor talked to the interlocutors there to gain an idea of the constraints of interpreting in that particular setting. Although analysis of any data will by nature never be a mirror reflection of reality, drawing conclusions on SCI [Simultaneous

Conference Interpreting] as situated action based on de-contextualized recordings must be taken with an even larger grain of salt. (Diriker 2004: 215, footnote)

Diriker targets the presumed failure of corpus linguists to adequately take into account the context in which interpreting takes place. However, her criticism is not entirely convincing for a number of reasons. On the one hand, every language act is situated. Interpreting is by no means more situated than any other type of linguistic production. If Diriker's concerns were to be taken at face value, the whole discipline of corpus linguistics would probably collapse. As a matter of fact, the whole point of corpus linguistics is to identify trends and tendencies across contexts, to find out to what extent interpreting is similar to or different from other types of language production, translation in particular. On the other hand, corpus linguists do not ignore the context altogether. It is commonly accepted that the best corpora are those that contain metadata regarding contextual features, so that contextual information can be retrieved from the corpus whenever relevant for the analysis.

Nevertheless, it is true that interpreting data are to be handled with care. Interpreting is not just a spoken form of translation. Translators work in similar circumstances as the authors of the source texts they translate; in some cases, professional translators might even have an edge on authors, as the latter are not always language professionals. In the case of interpreting, and simultaneous interpreting in particular, the advantages interpreters draw from their training are outweighed by the exceptionally challenging circumstances in which they work. Simultaneous interpreting is, after all, an extreme case of speech production in a noisy and stressful environment (Tóth 2011), circumstances ordinary speakers do not face. The nature of the noise – human speech – intensifies interferences with their own output (Seeber 2011), resulting in peculiar features, such as disfluencies (Plevoets and Defrancq 2016; 2018), sentence-final rising-level intonation (Ahrens 2004), etc. Consecutive interpreters experience high memory load. Even in cases where they can rely on notes, the actual source text is no longer available, as is the case in translation, increasing the risk of omissions.

Due to the unforgiving circumstances the activity takes place in, interpreting is much more prone to errors and omissions than translation. The accuracy problems highlighted by Fischer (2000), for instance, are well-known in Interpreting Studies: discourse markers, the items studied by Fischer (2000) are particularly vulnerable in interpreted renditions for a number of reasons. They occur sentence-initially, which exposes them to so-called imported load (Gile 2008): as interpreters finish rendering the previous utterance, they pay less attention to the start of the upcoming one. Discourse markers are also not part of the propositional content of the utterance, which is what interpreters are trained to focus on. Interestingly, discourse markers are also regularly added to interpretations, explicitating inferred relationships between clauses or simply covering up major omissions (Defrancq, Plevoets, and Magnifico 2015). Errors and omissions have been claimed to be inherent to interpreting and to constitute an important source of information for researchers modelling the cognitive processes behind the activity (Gile 1995). The boundary between errors and interpreting strategies is actually fuzzy: especially in cases where cognitive load is extremely high, it is acceptable to deploy coping strategies to keep the communication going at the cost of accuracy (Schjoldager 1995).

Accuracy problems do occur in interpreting and probably more so than in translations. In a study conducted on corpus data, Defrancq, Plevoets, and Magnifico (2015) found that for a range of causal and concessive connectives, interpreted texts (English and Dutch) only propose semantic equivalents for (French) source text items in 53% (Dutch) to 61% (English) of the cases, while in translation the equivalence rates range from 80% (Dutch) to 85% (English). In both modes, most of the non-equivalent renditions are in fact omissions, some of which may very well not be inaccuracies after all. Indeed, it is widely acknowledged that languages present different frequencies of connectives. Some omissions in translation and interpreting may be a reflection of language-specific tendencies.

For some reason, contrastive linguists generally do not seem to find accuracy issues problematic when dealing with translation data. Nearly all studies report omissions (euphemistically called "zero-translations"), but omissions are rarely a motive to cast doubt on the reliability of translation corpora. On the contrary, some studies even focus on omissions as a source of information on language contrasts (Aijmer and Altenberg 2002). Similarly, many studies brush aside problematic data, typically in categories such as "other translations", which are usually completely disregarded in the analysis. This tolerance for problematic data is surprising, even more so in light of the fact that interpreting data are widely held unusable in contrastive linguistics precisely because of the errors and omissions they contain. There seems to be little justification for approaching inaccuracies in translation and interpreting differently, as the difference is a matter of scale rather than a matter of principle. Therefore, interpreting data are not less or more suited for contrastive research than translation data; only more of it will have to be discarded.

As for the dimension of acceptability, i.e. the extent to which features of interpreted data differ from features of non-interpreted spoken data, not much can be said with any degree of certainty. Research has been carried out on various aspects of simultaneous interpreting, including lexical density, lexical variation (Kajzer-Wietrzny 2012; Bernardini et al. 2016), phraseology (Ferraresi and Milisevic 2017), explicitness (Kajzer-Wietrzny 2012; Defrancq, Plevoets and Magnifico 2015), and normalization (Kajzer-Wietrzny 2012). Only some of the evidence points to significant differences between interpreting and non-interpreted spoken language. Bernardini et al (2016), for instance, find evidence in support of the universal of simplification for English and Italian interpretations; Kajzer Wietrzny's (2012) study, in contrast, concludes for English interpretations from Spanish, French, Dutch and German that "[N]one of the hypothesized universals has been uniformly confirmed by all tested parameters" (Kajzer-Wietrzny 2012: 138). Both studies stress that there is a significant language effect as well in the data. Bernardini et al. (2016) point out that while Italian interpreters use shorter sentences than speakers and thus simplify sentence structure, English interpreters favor simplification on lexical parameters. The source language also plays a role, as Kajzer-Wietrzny's (2012) study illustrates.[1] English interpretations from French appear to be lexically more varied than English speeches, while English interpretations from the other languages are found to be less varied. On the basis of such divergent research results, formulating coherent advice on the usability of interpreting data for contrastive purposes seems difficult to achieve.

In addition, the focus of these studies has been on lexical properties at the text level. However, the question whether interpretations can be relied upon in contrastive research to study features of lexical items also hinges upon their acceptability on the micro-level, i.e. the extent to which they are used in similar or dissimilar ways across corpora of interpreting and non-mediated corpora. If interpreters are found to use lexical items in other ways than speakers, interpretation data cannot be considered a viable alternative to the definition of a *tertium comparationis* in contrastive lexical studies. Differences in use may indeed point to semantic differences between identical items in mediated and non-mediated language, while contrastive linguists expect there to be no such difference.

Little is known about the effect of interpreting on the level of the lexical item. The principal research question of this study will therefore focus on individual lexical items and ask whether interpreting has an influence on the use of individual lexical items and to what extent such an influence may make interpreted data unusable for contrastive research.

---

[1] Actually, as Bernardini et al. (2016) only investigate one language pair, the observed cross-linguistic differences between target texts could also be due to the source languages.

4 Methodology

To answer the central research question, we designed a method based on behavioral profiles (Gries 2006; Divjak and Gries 2006) which has become fairly standard when studying lexical items, including cross-linguistically. Behavioral profiles rest on the idea that semantic properties of lexemes can be studied through the co-occurrence of a lexeme with particular ID tags in corpora. ID tags are configurations of lexical, semantic, syntactic or pragmatic features presumed to be associated with particular meanings of lexemes. Unlike the elaborate configurations of ID tags found in most scholarly work (Gries 2006; Gries and Otani 2010), we will only use one variable that was proven to be highly relevant for the semantic properties of a specific category of verbs in previous work (Defrancq 2005; Defrancq 2008). The verbs involved belong to the class of verbs governing embedded interrogatives (*wonder, ask, understand, ...*) and the behavioral profile is based on the co-occurrence of these verbs with *wh*-items. We will first recall earlier findings to argue that even such a limited behavioral profile can detect semantically related verbs in a contrastive perspective. As the purpose of this study is to determine whether the semantic properties of lexical items are affected by the interpreting process, the behavioral profiles will be used to compare the properties of identical verbs in interpreted and non-interpreted data. If the behavioral profiles of these verbs turn out to be significantly different, this will be considered to be indicative of an interpreting effect.

4.1 Verbs governing embedded interrogatives

Verbs governing embedded interrogatives, such as *ask, understand, wonder, ...* constitute a particular class of mostly cognitive verbs. In semantic terms, a combination of such a verb with an embedded interrogative can be broadly described as referring to a cognitive state or activity relating to a particular type of information. In (1), for instance, the experiencer is said to request information about the identity of a person, while in (2) she is said to fail to gain knowledge about the reasons leading to a particular state of affairs.

(1) *I'll ask him who that was.*

(2) *She does not understand why he said that.*

As demonstrated in Defrancq (2005: 237, 2008: 469), verbs governing embedded interrogatives co-occur more often with some *wh*-items than with others. This is illustrated in Table 1 with data drawn from the newspaper section of the BNC.

Table 1: Frequencies of *wh*-items in combination with *ask* and *tell*.

	ask	%	tell	%
how	34	**11.3**	130	**45.4**
what	69	23.0	91	31.8
where	11	3.7	13	4.5
whether / if[a]	141	**47.0**	24	**8.4**
which	5	1.7	5	1.7
when	1	0.3	3	1.0
who	8	2.7	6	2.1
Why	31	**10.3**	14	**4.9**
∑	300	100.0	286	100.0

[a] The frequencies of *whether* and *if* were added up because their meanings are nearly identical.

For four out of eight *wh*-items (highlighted in bold type face), the relative frequencies are at least twice as high in one case as in the other. The frequency distributions of *wh*-items have been shown to be determined by the semantic properties of the verbs: verbs with similar meanings present similar *wh*-profiles, verbs with different meanings present different *wh*-profiles (Defrancq 2005). In a study carried out on a dataset including 33 verbs from four languages (FR, EN, NL and ES), we were able to correctly identify semantic equivalents across languages in 70% of the cases by analyzing correlations between *wh*-profiles (Defrancq 2008).

In this study, *wh*-distributions will be used to study the effect of different predictors on the *wh*-distributions associated with particular Dutch and English verbs. Among the predictors, the most important one is expected to be the meaning of the verb, but we will also focus on the mediated (interpreting) or non-mediated (spoken language) nature of the data and the context in which the data were produced (European Parliament vs. British Parliament). Therefore, *wh*-distributions will be compared in various combinations of sub-corpora. The effect of verb meaning will be studied for both languages by comparing *wh*-profiles for verbs with different meanings. The effect of the mediated nature of the data will be analyzed by comparing *wh*-profiles in interpreted data, on the one hand, and in all the non-interpreted data (EP and national parliaments) on the other. The effect of context will be studied by comparing *wh*-profiles in EP data (interpreted and non-interpreted), on the one hand, and in data from the national parliaments, on the other.

It is expected, based on previous studies (Defrancq 2005, 2008), that the meaning of the verb will appear to significantly determine the *wh*-distributions.

The effects of both other variables are harder to predict. If significant differences are found on the mediatedness dimension, it would mean that identical verbs are used differently in spoken and interpreted data, casting doubt on the usability of the interpreted data for contrastive research. Significant differences found on the context dimension would, in turn, imply that the European Parliament as a whole (interpreters and members) uses verbs differently than members of national parliaments.

4.2 Data used in the study

The data for the study are drawn from several corpora. The interpreting corpus consists of source speeches and simultaneous interpretations from the European Parliament, collected and transcribed at Ghent University (EPICG, see Bernardini et al. 2018). For this study, we selected two languages, Dutch and English, both as source (non-mediated) and target (mediated) languages. As EPICG also contains French source data, there are more Dutch and English target data than there are source data. As members of the European Parliament listen a fair amount of time to interpreters and *vice versa*, mutual influence of lexical patterns might be a confounding factor (Defrancq 2018): it is fairly likely that speakers in the EP who listen days in a row to the interpretations of speeches delivered by their colleagues are influenced by the linguistic patterns of these interpretations when they deliver their own speech. It is also not impossible (although less likely) that interpreters are influenced by members of the EP delivering speeches in their own language. We therefore decided to also include Dutch and English non-mediated data from other corpora that offer parliamentary data. For Dutch we drew from the *Corpus Gesproken Nederlands* (Oostdijk 2000) and, in particular, from sub-corpus g of political debates and for English from the S_Parl (Spoken Parliament) Section of the *British National Corpus* respectively. As Table 2 shows, the corpus sizes are small to very small.

Table 2: Corpus sizes in number of tokens.

Corpus	NL non-mediated	NL mediated	EN non-mediated	EN mediated
EPICG	18,206	36,555	20,615	33,693
CGN g	360,328	–	–	–
BNC S_Parl	–	–	96,239	–

As a result, there a very few data to work on for the different verbs included in the previous studies. From the overview shown in Table 3 it appears that only *say + wh* is sufficiently frequent in all English corpora. As we need at least a second verb to carry out the analysis, we decided to include a verb that was not previously analyzed: *know*. Its frequencies (*know + wh*) and those of its Dutch equivalent, *weten + wh*, are reasonably high, except in the interpreting sub-corpora. We therefore also decided to recategorize the *wh*-items in broader categories (see Section 4.3). In order to obtain a balanced data set, we also included the Dutch equivalent of *say + wh* in the analysis, even though its frequency in the non-mediated EP corpus (EPICGnm) is obviously too low.

Table 3: Frequencies of verb-*wh* combinations in the different sub-corpora.

	English				Dutch		
Verb	BNC	EPICGnm	EPICGm	Verb	CGN	EPICGnm	EPICGm
Previously studied verbs (Defrancq 2008)							
ask	17	2	8	vragen	83	3	8
decide	9	0	3	beslissen	9	0	0
determine	3	0	1	bepalen	15	0	2
say	184	30	47	zeggen	390	6	43
tell	53	7	8	vertellen	18	0	3
understand	28	1	8	begrijpen	83	7	3
wonder	19	0	0	z. afvragen	27	1	1
Verb added for this study							
know	99	17	40	weten	266	20	26

4.3 Re-categorization of *wh*-items

In previous studies (Defrancq 2005, 2008), frequency distributions were studied as raw data. Due to the limited amounts of data for this study, we decided to pre-process the data by summing frequencies for similar types of *wh*-items. Defrancq (2005) exposes in detail the semantic basis for such a categorization. In short, three types of *wh*-items are distinguished: identificational, predicative and presentational. Identificational *wh*-items are *who, which, where, when* and some occurrences of *what* (identify an object) and *how* (manner). They inquire about specific identities or co-ordinates and are more easily clefted in many languages than the other items. Verbs promoting identificational *wh*-items include *figure out, guess,* etc. Predicative items include *why* and some occurrences of *what* and *how,* mainly those used in combination with copular verbs, pro-verbs and attributive adjectives. Predicative items inquire about attributes of referents and states of affairs. Verbs found to promote predicative items include *find, show, understand,* etc. Finally, presentational items include *how* and some instances of *what* combined with predicates such as *happen* or *occur.* They narrate or inquire about events. In this context, *how* predominantly occurs in embedded predicates following verbs such as *tell, recall,* etc. *Whether* and *if* cut across the three categories, presenting a choice of options. They constitute a fourth category.

Two additional steps had to be taken for lack of data. First, the second (predicative) and third (presentational) categories were conflated, resulting in a three-way categorization in identificational items (or identificationally used items); non-identificational items and the choice-of-option items. Conflating the predicative and presentational categories was the most logical option, as, for the exception of *why,* the categories contain the same items.

Second, it was decided to also include subordinate *that*-clauses in the study (both with explicit and implicit *that*). Since Baker (1970) and Grimshaw (1979), it is widely accepted that the possibility to combine a verb with a *that*-clause, an embedded interrogative or both is semantically motivated and influenced by polarity and modality: many cognitive verbs allow both, but some, mainly the ones denoting processes of thought, belief and verbal expression, only allow particular *wh*-clauses in particular configurations of polarity and modality. In example (3), for instance, a *wh-clause* is disallowed with a *believe*-predicate (a), unless negative polarity and epistemic modality are added (b).

(3) a. *She believed who did it.
    b. You won't believe who did it.

Clauses headed by *whether* or *if* are usually not compatible with these verbs, even in specific configurations of polarity and modality. *That*-clauses, in contrast, combine unrestrictedly with such verbs. On the other hand, *that*-clauses are incompatible with other groups, most notably verbs of questioning, such as *wonder* and *ask* (the latter of which, combined with a *that*-clause, expresses a request rather than a question).

Despite the rather sketchy description of the relations between verbs and different types of clauses, we shall assume that frequencies of *that*-clauses and, more in particular, their relative frequency compared to different types of *wh*-clauses is determined by the semantic properties of the verbs they combine with. As *that-*

clauses tend to be much more frequent than *wh*-clauses, their inclusion in this study is expected to benefit the statistical analyses.

In all, the following categories will thus be used to draw up the behavioral profiles of the verbs included in this study:

C1 (identificational):	*what* (identify-object), *which*, *where*, *when*, *who*, *how* (manner, number)
C2 (predicative & narrative):	*what* (attribute & narrative), *why*, *how* (attribute & narrative),
C3 (choice of option):	*whether, if*
C4 (*that*-clause):	*that* (explicit and implicit)

Equivalent categories were constituted for Dutch:

C1:	*hoe* (manner, number), *waar, wanneer, wat* (identify-object), *welk, wie*
C2:	*hoe* (attribute & narrative), *waarom, wat* (attribute & narrative)
C3:	*of*
C4:	*dat* (explicit and implicit)

Categories C1–C4 are the dependent variable for this study. For each verb, the frequencies of *wh*-items in categories C1–C4 will therefore be collected. The independent variables include the meanings of the verbs, the mediated or non-mediated nature of the data and the context in which they were produced. As the dependent variable is nominal and has four possible outcomes, a multinomial linear regression in SPSS will be used to determine the effects of the different predictors.

5 Results

Descriptive statistics are shown in Table 4. The frequency distribution across languages of Categories 1–4 is very similar for equivalent verbs (*know – weten*: chi-square = 0.54; p = 0.91; *say – zeggen*: chi-square = 4.76; p = 0.19), confirming findings from previous studies (Defrancq 2005, 2008), namely that equivalent verbs across languages have similar *wh*-profiles. It follows from Table 4 that this also holds when subordinate *that*-clauses are added to the data. For non-equivalent pairs the distributions are significantly different (*know – zeggen*: chi-square = 115.74; p < 0.00001; *say – weten*: 113.73; p < 0.00001).

Table 4: Descriptive statistics for the entire dataset.

		know		say		weten		zeggen	
		N	%	N	%	N	%	N	%
Category	1	43	27.6	6	2.3	84	26.9	18	2.3
	2	10	6.4	10	3.8	25	8.0	8	1.8
	3	15	9.6	1	0.4	33	10.6	4	0.9
	4	88	56.4	244	93.5	170	54.5	409	93.2
Context	EP	57	36.5	74	29.5	46	14.7	49	12.2
	Other	99	63.5	184	70.5	266	85.3	390	88.8
Mediated	No	116	74.4	214	82.0	286	91.7	396	90.2
	Yes	40	25.6	47	18.0	26	8.3	43	9.8
Total		156		261		312		439	

The results of the multinomial tests are shown in Tables 5 (English) and 6 (Dutch). They run parallel for both languages. Due caution is in order with the Dutch data, as the model's fit is low due to cells with low frequencies. Unsurprisingly, the verb is the most powerful predictor of the model in both languages with p-values lower than 0.0001. This means that the frequency distribution of Categories 1–4 is first and foremost determined by the difference in meaning between the verbs in both languages. The effect of context is not significant: data from the European Parliament (interpreted and non-interpreted) and data from the national parliaments do not present significantly different frequency distributions (p > 0.5 in both cases). This seems to run counter the idea that speakers and interpreters in the EU converge on particular linguistic patterns because of mutual influence. In contrast, it does seem to matter whether the data are interpreted or not, as the differences on the mediatedness dimension are significant (p=0.048 and 0.024 for English and Dutch respectively).

Table 5: Effects of predictors in English.

Effect	-2 Log Likelihood of Reduced Model	Likelihood Ratio Tests		
		Chi-Square	Df	Sig.
Intercept	50.774	.000	0	.
Verb	145.603	94.829	3	.000
EP	56.337	5.563	3	.135
Mediated	58.672	7.898	3	.048

Table 6: Effects of predictors in Dutch.

Effect	-2 Log Likelihood of Reduced Model	Likelihood Ratio Tests		
		Chi-Square	Df	Sig.
Intercept	60.391	.000	0	.
Verb	219.318	158.927	3	.000
EP	66.920	6.528	3	.089
Mediated	69.798	9.406	3	.024

Mediatedness thus seems to influence the behavioral profiles of verbs in both languages, but the influence appears to be much smaller than the meaning difference between the verbs in both languages. As *wh-that*-profiles are strongly determined by the meaning of the verbs that govern them, a shift in profiles due to interpreting ultimately implies that interpreters use these verbs slightly differently as compared to speakers.

From an inspection of the parameter estimates (not shown here), it appears that in Dutch, mediatedness has the strongest negative effect on the frequency of items in Category 2. In English, in contrast, *wh*-items in Category 3 are most negatively affected.

6 Discussion

Even though the dataset is obviously extremely small, it seems to show an interpreting effect in the use of types of *wh*-items, including subordinating *that*, both in Dutch and in English. As the tendencies are parallel in both languages, i.e. a significant and strong effect of verb meaning, a significant, but weaker effect of mediatedness and no effect related to context, the results seem fairly robust.

The first question that arises in this context is whether the interpreting effect is strong enough to distort cross-linguistic relations. As mentioned before, on the whole dataset, including non-mediated data, pairs of equivalent verbs present similar frequency distributions and pairs of non-equivalent verbs showed significant differences. To verify whether the interpreting effect distorts these relations, the same analysis also needs to be carried out on the interpreting corpus only. The results are shown in Table 7.

The situation reflects the tendencies observed in the whole dataset: frequency distributions of equivalent verb pairs (*know-weten*; *say-zeggen*) are similar, while they are significantly different for non-equivalent verbs. In other words, the inter-

Table 7: Cross-linguistic relationships in interpreting.

	Cat. 1	Cat. 2	Cat. 3	Cat. 4	Fisher Exact	
know	8	3	7	22		
say	2	0	0	45	know	say
weten	5	1	1	19	p=0.34	p<0.01
zeggen	2	4	0	37	p<0.001	p=0.17
Total	17	8	8	123		

preting effect that was observed in the previous section is real but it does not seem to compromise cross-linguistic equivalence relations.

The second question that arises is what could possibly cause the observed interpreting effect. What is it about interpreting that can influence the use of particular items by interpreters? A usual suspect in this regard is the influence of the source text, i.e. the promotion of structures in target texts that are formally similar to structures of the source text. If source speakers use equivalents of *say/zeggen* and *know/weten* in combination with slightly different *wh-that*-profiles, this will inevitably affect the frequencies of *wh*-items and subordinating *that* in interpreting. However, in our case, source text influence is unlikely: first, our source texts are in different languages, namely French and, depending on the target, Dutch or English. A hybrid source corpus is unlikely to produce clear signals of transfer in the target texts. Furthermore, a detailed qualitative analysis of source-target correspondences quickly reveals that interpreters usually shy away from transfer, even though a formally similar structure is perfectly acceptable in the target language. For instance, examples (4)–(6) show English target structures where the embedded interrogative is introduced by a sequence composed of *how* and an adjective or a quantifier. In Dutch the parallel structure with the lexical equivalent *hoe* is used in only one case (4b), while both other cases present occurrences of *dat*.

(4) a. *allow me to say* **how** *much I'm [I am] looking forward to working with you all over ((0,3s)) at the next six months* [EPICG_20131501_Credit rating agencies_Lucinda Creighton_I_nl]
   b. *dus zou ik willen zeggen [breath]* **hoe**zeer *ik uitkijk naar de samenwerking met u allen ((0,2s)) binnen de komende zes maanden ((0,4s))*
   'so I would like to say how much I am looking forward to the cooperation with you all within the coming six months'

(5) a. *can I say **how** grateful I have been for the enormous cooperation ((0,3s)) from the other rapporteurs on this package* [EPICG_20092104_Common rules for the internal market in electricity – Agency for the cooperation of energy regulator_ElunedMorgan_I_nl]
 b. *en ik moet zeggen **dat** ik erg erkentelijk ben voor de zeer goede samenwerking met de overige rapporteurs*
 'and I have to say that I am very grateful for the very good cooperation with the other rapporteurs'

(6) a. *but I'm [I am] really a bit perturbed to hear people get up here ((0,3s)) wringing their hands ((0,2s)) saying **how** shocking it is* [EPICG_20131601_Recent Casualties In Textile Factory Fires_Gay Mitchell_I_fr]
 b. *maar ja mensen ((0,5s)) staan hier handenwringend en zeggen **dat** het allemaal zo verschrikkelijk is*
 'well yes people stand here wringing their hands and saying that it is all so terrible'

In (5) and (6) it would be perfectly acceptable to use the Dutch equivalent of *how*. The examples illustrate quite well that the actual explanatory factor of the interpreting effect may be so-called *conventionality* or *normalization*, i.e. an alleged universal propensity of translators (and, apparently also interpreters) to use the typical and frequent structures of the target language more frequently (Baker 1993; Toury 1995). In (5) and (6) embedded interrogatives of Category 2 are converted into *that*-clauses. As the latter are the most frequent clausal arguments of the verbs in Dutch (Table 1), the translation shifts indeed reinforce the category that is already the most frequent one. It is interesting to note that in both languages one of the smallest categories (Categories 2 and 3) is found to be most significantly impacted by the mediated nature of interpreting data. This is of course completely in line with the *normalization* hypothesis predicting that less frequent structures tend to be replaced by more frequent ones. The overall semantic result is that in interpreting the verbs studied here are situated slightly more towards the area of verbs of thought and belief than in non-mediated language.

7 Conclusions

The main purpose of this study was to verify whether interpreting data are a reliable source of information for contrastive researchers interested in features of spoken language. Translations are widely used for contrastive research, but are less suited to study spoken language. The literature offers little hope, as scholars from both contrastive studies and interpreting studies point out important caveats to the use of interpreting corpora. On the one hand, interpreting data are believed to lack accuracy (Fischer 2000; Mikhailov and Cooper 2016), which makes it hard to rely on them for an implied *tertium comparationis*. On the other hand, the same interpreting data are believed to be so extremely context-bound that analyzing them mainly in their textual dimension, as is the case in corpus-based contrastive research, is felt to misrepresent the interpreting activity itself (Diriker 2004). However, both sides offer very little empirical evidence for their claims.

We therefore set out to study potential differences in the use of particular verbal lexemes that could be attributed to interpreting. These differences could be triggered by small differences in semantic properties of these verbs, making the use of interpreted data problematic in contrastive analyses. We focused on Dutch and English verbs that are equivalent in meaning, can be combined with an embedded interrogative and a subordinate *that*-clause and are frequent enough in the interpreting corpora to afford statistical analysis. *Know-weten* and *say-zeggen* were selected as equivalent pairs. Behavioral profiles were defined on the basis of different types of *wh*-items and subordinating *that*. Given previous research on *wh*-profiles, it was assumed that these profiles are determined by the meaning of the verbs.

All occurrences of the relevant verbs in combination with a *wh*-item or *that* were collected in 3 types of corpora: (i) a corpus of non-mediated spoken language drawn from national parliaments; (ii) a corpus of non-mediated spoken language drawn from the European Parliament; (iii) a corpus of interpreting as carried out at the European Parliament. Most of the data under (ii) are the source data of the interpretations under (iii). This collection of corpora allowed us to study the effect of three predictors on the frequencies of *wh*-items and *that*: the meaning of the verb; the context (European Parliament vs. national parliaments) and the mediated nature of the data (non-mediated data vs. interpreting). A multinomial logistic regression was carried out to determine the significance of the effects.

Of the three predictors, two turned out to have a significant effect on the frequency distributions both in Dutch and in English: the verb and mediatedness. In contrast, the context in which the observed speech takes place does not affect the frequency distributions. Moreover, mediatedness is a weaker predictor than the verb.

It should be noted that this conclusion was reached on the basis of a small dataset. The effects can be interpreted as a tendency in interpreters to normalize their speech, i.e. to use frequent structures even more frequently to the detriment of infrequent ones. To the extent that the frequency distributions of *wh*-items and *that* are held to be determined by the semantic properties of the verb, the general conclusion of this study is that the verbs are used with slightly different semantic properties in interpreting. Overall, the effect is however fairly limited as it does not seem to distort cross-linguistic equivalence relations in the cases studied here. Therefore, on the basis on this limited pilot study, it would appear that interpreting data are not *per se* unreliable for contrastive analysis.

References

Ahrens, Barbara. 2004. *Prosodie beim Simultandolmetschen*. Peter Lang: Frankfurt/M.

Aijmer, Karin and Bengt Altenberg. 2002. Zero translations and cross-linguistic equivalence: Evidence from the English-Swedish Parallel Corpus. In Levi Egil Breivik and Angela Hasselgren (eds.), *From the COLTs mouth ... and others. Language corpora studies in honour of Anna-Brita Stenström*, 19–41 Amsterdam: Rodopi.

Baker, Carl. 1970. Notes on the description of English questions: the role of an abstract question morpheme. *Foundations of Language* 6. 197–219.

Baker, Mona. 1993. Corpus linguistics and translation studies: Implications and applications. In Mona Baker, Gill Francis & Elena Tognini-Bonelli (eds.), *Text and Technology: in honour of John Sinclair*, 233–250 Amsterdam/Philadelphia: John Benjamins.

Bernardini, Silvia, Adriano Ferraresi & Maja Miličević. 2016. From EPIC to EPTIC – Exploring simplification in interpreting and translation from an intermodal perspective. *Target* 28 (1). 61–86.

Bernardini, Silvia, Adriano Ferraresi, Mariachiara Russo, Camille Collard & Bart Defrancq. 2018. Building interpreting and intermodal corpora: a How-to for a formidable task. In Claudio Bendazzoli, Mariachiara Russo & Bart Defrancq (eds.), *Making Way in Corpus-based Interpreting Studies*, 21–42. Singapore: Springer.

Blum-Kulka, Shoshana. 1986. Shifts of cohesion and coherence in translation. In Juliane House & Shoshana Blum-Kulka (eds.), *Interlingual and Intercultural Communication*, 17–35. Tubingen: Gunter Narr Verlag.

Bührig, Kristin, Ortrun Kliche, Birte Pawlack and Bernd Meyer. 2012. The corpus "Interpreting in hospitals" – possible applications for research and communication trainings. In Thomas Schmidt & Kai Wörner (eds.), *Multilingual Corpora and Multilingual Corpus Analysis. Hamburg Studies in Multilingualism 14*, 305–315. Amsterdam: John Benjamins.

Chomsky, Noam. 1965. *Aspects of the Theory of Syntax*. Cambridge: MIT Press.

Defrancq, Bart. 2005. *L'Interrogative enchâssée. Structure et interpretation*. Bruxelles: DeBoeck/ Duculot.

Defrancq, Bart. 2008. Establishing cross-linguistic semantic relatedness through monolingual corpora: Verbs governing embedded interrogatives. *International Journal of Corpus Linguistics* 13(4). 465–490.

Defrancq, Bart. 2018. The European Parliament as a discourse community: its role in comparable analyses of data drawn from parallel interpreting corpora. *The Interpreters Newsletter* 22. 115–132.

Defrancq, Bart, Koen Plevoets & Cédric Magnifico. 2015. Connective markers in interpreting and translation: where do they come from? In Jesus Romero Trillo (ed.), *Corpus pragmatics in translation and contrastive studies*, 195–222. Singapore: Springer.

Delaere, Isabel. 2015. *Do translations walk the line? Visually exploring translated and non-translated texts in search of norm conformity*. Ghent: Ghent University dissertation.

Diriker, Erbrun. 2004. *De-/Re-Contextualizing Conference Interpreting: Interpreters in the Ivory Tower?* Amsterdam: John Benjamins.

Divjak, Dagmar & Stefan Gries. 2006. Ways of trying in Russian. Clustering behavioural profiles. *Corpus Linguistics and Linguistic Theory* 2 (1). 23–60.

Ferraresi, Adriano & Maja Miličević. 2017. Phraseological patterns in translation and interpreting. Similar or different? In Gert De Sutter, Marie-Aude. Lefer & Isabel Delaere (eds.), *Empirical Translation Studies. New Methodological and Theoretical Traditions*, 157–182. Berlin: De Gruyter.

Fischer, Kerstin. 2000. *From Cognitive Semantics to Lexical Pragmatics: The Functional Polysemy of Discourse Particles*. Berlin: De Gruyter.

Frawley, William. 1984. Prolegomenon to a theory of translation. In Frawley W. (ed.) *Translation, Literary, Linguistic and Philosophical Perspectives*, 159–175. London: Associated University presses.

Gast, Volker & Natalia Levshina. 2014. Motivating w(h)-clefts in English and German: A hypothesis-driven parallel corpus study. In Anna-Maria de Cesare (ed.), *Frequency, Forms and Functions of Cleft Constructions in Romance and Germanic. Contrastive, Corpus-Based Studies*, 377–414. Berlin: de Gruyter Mouton.

Gellerstam, Martin. 1986. Translationese in Swedish novels translated from English. In Lars Wollin & Hans Lindquist (eds.), *Translation Studies in Scandinavia*, 88–95. Lund: CWK Gleerup.

Gile, Daniel. 1995. *Regards sur la recherche en interprétation de conférence*. Lille: PUL.

Gile, Daniel. 2008. Local cognitive load in simultaneous interpreting and its implications for empirical research. *Forum* 6. 59–77.

Gries, Stefan. 2006. Corpus-based methods and Cognitive Semantics: The many senses of *to run*. In Stefan Gries & Anatol Stefanowitsch (eds.), *Corpora in Cognitive Linguistics: Corpus-based approaches to syntax and lexis*, 57–99. Berlin/New York: Mouton de Gruyter.

Gries, Stefan and Naoki Otani. 2010. Behavioral profiles: a corpus-based perspective on synonymy and antonymy. *ICAME Journal* 34. 121–150.

Grimshaw, Jane. 1979. Complement selection and the lexicon. *Linguistic Inquiry* 10. 279–326.

Johansson, Stig. 1998. On the role of corpora in cross-linguistic research. In Stig Johansson & Signe Oksefjell (eds.), *Corpora and cross-linguistic research: Theory, method, and case studies*, 3–24. Amsterdam: Rodopi/Brill.

Kade, Otto. 1968. *Zufall und Gesetzmässigkeit in der Übersetzung*. Leipzig.

Kajzer-Wietrzny, Marta. 2012. *Interpreting Universals and Interpreting Style*. Poznan: University of Poznan dissertation. https://repozytorium.amu.edu.pl/jspui/bitstream/10593/2425/1/Paca%20doktorska%20Marty%20Kajzer-Wietrzny.pdf (Accessed 2. 4.2018)

Lapshinova, Ekaterina. 2017. Exploratory analysis of dimensions influencing variation in translation. The case of text register and translation method. In Gert De Sutter & Isabel Delaere (eds.), *Empirical Translation Studies. New Methodological and Theoretical Traditions*, 207–234. Berlin: De Gruyter.

Mauranen, Anna. 2004. Corpora, universals and interference. In Anna Mauranen & Pekka Kujamäki (eds.), *Translation Universals: Do They Exist?*, 65–82. Amsterdam: Benjamins.

Mikhailov, Mikhail & Robert Cooper. 2016. *Corpus Linguistics for Contrastive and Translation Studies*. Oxon: Routledge.

Newman, John & Sally Rice. 2001. English SIT, STAND and LIE in large and small corpora. *ICAME Journal* 25. 109–133.

Oostdijk, Nelleke. 2000. The Spoken Dutch Corpus: Overview and first evaluation. In Maria Gravilidou, George Carayannis, Stella Markantonatou, Stelios Piperidis & Gregory Stainhaouer (eds.), *Proceedings of the Second International Conference on Language Resources and Evaluation*, 887–894. Paris: ELRA.

Plevoets, Koen & Bart Defrancq. 2016. The effect of informational load on disfluencies in interpreting: A corpus-based regression analysis. *Translation and Interpreting Studies* 11 (2). 202–224.

Plevoets, Koen & Bart Defrancq. 2018. Over-uh-load, filled pauses in compounds as a signal of cognitive load. In Claudio Bendazzoli, Mariachiara Russo & Bart Defrancq (eds.), *Making way in corpus-based interpreting studies*, 43–64. Singapore: Springer.

Sandrelli, Annalisa & Claudio Bendazzoli. 2005. Lexical patterns in simultaneous interpreting: A preliminary investigation of EPIC (European Parliament Interpreting Corpus). *The Corpus Linguistics Conference Series 1* http://goo.gl/53glY5 (Accessed 2 April 2018).

Schjoldager, Anne. 1995. An exploratory Study of translational norms in simultaneous interpreting: Methodological reflections. *Hermes, Journal of Linguistics* 14. 65–87.

Seeber, Kilian. 2011. Cognitive load in simultaneous interpreting: Existing theories – new models. *Interpreting*, 13 (2). 176–204.

Setton, Robin. 2011. Corpus-based interpretation studies: Reflections and prospects. In Alet Kruger, Kim Wallmach & Jeremy Munday (eds.), *Corpus-Based Translation Studies: Research and Applications*, 282–306. London/New York: Continuum.

Teubert, Wolfgang. 1996. Comparable or parallel corpora? *International Journal of Lexicography* 9. 238–264.

Tóth, Andrea. 2011. Speech disfluencies in simultaneous interpreting: a mirror on cognitive processes. *SKASE Journal of Translation and Interpretation* 5 (2). 23–31.

Toury, Gideon. 1995. *Descriptive translation studies and beyond*. Amsterdam: John Benjamins.

Viberg, Åke. 2013. Posture verbs: a multilingual contrastive study. *Languages in Contrast* 13 (2). 139–169.

Tom Bossuyt and Torsten Leuschner
WH-ever in German, Dutch and English: a contrastive study showcasing the *ConverGENTiecorpus*

Abstract: The present paper investigates the English irrelevance particle *-ever* and its functional equivalents *immer/auch* in German and *(dan) ook* in Dutch with regard to their distributional patterns and functional motivations, using data from the small-scale, multilingual, comparative *ConverGENTiecorpus* in conjunction with larger, non-comparable, monolingual corpora. An overview of the corpora, the search queries and the methods of analysis is provided first. The distributional and combinatorial patterns of irrelevance particles in two types of irrelevance constructions are presented, focusing on Dutch and German, and the present-day dynamics of irrelevance marking are discussed through the differences and similarities of the language-specific particles, including some peculiarities of the much less variable English *WH-ever* paradigm. A survey of the further grammaticalization of *whatever* and *however* and its German and Dutch equivalents is also provided. The results suggest that the synchronic state of the irrelevance-marking subsystems in English, German and Dutch represents snapshots of a long-term grammaticalization process. While this process is nearly complete in English, in German it is not only incomplete but appears to have lost its former directionality. Although signs of grammaticalization are weakest in Dutch *W ... ook*, Dutch *W dan ook* shows the highest degree of specialization of all irrelevance-marking combinations in the set. English *WH-ever* is much less versatile, with two notable exceptions: the freestanding discourse marker *whatever* and the concessive/contrastive conjunctional adverb and discourse marker *however*.

Keywords: irrelevance particles, grammaticalization, comparative corpora, multilingual corpora, ConverGENTiecorpus

1 Introduction

The present paper is part of a functional-typological research project on the expression of irrelevance in the Germanic languages. More specifically, it is one in a series of studies investigating so-called "irrelevance particles" like English *-ever* and its functional equivalents *immer/auch* in German and *(dan) ook* in Dutch with regard to their emergent distributional patterns and functional motivations (Bossuyt 2016; Bossuyt, De Cuypere, and Leuschner 2018; Bossuyt forthc.). The main environment in which such particles occur is a type of complex sentence construction known as "universal concessive conditional" (henceforth: UCC):

(1) a. English: *What**ever** you do, I support your decision.*
b. German: *Was **immer** du **auch** tust, ich unterstütze deine Entscheidung.*
    'Whatever you do, I support your decision.'
c. Dutch: *Wat je **ook** doet, ik steun je beslissing.*
    'Whatever you do, I support your decision.'

Complex sentences as in (1) resemble prototypical *if*-conditionals in expressing a conditional relationship $p \rightarrow q$. The difference is that the protasis in UCCs expresses a multiplicity of antecedent values $\{p_1, p_2, p_3, ...\}$, including a contextually extreme condition p_n under which one would normally expect $\neg q$ rather than q to be true (König 1986: 231–234). For example, under a condition p_n like *If you commit a serious crime*, one would not expect *I support your decision* (=q) to be true. While there are thus good reasons for the label "concessive conditionals", the common epithet "universal" is a slight misnomer given that the semantics of UCC protases are more reminiscent of a "free-choice" quantifier like positive-polarity *any* than of a typical universal quantifier like *every* or *all* (König and Eisenberg 1984: 315). The quantificational effect of the protasis allows the recipient to check the truth value of the consequent q under a randomly selected condition p_x (König 1986: 231; cf. the classic analysis of free-choice quantification in Vendler 1967). Under a Heimian analysis of indefinite NPs (Heim 1982), the *WH*-word expresses a variable in the open proposition p_x. The function of the irrelevance particle is to preempt existential closure of the variable, forcing the free-choice effect of the protasis and thus the "deconditionalization" (Zaefferer 1991) of q with respect to any conceivable antecedent condition.

According to Haspelmath and König (1998: 609), irrelevance particles in the protasis are cross-linguistically the main strategy for the free-choice-based expression of irrelevance. They either follow the *WH*-phrase immediately or occur "clause-internally", i.e. further to the right in the subordinate clause. English *-ever* as in (2) is of the former type, whereas Dutch *(dan) ook* '(then) also' as in (3) seems to belong to the latter:

(2) *What**ever** you do, do it with all of your heart* (COCA, NEWS)

(3) a. *Wat je **ook** probeert, alles lukt.* (WR-P-P-G-0000169195)
 'Whatever you try, everything works out.'
 b. *Wat je **dan ook** probeert, de reactie is altijd: that's not right.* (WR-P-P-H-0000024281)
 'Whatever you try, the reaction is always: that's not right.'

However, *(dan) ook* occasionally occurs further to the left before non-pronominal subjects. In such cases, it is adjacent to the *W*-pronoun and thus more reminiscent of *-ever*:

(4) a. *Wat **ook** de oorzaak is, Smith Island ligt nu nog maar een centimeter of dertig boven zeeniveau.*
 (WR-P-P-B-0000000235)
 'Whatever the cause is, Smith Island is now only about thirty centimeters above sea level.'
 b. *Wat **dan ook** de oorzaak is, leg de zieke met de voeten omhoog en zorg dat hij voldoende lucht krijgt.* (WR-P-P-H-0000061428)
 'Whatever the cause is, lay down the sick person with their feet up and make sure they get enough air.'

German is even more complex in this regard, as it has irrelevance particles of both types, viz. right-leaning *auch* 'also', a cognate of Dutch *ook*, and left-leaning *immer* 'ever', a partial cognate of English *-ever* (Leuschner 1996). Both *auch* and *immer* may occur alone or in combination and in different positions (cf. Bossuyt, De Cuypere, and Leuschner 2018):

(5) a. *Was **auch** dein Unglück sei, du mußt es tragen.* (HMP09/JAN.02505)
 'Whatever your misfortune is, you have to bear it.'
 b. *Was du **auch** siehst, du siehst nie alles.* (M03/NOV.79556)
 'Whatever you see, you never see everything.'
 c. *Doch was **immer** sein Ziel war – dorthin kam er nicht mehr.* (K97/JAN.04569)
 'But whatever his goal was – he did not make it that far.'
 d. *Was er **immer** sagt – George W. Bush zahlt für die Fehler, die er und seine Regierung im Vorfeld des Irak-Abenteuers begangen haben.* (RHZ06/MAR.23289)
 'Whatever he says – George W. Bush pays for the mistakes he and his government made prior to the Iraq-adventure.'

e. *Was auch **immer** Ihr vorhabt, Luana, ich bleibe an Eurer Seite!* (DIV/APS.00001)
'Whatever you are planning to do, Luana, I will continue to back you!'
f. *Was Maurice **auch immer** getan hat, Jonas wird da nichts damit zu tun haben.* (A08/AUG.06990)
'Whatever Maurice has done, Jonas probably has nothing to do with it.'
g. *Was **immer auch** Sie für sich als Vorbereitung wählen, ich wünsche Ihnen noch eine gute Adventszeit und ein gesegnetes Weihnachtsfest.* (RHZ96/DEZ.14165)
'Whatever you choose as a preparation for yourself, I wish you a good Advent season and a blessed Christmas.'
h. *Frau von Fürstenberg, was **immer** Sie die Journalisten auch fragen, in Ihren Antworten taucht meistens Ihre Mutter auf.* (WWO13/MAI.00083)
'Lady von Fürstenberg, whatever journalists ask you, your mother usually pops up in your answers.'
i. *Was man **immer auch** davon halten mag, die Häufigkeit von UFO-Sichtungen scheint in Woronesch ein publiziertes Phänomen zu sein.* (WDD11/W56.77761)
'Whatever one may think of it, the frequency of UFO sightings appears to be a much-reported phenomenon in Voronezh.'

The combination *auch immer* as shown in (5e) is the preferred option in irrelevance-based discourse markers (e.g. *Doch was auch immer: …*), disjunctive general extenders (e.g. *… oder was auch immer*) and indefinite pronouns (e.g. *Krieg gegen wen auch immer*), which we call "secondary" irrelevance constructions in order to distinguish them from the "primary" irrelevance constructions illustrated in (5). The former are an onward grammaticalization from the latter and will be introduced separately in Section 2.3 below, examples (10)–(12).

For our investigation to be informed by functional typology (see Siemund 2018 for a recent exposition with a focus on English) means that it is set in a line of comparative linguistic research concerned with the patterns, limits and motivations of variation in language, both cross-linguistically and language-internally ("micro-typology"; cf. König 2012). In functional typology, broad typological investigations based on large-scale language samples (e.g. Haspelmath and König 1998 on concessive conditionals in 42 European languages) are often supplemented with in-depth contrastive studies, which have in recent years drawn increasingly on the qualitative and/or quantitative analysis of corpus data (see e.g. Defrancq 2010 on universal concessive conditionals in English and French; cf. also Hilpert 2008 on future tenses in Germanic, inter alia). In the present study, we expand on this tradition by including data from the English, German, and Dutch components of the *ConverGENTiecorpus*, a multilingual comparable corpus which was compiled at Ghent University in 2015 and is here and in Bossuyt (forthc.) employed for the first time in an investigation of the three languages in focus. As is often the case with comparable corpora, however, the language-specific components of the *ConverGENTiecorpus* are rather small (cf. below), and suitable parallel or translation corpora to complement it are lacking altogether. The data from the *ConverGENTiecorpus* are therefore supplemented with data from larger, monolingual reference corpora for each of the three languages in question (for more details, cf. below). This procedure is different from the methodology advocated in e.g., Johansson (2007), but it allows us to achieve two purposes at once: (1) to reveal the synchronic (and ultimately diachronic) dynamics of emergent irrelevance marking by means of *-ever, immer/auch*, and *(dan) ook* in English, German, and Dutch, and (2) to compare the data drawn from both types of corpora and reflect on the respective merits of the comparable *ConverGENTiecorpus* and the monolingual reference corpora (cf. Conclusion).

Although closely related to several other recent studies of irrelevance particles, the present paper nevertheless offers some added value of its own. While Bossuyt, De Cuypere, and Leuschner (2018) is about German only, covering irrelevance particles with *was* 'what' and *wer* 'who' (including its inflectional forms), the present paper shares with Bossuyt (forthc.) a broad trilingual coverage of all *WH*-words in the *ConverGENTiecorpus*, with an in-depth focus on 'what' and 'who' in the large monolingual corpora. However, whereas Bossuyt (forthc.) provides a detailed survey of the quantitative results and statistical patterns, the present paper specifically highlights the contribution of the *ConverGENTiecorpus*, and care has been taken to cite different examples throughout. Together with the small-scale pilot study by Bossuyt (2016) on irrelevance particles with *was* in German only, all four papers constitute extended semi-replications of a seminal study by Leuschner (2000), which was based on just 104 tokens of *immer/auch* with all *W*-words of German. The fact that Bossuyt, De Cuypere, and Leuschner (2018) is based on 23,299 tokens from German despite its more narrow coverage of just *was* and *wer* (including inflectional forms) is a measure of the enormous progress made in the meantime, as is the fact that the present paper and Bossuyt (forthc.) are based on 38,748 tokens from three languages in total (including concessive *however*, cf. further below).

Section 2 provides an overview of the corpora used, the design of the search queries, and the methods of analysis. The distributional and combinatorial patterns of irrelevance particles in two types of irrelevance constructions, viz. subordinate clauses as seen above in (1) and elliptically reduced constructions (cf. below), are presented in Section 3, focusing on Dutch and German. Section 4 discusses the present-day dynamics of irrelevance marking through the differences and similarities of the language-specific particles, including some peculiarities of the much less variable English *WH-ever* paradigm. The further grammaticalization of *whatever* and *however* compared to their German and Dutch equivalents is surveyed in Section 5. A summary of the results and future directions is provided in Section 6.

2 Methodology

2.1 Corpora

As mentioned above, the present paper combines data from large, monolingual corpora with data from the smaller, but more comparable multilingual *ConverGENTiecorpus*. The following monolingual corpora were used:

- The *Deutsches Referenzkorpus* (henceforth: *DeReKo*), hosted at the Institute for German Language (IDS) in Mannheim, is the main reference corpus for contemporary written Standard German. It contains approximately 42 billion tokens (as of February 3rd, 2018),[1] of which ca. 9.2 billion are publicly accessible in the so-called "Archiv W" (as of August 3rd, 2018).[2] "Archiv W" consists of a large variety of text types, mostly printed news media from Germany, Austria, and the German-speaking part of Switzerland, but also various other non-fiction genres and some fiction. Articles and discussions from Wikipedia as well as parliamentary minutes have been added since 2014 (Kupietz and Lüngen 2014).
- The BYU corpora are probably the most widely used online corpora of English.[3] This study combines data from the *COCA* (560 million tokens of US-American English, 1990–2017), *Strathy Corpus* (50 million tokens of Canadian English, 1970s–2000s), *Wikipedia Corpus* (1.9 billion tokens, 2012–2013), and *Hansard Corpus* (1.6 billion tokens of British parliamentary minutes, 1803–2005), with data from the *BNC* (100 million tokens of British English, 1980s–1993), which is not part of the BYU corpora but is searchable via the BYU interface. The English corpora used in the present investigation contain over 4.2 billion tokens in total.

---

[1] http://www1.ids-mannheim.de/kl/projekte/korpora.html, last accessed March 20th, 2019.
[2] https://www.ids-mannheim.de/cosmas2/projekt/referenz/archive.html, last accessed March 20th, 2019.
[3] The BYU corpora can be accessed at https://corpus.byu.edu/, last accessed March 20th, 2019.

- The *SoNaR* corpus is a 500-million-word reference corpus of contemporary written Dutch.[4] It consists of both conventional printed media (e.g. newspapers) and online text types (e.g. tweets, blogs, chat conversations) and is balanced between Dutch and Flemish (Oostdijk et al. 2013).

The *ConverGENTiecorpus* is a multilingual comparable corpus that was compiled at Ghent University in 2015.[5] It consists of seven monolingual subcorpora in English, Dutch, German, French, Spanish, Portuguese, and Italian, which all adhere to the same sampling frame and each contain approximately 1.5 million tokens, distributed over a wide variety of non-translated text genres as specified in Table 1.

Table 1: Structure and content of the ConverGENTiecorpus.

register	sub-register	text types (exhaustive)
literary prose, post-1980 [300,000 words]	fiction [200,000 words]	novels, short stories
	non-fiction [100,000 words]	– essays – (auto)biographies (no travel)
journalistic texts [450,000 words]	news articles [300,000 words]	domestic and foreign news, economics, culture (no sports)
	comment articles [150,000 words]	editorials, columns, background
instructive texts [300,000 words]	manuals [100,000 words]	– machines/appliances (major firms) – software, web applications – administrative procedures
	legislative texts [100,000 words]	– school regulations – laws
	contracts [100,000 words]	– sales contracts – leases
corporate communication [150,000 words]	press texts [100,000 words]	– annual reports (governments, firms) – newsletters – press releases – mission statements
	promotional texts [50,000 words]	– tourist guides, tourism websites – product presentations

---

4 The *SoNaR* corpus can be easily consulted via the *OpenSoNaR* web interface at http://opensonar.inl.nl/, last accessed March 20th, 2019.

5 Cf. http://research.flw.ugent.be/en/projects/convergentiecorpus, last accessed March 20th, 2019. The corpus is non-copyright-cleared and only available internally.

Table 1 (continued)

register	sub-register		text types (exhaustive)
scientific prose [300,000]	academic texts [150,000 words]	humanities [75,000 words]	Ph.D. theses
		sciences [75,000 words]	Ph.D. theses
	popularizing texts [150,000 words]	humanities [75,000 words]	books [37,500 words] articles [37,500 words]
		sciences [75,000 words]	books [37,500 words] articles [37,500 words]

2.2 Search queries

The subcorpora of the *ConverGENTiecorpus* were searched with AntConc for every *WH*-word in the respective language, as in Leuschner's (2000) original study on German. For the German and Dutch data, the distance operator between the *WH*-word and the irrelevance particle was increased until there were no longer any new hits, and eventually set at 5 words; in English, distance is not an issue because *-ever* is invariably univerbated with the *WH*-word. A total of 1,853 tokens were exported from the subcorpora for further manual analysis (cf. below), of which 321 are from German, 292 from Dutch, and the remaining 1,240 from English. This large figure is due to concessive *however*. However is responsible for 956 (=77.1%) of the 1,240 English tokens, yet just 17 out of the 956 (=1.78%) are concessive-conditional. The remaining 939 are concessive rather than concessive-conditional and will be discussed separately below (Section 5). Adding the 17 concessive-conditional *however*-tokens to the 284 (=1,240 – 956) tokens with WH-*ever* words other than *however*, we arrive at 301 concessive-conditional WH-*ever* tokens that were exported for manual analysis from the English part of the *ConverGENTiecorpus*. It is this figure which is cited in Table 2 below alongside the corresponding figures for German (321) and Dutch (292).

In contrast to the broad coverage of WH-*ever* words including *however* that were exported from the *ConverGENTiecorpus*, the search queries for the monolingual corpora were limited to the *WH*-words for 'what' and 'who' (including inflectional forms, if applicable, e.g. *whom*), thus maximizing coverage for a few central *WH*-words. While this sacrifices direct cross-corpus comparability, its effects are likely to be limited and calculable (cf. Section 3.2.1 below on

Table 2: Overview of corpora and tokens – totals and per language.

–	totals	German	Dutch	English
comparable corpus (no. of words accessible)	–	ConverGENTiecorpus (1.5m per language)		
WH-words	–	all	all	all
initial samples: total tokens exported	1,853	321	292	301 (excl. concessive *however*)
final samples: valid tokens (% of total)	563 (=61.60%)	91 (=28.35%)	171 (=58.56%)	301 (=100%)
monolingual corpora (no. of words accessible)	–	*DeReKo* (9.2b)	*SoNaR* (500m)	*BYU*, *BNC* (4.2b)
WH-words	–	wer, wessen, wem, wen, was	wie, wiens, wat	who, whom, what
initial samples: total tokens exported	89,359	53,732	30,985	4,642
final samples: valid tokens (% of total)	37,246 (=41,68%)	23,299 (=43.36%)	9,305 (=30.03%)	4,642 (=100%)
total tokens exported	90,273	54,053	31,277	4,943
total valid tokens (% of total exported)	37,809 (=41.88%)	23,390 (=43.27%)	9,476 (=30.30%)	4,943 (=100%)

the ratio of instances of *immer* in field II between *DeReKo* and the *ConverGEN-Tiecorpus*).

For the monolingual German data, Leuschner's (2000) conclusions on the positional tendencies of *immer* and *auch* were taken into account in the design of the search queries. For *auch*, a distance operator of 4 yielded the best balance between precision and recall. For *immer*, only instances with the irrelevance particle immediately after the *W*-word were initially included. A later stage included search strings in which the *W*-word was immediately followed by a 3rd person pronominal subject (i.e. *er* 'he', *es* 'it', *sie* 'she', *das* 'this, that', *dies* 'this', *man* 'one') which was in turn immediately followed by *immer* (e.g. *was sie immer*). An exception is *wessen*, which can modify nouns (e.g. *wessen Buch* 'whose book') and therefore had the distance operator set to 3 with *immer* and 4 with *auch*. In total, 53,732 instances were exported for manual analysis (cf. below).

For the monolingual Dutch data, the queries were designed to resemble those for *auch* in *DeReKo*, i.e. search queries allowed a distance of 4 from the W-word (*wat* 'what', *wie* 'who', *wiens* 'whose') to, and including, the irrelevance particle *ook*. A total of 30,985 instances were exported for manual analysis.

For the monolingual English data, search queries for *whatever*, *whoever*, *whomever*, and *whosever* were conducted separately in each of the above-mentioned corpora, resulting in a total of 4,642 tokens being exported. The possessive form *whoever's* had to be excluded from the search because the query resulted almost exclusively in tokens of *whoever* followed by the contracted form of *is*. Specifying *whoever* as a noun (_n*), WH-pronoun (_pnq*) or possessive determiner (_app*) did not lead to improved results.

The need for manual analysis as alluded to above is due to the functional ambiguity of German *immer* and *auch* and of Dutch *ook* (but not English *-ever*).[6] *Immer* can also be a temporal adverb (6), while *auch* resp. *ook* can also be focus particles (7)–(8):

(6) #*Was **immer** bleiben wird, ist mein Code civil.* (Z10/FEB.00579)
 'What will always remain, is my Code civil.'

(7) #*Was es heute jedoch **auch** häufiger gibt, sind Mütter, die arbeiten.* (BRZ08/SEP.06321)
 'However, what is nowadays more common as well are working mothers.'

(8) #*Wat **ook** speciaal zal zijn, is het Japanse theehuisje van S. D.* (WR-P-P-G-0000666221)
 'What will be special, too, is S. D.'s Japanese tea cottage.'

Due to such ambiguities and the need to remove duplicates from the exported *DeReKo*, *SoNaR*, and *ConverGENTiecorpus* samples, the final samples contain fewer tokens than were initially exported. We call these remaining tokens "valid". In total, 90,273 tokens were exported from all the corpora (comparable and monolingual combined), of which 37,809 (41.88%) are valid (38,748 or 42.92% when including concessive *however*). Table 2 summarizes the amount of exported and valid instances per corpus and per language.

---

6 Cf., however, briefly Section 4.2.1 below on non-quantificational *ever* in interrogatives, which is excluded from the present investigation.

2.3 Structure types

All the valid tokens do not necessarily represent prototypical UCCs as initially exemplified in (1)–(5). A considerable amount of instances, in particular in the German and English samples, are so-called "non-specific free relatives" (henceforth: NFRs):

(9) Was **immer** er finden konnte, hat er verschlungen. (A97/JUL.14948)
    'Whatever he could find, he devoured.'

The most notable difference between UCCs and NFRs is the syntactic function of the subordinate clause: UCCs are loose adjuncts, whereas NFRs are embedded arguments, e.g. direct object in (9). However, the commonality that both subordinate clause types are introduced by a *WH*-word followed by one or more irrelevance particles and that they both convey a similar quantificational effect is more important for the present study than said syntactic differences. UCCs and NFRs will therefore be jointly referred to as *primary irrelevance constructions* (cf. below on *secondary* irrelevance constructions).

The positional and combinatorial variability of irrelevance particles in primary irrelevance constructions in Dutch and German was analyzed using Leuschner's (2000) version of the Topological Field Model familiar from German syntax (cf. Wöllstein 2014), as shown in Table 3a.

Table 3a: Leuschner's adaptation of the Topological Field Model for primary irrelevance constructions in which the *W*-word is not the subject of the subordinate clause, exemplified by the subordinate clause in (1b).

–	pre-field	left bracket	mid-field			right bracket	post-field
–	W	–	II	S	IV	V	–
(1b)	was	–	immer	du	auch	tust	–

The model assumes the classic bracket structure of German clauses in the version for verb-late subordinate clauses. The finite verb fills the right-hand part of the bracket (i.e. the "right bracket"), the left-hand part of the bracket (i.e. the "left bracket") remains empty, and the *W*-word occupies the "pre-field" just before the left bracket (cf. Wöllstein 2014: 32–37). The field between the two parts of the bracket is the mid-field. Leuschner (2000: 345) subdivides the mid-field into a field S for the subject of the subordinate clause and two fields that can be occupied by irrelevance particles: field II to the left of S and field IV to the right of S.

In Table 3a, the *W*-word is not the subject of the subordinate clause. If it is the subject, the mid-field does not need to be split up and is therefore re-labeled "II/IV" (Leuschner 2000: 345–346), as seen in Table 3b.

Table 3b: Leuschner's (2000: 346) adaptation of the Topological Field Model for primary irrelevance constructions in which the *W*-word is also the subject of the subordinate clause, exemplified by (10), taken from the *SoNaR* corpus (translation: 'whoever governs Iraq').

–	pre-field	left bracket	mid-field	right bracket	post-field
–	W	–	II/IV	V	–
(10)	wie	–	Irak *dan ook*	bestuurt	–

While the majority of tokens fit the structure in Tables 3a or 3b, a considerable minority do not fit either (8,975 out of 32,866 instances = 27.31% of the total "valid" samples for German and Dutch). This is because they represent a different type of structure, which is historically derived from primary irrelevance constructions by ellipsis and grammaticalization (Haspelmath 1997: 139; Hoeksema 2012: 100–103 for Dutch; Breindl 2014: 980–981 for German; Brinton 2017: 268–282 for English) and occurs in three distinct functions. The relevant constructional varieties will henceforth be labeled *secondary irrelevance constructions*:

(11) discourse markers
 a. [...] *we'd just talk about, I don't know* [pause] **whatever**, *she'd probably agree with everything I said as well because that's what Catherine's like* (BNC KP4 S_conv)
 b. *Luister, als ik meer ...* **wat dan ook**, *je weet wel ...* (WR-P-E-G-0000010571)
 'if I [had] more ... whatever, you know what I mean ...'
 c. *Doch* **was auch immer**: *Ein Crash ist trotzdem jederzeit möglich.* (SOZ06/OKT.04291)
 'But whatever: a crash is nevertheless a possibility at all times.'

(12) disjunctive general extenders
 a. *we are Rutgers rather than Stanford, Pittsburgh or* **whatever** (EN_Sci_Aca_0076)
 b. *Een bedrijf moet niet iets ondernemen omdat het Belgisch of Frans of* **wat dan ook** *is. Dat vind ik een slechte motivering.* (WR-P-P-G-0000175623)
 'A company should not undertake something because it is Belgian or French or whatever. I find that a bad motivation.'

    c. *Hey also ich weis* [sic] *nicht von wo du bist. aber ich bin einer von denen so genannten „deutsch Belgier"* [sic] *oder „belgisch Deutschen" oder **was auch immer**.* (WDD11/D01.18693)
    'Hey, so I do not know where you are from, but I am one of those so-called "German Belgians" or "Belgian Germans" or whatever.'

(13) indefinite pronouns
    a. *The casual revolution has meant that many of us can wear jeans to the office with **whatever** on top.* (EN_Jou_New_0080)
    b. *Wij wensen geen oorlog met **wie dan ook**.* (WR-P-P-G-0000587476)
    'We do not wish war against anyone (lit. whoever)'.
    c. *Sicher ist es richtig, dass die weit überwiegende Mehrheit unseres Volkes keinen Krieg gegen **wen auch immer** will.* (U02/SEP.02251)
    'It is definitely right that the vast majority of our people do not want a war against anyone (lit.: whoever.ACC).'

Irrelevance-based indefinite pronouns are especially common in Dutch, where they represent a relatively recent development since ca. 1800 (Hoeksema 2012: 102). In German, they are marginal, while indefinite pronouns from the *any*-series (cf. Haspelmath 1997) are standardly used in English, as seen in the translations of (13b) and (13c).

3 Distributional and combinatorial patterns

This section presents the distributional patterns of irrelevance particles in the different corpora, discussing primary and secondary irrelevance constructions separately. Since English *-ever* is always univerbated with the *WH*-word, distributional patterns are not an issue in English, and the focus is therefore on Dutch and German. English irrelevance marking instead presents special characteristics of its own which are addressed partly in Section 4.2, partly in the separate Section 5.

3.1 The *ConverGENTiecorpus*

Table 4a shows the distribution of irrelevance particles in Dutch primary irrelevance constructions in the *ConverGENTiecorpus*. Table 4b shows the distribution of irrelevance particles in German primary constructions in this corpus.

An example of each sentence type is provided in (14) resp. (15). Note that the left bracket and the post-field, which are standardly unoccupied in subordinate clauses (cf. Section 2.3) and thus do not influence the distribution of the particles, are left out of this and all subsequent tables.

Table 4a: Distribution of irrelevance particles in Dutch primary irrelevance constructions in the *ConverGENTiecorpus*.

–	W	II	S	IV	V	raw freq.	rel. freq.
a.	W	–	S	ook	V	74	96.10%
b.	W	ook	S	–	V	3	3.90%
						77	100.00%

Table 4b: Distribution of irrelevance particles in German primary irrelevance constructions in the *ConverGENTiecorpus*.

–	W	II	S	IV	V	raw freq.	rel. freq.
a.	W	immer	S	–	V	22	44.90%
b.	W	auch immer	S	–	V	13	26.53%
c.	W	immer	S	auch	V	8	16.33%
d.	W	–	S	auch	V	6	12.24%
						49	100.00%

(14) a. *Welke nieuwe aanpak de VS **ook** kiezen, kondig aan dat de VS dat doen bij wijze van proef.* (NE_Jou_Com_1072)
'Whichever new approach the US choose, (please) announce that the US are doing so as a test.'

b. *Wie **ook** zijn medewerkers waren in de regering, [...], allen bewaren ze goede herinneringen aan hun vroegere 'baas'.* (NE_Lit_Non_1208)
'Whoever his co-workers in the government were, they all treasure good memories of their former "boss".'

(15) a. *Wo **immer** ich erschien, gab es plötzlich keinen Bedarf an Arbeitskräften.* (GE_Lit_Fic_0005)
'Wherever I showed up, there was suddenly no need for workers.'

b. *Dazu klinkten sie ihre gefährliche Fracht einfach aus – wo **auch immer** sie sich gerade befanden.* (GE_Sci_Pop_0476)
'To this end, they simply released their dangerous cargo – wherever they happened to be at the time.'

c. [...] *dann bleibe ich von Karmafolgen unbehelligt, wo **immer** ich **auch** sein mag, hier oder nach dem Tod.* (GE_Lit_Non_0729)
   '... then I will remain untroubled by karma, wherever I may be, here or after death.'
d. *Wo Forscher **auch** hinsehen, überall entdecken sie bisher unbekannte Arten.* (GE_Sci_Pop_0630)
   'Wherever scientists look, they discover previously unknown species everywhere.'

While Dutch primary irrelevance constructions in the *ConverGENTiecorpus* are almost exclusively marked in field IV (96.10%), this is only a minor option in the corresponding primary irrelevance constructions in German (12.24%). Instead, German prefers irrelevance marking in field II (71.43%). This is also reflected in the fact that there are more tokens in which both fields are occupied (=type c.; 16.33%) than where only field IV is occupied.

Note that Tables 4a and 4b only show irrelevance constructions in which the *W*-word is not the subject (cf. Table 3a above). The reason is that there are no tokens of the *W II/IV S*-pattern in the Dutch component of the *ConverGENTiecorpus*. This is partly due to the fact that tokens with Dutch *er*, as in *wat er ook gebeurt* 'whatever happens', were analyzed as instances of the *W II S IV V*-pattern. The German component contains only 7 tokens of the *W II/IV S*-pattern, of which 3 have *immer* (42.86%), 2 have *auch immer*, and 2 have *auch* (each 28.57%). Because the total number of tokens is so low, little can be said about them and they will therefore not be discussed separately.

The distributional patterns in secondary irrelevance particles in the *ConverGENTiecorpus* are given in Table 5a for Dutch and Table 5b for German.

Table 5a: Distribution of irrelevance particles in Dutch secondary irrelevance constructions in the *ConverGENTiecorpus*.

–	dan ook	ook	total
Raw freq.	55	38	93
Rel. freq.	59.14%	40.86%	100.00%

Whereas single particles like Dutch *ook* resp. German *immer* are most frequent in primary irrelevance constructions (cf. Tables 4a–4b above), *dan ook* and *auch immer* are more frequent in secondary irrelevance constructions, as shown by the b. and c. examples in (11)–(13) above. Both *dan ook* and *auch immer* are "closed" particle combinations in the terminology of Thurmair (1989: 290 on German

Table 5b: Distribution of irrelevance particles in German secondary irrelevance constructions in the *ConverGENTiecorpus*.

–	auch immer	immer	auch	total
raw freq.	26	6	3	35
rel. freq.	74.29%	17.14%	8.57%	100.00%

modal particles), i.e. no other constituent is allowed between the two components, which invariably occur side by side. Both have arguably been reanalyzed as complex particles in secondary irrelevance constructions, in which they now function as the prototypical "indefiniteness marker" to the *W*-stem (Bossuyt forthc., cf. Haspelmath 1997). By contrast, *immer* (...) *auch*, which does allow constituents between its components and thus qualifies as an "open" particle combination in the terminology of Thurmair (1989), does not occur in secondary constructions in the *ConverGENTiecorpus*.

3.2 *SoNaR* and *DeReKo*

3.2.1 Primary irrelevance constructions

Based on our manual analysis of the data as described above, Table 6a lists the distributional patterns of Dutch irrelevance particles in primary irrelevance constructions in which the *W*-word is not the subject of the subordinate clause. Each type is exemplified by an instance from the *SoNaR* corpus in (16).

Table 6a: Distribution of irrelevance particles in Dutch primary irrelevance constructions in which W ≠ S in the *SoNaR* corpus.

–	W	II	S	IV	V	raw freq.	rel. freq.
a.	W	–	S	ook	V	4,808	94.03%
b.	W	ook	S	–	V	169	3.31%
c.	W	–	S	dan ook	V	132	2.58%
d.	W	dan ook	S	–	V	4	0.08%
						5,113	100.00%

(16) a. *Wat ze* **ook** *met Saddam doen, het zal nooit genoeg zijn.* (WR-P-P-G-0000156353)
   'Whatever they do with Saddam, it will never be enough.'

b. *Wie **ook** de daders mogen zijn, ze moeten opgespoord, berecht en zeer zwaar bestraft worden.* (WR-P-E-A-0000552748)
'Whoever the perpetrators may be, they must be tracked down, brought to court and punished severely.'

c. *Alsof onze namen ook maar iets onthullen. Dan ga je vanzelf denken aan zoiets als 'een ware naam', wat dat **dan ook** mag betekenen.* (WR-P-P-G-0000004169)
'As if our names reveal anything at all. It automatically makes you think of something like "a true name", whatever that may mean.'

d. *Wat **dan ook** de oorzaak van de ramp is, de verzekering van de eigenaar dekt de schade.* (WR-P-P-H-0000107290)
'Whatever is the cause of the disaster, the owner's insurance covers the damage.'

In contrast to the Dutch *ConverGENTiecorpus* data, the *SoNaR* data in Table 6a show that the single particle *ook*, although clearly more frequent (97.34%) than *dan ook*, is not the sole possibility in primary irrelevance constructions. Both *ook* and *dan ook* show a strong preference for field IV (4,808/4,977 = 96.60% occurrences of *ook* in field IV; 132/136 = 97.06% occurrences of *dan ook* in field IV) rather than field II (169/4,977 = 3.40% for *ook*; 4/136 = 2.94% for *dan ook*).

Ook is more frequent, too, than *dan ook* in primary irrelevance constructions in which the *W*-word is simultaneously the subject of the subordinate clause, as can be seen in Table 6b. An example from the *SoNaR* corpus is given for each type in (17).

Table 6b: Distribution of irrelevance particles in Dutch primary irrelevance constructions in which W = S in the *SoNaR* corpus.

	W	II/IV	V	raw freq.	rel. freq.
a.	W	ook	V	257	94.83%
b.	W	dan ook	V	14	5.17%
				271	100.00%

(17) a. *Wie de verkiezingen **ook** wint, de nieuwe premier van Israel krijgt het moeilijk.* (WS-U-E-A 0000022039)
'Whoever wins the elections, Israel's new prime minister will have a tough time.'

b. *En wie **dan ook** in november wordt gekozen, de verhoudingen in de internationale politiek zullen er aanmerkelijk door veranderen.* (WR-P-P-H-0000157358)
'And whoever is elected in November, it will change the balance in international politics substantially.'

Table 6c shows the distribution of German irrelevance particles in primary constructions in which the *W*-word is not the subject of its clause. (18) provides an example from *DeReKo* for each type.

Table 6c: Distribution of irrelevance particles in German primary irrelevance constructions in which W ≠ S in *DeReKo*.

–	W	II	S	IV	V	raw freq.	rel. freq.
a.	W	*immer*	S	–	V	6,075	67.05%
b.	W	*immer*	S	*auch*	V	1,005	11.09%
c.	W	*auch immer*	S	–	V	954	10.53%
d.	W	–	S	*auch*	V	647	7.14%
e.	W	–	S	*auch immer*	V	154	1.70%
f.	W	*immer auch*	S	–	V	149	1.64%
g.	W	–	S	*immer*	V	39	0.43%
h.	W	*auch*	S	–	V	22	0.24%
i.	W	–	S	*immer auch*	V	15	0.17%
						9,060	100.00%

(18) a. *Komm, komm, wer **immer** du bist.* (BRZ06/MAI.16559)
'Come, come, whoever you are.'
b. *Weil Macht so eine herrliche Sache ist. Und alle klatschen, was **immer** man **auch** sagt.* (A99/MAR.17500)
'Because power is such a splendid thing. And everyone applauds, whatever you say.'
c. *Was **auch immer** du tust, tue es klug und bedenke das Ende.* (M13/JUL.01194)
'Whatever you do, do it thoughtfully and consider the end.'
d. *Wer oder was man **auch** ist; man blamiert sich doch nur.* (DIV/SAW.00001)
'Whoever or whatever you are; all you do is embarrass yourself.'

e. *Beide haben gut trainiert. Für wen ich mich **auch immer** entscheide, es ist keine Entscheidung gegen den anderen.* (BRZ06/FEB.10416)
'They both trained well. Whomever I choose, it is not a choice against the other one.'
f. *Was **immer auch** die Vereinten Nationen beschließen, wir jedenfalls werden uns nicht beteiligen.* (PBT/W15.00004)
'Whatever the United Nations decide, as far as we are concerned we won't get involved.'
g. *Was es **immer** war, es ist ihnen unter die Haut gegangen.* (E96/JUL.17159)
'Whatever it was, it got under their skin.'
h. *Von wem **auch** die Formulierung stammen mag: das juristische Studium endet mit der ersten Staatsprüfung.* (WDD11/F11.05937)
'To whomever the phrasing may be due: law studies end with the first state exam.'
i. *Heute lähmt mich immer mehr die Einsicht, dass man, was man **immer auch** sagt, gar nicht ernst genommen wird.* (SOZ13/FEB.04565)
'Nowadays, the knowledge that, whatever you say, you do not get taken seriously at all, paralyzes me more and more.'

DeReKo data in Table 6c confirm that German prefers irrelevance marking in field II rather than field IV. In 90.56% of all tokens, field II is occupied by irrelevance particles. Even without the *W immer S auch V*-pattern, in which discontinuous *immer ... auch* straddles field S (type b.), the proportion of irrelevance particles exclusively occupying field II is still 79.47%. The *DeReKo* data also confirm the positional preferences of each particle or particle combination individually in the *ConverGENTiecorpus*, viz. left-leaning *immer* and *auch immer*, discontinuous *immer ... auch*, and right-leaning *auch*. All these particles or particle combinations also occur in dispreferred positions (types e.–i.), albeit rarely (4.18% combined).

A notable difference between *DeReKo* and the *ConverGENTiecorpus*, however, is the respective proportion of *immer* in field II. *Immer* is the most frequent particle in both corpora, yet its proportion is much higher in *DeReKo* (6,075/9,060 = 67.05%) than in the *ConverGENTiecorpus* (22/49 = 44.90%); both are higher than in the *Mannheimer Korpus* as used by Leuschner (2000: 348; 34/92 = 39.96%). A one-tailed two-proportions Z-test suggests that the proportion of *immer* in the *DeReKo* deviates significantly from both the *ConverGENTiecorpus* and the *Mannheimer Korpus* ($p < 0.0001$ for both). This continues to hold after Bonferroni correction is applied to counteract alpha inflation when comparing more than two samples. The *ConverGENTiecorpus* and the *Mannheimer Korpus*, on the other hand, do not deviate significantly from each other ($p = 0.18$). The difference in *immer*-proportions is likely to be the combined result of several factors:

- The design of the search queries (cf. Section 2.2) may cause *immer* to be somewhat overrepresented in the *DeReKo* sample. Since larger distance operators make recall less precise, searches for *W immer*, with *immer* immediately following the *W*-word, contain far fewer invalid instances than queries for *W ... auch* with a larger distance operator of 4, which inevitably yield more "noise". Depending on the *W*-word, the proportion of invalid instances with *auch* varies between ca. 30% and ca. 85%, whereas this proportion is only 12% to 20% with *immer*.
- Text genre may play a role, too: *DeReKo* has a much higher proportion of written press texts than the more balanced *ConverGENTiecorpus* and *Mannheimer Korpus*. Further research should investigate the use of irrelevance particles across genres and registers.
- The proportional differences between the *Mannheimer Korpus* (which was compiled in the 1960s) and *DeReKo* (which consists primarily of texts from the 1990s–2010s) may reflect a micro-diachronic increase of *immer*. Since the emergence of irrelevance marking is said to show a lack of directionality (Leuschner 2006), any such directionality would be remarkable indeed. It is unlikely, however, given that the *ConverGENTiecorpus* consists of texts from the 1990s until 2015 much like *DeReKo*, yet shows a distribution more similar to the *Mannheimer Korpus*.

However, the most elementary and probably strongest factor causing *immer*-proportions to differ is probably the restriction of the *DeReKo* sample to *was* and *wer* (incl. inflectional forms, cf. above). In contrast to the samples taken from the *Mannheimer Korpus* (by Leuschner 2000) and the *ConverGENTiecorpus*, the *DeReKo*-sample thus excludes most *W*-words that can form complex *W*-phrases such as *welch-* (e.g. *welches Auto* 'which car') and *wie* (e.g. *wie schön* 'how nice'). Since *immer* systematically fails to occur in complex *W*-phrases (cf. below), the restriction to *was* and *wer* in the present *DeReKo* sample thus translates directly into a bias against complex *W*-phrases in the *DeReKo* data and in favor of *immer* in the resulting statistics. The skewing can be tested indirectly by applying a corresponding restriction to the *ConverGENTiecorpus* data: once *wie* and *welch-* clauses are excluded from Table 4b, the ratio of *immer* in these clauses increases to 54.05% (n = 20 out of 37), nearly halving the difference between the original 44.90% and the *DeReKo*'s 67.05%. This difference, however, remains statistically significant (one-tailed two-proportions Z-test: p = 0.047). At the moment, the only *W*-word in the *DeReKo*-sample which favors complex phrases is *wessen* 'whose'; it is also, however, by far the least frequent *W*-word in the sample (n = 252 or 1.08%). A more reliable reduction of the present pro-*immer* bias is likely to occur as *welch-* is added to the *DeReKo* sample at a future stage of the investigation.

The combinatorial patterns found in Table 6c are relatively similar to those in primary irrelevance constructions in which the *W*-word is also the subject of the subordinate clause, as can be seen in Table 6d. An example from *DeReKo* for each type can be found in (19); in order to focus on the differences in the particles, we deliberately present examples containing the same verb, viz. *passieren* 'happen'.

Table 6d: Distribution of irrelevance particles in German primary irrelevance constructions in which W = S in *DeReKo*.

	W	II/IV	V	raw freq.	rel. freq.
a.	W	*Immer*	V	7,299	78.37%
b.	W	*auch immer*	V	1,295	13.91%
c.	W	*immer auch*	V	640	6.87%
d.	W	*auch*	V	79	0.85%
				9,313	100.00%

(19) a. *Was **immer** passiert, ich habe heute etwas zu feiern.* (A10/SEP.03856)
 'Whatever happens, I have something to celebrate today.'
 b. *Ich lasse mich einfach treiben. Was **auch immer** passiert.* (SOZ12/JAN.03892)
 'I just allow myself to drift. Whatever happens.'
 c. *Was **immer auch** passiert, gib bitte keinem von uns eine gelbe Karte.* (T04/MAI.28737)
 'Whatever happens, please do not give any one of us a yellow card.'
 d. *Es geht schon wieder weiter, was **auch** passiert.* (NON12/DEZ.09866)
 'Things will move on, whatever happens.'

The order of the most frequent irrelevance particle(s) in Table 6d reflects the four most frequent options in Table 6c, viz. *immer* > *immer* (...) *auch* > *auch immer* > *auch*, to a great extent. The only difference is that *auch immer* is in second place in W II/IV V-clauses (Table 6d), while *immer* (...) *auch* holds this position in W II S IV V-clauses (Table 6c).

There are, however, clear proportional differences in *W II/IV V*-clauses between *DeReKo* on the one hand and the *ConverGENTiecorpus* and *Mannheimer Korpus* on the other hand, much like with the *W II S IV V*-clauses discussed earlier. These may well be explained by the same factors, but this is impossible to ascertain because the samples from the *ConverGENTiecorpus* and the *Mannheimer Korpus* are so small as to rule out testing for statistical significance.

3.2.2 Secondary irrelevance constructions

Tables 7a and 7b show the distributional patterns of irrelevance particles in secondary constructions for Dutch and German respectively.

Table 7a: Distribution of irrelevance particles in Dutch secondary irrelevance constructions in *SoNaR*.

–	dan ook	ook	total
raw freq.	2,946	975	3,921
rel. freq.	75.13%	24.87%	100.00%

Table 7b: Distribution of irrelevance particles in German secondary irrelevance constructions in *DeReKo*.

–	auch immer	immer	auch	immer auch	total
raw freq.	4,485	399	24	18	4,926
rel. freq.	91.05%	8.10%	0.49%	0.37%	100.00%

As in the *ConverGENTiecorpus*, *dan ook* and *auch immer* are the most frequent options in Tables 7a and 7b, respectively. *Dan ook* is even more frequent in *SoNaR* than in the *ConverGENTiecorpus*, but a considerable minority of all tokens still has *ook* alone. These are mostly confined to a specific functional niche, viz. use with indefinite pronouns in comparative constructions:

(20)   Räikkönen heeft meer dan **wie ook** het potentieel om wereldkampioen te worden. (WR-P-P-G-0000179920)
       'Räikkönen has more potential than anyone (lit. whoever) to become world champion.'

The fact that speakers tend to use *dan ook* less often in comparative constructions may well be due to *horror aequi*: as *dan* happens to be homonymous with the comparative particle *dan* 'than' in Dutch, speakers tend to prefer *dan wie ook* over *dan wie dan ook* 'than anyone' (Hoeksema 2012: 96–100). This is borne out by our data at a ratio of nearly 5:1: out of 856 *dan W (dan) ook* comparatives in the *SoNaR* sample, only 183 (21.38%) are *dan W dan ook*, the remaining 673 (78.62%) are *dan W ook*.

No corresponding homonymy exists in German, and so it is not surprising that the proportion of *auch immer* in *DeReKo* (91.05%) is significantly higher than that of *dan ook* in *SoNaR* (75.13%) according to a two-tailed two-proportions

Z-test (p < 0.0001). In fact, *auch immer* sharply prefers secondary over primary constructions: 4,485 out of 6,889 *auch immer*-tokens occur in secondary irrelevance constructions (65.10%). All other options are marginal: just 2.89% of *immer* (399/13,813), 3.31% of *auch* (24/772) and 0.99% of *immer* (...) *auch* (18/1,827) are in secondary constructions.

4 The dynamics of irrelevance marking

This section highlights the present-day dynamics of irrelevance marking through a cross-linguistic conspectus of the three languages. Since German has the most complex patterns of irrelevance marking, it serves as the pivot in the first part, being compared first with Dutch and then with English, followed by a closer look at some peculiarities of the English *WH-ever* paradigm.

4.1 A cross-linguistic conspectus

4.1.1 German and Dutch

Not only are German *auch* and Dutch *ook* cognates (cf. Section 1), they also show a strikingly similar preference for field IV: *auch* occupies this field in 96.71% of all its tokens in *DeReKo*, and *ook* does so in 96.60% of all its tokens in *SoNaR*. Their distributional tendencies are statistically identical both in the large, monolingual corpora and in the components of the *ConverGENTiecorpus*: $\chi^2 < 0.001$; df = 1; p > 0.99 for *DeReKo* and *SoNaR*; Fischer's Exact Test: p > 0.99 for the *ConverGENTiecorpus*. This rightward tendency helps disambiguate the irrelevance particle from the homonymous focus particles: *auch* and *ook* are more likely to be misinterpreted as focus particles at the beginning of the subordinate clause, i.e. in field II, whereas they are more likely to be read as irrelevance particles further towards the verb phrase at the end of the subordinate clause, i.e. in field IV (Leuschner 2000: 354 on German *auch*).

Occupation of field II by *auch/ook* is both less frequent and more restricted. While *auch* and *ook* can occupy field II before lexical subjects, they cannot do so before pronominal subjects (Leuschner 2000: 350 on *auch*):

(21) a. Wer **auch** Präsident sei, die Präsidialgewalt muss so diktatorisch als möglich organisiert sein. (Z13/MAI.00324)
 'Whoever may be president, the presidential power must be organized as dictatorially as possible.'

b. *Wat **ook** de uitslag is, ik wil met een goed gevoel van het terrein komen.* (WR-P-P-G-0000566885)
   'Whatever the result is, I want to come off the pitch with a positive feeling.'

(22) a. **Wer **auch** er ist, […]*   'Whoever he is …'
     b. **Wat **ook** dat is, […]*   'Whatever that is …'

The base position of lexical subjects in German (and Dutch) is [Spec, VP] (Lenerz 1993: 118), i.e. the right periphery of the mid-field or field IV. Since this is also the preferred position of *auch/ook*, the irrelevance particle *auch* or *ook* may scramble to field II. Pronominal subjects, by contrast, generally prefer the left periphery of the mid-field, i.e. field II, which is also known as "Wackernagel's position" (Lenerz 1993: 117–118). Hence *auch* resp. *ook* are always able to occupy their preferred field IV if the subject of the subordinate clause is a pronoun.

The "closed" particle combinations *auch immer* and *dan ook*, too, share similarities. Both are the most frequent option in secondary constructions in their respective language. However, *dan ook* is less predominant in Dutch (59.14% of secondary constructions in the *ConverGENTiecorpus*, 75.13% in *SoNaR*) than *auch immer* is in German (74.29% of secondary constructions in the *ConverGENTiecorpus*, 95.10% in *DeReKo*), and this may well be due to *horror aequi* (cf. above) as *dan W dan ook* is avoided in comparatives (just 21.38%, cf. above). Both *auch immer* and *dan ook* specialize for secondary constructions, but whereas *dan ook* occurs exclusively in secondary constructions in the *ConverGENTiecorpus* and nearly exclusively in secondary constructions in *SoNaR* (95.16% of all instances), *auch immer* occurs in both primary and secondary constructions.

4.1.2 German and English

German *immer* almost exclusively occurs in field II (99.36% in *DeReKo*). Pronominal subjects compete with *immer* for this position, but occupy it only in very few instances (0.64% in *DeReKo*). Lexical subjects never occur before *immer*.

(23) *[…] und was man **immer** letztlich sagen oder denken mag, jedenfalls gilt der Satz: „Was wir verstehen und lieben, versteht und liebt auch uns."* (NZZ06/MAI.04751)
   'Whatever one may ultimately say or think, in any case the following sentence applies: "what we understand and love, understands and loves us too."'

(24) *Was die Menschen **immer** sagen oder denken mögen [...]
'Whatever people may say or think ...'

As mentioned above (cf. Section 1), English -*ever* and German *immer* are partial cognates, and historically they displayed the same leftward tendency. *Ever* moved left faster and further than *immer*, however, becoming attached to the *WH*-word in the process. Both *ever* and *immer* were initially employed in field IV to strengthen the quantificational effect of the original irrelevance markers 'so ... so' (e.g. Old English *swa hwycl swa* 'whoever, whichever', Old High German *so wér so* 'whoever'). In the process of replacing 'so ... so', they then began occupying field II more and more often (Leuschner 2006: 134–146; cf. Jäger 2018: 83–91, 472–484 on German). While the last instances of irrelevance-marking *ever* in field IV seem to be attested around the 12th century, the positional tendencies of the German irrelevance particles did not emerge clearly until well into the 19th century (Leuschner 2006: 136). Indeed the grammaticalization of irrelevance-marking *immer* is still far from complete, as shown by the fact that *immer* on its own is problematic in the German counterparts of complex *WH*-phrases like *whichever book*. In such cases, field II starts after the noun in primary constructions, hence the complex *W*-phrase cannot be split (*welches *immer Buch* 'whichever book'). *Immer* is unattested after such complex *W*-phrases (*welches Buch *immer*). Instead, *auch immer* is the only attested option in field II (*welches Buch auch immer*). Alternatively, *auch* or *auch immer* can be used in field IV. However, *immer* is marginally attested as sole irrelevance marker in secondary constructions in which *welch-* 'which' modifies a complex *W*-phrase (n = 4 in the *ConverGENTiecorpus*, compared to *auch immer*: n = 23):

(25) *Die Untervermietung oder sonstige Weitergabe des Mietgegenstandes an natürliche oder juristische Personen in **welcher Form immer** ist dem Mieter untersagt.* (GE_Ins_Con_0104)
'Subleasing or other forms of transfer of the rented property to natural or legal persons in whichever form is prohibited to the tenant.'

Similarly, *immer* alone is marginally attested in secondary constructions in which *wessen* 'whose' modifies a noun (n = 3 in *DeReKo*). In primary constructions, on the other hand, *auch immer* is used in field II when *wessen* modifies a noun, cf. in (26a), not *immer* (**wessen Idee immer*). On the other hand, *immer* is unproblematic when *wessen* functions as a genitive object and no constituents intervene between it and the irrelevance particle, cf. (26b):

(26) a. *Wessen Idee **auch immer** es war [...]* (NON10/MAI.21163)
 'Whoever's idea it was'
 b. *Wessen **immer** man die BR-Redakteure bezichtigen mag [...]* (NUZ07/JUN.00202)
 'Whatever one may accuse the BR-editors of'

Restrictions like these encourage the use of other irrelevance particles like *auch immer*, preventing *immer* from becoming the sole irrelevance particle in German and attaining univerbation with the *W*-word, as happened in English centuries ago.

4.2 The English WH-*ever* paradigm

4.2.1 Layering

Compared with German and Dutch, irrelevance marking in English is special in two respects: it has just one irrelevance particle, viz. *-ever*, and this particle only occurs in one fixed position, viz. in univerbation with the *WH*-pronoun. Nevertheless, the *WH-ever* paradigm shows a few well-known quirks and defects that are reflected in our corpus data. One way to think of the quirks is in terms of layering (Hopper 1991), as vestiges of older, West Germanic irrelevance marking co-exist with more recent, language-specific *-ever* in a way unparalleled in German and Dutch. The older layer is represented by the residual presence of the ancient irrelevance particle *-so-*, which occurred without *-ever* in archaicizing style until ca. 1900 (e.g. *whoso* 'whoever', Jespersen 1949: 65). It was thenceforth used invariably in combination with *-ever*, if at all, and survives in the *ConverGENTiecorpus* (except for one instance, cf. below) only in the intensifying postnominal polarity item *whatsoever*, as in *any/no idea whatsoever* 'any/no idea at all', which we excluded from our investigation. Otherwise *-soever* is now so marginal as to be attested only in archaic (e.g. biblical) usage even in the large BYU collection of corpora:

(27) *The Gospel tells us this clearly: **Whosoever** will save his life shall lose it: and whosoever will lose his life for my sake shall find it.* (COCA, FIC)

Another intensifier that was excluded from our investigation is non-quantificational *ever* as sometimes attested in *WH*-interrogatives:

(28) a. [W]hatever *happened to those 30 million jobs President Bush said we could expect back in 1988?* (COCA, SPOK)b.
   b. *"Whyever did you buy it then?" said Clara.* (cited in Defrancq 2010: 393)

This variety of *-ever* represents a further step in the grammaticalization of the more recent *-ever* layer of irrelevance marking. This process first led the original quantificational, temporal adverb *aefre* to develop into the quantificational, but no longer temporal irrelevance particle *-ever* and thence into an intensifier that is neither temporal nor quantificational and no longer involved in irrelevance-marking. It is known in parts of the literature as the "floating" (as opposed to bound) *ever* because its normative spelling is separate from the *WH*-word ("What ever happened to ... ?"). However, as often predicted (cf. Leuschner 2006: 36–37, fn. 10, with references), it regularly fails to "float". As seen in (28a–b), this makes it formally indistinguishable from univerbated, quantificational *WH-ever*, which itself cannot occur in interrogatives. And as seen specifically in (28b), the result may well be *whyever*, whose quantificational version is often regarded as (near-)ungrammatical (cf. below).

4.2.2 Asymmetries

Another source of dynamics in English irrelevance marking is the use, or avoidance, of specific *WH*-pronouns in combination with *-ever*. Cases in point are *whose* and *whom*. *Whosever* is unattested in the *ConverGENTiecorpus* and has 17 attestations in the BYU-corpora, of which (29) is one:

(29) **Whosever** *fingerprints they are, they aren't hers.* (COCA, FIC)

Its replacement *whoever's* is not attested in the *ConverGENTiecorpus*, either, and was excluded from the BYU sample for practical reasons (cf. Section 2.2 above). *Whomever* is attested three times in the *ConverGENTiecorpus* (out of 1240 tokens = 0.24%), yet at 4,642 tokens (= 13.46%) turns out to be surprisingly frequent in the BYU-corpora. (30) is an example, while (31) represents the sole example of *whomsoever* in the *ConverGENTiecorpus*, not surprisingly from archaicizing style in fiction:

(30) *He'll choose* **whomever** *he decides to choose and that will be that.* (COCA, FIC)

(31) *I took the paper from his hand and read: TO* **WHOMSOEVER** *IT MAY CONCERN, I [...] DO MAKE THE FOLLOWING STATEMENT [...].* (EN_Lit_Fic_0010)

In line with the now commonly accepted use of *who* for *whom*, example (32) illustrates the use of *whoever* in potential *whomever* contexts:

(32) **Whoever** you meet, **whoever** you speak to, **whoever** you write to, ask yourself: "Is there any way I can help this person?" (BNC, EW5 W_commerce)

Especially in spoken usage, *whomever* is sometimes used hypercorrectly in *whoever*-contexts:

(33) a. *What I'm interested in is making sure that the transition,* **whomever** *is president, goes smoothly and we can get the things done we talked about.* (COCA, SPOK)
 b. *I don't have to look to my vice president, Joe Biden or* **whomever** *it may be and say, what do I do next?* (COCA, SPOK)

The high incidence of *whomever* in the BYU corpora is due to North American sources, as *whomever* has much higher scores per 1 million words in the COCA corpus (U.S., 1.67) and in the Strathy corpus (Canada, 1.04) than in the exclusively British BNC (0.27). Why North American English should be so *whomever*-rich is an intriguing matter that we cannot investigate here, but the corresponding normalized scores for the general Wikipedia corpus (0.40) shows that the skewing is indeed due to the North American corpora, especially from the U.S.

Another interesting empirical observation concerns the widely reported absence of **whyever* from the *WH-ever* paradigm (see Leuschner 2006: 41; Oppliger 2018: 276). Leuschner (2006: 41) asserts that *whyever* is invariably replaced with *for whatever reason* or similar periphrastic alternatives in his data. Corresponding asymmetries and substitutes are reported by Defrancq (2010) for French and Spanish, and by Citko (2010) for Polish. The replacement of *whyever* with *for whatever reason* is confirmed by the *ConverGENTiecorpus*, which invariably has the latter, or a similar substitute, instead of the former:

(34) a. *Interestingly, for* **whatever** *reason, I think there is quite a lot more optimism on this side of the Atlantic.* (EN_Sci_Aca_0076)
 b. *And it will sell tiny berths on the craft to people who, for* **whatever** *reason, want to send small objects to the Moon.* (EN_Sci_Pop_0041)

The Dutch equivalent *waarom ... ook* is also invariably replaced with a 'whatever'-based alternative in primary constructions (Leuschner 2006: 43), but can occur in secondary constructions. German *warum immer/auch* occasionally occurs in both primary and secondary constructions:

(35) *Eigenlijk, wordt het jullie verboden contact te hebben met Simone op elk moment, **waarom dan ook**.* (WR-P-E-G-0000010976)
'In actual fact you.PL are being forbidden to have contact with Simone at any time, for whatever reason (lit. 'whyever').'

(36) *"Wir haben verdient verloren", schimpfte Christian Heidel, "weil wir in der ersten Hälfte, **warum auch immer**, im Tiefschlaf waren."* (RHZ02/NOV.18438)
'"We deserved to lose," grumbled C.H., "because we were in a deep sleep, for whatever reason (lit. 'whyever'), during the second half [of the match]".'

(37) ***Warum auch immer** man es tut[,] die Hände duften noch lange nach Jasmin.* (Z07/MAI.00455)
'For whatever reason (lit. 'whyever') one does it, one's hands smell of jasmine for a long time afterwards.'

Note that we searched *DeReKo* and *SoNaR* specifically for 'whyever'-equivalents in order to provide a comparison with English, even though the respective W-words *warum* and *waarom* were not among our original search targets in these corpora (cf. Section 2.2). For this reason, no statistics are provided.

Why users should avoid 'whyever' to a greater or lesser extent across languages is an intriguing issue that we cannot pursue in detail here. It appears to be linked to, though not identical with, the fact that irrelevance of reason seems rarely to be raised openly in discourse, as suggested by the low incidence of primary irrelevance constructions. Part of the motivation may well be that reasons are cognitively so complex as to be hard to conceptualize in terms of partially ordered scalar, sets (as Defrancq 2010: 372 seems to suggest); in languages with highly grammaticalized WH-'ever' paradigms, this may well translate into the exclusion of 'whyever' from the paradigm. Nevertheless, *whyever* is occasionally attested (Defrancq 2010: 372), as confirmed by a search in the BYU corpora which turns up three genuine attestations of *whyever* in the *COCA*-corpus. Two are in primary constructions, one is in a secondary, discourse marker-type construction:

(38) a. **Whoever** *the builders were and **whyever** they left, they could have left an influence on our own evolving cultures.* (COCA, FIC)
b. *Why had that broke her loose? **Whyever**, Riley knew he must trust her.* (COCA, FIC)
c. *What are you talking about? **Whyever** Rand went, it was nothing you did or didn't do.* (COCA, FIC)

In (38a) and (38b) we may assume priming from preceding *whoever* and *why*, respectively. Whether *whyever* may be primed by the preceding interrogatives in (38b) and (38c) remains a matter of speculation.

5 Further grammaticalization: 'whatever' and 'however'

As a consequence of the high degree of grammaticalization of *-ever* (cf. above), there are some onward developments to report from the English WH-*ever* paradigm involving *whatever* and *however* which have some interesting, if partly limited, parallels in German and Dutch.

As illustrated above discourse markers meaning 'whatever' exist in all three languages. However, English *whatever* not only appears to be more frequent in this function than Dutch *wat dan ook* and German *was auch immer*, but is also different in that it regularly occurs as a "freestanding" discourse marker, i.e. "as a sentence in its own right" (Brinton 2017: 268, 272, with more references).

(39) *Some people are calling her husband a cradle robber, pervert, a dirty old man.* **Whatever.** *Those are just words. We know the truth.* (COCA, SPOK)

The discourse marker *whatever* is typically used to bring a given discourse topic to an end (Brinton 2017: 271). In our data it primarily signals the speaker's reluctance to carry their argument further without conceding the other party a fair point. The following example is from an American talk show in which several family members and/or friends accuse Jamie of being unable or unwilling to take care of her two-year-old child:

(40) JAMIE: *Oh, now – now why – now why do you have guardianship?*
 CAROL: *Because you didn't want to be a mother anymore.*
 JAMIE: *Oh,* **whatever. Whatever.** (COCA, SPOK)

Freestanding *whatever* seems to be a uniquely English phenomenon: the *DeReKo* sample does not contain any instances of *was auch immer* as a discourse marker and while freestanding *wat dan ook* is found occasionally in the *SoNaR* corpus, nearly all instances are in subtitles of English films and thus probably primed by the source language. Moreover, German and Dutch irrelevance constructions do not seem to be used in a sequence-closing function very often, although they do appear as resumptive discourse markers, especially with 'how' (Leuschner 2000: 352 on German).

This takes us to *however* and a comparison with *wie dan ook* and *wie auch immer*. As mentioned in Section 2.2, no less than 956 out of 1,240 instances (or 77.10%) of all WH-*ever* tokens in the English component of the *ConverGEN-Tiecorpus* represent *however*. Out of these 956, only 10 (1.05%) represent primary irrelevance constructions as in (41a), and a mere 7 (0.73%) represent secondary constructions as in (41b).

(41) a. *[…] although the "youth" in the title is a misnomer – you can join,* **however** *old you are.* (EN_Cor_Pro_0071)
      b. *And any encouragement,* **however** *minor, will be treated as a justification for sending you everything else that the writer has ever written.* (En_Lit_Non_0028)

The vast majority (939 instances or 98.22%) instead consists of cases in which *however* is concessive, often shading into simple contrast (Leuschner 2013: 57), representing an onward development from secondary irrelevance constructions. 'However'-subordinators are cross-linguistically known to break ranks with their original concessive-conditional paradigm and develop separate concessive readings (König 1985: 274), e.g. Latin *quamvis* (Leuschner 2008) and Middle High German *swie* (De Groodt 2002). Yet both are subordinators and thus distinct from concessive *however*, which has instead evolved into a conjunctional adverb which can occur in sentence-initial, sentence-medial, or sentence-final position:

(42) a. *[N]early four out of five (78%) 14 to 16 year olds say they would consider a career in a STEM-related industry.* **However***, more than half (51%) say they know little or nothing about the types of jobs that are on offer.* (EN_Cor_Pre_0069)
      b. *We know this was in his briefing note for yesterday's appearance because it was photographed in the back of his car. But he didn't mention it. He did,* **however***, blandly assert that women in the City who take six months off to have children find themselves "behind the rest of the pack and earning less money."* (EN_Jou_New_0084)
      c. *[…] short-term real and nominal interest rates increased. Long-term real rates remained low,* **however***.* (EN_Jou_Com_0078)

However in (42a–c) profiles its proposition against another, contextually salient proposition, often taking as its starting-point a potential conclusion from the latter, e.g. that a short-term increase of interest rates could indicate a long-term increase (cf. König and Siemund 2000 for an analysis of concessivity along these lines). Compare this with the quantificational, concessive-conditional semantics of German *wie auch immer* and Dutch *hoe dan ook*, which generalize over a set of propositions implicit in the prior discourse. What is salient in this case is not a single proposition but an unresolved issue or debate, and the statement with *wie auch immer* or *hoe dan ook* rejects the need to pick a true proposition from the (sometimes binary) set for the discourse to continue:

(43) a. *Offenbar lässt sich nicht eindeutig klären, was sich nun wirklich abgespielt hat – **wie auch immer** – Maria Hofers "Curriculum Vitae" ist jedenfalls zu entnehmen, dass sie noch während des Krieges wieder Konzerte und Vorträge gegeben habe.* (GE_Lit_Non_0731)
'Apparently it is not entirely clear what really happened – anyway – in any case it can be derived from Maria Hofer's curriculum vitae that she was playing concerts and giving talks again while the war was still going on.'

b. *Heeft de Braziliaanse justitie dat geld dan onrechtmatig geïnd? **Hoe dan ook**, het geld zou jaren na de uitlevering van Haemers aan ons land via diplomatieke druk teruggegeven zijn.* (NE_Jou_Com_1105)
'Has the Brazilian judiciary collected that money unlawfully, then? Either way, the money would have been returned under diplomatic pressure years after Haemers' extradition to our country.'

Note that *wie auch immer* and *hoe dan ook* function as discourse markers in these examples. There are clearly two distinct grammaticalization paths at work: one leads from 'however' primary irrelevance constructions to 'however' discourse markers, the other leads from 'however' primary irrelevance constructions to 'however' adverbs which may then – as has indeed happened in English – be re-interpreted as concessive/contrastive.

This latter path is reminiscent of Dutch *W dan ook* indefinite pronouns (cf. above), and it is not surprising that Dutch *hoe dan ook* 'however' shows evidence of the change towards a *however*-style adverb, though mostly (as yet) without the concessive/contrastive semantics. This is suggested by (44a) and (44b), where *hoe dan ook* occurs, respectively, sentence-medially and sentence-initially in the structural position immediately in front of the finite verb (the pre-field, known in German as the *Vorfeld*). In such contexts *hoe dan ook* takes scope at propositional level at most and is subject to the verb-second rule; in short, it functions as a sentential adverb rather than as a discourse marker. Although the vast majority of tokens are still concessive-conditional ('in any case') as in (44a), it is at this stage of the grammaticalization process that the reading may shift to purely concessive ('nevertheless') as in (44b):

(44) a. *Wat moet Kléber, die weet **hoe dan ook** verslagen te zijn, voor bijdrage leveren aan de snelheid van Reilhan?* (NE_Lit_Fic_0007)
'What can Kléber, who knows that he is beaten in any case, contribute to the speed of Reilhan?'
b. *Een doos met een tv-toestel stond op de speelplaats klaar om meegenomen te worden, maar daar hadden de inbrekers blijkbaar geen tijd meer voor. De tv stond een tijdlang in de regen. Gelukkig liep het toestel geen schade op. **Hoe dan ook** is de school lelijk ontriefd. Een exacte schatting van de geleden schade hebben we nog niet kunnen maken.* (WR-P-P-G-0000521591)
'A box with a television set stood in the playground, ready to be taken away, but apparently the thieves no longer had time for that. The television stood in the rain for a while. Fortunately the set did not suffer any damage. Nevertheless, the school was massively inconvenienced. We have as yet been unable to draw up a precise estimate of the damage.'

Although (44a) and (44b) do not by any means represent the complete usage patterns of *hoe dan ook*, they do suggest that purely concessive readings are still marginal with *hoe dan ook*. With German *wie auch immer* they are as yet unattested in our data.

6 Concluding remarks

The present study has documented and contrasted the distributional patterns of the irrelevance particles *-ever*, *immer/auch* and *(dan) ook* using data from the small-scale, multilingual comparative *ConverGENTiecorpus* in conjunction with larger, non-comparable, monolingual corpora. The results suggest that the synchronic state of the irrelevance-marking subsystems in English, German, and Dutch represents snapshots of a long-term grammaticalization process. While this process is nearly complete in English, in German it is not only incomplete but appears to have lost its former directionality, as *immer* has so far resisted univerbation with the W-word. The fact that *immer* does not, or, in some cases, only marginally combines with complex W-words or W-phrases seems to encourage the use and survival of *auch* and *auch immer* as alternatives to *immer* and to perpetuate the status of the *W immer/auch* paradigm as a long-term "building-site of grammaticalization" (Leuschner 2006). Finally, signs of grammaticalization are weakest in Dutch discontinuous *W ... ook*. Nonetheless *W ... ook* has been undergoing changes like the development of a distinct irrelevance-marking function for the erstwhile focus particle *ook* (cf. its German counterpart *auch*), the obligatorification of *ook* and the further development, by reanalysis, of a complex particle *dan ook* which specializes for secondary irrelevance constructions. Indeed Dutch *W dan ook* shows the highest degree of specialization of all irrelevance-marking combinations in the set, as it occurs almost exclusively in secondary constructions. German *W auch immer* also regularly occurs in secondary constructions, but barely as an indefinite pronoun. English *WH-ever*, on the other hand, is much less versatile in these contexts, mainly due to the systemic presence of *any*-pronouns, with the notable exception of freestanding *whatever* and the development of *however* into a concessive/contrastive conjunctional adverb.

With regard to methodology, our contribution highlights the strengths and weaknesses of comparable, if small, multilingual corpora like the *ConverGEN-Tiecorpus*. When such corpora are combined with large, monolingual corpora such as *DeReKo* or *SoNaR*, on the other hand, one gets the best of both worlds, as sufficiently large data sets can be extracted from the latter, while comparability is maintained between the language-specific components of the former. In this way, one can compare samples from different corpora in the same language and samples from comparable corpora in different languages. For instance, the fact that *auch* exclusively occupies field II in the small *ConverGENTiecorpus* is nuanced by its preference for field IV in the much larger *DeReKo*. *Auch* in the German component of the *ConverGENTiecorpus* can be compared with *ook* in the Dutch component, and the latter can in turn be cross-checked against the much larger *SoNaR* corpus.

Two methodological directions suggest themselves from here.[7] One starts from the observation that the procedure described above is rather labor-intensive. In our project, the searches in large monolingual corpora have so far been limited to queries with the *WH*-words for 'what' and 'who' (incl. inflectional forms, if applicable), maximizing coverage for a few central *WH*-words while partially sacrificing cross-corpus comparability. The alternative is to prioritize cross-corpus comparability by extracting sub-corpora from the monolingual corpora in such a way that coverage of all *WH*-words becomes manageable. If all *WH*-words can be included in the analysis of such a sub-corpus, the discrepancy in the ratio of

---

[7] We are grateful to an anonymous reviewer for suggestions in both directions, even if s/he may not necessarily agree with the use we are making of them.

instances of *immer* in field II between *DeReKo* and the *ConverGENTiecorpus* (cf. Section 3.2.1) may well diminish.

The other methodological direction leads away from large, monolingual corpora to a conjunction of comparable corpora with parallel or translation corpora, as suggested by Johansson (2007), Steiner, Hansen-Schirra and Neumann (2012), and others. Provided suitable translation corpora become available in the future, what is likely to matter above all in any such endeavor is size, as suggested by the partial failure of the *ConverGENTiecorpus* to reveal reliable distributional patterns or lend itself to statistical significance testing (e.g. with German clauses of the $W = S$ type, cf. Sections 3.1 and 3.2). Whatever the purpose of the investigation and the types of corpora used, it will be imperative for any multilingual corpus to be large enough to yield statistically viable results for a sufficiently wide range of linguistic phenomena that are likely to come under investigation in any given research context.

References

Bossuyt, Tom. 2016. Zur Distribution von Irrelevanzpartikeln in *was immer/auch-*Konstruktionen: Positionelle und kombinatorische Varianz im Deutschen Referenzkorpus. *Germanistische Mitteilungen* 42 (1). 45–70.

Bossuyt, Tom. forthc. Lice in the fur of our language: German irrelevance particles between Dutch and English. In Gunther De Vogelaer, Dietha Koster & Torsten Leuschner (eds.), *German and Dutch in contrast: Synchronic, diachronic and psycholinguistic perspectives*. Berlin & Boston: de Gruyter.

Bossuyt, Tom, Ludovic De Cuypere & Torsten Leuschner. 2018. Emergence phenomena in German *W- immer/auch-*subordinators. In Eric Fuß, Marek Konopka, Beata Trawiński & Ulrich H. Waßner (eds.), *Grammar and corpora 2016*, 97–120. Heidelberg: Heidelberg University Publishing.

Breindl, Eva. 2014. Irrelevanzkonditionale Konnektoren. In Eva Breindl, Anna Volodina & Ulrich H. Waßner (eds.), *Handbuch der deutschen Konnektoren: Semantik der deutschen Satzverknüpfer*, 964–1009. Berlin & New York: de Gruyter.

Brinton, Laurel J. 2017. *The evolution of pragmatic markers in English: Pathways of change*. Cambridge: Cambridge University Press.

Citko, Barbara. 2010. On the distribution of *-kolwiek* 'ever' in Polish Free Relatives. *Journal of Slavic Linguistics* 28 (2). 221–258.

De Groodt, Sarah. 2002. Reanalysis and the five problems of language change: A case study on the rise of concessive subordinators with *ob-* in Early Modern German. *Sprachtypologie und Universalienforschung* 55 (3). 277–288.

Defrancq, Bart. 2010. Contrastive corpus analysis of cross-linguistic asymmetries in concessive conditionals. In Richard Xiao (ed.), *Using corpora in contrastive and translation studies*, 363–395. Newcastle: Cambridge Scholars Publishing.

Haspelmath, Martin. 1997. *Indefinite pronouns*. Oxford: Oxford University Press.

Haspelmath, Martin & Ekkehard König. 1998. Concessive conditionals in the languages of Europe. In Johan van der Auwera (ed.), *Adverbial constructions in the languages of Europe*, 563–641. Berlin & New York: de Gruyter.
Heim, Irene R. 1982. *The semantics of definite and indefinite noun phrases.* Amherst: University of Massachusetts dissertation.
Hilpert, Martin. 2008. *Germanic future constructions: A usage-based approach to language change.* Amsterdam & Philadelphia: Benjamins.
Hoeksema, Jack. 2012. Wie dan ook, wat dan ook, etc. als free choice indefinites en negatief-polaire uitdrukkingen. *TABU* 40 (3). 89–109.
Hopper, Paul J. 1991. On some principles of grammaticization. In Elizabeth Traugott & Bernd Heine (eds.), *Approaches to grammaticalization*, 17–35. Amsterdam & Philadelphia: Benjamins.
Jäger, Agnes. 2018. *Vergleichskonstruktionen im Deutschen. Diachroner Wandel und synchrone Variation.* Berlin & Boston: de Gruyter.
Jespersen, Otto. 1949. *A Modern English grammar on historical principles. Part III: syntax, second volume.* Copenhagen: Munksgaard / London: Allen & Unwin.
Johansson, Stig. 2007. *Seeing through multilingual corpora: On the use of corpora in contrastive studies.* Amsterdam & Philadelphia: Benjamins.
König, Ekkehard. 1985. Where do concessives come from? On the development of concessive conditionals. In Jacek Fisiak (ed.), *Historical semantics – historical word-formation*, 263–282. Berlin: de Gruyter.
König, Ekkehard. 1986. Conditionals, concessive conditionals and concessives: Areas of contrast, overlap and neutralization. In Elizabeth Closs Traugott, Alice ter Meulen, Judy Snitzer Reilly & Charles A. Ferguson (eds.), *On conditionals*, 229–246. Cambridge: Cambridge University Press.
König, Ekkehard. 2012. Contrastive Linguistics and Language Comparison. In *Languages in Contrast* 12. 3–26.
König, Ekkehard & Peter Eisenberg. 1984. Zur Pragmatik von Konzessivsätzen. In Gerard Stickel (ed.), *Pragmatik in der Grammatik: Jahrbuch 1983 des Instituts für Deutsche Sprache*, 313–332. Düsseldorf: Schwann.
König, Ekkehard & Peter Siemund. 2000. Causal and concessive clauses: Formal and semantic relations. In Elizabeth Couper-Kuhlen & Bernd Kortmann (eds.), *Cause, condition, concession, contrast: Cognitive and discourse perspectives*, 341–360. Berlin & New York: de Gruyter.
Kupietz, Marc & Harald Lüngen. 2014. Recent developments in DeReKo. In Nicoletta Calzolari, Khalid Choukri, Thierry Declerck, Hrafn Loftsson, Bente Maegaard, Joseph Mariani, Asuncion Moreno, Jan Odijk & Stelios Piperidis (eds.), *Proceedings on the ninth International Conference on Language Resources and Evaluation*, 2378–2385. Reykjavík: ELRA.
Lenerz, Jürgen. 1993. Zu Syntax und Semantik deutscher Personalpronomina. In Marga Reis (ed.), *Wortstellung und Informationsstruktur*, 117–154. Tübingen: Niemeyer.
Leuschner, Torsten. 1996. *Ever* and universal quantifiers of time: Observations from some Germanic languages. *Language Sciences* 18. 469–484.
Leuschner, Torsten. 2000. ... *wo immer* es mir begegnet ... – *wo es auch sei.* Zur Distribution von 'Irrelevanzpartikeln' in Nebensätzen mit *W auch / immer. Deutsche Sprache* 28. 342–356.

Leuschner, Torsten. 2006. *Hypotaxis as building-site: The emergence and grammaticalization of concessive conditionals in English, German and Dutch*. Munich: Lincom.

Leuschner, Torsten. 2008. From speech-evocation to hypotaxis: The case of Latin *quamvis* 'although'. In Elena Seoane & María José López-Couso (eds.), *Theoretical and empirical issues in grammaticalization*, 231–252. Amsterdam & Philadelphia: Benjamins.

Leuschner, Torsten. 2013. Was Partikeln wohl (auch immer) mit Gleichgültigkeit zu tun haben: Funktionale und linguistikdidaktische Perspektiven. *Germanistische Mitteilungen* 39 (1). 37–62.

Oostdijk, Nelleke, Martin Reynaert, Véronique Hoste & Ineke Schuurman. 2013. The construction of a 500-million-word reference corpus of contemporary written Dutch. In Peter Spyns & Jan Odijk (eds.), *Essential speech and language technology for Dutch: Results by the STEVIN-programme*, 219–247. Berlin & Heidelberg: Springer.

Oppliger, Rahel. 2018. *Whatever the specific circumstances, …:* A Construction Grammar perspective of *wh-ever* clauses in English. In Elena Seoane, Carlos Acuña-Fariña & Ignacio Palacios-Martínez (eds.), *Subordination in English: Synchronic and diachronic perspectives*, 263–284. Berlin & Boston: de Gruyter.

Siemund, Peter. 2018. *Speech acts and clause types: English in a cross-linguistic context*. Oxford: Oxford University Press.

Steiner, Erich, Silvia Hansen-Schirra & Stella Neumann. 2012. *Cross-linguistic corpora for the study of translations: Insights from the language pair English-German*. Berlin & Boston: de Gruyter.

Thurmair, Maria. 1989. *Modalpartikeln und ihre Kombinationen*. Tübingen: Niemeyer.

Vendler, Zeno. 1967. *Linguistics in philosophy*. Ithaca & London: Cornell University Press.

Wöllstein, Angelika. 2014. *Topologisches Satzmodell*. 2nd edition. Heidelberg: Winter.

Zaefferer, Dietmar. 1991. Conditionals and unconditionals: Cross-linguistic and logical aspects. In Dietmar Zaefferer (ed.), *Semantic universals and universal semantics*, 210–236. Berlin & New York: Floris.

Olli O. Silvennoinen
Comparing corrective constructions: Contrastive negation in parallel and monolingual data

Abstract: This article is a quantitative study of contrastive negation in 11 European languages, using parallel and monolingual corpus data. Contrastive negation refers to expressions that combine a negated and an affirmed element so that the affirmed element replaces the negated one. In the languages being studied, there is typically a large number of constructions that fall under this definition. One of the ways of expressing contrastive negation is through a corrective conjunction (e.g. *but* in *not once but twice*). In this paper, constructions with a corrective conjunction are compared to other contrastive negation constructions by constructing a probabilistic semantic map on the basis of a multivariate statistical analysis of parallel corpus data using multiple correspondence analysis (MCA). The data comes from the Europarl corpus, which represents the proceedings of the European Parliament. The results suggest that in this discourse type, corrective conjunctions are associated with additive contrasts (e.g. *not only once but twice*), while constructions without an additive are mostly replacive (e.g. *It's not you, it's me*). However, some languages also display correctives that are more weakly or not at all associated with additivity. The results display an areal and genealogical core of Germanic languages and French, with the other Romance and the Finnic languages studied deviating from this core in various ways. The results are evaluated against monolingual corpus data from the Finnish component of the same corpus. Overall, the study suggests that parallel corpora are a promising source of data even for a grammatical domain in which the languages studied have seemingly analogous constructions.

Keywords: contrastive negation, corrective conjunctions, Europarl, multiple correspondence analysis, parallel corpus

---

Note: I wish to thank the following people for their help in a pilot study of this article: Pieter Claes, Andrei Călin Dumitrescu, Agata Dominowska, Lotta Jalava, Maarit Kallio, Katharina Ruuska, Ksenia Shagal and Max Wahlström. I also express my gratitude to Matti Miestamo, Minna Palander-Collin, Jouni Rostila and Johan van der Auwera as well as two anonymous referees for their comments on previous versions of this paper. All remaining mistakes are naturally my responsibility.

Olli O. Silvennoinen, School of Humanities, English Language and Culture, University of Eastern Finland, Joensuu, Finland

https://doi.org/10.1515/9783110682588-008

1 Introduction

Corpus data are increasingly used in cross-linguistic studies involving more than two languages. While even early typological studies made occasional use of corpora (Greenberg 1966), corpus-based cross-linguistic studies cannot be said to have taken off until the past two decades or so, largely because of the advent of readily usable parallel corpora (see e.g. Cysouw and Wälchli 2007; Aijmer 2008), i.e. corpora made up of translated texts aligned at the level of words, sentences or paragraphs. These have ranged from small-scale datasets comprising only a handful of languages to "massively parallel texts" (Cysouw and Wälchli 2007: 95) such as parts of the Bible, which exist in thousands of languages. An alternative to parallel corpora is comparable corpora, i.e. monolingual corpora of the same genre in different languages.

Both monolingual and parallel corpus data are used in this study to examine contrastive negation. Empirically, the goal of the paper is to achieve an account of how contrastive negation is expressed in 11 European national languages, belonging to the Germanic, Romance and Uralic groups. Methodologically, the goal is to see the extent to which parallel and monolingual data can be used to answer research questions and how monolingual corpus data can be used to validate (or disconfirm) the results of parallel corpus analysis.

Contrastive negation refers to expressions that combine a negated and an affirmed element so that the affirmed element replaces the negated element in the discourse universe (see Gates Jr. and Seright 1967; McCawley 1991; Silvennoinen 2017). Consider examples (1)–(3):

(1) *Shaken, not stirred*

(2) *Not once but twice*

(3) *It's not you – it's me.*

As the examples show, in English, there are many ways of expressing contrastive negation. These examples by no means exhaust the constructional options that English offers, but they do enable us to chart the terrain in three respects. First, the negative may follow the affirmative (as in (1)) or it may precede it (as in (2) and (3)). Second, the constructions may be asyndetic (i.e. without conjunction, as in (1) and (3)) or syndetic (i.e. with a conjunction, in this case a corrective use of *but*, as in (2)). Third, the contrasted elements may take the form of clauses (as in (3)) or sub-clausal units (as in (1) and (2)). Similarly, in other European languages, contrastive negation may appear in several constructional formats.

The approach to contrastive negation adopted in this paper draws on contrastive linguistics and typology, but with a particular focus on European languages. Especially when comparing more than two languages, cross-linguistic studies have traditionally relied on reference grammars and elicitation as sources of data. The latter typically includes questionnaires encompassing a list of translation sentences, for which a verbatim equivalent is requested from an expert or a native speaker of the language.[1] For several reasons, these data types are not ideal for contrastive negation. First, they are most appropriate for domains that are marked overtly with a dedicated or semi-dedicated marker, while contrastive negation may be expressed without any explicit marking as a sequence of an affirmative and a negated element. Second, the variation among contrastive negation constructions is multifactorial and gradient (Silvennoinen 2018), and this type of syntactic variation is unlikely to be found in reference grammars or questionnaire data. Third, the stable parts of contrastive negation constructions are negators, focus particles and conjunctions. These are typically polysemous items, for which contrastive negation constructions are usually only one, often marginal syntactic environment among several. In other words, contrastive negation often does not have a dedicated marker, which means that it may not be covered even in an extensive reference grammar. For these reasons, a cross-linguistic study of contrastive negation requires corpus data.

Compared with reference grammars and elicitation, the traditional data sources of typology, parallel corpora buttressed with multivariate statistical techniques have enabled typologists and others interested in comparing more than two or three languages at a time to take intralinguistic variation into account better, especially in the case of grammatical domains in which the variation even within a single language is multifactorial (e.g. Levshina 2016a). Parallel corpora have been used successfully to investigate domains as diverse as epistemic modality (van der Auwera, Schalley and Nuyts 2005), motion verbs (Wälchli and Cysouw 2012) and causatives (Levshina 2015; 2016a).

Despite their potential, parallel corpora raise questions, and with reason. Lewis (2006: 140–141), who studies English *on the contrary* and its French counterpart *au contraire* in comparable corpora of political discourse, offers a number of arguments against parallel data: translations differ in how faithfully they aim to represent the source text, they frequently vary in quality, they may represent translationese rather than the studied language itself, and they may follow the

---

[1] Some cross-linguistic have also used non-linguistic elicitation materials, such as picture books, to create comparable corpora (Berman and Slobin 1994). These kinds of datasets have similar advantages and drawbacks as other types of comparable corpus data, an issue to which I return below.

structural choices of the source text in ways that untranslated texts do not. A counter-point to this is the feasibility of studying many languages: while there have been some studies using comparable corpora even in typology (e.g. Stivers et al. 2009), these tend to be multi-author studies requiring extensive resources. By contrast, a parallel corpus gives the researcher access to many languages relatively cheaply. While a parallel corpus study might not give an ideal picture of an individual language, this is not the point: a broader comparative perspective necessarily has a smaller resolution than an approach that only contrasts a couple of often closely related languages. In more general terms, Mauranen (1999: 165–167) points out that criticisms of parallel corpora rest on a dubious distinction between "pure" language on one hand and translations on the other. She argues that translations are normal language use, created in a specific setting and for a specific purpose, just like all naturally occurring language. That said, parallel corpora are a data type that needs to be handled with care. As many authors have argued (e.g. Van Olmen 2011: 114–115), they are most useful as complements to, rather than replacements of, other kinds of data.

In this paper, I shall show that parallel corpora offer an appropriate methodological tool for cross-linguistic comparison even in the domain of contrastive negation, in which formally and functionally analogous translation equivalents are readily available. To do so, I use the Europarl corpus (Koehn 2005; Tiedemann 2012), which consists of proceedings of the European parliament translated into the official languages of the member states of the European Union. My analytic approach draws on quantitative corpus linguistics (Gries 2009). In particular, I shall use multiple correspondence analysis (Glynn 2014; Greenacre 2017), an exploratory dimensionality reduction technique that allows the visualisation of similarities and differences in the expression of contrastive negation in the data. The paper will proceed as follows: Section 2 will present previous monolingual and cross-linguistic research on contrastive negation. Data and methods are presented in Section 3. In Section 4, the findings of the case studies will be reported, and in Section 5, they will be discussed.

2 Contrastive negation and corrective coordination

In cross-linguistic studies, a distinction is often made between comparative concepts and descriptive categories (Haspelmath 2010). Comparative concepts are typically functional notions that are meant for cross-linguistic comparison. Thus, they are not meant to be psychologically real to any speaker nor do they need to correspond exactly to a natural class of constructions in any given language being studied, though they may do so. Descriptive categories, on the other hand, are language-specific and (possibly) psychologically real to the speakers of those languages, such as specific constructions. In practice, however, the distinction between comparative concepts and descriptive categories is not always so neat (see van der Auwera and Sahoo 2015). In this study, the term contrastive negation refers to both: it is a functional notion meant for cross-linguistic comparison but it also groups together construction types in specific languages so that we may talk about English or Portuguese contrastive negation, for instance. Contrastive negation as a comparative concept is defined in (4):

(4) Contrastive negation refers to expressions which are combinations of affirmation and negation in which the focus of negation is replaced in the affirmative part of the expression. The relationship between the affirmed and the negated part of the expression is not causal or concessive, and the negation must have overt scope.

This definition presupposes certain other comparative concepts, the most important ones being negation (and by extension, affirmation) as well as focus and scope. According to Miestamo's (2005) definition, negation as a comparative concept is a construction that flips the truth value of the corresponding affirmative. However, in the case of contrastive negation, this definition needs some caveats. Most of the literature on contrastive negation deals with metalinguistic negation (Horn 1985; 1989: 362–444). Metalinguistic negation refers to cases such as those in (5) (taken and adapted from Horn 1989: 370–373). In (5a), the speaker corrects the pronunciation of another speaker. In (5b), the negation targets a stylistically inappropriate expression. In the last two examples, what is negated is an implicature: if left unnegated, A's utterance in (5c) would implicate that the woman in question is not the wife of X, and in (5d), the negation corrects the scalar implicature that there are men who are not chauvinists.

(5) a. *He didn't call the [pólis], he called the [polís].*
    b. *Grandpa isn't feeling lousy, Johnny, he's just a tad indisposed.*
    c. A: *X is meeting a woman this evening.*
       B: *No, he's not – he's meeting his wife!*
    d. *SOME men aren't chauvinists – ALL men are chauvinists.*

In all these cases, the negation does not target the propositional content of the sentence, at least not purely (in (5c) and (5d), the negation targets an implicature that is not part of the literal meaning of the sentence – the wife is a woman and 'all men are chauvinists' logically entails that some are; of course, the implicature can be expressed as a proposition in its own right). Thus, it is debatable, and indeed has been debated, whether such cases have to do with truth conditions at all. A review of the literature on metalinguistic negation is beyond the scope and focus of this paper (but see e.g. Carston 1996; Geurts 1998; Pitts 2011; Moeschler 2015; Larrivée 2018). Here, I simply follow Carston (1996), who argues that negation is truth-functional even when metalinguistic, but the relevant truth value pertains to a representation. Thus, to take (5a) as an example, it is not true that [pólis] appropriately represents *police*. For present purposes, it is important to note that metalinguistic negation is probably prototypically (though not obligatorily: Carston 1996: 314) expressed by contrastive negation, as the affirmative part of the construction renders the metalinguistic reading clear. However, the opposite is not true: contrastive negation mostly targets the literal or "descriptive" (Horn 1985) content of an utterance (Silvennoinen 2018).

As to focus, I rely on Lambrecht (1994), who defines focus as that part of an assertion (whether affirmative or negative) that is new, i.e. not recoverable from presupposed information. Scope is larger than focus: it refers to all elements in a clause or other negative unit that can be the focus of negation (e.g. Huddleston and Pullum 2002: 790–799). For example, in the clause *I don't want my martini shaken*, the scope is usually all the words following *don't* but the focus may be *shaken* ('I want my martini stirred'), *my martini* ('I want my margarita shaken') or even the verb phrase headed by *want* ('I don't just want but need my martini shaken'). However, the scope (and, by extension, focus) may also fall on the subject *I* ('It is she who wants her martini shaken'). As pointed out in Fillmore, Kay and O'Connor (1988: 521–522), there may also be several focal elements ('I don't want my martini shaken but my gin and tonic stirred'). Moreover, my definition of contrastive negation includes (6), which has an ellipted focus, but excludes (7), which has a negative pro-sentence that by definition does not have an overt scope.

(6) A: *Do you go to the gym often?*
B: ***I don't [go to the gym]**, I go running instead.*

(7) A: *Do you go to the gym often?*
B: ***No**, I go running instead.*

An alternative way of phrasing the definition in (4) would be that contrastive negation refers to an affirmation and a negation that are in an antithetical relation to one another. My understanding of antithesis is informed by Rhetorical Structure Theory (Thompson and Mann 1987): thus, the size or syntactic rank of the elements in an antithetical relation is not constrained. As a consequence, my definition of contrastive negation does not presuppose that the contrasted elements need to be in the same orthographic sentence. Also, my definition is intentionally vague as to whether the relationship between the affirmed and the negated parts is coordinate or subordinate since this would prioritize certain kinds of constructions over others. In addition, the literature on English is not unanimous as to whether the [Y not X] construction (e.g. (1)) is coordinate (Huddleston and Pullum 2002), subordinate (Gates Jr. and Seright 1967) or between the two (McCawley 1991). This uncertainty would be problematic if (4) were to constrain the investigation to, say, coordinate constructions, but a definition of contrastive negation that is uncommitted in this regard avoids this problem.

That said, prototypically, contrastive negation in European languages is expressed using coordinate constructions, whether syndetic or asyndetic. Coordination as a functional domain is generally split into three semantic subdomains, which Mauri (2009) calls combination relations, contrast relations and alternative relations. In broad terms, these correspond to English *and*, *but* and *or*, respectively. Contrastive negation is a kind of contrast relation. For the purposes of this study, I divide contrast relations into two groups, following Anscombre and Ducrot (1977). These two groups are exemplified in (8) and (9), in which the (a) versions come from English, the (b) versions from Spanish:[2]

(8) a. *Peter is intelligent **but** he doesn't work.*
    b. Spanish
       *Pedro   es   inteligente **pero** no   trabaja.*
       Pedro   be.3SG intelligent but NEG work.3SG

(9) a. *Peter is not intelligent **but** stupid.*
    b. Spanish
       *Pedro   no   es   inteligente **sino** estúpido.*
       Pedro   NEG be.3SG intelligent but stupid

Anscombre and Ducrot analyze such examples in terms of argumentation. In (8), the two conjoined clauses are arguments for different conclusions: if Peter/Pedro is intelligent, he would be expected to work under the speaker's model of the world, so the fact that he does not is construed as dampening the argumentative

---

[2] The glossing conventions in this paper follow the Leipzig rules. Default categories such as singular (in nouns), indicative or nominative are not glossed separately. Glosses that do not appear in the rules but are used here: ADE (adessive case), ALL (allative case), CNG (connegative), COND (conditional mood), ELA (elative case), ILL (illative case) and PRT (partitive case).

force of the first clause. The relationship between the clauses is thus concessive and (8) is therefore not a case of contrastive negation. In (9), by contrast, the conjoined phrases argue for the same conclusion: not being intelligent is compatible with being stupid, and 'intelligent' is replaced by 'stupid'. Thus, (9) is a case of contrastive negation. Both examples contain the conjunction *but* in English. By contrast, in Spanish, the first example contains the general adversative *pero* whereas the second example contains the corrective conjunction *sino*. German makes a distinction similar to Spanish, with *pero* corresponding to *aber* and *sino* to *sondern*.

In the subsequent discussion, I adopt the following terminological conventions. Following Anscombre and Ducrot, conjunctions like Spanish *pero* will be PA conjunctions (*pero*/*aber*) and those like *sino* SN conjunctions (*sino*/*sondern*). Conjunctions like English *but* will be PA/SN conjunctions.[3] The semantic relation between the elements contrasted by an SN conjunction is called corrective, but this relation can also be expressed asyndetically, with a PA/SN conjunction or sometimes another type of conjunction, as we will see below. The whole construction will be called contrastive negation or contrastive negation construction. Following Croft (2016), I regard the use of SN and PA/SN conjunctions as different strategies for expressing the comparative concept of contrastive negation in a language.

Mauri (2007; 2009: 283–284) notes that there is some areality in whether a language makes the distinction between PA and SN or not: in Europe, languages with the PA/SN strategy, i.e. a conjunction that expresses both adversativity and correctivity, form a continuous area in western central Europe (e.g. Danish, Dutch, English, French). By contrast, languages that make a distinction between PA and SN are located either in the north and east (e.g. Estonian, Finnish, German, Swedish, as well as many Slavonic languages) or in Spain (e.g. Spanish and Basque). Italian displays both strategies.

Previous research on contrastive negation has largely focused on conjunctions (e.g. Dascal and Katriel 1977; Koenig and Benndorf 1998; Birkelund 2009; Jasinskaja 2010, 2012). As seen in the introduction, however, asyndetic forms of contrastive negation are also possible and indeed commonplace (Silvennoinen 2017). On a more general level, languages differ as to the degree to which conjunctions are conventionalized as markers of specific types of coordination

---

3 Some languages make further splits in the PA domain (Foolen 1991; Malchukov 2004; Mauri 2007; Izutsu 2008; Mauri 2009). However, as these do not apply to contrastive negation, I do not discuss them here. Also outside of the scope of this paper are languages like Russian, in which the same conjunction can be used not only in adversative and corrective but also additive contexts (Jasinskaja 2010, 2012).

(Lehmann 1988; Mithun 1988). In most of the previous studies, the distinction between PA and SN coordination is presented as a categorical one, at least implicitly: if a language makes a distinction between a PA and an SN conjunction, this distinction is always observed. An exception is Mauri (2009), who notes that a language may have several conjunctions to express correctivity and that even languages that have a dedicated SN conjunction may also use the conjunction used in adversative contexts for this (e.g. Italian). Thus, it is possible for a language to have a system with both a PA/SN and an SN conjunction (I see no reason why the reverse situation could not hold as well). When and why the two conjunctions are used is not addressed in Mauri's study, however. This study will thus look more deeply into the differences in usage among the various forms of contrastive negation.

3 Data and methods

3.1 Data collection

As stated in the introduction, this study uses both parallel and monolingual corpus data. The data comes from the Europarl corpus (Koehn 2005; Tiedemann 2012), which consists of the proceedings of the European Parliament translated into the official languages of the European Union. The corpus thus gives us access to a relatively large number of European languages. Parliamentary discourse is particularly suited to studying contrastive negation since it has been found to favor argumentative genres (Silvennoinen 2017). In addition, Europarl offers ways of circumventing or at least mitigating several criticisms of parallel corpora made in previous research. Firstly, all the translations have been prepared professionally and for the same purpose, with strict in-house rules regarding how free or literal they may be. Secondly, the source languages vary. While this does not remove the source text bias, it means that it will not be based on one language only.[4]

---

[4] I conducted a pilot study using subtitling data from Levshina (2016b). While subtitles represent a more informal register than parliamentary discourse, the space restrictions in this type of data make them less well suited for studying contrastive negation, which is a domain with constructions of varying degrees of compactness. In practice, subtitlers often translate an expanded construct (i.e. one that consists of two full clauses: *I don't like it, I love it*) with a syndetic construction (e.g. *I don't like but love it*) because the latter tend to be more compact.

Thirdly, and most importantly, the corpus contains data from only one parliament. Thus, the institutional and legal context is constant. This is arguably a major strength compared to most comparable corpora of parliamentary or political discourse that might be compiled since political cultures in general and their discursive characteristics in particular are subject to cross-cultural as well as institutional variations (Bayley 2004). It is not at all clear, for instance, that parliamentary discourse in the British House of Commons and the Finnish Eduskunta could be called instances of the same genre: the former is the lower of two chambers, has two parties and houses debates that are famously adversarial, while the latter is unicameral, has substantial representation from multiple parties and has a notably calmer atmosphere.

A problem that cannot be fully resolved is that of translationese or translation universals. Therefore, the results of the present study should be seen as indicative of the patterns of the target languages. I assume that translation shifts allow us to gauge the extent to which otherwise analogous constructions in different languages are conventionalized. Methodologically, my study falls under quantitative corpus linguistics (see e.g. Gries 2009). Previous research indicates that there is a large degree of cognitive synonymy between the various constructions of contrastive negation (Silvennoinen 2018). Because of the abstract nature and comparatively large number of these constructions, the variation is difficult to describe in categorical terms and therefore an exploratory multivariate statistical analysis is the best way to get a handle on the data.

Another issue with Europarl is the fact that some of the speakers give their speeches in English even though it is not their native language. This may potentially cause L2 interference or English as a lingua franca effects in the data. However, the problem this causes is likely to be small given the careful editing that Europarl texts undergo, both before the speeches are given and during transcription.

The analysis was restricted to 11 languages. Of those, two are Uralic (Estonian, Finnish). The remaining 10 languages are Indo-European, from the Germanic (Danish, Dutch, English, German, Swedish), and Romance (French, Italian, Portuguese, Spanish) branches. Table 1 lists the conjunctions used in the languages in question.

To get an idea of translation effects in the parallel corpus study, I also conducted a small-scale case study on comparable monolingual corpus data in Finnish. The Finnish data also comes from Europarl; the query was restricted to interventions made in Finnish.[5] Because of the randomization in the extraction

---

5 Unfortunately, the OPUS interface for EuroParl did not display the language the speaker used at the time the study was conducted. For this reason, the Finnish data was sought from the Finnish

Table 1: The languages and conjunctions.

Languages without the PA/SN distinction		Languages with a distinction between PA and SN		
Language	PA/SN conjunction(s)	Language	PA conjunction	SN conjunction
Danish	men	Estonian	aga	vaid
Dutch	maar	Finnish	mutta	vaan
English	but	German	aber	sondern
French	mais	Italian	ma	bensì
Portuguese	mas[a]	Spanish	pero	sino
		Swedish	men	utan

[a]Rudolph (1996: 301) points out that at least one author in her data uses *senão*, a calque on the Spanish *sino*. This is not an entrenched part of Portuguese grammar and does not appear in my data.

of examples, the datasets in the parallel and the monolingual corpus study are different. While obtaining comparable corpus data from all the languages in the Europarl data is beyond what can be achieved in this study, the Finnish data is used as a control to gauge the extent to which the parallel corpus data can present a realistic view of the constructions of a language.

Contrastive negation presents something of a challenge for corpus-linguistic studies. There are several constructional formats available in all languages in this study. Furthermore, these formats utilize items that are often highly polysemous. The English corrective conjunction *but*, for instance, is polysemous not only with the general adversative meaning but also with meanings such as exceptivity (e.g. *That person is nothing but trouble*) and restrictiveness (e.g. *She is but a child*). This restricts the number of exemplars that can reasonably be included in the study as the forms cannot be extracted purely through a query but must be identified semi-manually. The cross-linguistic nature of this study poses an additional difficulty since different languages carve the same conceptual space in slightly different ways. Thus, where one language uses contrastive negation, another might opt for another construction type.

Keeping these caveats in mind, I searched the corpus for contrastive negation semi-manually. The procedure draws on that used in Silvennoinen (2017) and therefore the query language was English for the parallel corpus part of the study, regardless of whether the original language of the examples was English

---

Language Bank's Korp interface (https://korp.csc.fi), which includes Finnish EuroParl data as part of the FinnTreeBank 3 corpus.

or whether the examples had been translated into English. Thus, to borrow Gast's (2015) metaphor, English contrastive negation is used as the anchor with which variation in other languages is studied in the parallel corpus study. I queried the corpus for all negators in English: *not, no, neither, never, nobody, none, no one/ no-one, nor, nothing, nowhere*, as well as the contracted form *n't*.[6] For the monolingual Finnish data, I searched for all inflected forms of the Finnish negative auxiliary *e-* (including the syncretic negative form *äl-*). The query window was set to one orthographic sentence on either side of the target sentence to allow for the detection of constructs that extend over two sentences and for seeing the context of the examples. For the parallel Europarl dataset, I analyzed manually 1,500 random results of this query for whether they included contrastive negation. This yielded 240 cases. For the Finnish data, I randomly analyzed 1,000 concordance lines. This yielded 155 cases.

3.2 Analysis

The variation in the domain of contrastive negation is likely to be multifactorial in the languages being studied. For this reason, the datasets were coded for several variables that were expected to be associated with the constructional variation of this domain, either because of previous research on contrastive negation (Silvennoinen 2018) or other domains.

First, the constructional schemas (Cxn) of the cases in each language were coded. In this case, I opted for a simple coding scheme, recording whether a construct is negative-first or negative-second and what type of linking is found between the parts, if any. Thus, I gloss over the syntactic rank of the contrasted elements. In addition, I only focus on linking by means of conjunctions, leaving the marking of correctivity by discourse markers such as *rather* and *on the contrary* outside the scope of this study. The only exception to this is from Portuguese, in which the discourse marker *sim* is often but not always fused onto the conjunction *mas* (Rudolph 1996: 301).

The constructional schemas in which the negative precedes the affirmative are exemplified in Swedish in (10)–(12). (10) shows an SN and (11) a PA conjunction, and (12) an asyndetic linking between the contrasted elements.

---

6 The contracted form *n't* was queried by searching for the combination of an apostrophe and the letter "t" as a separate word. The word *cannot* was queried separately. Words such as *hardly* and *scarcely* were excluded from the search since they are only marginally used contrastively. A similar restriction is made by Tottie (1991), for instance.

(10) CXN: [Neg X SN Y]
Swedish
Och den har varit och fortsätter att vara en stabil stöttepelare,
'[A]nd it has been and continues to be a pole of stability,'
inte	*bara*	*för*	*den*	*europeiska*	*ekonomin,*	*utan*	*också*
NEG	only	for	DEF	European.DEF	economy.DEF	but_SN	also

för den globala ekonomin.
for DEF global.DEF economy.DEF
'not just for the European economy, but also for the global economy.'
(Europarl: Joaquín Almunia)

(11) CXN: [Neg X PA Y]
Swedish
Budgeten	*kommer*	*att*	*utökas*	*till*	*400*	*miljoner*
budget.DEF	come	to	raise.PASS.INF	to	400	million.PL
euro	*som*	*ni*	*vet,*	*inte*	*i*	*år*	*men*	*2013.*
euro	as	you.PL	know	NEG	in	year	but_PA	2013

'The budget will increase – as you know, not this year but in 2013 – to EUR 400 million.' (Europarl: Benita Ferrero-Waldner)

(12) CXN: [Neg X, Y]
Swedish
Den	*internationella*	*finanskrisen*	*började*	*inte*	*på*
DEF	international.DEF	financial.crisis.DEF	begin.PST	NEG	on
öarna.	*Den*	*började*	*i*	*USA [...].*
island.PL.DEF	it	begin.PST	in	USA

'The international financial crisis did not start on the islands. It started in the United States [...].' (Europarl: Robert Goebbels)

Analogously, the constructional formats in which the negative follows the affirmative are exemplified in French in (13)–(14). Again, (13) shows a syndetic and (14) an asyndetic coordination.

(13) CXN: [Y Conj Neg X]
French
Cela	*signifie*	*également*	*que*	*les*	*APE*	*devraient*
this	mean.3SG	also	that	DEF.PL	EPA	should.COND.3PL
être	*dynamiques –*	*et*	*non*	*statiques [...].*
be	dynamic.PL	and	NEG.FOC	static.PL

'It also means that EPAs should be dynamic and not static [...].' (Europarl: Catherine Ashton)

(14)   CXN: [Y Neg X]
       French
       *Les   pays   dévoyés   étaient   l'   **exception**,*
       DEF.PL   country.PL   errant.M.PL   be.PST.3PL   DEF   exception
       ***non**   la   **règle**.*
       NEG.FOC   DEF.F   rule
       'Errant countries were the exception and not the rule.' (Europarl: Edward Scicluna)

Each of the categories in (10)–(14) includes both clausal and sub-clausal contrasted elements. In addition, there are categories for "other contrastive negation" and, for languages other than English, "not contrastive negation", exemplified in (15) and (16), respectively. (15a) shows a construction from Portuguese in which there is a conjunction between the contrasted elements but not one that is either the PA or the SN conjunction in the language; rather, the conjunction *como* 'as' is an adverbial subordinator. Since the construction is a combination of a negated and an affirmed element, it nevertheless counts as contrastive negation under the definition adopted in this study. (15b) shows a case from French in which the translator has opted for *et* 'and' as the conjunction between a negative and the affirmative that follows it; the original Italian (not reproduced here) uses the unambiguous SN conjunction *bensì*. (16) shows a case from Finnish in which the translator has replaced a contrastive negation with a construction that does not fall under the definition of contrastive negation adopted here. The construction [*paitsi X myös Y*], literally 'except X, also Y', contains the semantically but not syntactically negative preposition *paitsi* 'except'. Since lexical negatives fall under the definition of contrastive negation, so does this construction. I return to some of the ways of avoiding a contrastive negation in translation in the results below.

(15)   CXN: other contrastive negation
       a.   Portuguese
            Graças aos intercâmbios de estudantes, como sucede no programa Erasmus,
            'Thanks to student exchanges, such as Erasmus,'
            *os   nossos   jovens   **não   apenas   aprofundam***
            DEF.PL.M   our.PL.M   young.PL   NEG   only   deepen.3PL
            os   seus   conhecimentos   em   domínios   específicos
            DEF.PL.M   their   knowledge.PL in   domain.PL   specific.M.PL
            ***como   também   alargam**   os   seus   **horizontes**.*
            as   also   broaden.3PL   DEF.PL.M   their   horizon.PL
            'our young people are not only furthering their knowledge in specific subject areas, but are also broadening their horizons.' (Europarl: Czesław Adam Siekierski)

b. French
C' est   pourquoi je   n'   ai   pas voté
it be.3SG why   1SG   NEG   AUX.1SG   NEG vote.PTCP
contre et   que   j'   ai   préféré   m'   abstenir.
against and   that 1SG   have.1SG prefer.PTCP 1SG.ACC abstain.INF
'This has led me not to vote against it, but rather to abstain.' (Europarl: Luca Romagnoli)

(16) CXN: not contrastive negation
Finnish
Mielestäni senkaltainen suhtautuminen maahanmuuttoon on
in.my.view such   disposition   immigration.ILL be.3SG
paitsi väärin myös vaarallista.
except wrong   also dangerous.PRT
'In my view, focusing on immigration in that way is not only wrong but also dangerous.' (Europarl: Juan Fernando López Aguilar)

For those parts of the analysis that focus on individual languages, more fine-grained language-specific categories may be used.

Second, the functional features of each case were coded along five parameters. The functional parameters used in this study are the following (mnemonic names in parentheses; these will figure in the analysis later on):

Semantic type of the construct (SEMTYPE) refers to scalarity and can be either replacive, additive or restrictive. Replacives are the basic type: there is no scalarity invoked between X and Y. In additives, the affirmed element is construed as higher on a scale, which is shown by a scalar element in the scope of the negation, as in the English [not only X but Y] construction. Conversely, in restrictives, the negated element is higher on a scale, as shown by a scalar in the affirmed element, as in the English [not X, just Y] construction. The categories are based on Dik et al. (1981). The three levels of the variable SEMTYPE are exemplified in (17)–(19):

(17) SEMTYPE: rep
Shaken, not stirred.

(18) SEMTYPE: add
*Not **only** stirred but shaken.*

(19) SEMTYPE: rst
*Not shaken, **just** stirred.*

Note that the expression of scalarity need not be a scalar adverb. In Finnish for instance, additivity may be expressed by negating the lexical verb *riittää* 'be enough', as in (20):

(20) Finnish
Ei nimittäin riitä, että valitsee hyllystä
NEG.3SG namely be.enough.CNG that choose.3SG shelf.ELA
ympäristömerkillä varustetun paketin, vaan sitä
environmental.label.ADE attach.PTCP.GEN package.GEN but$_{SN}$ it.PRT
on osattava myös käyttää.
be.3SG know.PTCP also use.INF
'It is not enough to choose a packet with an environmental label off the shelf: people also have to be able to use the product correctly.'
(Europarl: Eija-Riitta Korhola)

The target of negation (NEGTARGET) captures whether the negation targets only propositional content or not. By default, negation targets propositional content, but it may also target presuppositions, implicatures and formal features of a previous or imagined utterance. Such non-propositional cases include metalinguistic negation (see Section 2). They also include additive cases that target scalar implicatures but are not strictly speaking metalinguistic because of the presence of a scalar adverb (e.g. *only*) in the scope of the negation. Propositional, non-propositional metalinguistic and non-propositional non-metalinguistic negation are exemplified in (21)–(22). (21a) is metalinguistic because the simple negation *She doesn't have two children* is untrue under a strictly truth-conditional reading in case she has three, since three subsumes two.[7]

(21) NEGTARGET: prop
She doesn't have three children but two.

(22) NEGTARGET: non_prop
 a. *She doesn't have two children but three.*
 b. *She doesn't have only two children but three.*

---

[7] The truth conditions of metalinguistic negations are a matter of debate; see e.g. Carston (1996) and Moeschler (2015). This matter has no consequences for the analysis presented here and will therefore be set aside.

Structural difference (STRDIFF) refers to the kind of difference that obtains between the contrasted elements. Drawing on Lambrecht's (1994: chap. 5) classification of focus structures, I divide the possibilities into three: narrow, predicate and other.[8] When the difference is classified as "narrow", it is a constituent below the finite verb phrase, as in (23). When the difference is classified as "predicate", it is a finite verb phrase, as in (24). When the domain of the contrast cannot be stated as either the verb phrase or a narrower constituent of the clause, the focus structure is classified as "other", as in (25), in which the first (negative) part has *our sole concern* as subject whereas the latter (affirmative) part has *we* in that role. The structural difference types are ordered from the most restricted (narrow) to the most extensive (other) change.

(23) STRDIFF: narrow
These plants represent a danger to public health and to the ecosystem, **not only** *[in their country of origin],* **but also** *[throughout Europe and the world].* (Europarl: Marisa Matias)

(24) STRDIFF: predicate
Parliament managed to find the right compromises that **do not** *[flush the text of its content]* **but, instead,** *[put real pressure on those who, in the Commission, want the Single Market to continue to adopt a purely free market approach, without including social issues, tax issues or environmental issues].* (Europarl: Pascal Canfin)

(25) STRDIFF: other
In future, our sole concern should not just be the cooperation between the police and judicial authorities as regards mutual recognition; we must also look at the establishment of procedural standards. (Europarl: Jan Philipp Albrecht)

Deontic modality (DMOD) refers to the moral desirability of a future state of affairs (e.g. Nuyts 2006: 4–5) as well as permission and obligation.[9] My defini-

---

[8] Lambrecht uses the term "argument focus" instead of "narrow focus". However, not all such foci are in fact arguments in their respective clauses, which is why I have appropriated Van Valin's (2005) term "narrow focus". Lambrecht's typology also includes a third type, sentence focus, which is subsumed under "other" in this classification. Note that in this paper, I am not classifying foci, which can be quite subjective and difficult, but the difference between the contrasted elements, which can be larger than the focus.

[9] This differs from definitions of deontic modality that exclusively refer to permission and obligation (e.g. Palmer 2001: 9–10, 70–76). However, in parliamentary discourse, what is at issue

tion thus combines what Nuyts, Byloo and Diepeveen (2010) and Van linden and Verstraete (2011: 155) call deontic and directive, the former referring to moral desirability and the latter to the illocutionary forces of permitting and obligating "Moral" is here understood as a scale construed by the conceptualizer, ranging from acceptable to necessary (and, in the negative, to unacceptable). This variable has two levels: neutral (no deontic modality is indicated in the example) and deontic (there is a marker of deontic modality in the context). (26) exemplifies the neutral case, whereas (27) illustrates different kinds of deontic modality: imperative mood in (27a), modal auxiliary in (27b) and modal adjective in (27c) (see Van linden and Verstraete 2011).

(26) DMOD: neutral
*In this context, statistics **not only monitor specific tourism policies, but are also useful in the broader context of regional policies and sustainable development**.* (Europarl: Licia Ronzulli)

(27) DMOD: deontic
a. Do *not listen too much to the Member States;* listen *instead to the Spanish Presidency, because it has some good ideas on this subject.* (Europarl: Guy Verhofstadt)
b. *I am frankly concerned about the current situation in Egypt and about today's developments, so I believe that we **must not show calm but must rather show solidarity**.* (Europarl: Marisa Matias)
c. The most important *issue is **not to punish the illegal workers from third-party states, but to penalise the employers, who are in a much stronger position**.* (Europarl: Jörg Leichtfried)

Weight (WEIGHT) refers to the syntactic weight of the contrasted elements. This is operationalized as the number of words of the negative and affirmative focus (see Szmrecsanyi 2004 for why the number of words is an adequate measure). The variable has three levels: "aff-heavy" (when the affirmative focus has more words than the negative focus, as in (28)), "balanced" (when the number of words is equal in both, as in (29)) and "neg-heavy" (when the negative focus has more words than the affirmative focus, as in (30)). Scalar elements that count towards making a construct either additive or restrictive as

---

is rather the desirability of a certain course of action or policy, as the speakers are not in a position to give commands to one another. See Nuyts (2006: 4–5; Nuyts, Byloo, and Diepeveen 2010: 17–18, 23–24) on defining deontic modality.

well as linking adverbs (e.g. *instead, on the contrary*) were not counted. Including the scalar elements would bias additive constructs towards neg-heavy and restrictive constructs towards aff-heavy. Including the linking adverbs would bias the data towards whichever element comes second since adversative linking adverbs appear predominantly on the second element of an adversatively connected pair of clauses.

(28) WEIGHT: aff_heavy
 *OK, it was **not [their fault], but apparently [the fault of others]**.* (Europarl: Guy Verhofstadt)

(29) WEIGHT: balanced
 ***These are not even [British] dud banks, they are [foreign] dud banks**, and I hear today that the British taxpayer is being asked to fork out for Portugal.* (Europarl: Godfrey Bloom)

(30) WEIGHT: neg_heavy
 *You will **not** achieve good results **[with 27 national states acting unilaterally], but only [by pooling forces]**.* (Europarl: Helga Trüpel)

The functional variables were coded on the basis of the English data. Unfortunately, the Europarl metadata does not indicate the original language for all contributions. In addition, English is often used in the European Parliament even by MEPs who do not speak it as a native language. In practice, the variables are consistent across languages; however, an exception to this is seen in the analysis of the monolingual Finnish data in Section 4.2.

The functional variables were used to create a semantic map of contrastive negation (see Croft 2001; Haspelmath 2003). A semantic map is a graphic representation of a given domain or set of domains. The idea behind semantic maps is that similar meanings tend to be encoded in similar ways across languages. The maps can be either connectivity maps or probabilistic maps (van der Auwera 2013). Since it is expected that the ways of expressing contrastive negation vary across multiple parameters at the same time and compete against not only other constructions of contrastive negation but also other construction types, this study uses a probabilistic map, as these are better at representing gradient and partially overlapping patterns of variation. For connectivity maps relevant to the domains of adversativity and correctivity, see Malchukov (2004), Lewis (2006: 146) and Mauri (2009).

Probabilistic maps are constructed using statistical techniques that produce a graphical output. For this reason, various dimensionality-reduction techniques have been used in previous studies, such as multidimensional scaling (Croft and Poole 2008; Wälchli and Cysouw 2012; Levshina 2016b). The statistical method used to construct the map in this study is multiple correspondence analysis (MCA) with supplementary points, which is a member of the larger family of correspondence analysis (Glynn 2014; Greenacre 2017). MCA is a dimensionality-reduction technique for multivariate categorical data. Its input is a data frame that only includes categorical variables. MCA looks for associations between the variables to reduce the number of dimensions that are needed to represent the data. The dimensions are typically agglomerates of several "raw" variables. As a result, the data can be represented in a low-dimensional space. As an exploratory technique, MCA is useful when there are no clear hypotheses regarding the associations between explanatory and outcome variables, which is the case here as the outcome variables are different for each language of the dataset.

4 Results

4.1 Parallel data

In this section, I present the results of the analysis on the Europarl data. I begin by discussing the descriptive statistics of the constructions in the individual languages and then the functional variables. I then move on to the exploratory statistical analysis using MCA. All statistical analyses were done using the open-source statistical environment R (R Core Team 2016).

Table 2 shows the distributions of the strategies for expressing contrastive negation in the languages studied. Note that for some individual cases, there is not a translation in all languages of the corpus, which is why all rows do not add up to 240. As might be expected, translations are quite consistent across languages: for example, syndetic negative-first constructions in one language tend to be rendered as syndetic negative-first constructions in the others, too. The ordering of the contrasted elements tends to be retained in translation as well. Danish, Dutch, English, French, German, Spanish and Swedish seem very similar in this table, if one ignores whether they make a distinction between PA and SN or not. By contrast, Estonian, Finnish, Italian and Portuguese display divergences.

Perhaps surprisingly, the table shows that even languages with dedicated SN conjunctions exhibit their PA conjunctions in the dataset. Mostly, these are one-offs, as the Swedish example in (11), repeated here as (31):

Table 2: Raw frequencies of the strategies.

	[Neg X SN Y]	[Neg X PA/SN Y]	[Neg X, Y]	[Y, and Neg X]	[Y, Neg X]	other form of contrastive negation	not contrastive negation
Danish	0	122	59	27	20	1	7
Dutch	0	128	49	27	15	–	15
English	0	131	57	24	25	3	–
Estonian	113	1	53	8	34	3	24
Finnish	97	1	45	24	16	1	45
French	0	128	55	28	14	1	14
German	136	2	53	28	15	1	5
Italian	24	110	44	24	16	5	17
Portuguese	0	103	61	29	11	24	12
Spanish	128	3	54	26	21	3	5
Swedish	127	3	53	23	22	1	11

(31) Swedish
Budgeten kommer att utökas till 400 miljoner euro
budget.DEF come to raise.PASS.INF to 400 million.PL euro
som ni vet, **inte** *i år* **men** *2013.*
as you.PL know NEG in year but$_{PA}$ 2013
'The budget will increase – as you know, not this year but in 2013 – to EUR 400 million.' (Europarl: Benita Ferrero-Waldner)

Italian is the only language analyzed here that shows a sustained presence both for the SN and the PA/SN strategies. The SN conjunction *bensì*, which is rarer, only appears in replacive contexts, as in (32). The PA/SN conjunction *ma* occurs with both replacives and additives, the latter of which is shown in (33).

(32) Italian
Il bilancio sarà incrementato – come sapete,
'The budget will increase – as you know,'
non quest' anno, bensì nel 2013 a 400 milioni di euro.
NEG this year but$_{SN}$ in 2013 to 400 millions of euro
'not this year but in 2013 – to 400 million euros.' (Europarl: Benita Ferrero-Waldner)

(33) Italian
[...] nuove sfide, come il cambiamento climatico, probabilmente destabilizzeranno le scorte alimentari già in diminuzione,
'[...] new challenges, such as climate change, are likely to destabilise already dwindling food stocks,'

non	solo	in	Europa	ma	in	tutto	il	mondo.
NEG	only	in	Europe	but_{PA/SN}	in	all	the	world

'not only in Europe, but also worldwide.' (Europarl: Daciana Octavia Sârbu)

Another finding that we can make at the outset is that the languages differ quite a lot in the prevalence of construction types other than contrastive negation. Finnish and Estonian have the largest shares of translation strategies that do not involve contrastive negation, followed by Italian. The Italian data has a large number of cases in which the translators have opted for lexical negatives. A case in point is (34) which uses the semantically negative preposition *contro* 'against' in lieu of contrastive negation.

(34) Italian
Vorrei dire che il nostro Parlamento, votando questo compromesso sul pacchetto sulle telecomunicazioni, opera una scelta:
'I would like to say that our Parliament, in voting in favor of this compromise on the telecoms package, will be indicating a clear choice:'

una	scelta	a	favore	della	regolamentazione	del
INDF.F	choice	P	favor	of.DEF.F	regulation	of.DEF.M

mercato,	**e**	**contro**	**la**	**concorrenza**	**senza**	**regole.**
market	and	against	DEF.F	competition	without	regulation

'that of a regulated market, and not of unregulated competition.' (Europarl: Catherine Trautmann)

In the Estonian and Finnish data, on the other hand, constructions that the translators have used to replace contrastive negation include antithetical constructions without negation. For instance in Finnish, expressions that are used to translate replacive contrastive negation include the postpositions *lisäksi* 'in addition' and *sijaan* 'instead'. Additive contrastive negation can be translated by the correlative construction [*paitsi X myös Y*] 'except X also Y', which uses the semantically negative preposition *paitsi*.[10] (35) is an example of an additive case

---

10 The construction with *paitsi* falls outside of my definition of contrastive negation as it is only semantically but not grammatically negative. Finnish makes a distinction between bounded and

rendered with contrastive negation, while (36)–(38) present alternative strategies ((38) is repeated from (16) for convenience).

(35) Finnish
Ei ainoastaan yksittäisillä mailla vaan koko
NEG.3SG only single.PL.ADE country.PL.ADE but_SN whole
alueella on meille suuri strateginen merkitys.
region.ADE be.3SG 1PL.ALL large strategic meaning
'The whole region is of major strategic significance to us, not just the individual countries.' (Europarl: Elmar Brok)

(36) Finnish
Kyse on **uskottavuuden lisäksi valmiudestamme**
issue be.3SG credibility.GEN in.addition readiness.ELA.POSS:1PL
olla läsnä Kuubassa.
be.INF present Cuba.INE
'What is at stake is not only that credibility, but also our capacity to be present in Cuba.' (Europarl: Andris Piebalgs)

(37) Finnish
EAMV:n *pitäisi olla ainoa valvonnasta*
ESMA.GEN should.COND.3SG be.INF sole supervision.ELA
vastaava viranomainen **kansallisten viranomaisten sijaan** *[...].*
responsible authority national.PL.GEN authority.PL.GEN instead
'ESMA, not the national authorities, should be the only authority with responsibility for this matter [...].' (Europarl: Harlem Désir)

(38) Finnish
Mielestäni senkaltainen suhtautuminen maahanmuuttoon on
in.my.view such disposition immigration.ILL be.3SG
paitsi väärin *myös vaarallista.*
except wrong also dangerous.PRT
'In my view, focusing on immigration in that way is not only wrong but also dangerous.' (Europarl: Juan Fernando López Aguilar)

---

unbounded Objects through case marking. In grammatically negative clauses, this distinction is neutralised: negative Objects behave like unbounded ones, even when they are bounded. *Paitsi* does not cause this neutralisation: its complement can take both bounded and unbounded case marking.

Finally, Portuguese has a high number of cases that do not fall under the main strategies. I will come back to this observation below.

I now move to the functional variables. Table 3 shows the raw frequencies of each of the variable levels as well as their percentages. The variables are quite skewed: restrictives in particular are a rare category in the data. For this reason, the data was recoded so that restrictives were subsumed into replacives in the statistical analysis to follow.

Table 3: Frequencies and proportions of the functional variable levels in the Europarl data.

Variable	Level	Freq	%
SemType	rep	139	57.9
	add	96	40.0
	rst	5	2.1
NegTarget	prop	200	83.3
	non_prop	40	16.7
StrDiff	narrow	176	73.3
	predicate	44	18.3
	other	20	8.3
DMod	neutral	171	71.3
	deontic	69	28.8
Weight	aff_heavy	151	62.9
	balanced	36	15.0
	neg_heavy	53	22.1

Recall that the functional variables were coded according to the English data. The idea is that the co-occurrence patterns of the variable levels are used to create a semantic space that is common to all the languages studied in this paper. The method for doing this is multiple correspondence analysis (MCA). Creating one space for all languages allows us to visualize the similarities and differences between the different constructions not only within one language (e.g. the difference between [not X but Y] and [Y not X] in English) but also across languages (e.g. the difference between [nicht X sondern Y] in German and [non X bensì Y] in Italian). Thus, we get to see patterns that would be difficult if not impossible to detect merely by examining the dataset manually or by only looking at the data in numerical form. The particular flavor of MCA used in this study is adjusted MCA, which was performed using the packages ca (Nenadic and Greenacre 2007) and FactoMineR (Lê, Josse and Husson 2008). Visualization was done in part using the package factoextra (Kassambara and Mundt 2017).

According to the analysis, the five variables can be condensed into three underlying dimensions, which together explain 66.0% of the variation. The contributions of the variables are summarized in Table 4. The table shows the dimensions, their principal inertias (amount of variance), the proportion of the variance that each dimension explains as a raw and as a cumulative percentage, and, finally, a scree plot showing the percentage of variance explained by each variable in a visual way. The dimensions are ordered so that dimension 1 accounts for the biggest proportion of the co-variation patterns in the data. Dimension 2 then accounts as much of the remaining variation. As the table shows, dimension 1 is by far the most powerful one: it accounts for 49.5% of the variation, while dimension 2 only accounts for 11.1% and dimension 3 for 5.5%. As shown by both the percentages and the scree plot, dimension 4 has a negligible contribution and therefore it will be ignored in what follows. The first three dimensions together capture around two thirds of the variance in the data. The resulting biplots (see below) are thus interpretable but do not account for around one third of the variance, which needs to be kept in mind.

Table 4: Principal inertias (eigenvalues) of MCA.

Dimension	Principal inertia	%	Cumulative %	Scree plot
1	0.011964	49.5	49.5	*******************
2	0.002677	11.1	60.6	****
3	0.001320	5.5	66.0	**
4	5.8e-050	0.2	66.3	

Table 5 shows the contributions of each variable to the first three dimensions. Dimension 1 mainly takes SemType and NegTarget into account, with a moderate contribution from StrDiff. Dimension 2, on the other hand, is mostly about Weight and DMod. Dimension 3 takes into account Weight and StrDiff.

More precise information on the contributions of each of the variable levels is presented in Figure 1. The left-hand side shows dimensions 1 and 2, and the right-hand side dimensions 1 and 3. The positive end of dimension 1 is associated with non-propositional targets of negation, additive semantics and, to a lesser extent, narrow and balanced foci. The negative end of dimension 1 is associated with propositional targets of negation, replacives (including restrictives) and foci that are neither narrow nor predicates. The positive end of dimension 2 is associated

Table 5: Contributions of the functional variables to the MCA dimensions.

	Dimension 1	Dimension 2	Dimension 3
SEMTYPE	0.426	0.074	0107
NEGTARGET	0.486	0.206	0.000
STRDIFF	0.302	0.181	0.359
DMOD	0.074	0.310	0.102
WEIGHT	0.149	0.421	0.544

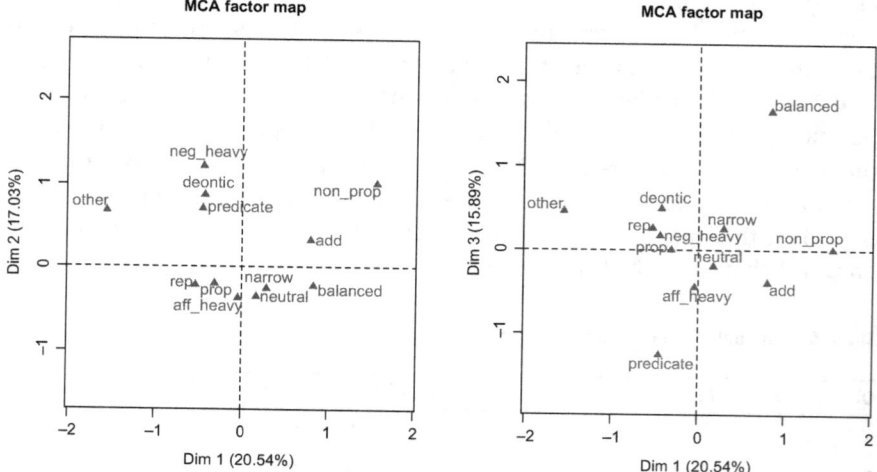

Figure 1: Variable levels in MCA dimensions.

with negative-heavy and deontic constructs. The negative end of dimension 2 is associated with their opposites: affirmative-heavy and deontically neutral constructs. Dimension 3 in its positive pole is associated with balanced constructs and narrow foci, and affirmative-heavy constructs with predicate-level structural differences in its negative pole.

The space created in this analysis is largely similar to the one in Silvennoinen (2018), which is based on English newspaper data: the semantic type of additivity forms a natural pairing with negation targeting scalar elements since both denote moving upwards from a value on a scale (e.g. *not only once but twice*). In the English data, the semantic types were associated with different constructions: additives with the [*not X but Y*] construction (to form [*not only X but also Y*]), restrictives with the [*not X, Y*] construction (to form [*not X, just Y*]). In the Europarl data, the former tendency is borne out while the latter is not, in part because the number of restrictives is so small as to not permit generalizations.

Let us now turn to how the languages fill the space created. Space does not permit a full analysis of each language, so I will focus on the most distinctive ones. For all languages, I first show dimensions 1 against dimension 2, and then dimension 1 against dimension 3. In this way, all three dimensions are shown, but emphasis is given to dimension 1, which explains the largest share of the co-occurrences in the data. Furthermore, for each language, the same colors will be used for the same constructional strategies: blue for syndetic negative-first PA/SN coordination (e.g. English *but*), red for syndetic negative-first SN coordination (e.g. German *sondern*), orange for asyndetic negative-first coordination, green for all negative-second coordination, brown for other forms of contrastive negation, and black for cases not expressed as contrastive negation. Further distinction are drawn as needed.

I begin with the English data, presented in Figures 2 and 3. As seen in both figures, dimension 1 makes a difference between syndetic and asyndetic negative-first constructions in English. Syndetic coordination (i.e. the [Neg *X* but *Y*] construction, represented in blue) mostly occupies the right-hand side

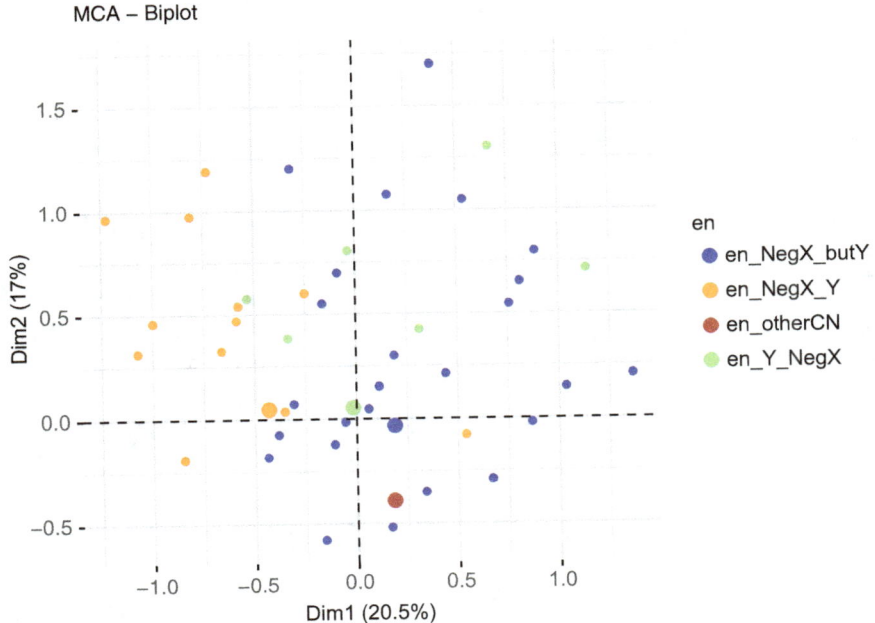

Figure 2: MCA biplot for English, dimensions 1 and 2.

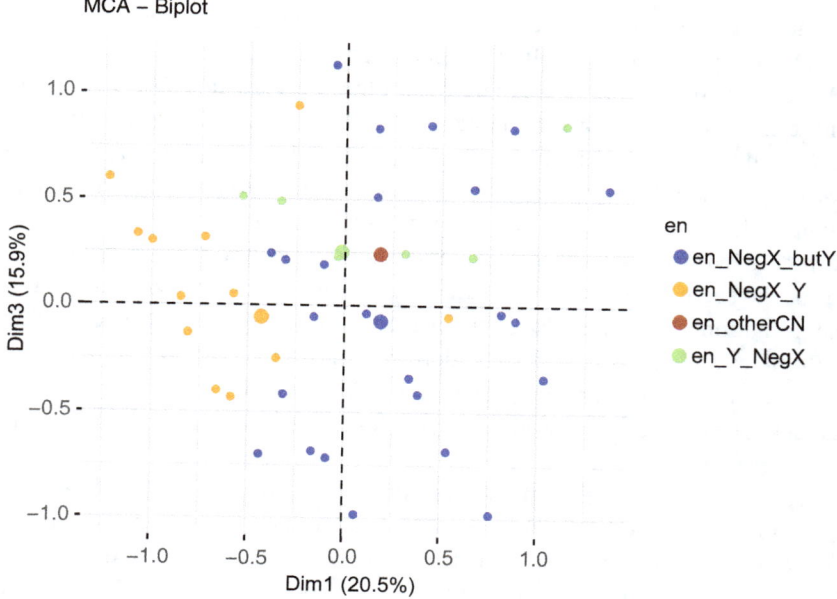

Figure 3: MCA biplot for English, dimensions 1 and 3.

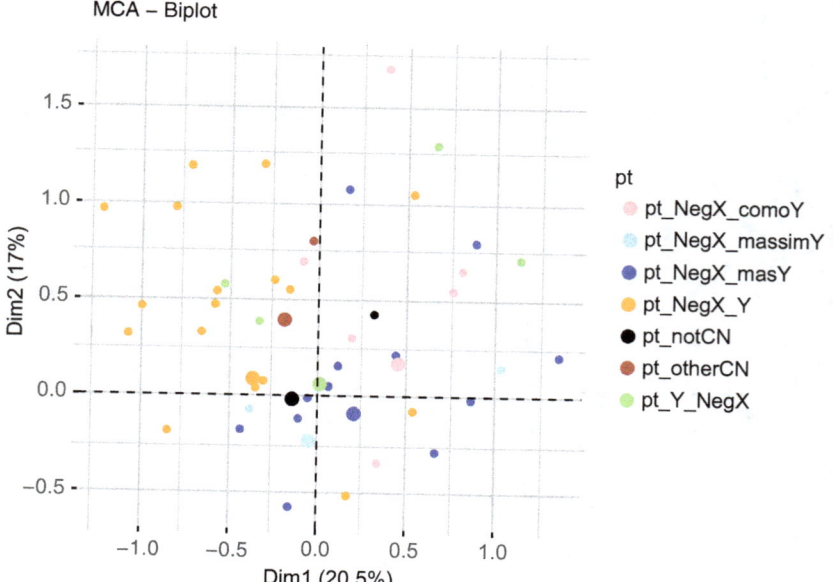

Figure 4: MCA biplot for Portuguese, dimensions 1 and 2.

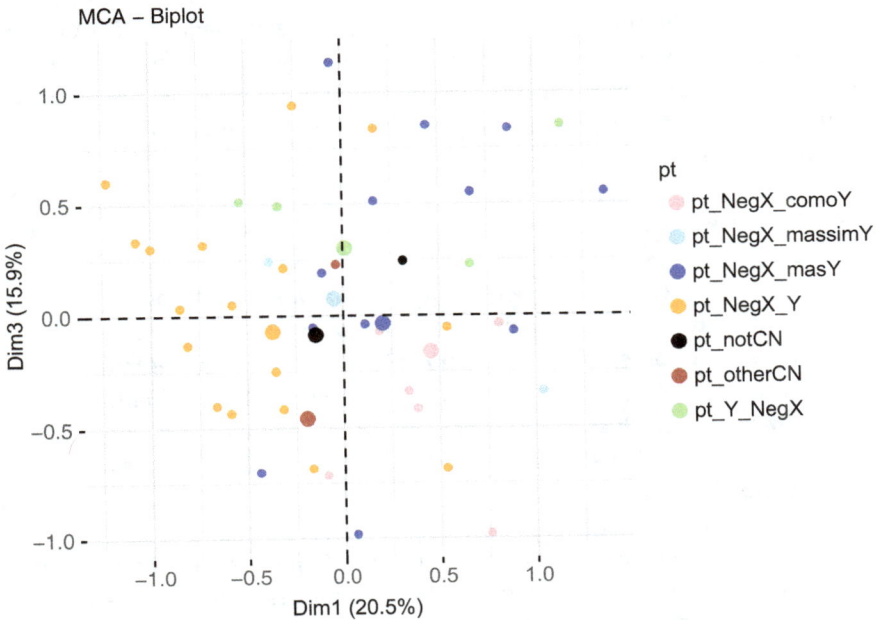

Figure 5: MCA biplot for Portuguese, dimensions 1 and 3.

of both figures, which is where the positive pole of dimension 1 lies. Thus, as expected, the [Neg *X but Y*] construction is associated with additive semantics and non-propositional targets. By contrast, asyndetic negative-first constructs in English (represented in orange) tend to have replacive semantics and propositional targets. In addition, the asyndetic strategy is mostly on the positive side of dimension 2. This side is favored by deontic and, surprisingly, negative-heavy cases. Dimension 3 does not change the picture much, except for the fact that negative-second constructs (represented in green) tend towards its positive end, i.e. balanced and narrow foci.

The patterns in the English data are largely replicated in the geographically closest languages Dutch, French and German as well as the genealogically related Danish and Swedish. Spanish also patterns in quite a similar way. In all these languages, the [Neg *X Conj Y*] strategy is predominantly used in additive contexts. Because of the similarities, I will not show the maps for these languages.

Portuguese and Italian show more divergent behavior. The Portuguese data is shown in Figures 4 and 5. Portuguese presents a wider array of contrastive negation constructions than some of the other languages. On the one hand, in the additive domain, Portuguese tends to make use of either the regular [Neg *X mas Y*] construction or another construction that uses the conjunction *como* 'as' as the corrective element (represented as pink). The latter construction was classified under "other forms of contrastive negation" in Table 2. These two constructions are exemplified in (39) and (40):

(39) Portuguese
e

Esta	*situação*	**não**	*penalizará*	**apenas**	*para*	*os*
this.F	situation	NEG	punish.FUT.3SG	only	P	DEF.PL.M

transportadores,	**mas**	**também**	*os*		*seus*	**clientes**
carrier.PL	but_{PA/SN}	also	DEF.PL.M		their	client.PL

directos,	**retalhistas**	**e**	**consumidores**	*finais*	*da*	
direct.PL	retailer.PL	and	consumer.PL	final.PL	of.DEF.F	

União	**Europeia.**
union	European.F

'It will not only be the carriers which will suffer as a result of this, but also their direct customers, retailers and end customers in the European Union.' (Europarl: Bilyana Ilieva Raeva)

(40) Portuguese
Graças aos intercâmbios de estudantes, como sucede no programa Erasmus,
'Thanks to student exchanges, such as Erasmus,'

os	*nossos*	*jovens*	**não**	**apenas**	**aprofundam**
DEF.PL.M	our.PL.M	young.PL	NEG	only	deepen.3PL

os	*seus*	**conhecimentos**	*em*	*domínios*	*específicos*
DEF.PL.M	their	knowledge.PL	in	domain.PL	specific.PL

como	**também**	**alargam**	*os*		*seus*	*horizontes.*
as	also	broaden.3PL	DEF.PL.M		their	horizon.PL

'our young people are not only furthering their knowledge in specific subject areas, but are also broadening their horizons.' (Europarl: Czesław Adam Siekierski)

The construction with *como* appears in the same region as the one with *mas* in Figure 4, and in Figure 5, because of its additive semantics. The use of *como* is reminiscent of the construction [*tanto X como Y*] 'both X and Y', which has a similarly additive function.

On the other hand, the PA/SN conjunction *mas* is frequently followed by *sim* 'yes' to the extent that this collocation is mentioned in reference works as a single connective (e.g. Rudolph 1996: 300–301). The cases with *mas sim* mostly appear in the center of both figures (represented in light blue). This follows from the fact that they are mostly replacive: 19 out of 21 cases of *mas sim* are replacive, while only 2 are additive. This contrasts with simple *mas*, which appears in 47 replaces and 35 additives (and 1 restrictive). In addition, *mas sim* prefers narrow structural differences (19 out of 21), as opposed to predicate-level (2 out of 21) and more extensively different (0 out of 21) cases. The latter tend to be rendered through two asyndetically combined clauses, as in the other languages of the dataset. An example of the construction with *mas sim* is (41).

(41) Portuguese
*Tudo   isto   **Não** é,   em   primeiro lugar e   Acima de*
all.M   this   NEG   be.3SG in   first.M   place and Above of
tudo,   uma   questão de   Acordo   ou   de   dinheiro,
all.M   INDF.F   question of   agreement or   of   money
mas   sim   *de   humanidade e   de   engenho.*
but_PA/SN yes   of   humanity   and   of   ingenuity
'All this is not, first and foremost, a question of agreement and money, but of our humanity and ingenuity.' (Europarl: Pál Schmitt)

Figures 6 and 7 present the Italian data. Unlike the other SN conjunctions in the data, *bensì* does not prefer additive contexts: out of the 24 cases of *bensì*, only 6 are in cases coded as "additive" based on the English data, and one of these is even translated as a replacive. Rather, *bensì* is predominantly replacive, which shows in the rather small area that it occupies on the map. Similarly to Portuguese *mas sim*, *bensì* prefers to appear with narrow (20 out of 24) and predicate (4 out of 24) foci and thus its domain does not extend to the left of the figures. In Italian, the default conjunction for contrastive negation constructions in which the negative precedes the affirmative is *ma*, both in terms of function and frequency.

Finally, I look at Uralic languages, concentrating on Finnish. The Estonian data is similar to Finnish, except for the fact that the difference from the Indo-European languages is somewhat less extreme. The Finnish data is shown in Figures 8 and 9. The construction with the Finnish SN conjunction *vaan* occupies a large area in the figures: it appears in replacive (58 cases out of 97) cases as well as additive ones (38 out of 97), in addition to one stray restrictive case. The few cases that use the PA conjunction *mutta* are far from the additive cases; they are grouped under "not contrastive negation" in the figures.

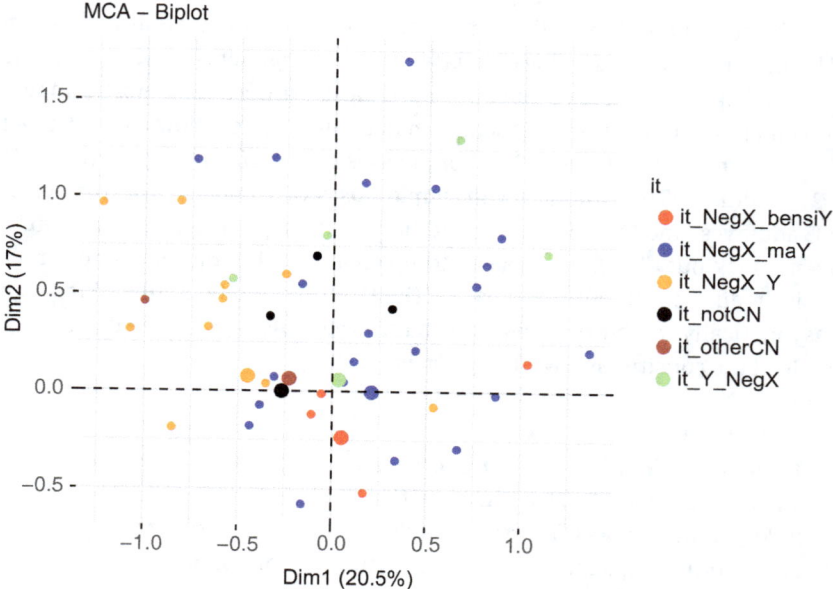

Figure 6: MCA biplot for Italian, dimensions 1 and 2.

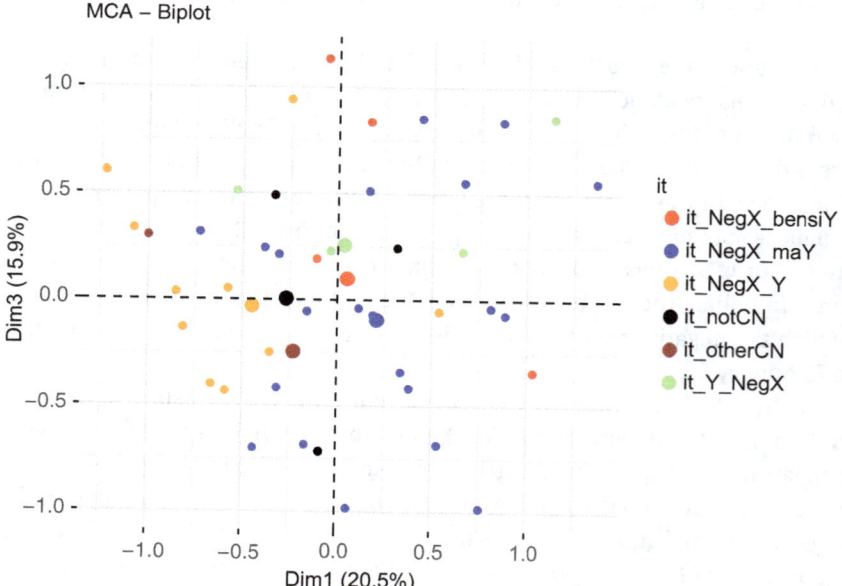

Figure 7: MCA biplot for Italian, dimensions 1 and 3.

Comparing corrective constructions: Contrastive negation — 253

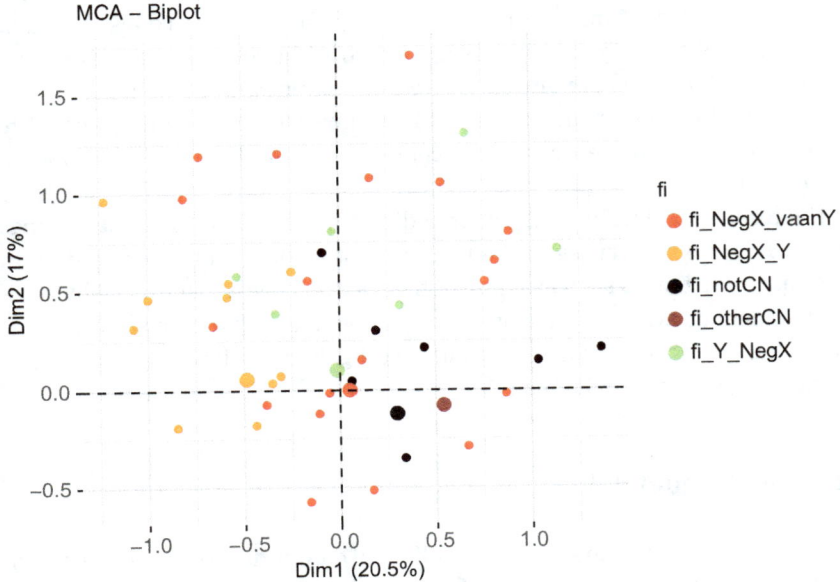

Figure 8: MCA biplot for Finnish, dimensions 1 and 2.

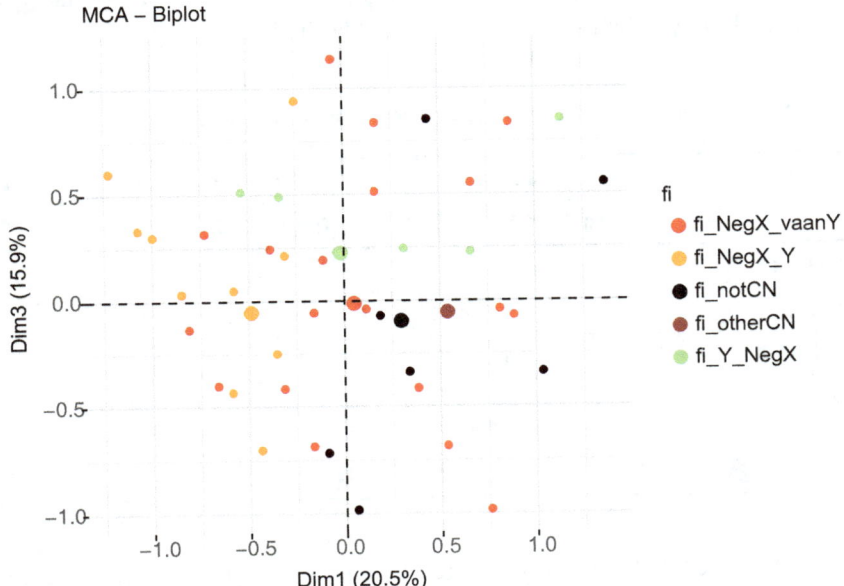

Figure 9: MCA biplot for Finnish, dimensions 1 and 3.

Like Portuguese, Finnish differs from English in how it codes the additive cases. Unlike Portuguese, however, English additive constructs of the type [*not only X but (also) Y*] are often rendered through means other than contrastive negation in the Finnish dataset. This is shown in that the black dots are distributed mainly to the right of the center, i.e. towards the positive pole of dimension 1.

The results obtained in this section indicate that parallel corpus data brings forth meaningful differences in the uses and forms of contrastive negation. In addition, for languages such as Finnish, the results suggest that especially additivity is a domain with a great number of competing constructions. In the next section, the results of the parallel corpus investigation will be compared to comparable control data from Finnish.

4.2 Monolingual data

This section turns to the analysis of monolingual corpus data of Finnish. The aim is to see the extent to which comparable corpus data replicates the findings of the parallel corpus analysis.

Table 6 compares the Finnish datasets. According to Fisher's exact test there is no statistically significant difference between the strategies used in the two datasets. Indeed, the distributions are remarkably similar.

Table 6: A comparison of the constructional strategies in the Finnish datasets.

	Parallel data		Monolingual data	
	Freq (N=184)	%	Freq (N=155)	%
[Neg X Conj Y]	98	53.3	81	52.3
[Neg X, Y]	45	24.5	31	20.0
[Y Conj Neg X]	24	13.0	19	12.3
[Y Neg X]	16	8.7	21	13.5
other form of contrastive negation	1	0.5	3	1.9

I now turn to the functional variables. Table 7 shows the functional variables in the parallel and monolingual datasets. Note that the parallel data columns only

Table 7: A comparison of the functional variables in the Finnish datasets.

Variable	Level	Parallel data Freq (N=184)	%	Monolingual data Freq (N=155)	%
SEMTYPE	rep	126	68.5	101	65.2
	add	54	29.3	44	28.4
	rst	4	2.2	10	6.5
NEGTARGET	prop	153	83.2	129	83.2
	non_prop	31	16.8	26	16.8
STRDIFF	narrow	126	68.5	71	45.8
	predicate	38	20.7	24	15.5
	other	20	10.9	60	38.7
DMOD	neutral	123	66.8	112	72.3
	deontic	61	33.2	43	27.8
WEIGHT	aff_heavy	113	61.4	87	56.1
	balanced	25	13.6	31	20.0
	neg_heavy	46	25.0	37	23.9

include those cases that are expressed using contrastive negation in Finnish. For this reason, the figures are slightly different from those in Table 3.

The table shows that the two datasets mirror each other in the distributions of the functional variable levels. Thus, the finding that Finnish contrastive negation is used less for additive meanings finds support also in the comparable data, and it would seem that the translators who have produced the Europarl data have managed to avoid overusing contrastive negation in additive contexts.

The only variable that shows a statistically significant difference between the two datasets is structural difference (Fisher's exact: $p = 1.657e-08$): in the monolingual dataset, there is much more of the category "other" and less of "narrow" and "predicate". This result stems from the structural differences between Finnish and most other European languages. Finnish is a Uralic language that largely relies on case marking to express syntactic roles in a clause. Different argument structures assign different cases so that when two clauses have different predicates, the surrounding arguments may also be coded differently. Consider (42):

(42) Finnish
*Jos jatkamme, niin **seuraava velkakriisi ei** *koske*
if continue.1PL so next debt.crisis NEG.3SG concern.CNG
***valtiota, vaan** kyseessä on Euroopan keskuspankin*
state.PRT but issue.INE be.3SG Europe.GEN central.bank.GEN
velkakriisi.
debt.crisis
'[We cannot go on as a European Union buying our own debt.] If we do, the next debt crisis will not be in a country, but will be a debt crisis of the European Central Bank itself. [lit. If we continue, then the next debt crisis does not concern a state but at issue is a debt crisis of the European Central Bank]' (Europarl: Nigel Farage)

The source language is English. In the original, the conjunction *but* connects two full VPs although the actual difference is only the subject predicative (*in a country* vs. *a debt crisis of the European Central Bank itself*) and so the example has been classified as exhibiting a "narrow" structural difference. By contrast, in (42), the conjunction *vaan* connects two full clauses that share no clause elements. The contrasted elements are not parallel: the first clause is transitive and the second copular, and their one shared lexical element (the noun *velkakriisi* 'debt crisis') has a different function in both clauses (Subject of the transitive verb in the first clause, Subject Predicative of the copula in the second). Thus, the contrast is not based on the pairing of an argument or even a predicate VP but on the contrastiveness of the clauses as wholes.

After this difference between the parallel and the monolingual data was found, I recoded the parallel data on STRDIFF, this time with Finnish as the basis for coding. The proportions of the three levels of STRDIFF in the three datasets are shown in Figure 10.

What Figure 10 shows is a fairly typical translation effect. Since a similar difference in this variable was not found in the Indo-European languages of the study, we can regard the left-hand bar as an approximation of the three types of structural difference in the corpus at large. As previously, it shows "narrow" as the largest category, followed by "predicate" and then "other". The Finnish monolingual data in the right-hand column, on the other hand, has almost equal shares of "narrow" and "other"; the proportion of "predicate" does not seem to differ much from the left-hand bar. Displayed in the central bar, the Finnish part of the parallel datasets is a compromise between the two: the proportions of both "narrow" and "other" fall between the extreme values of the parallel English data on one hand and monolingual Finnish data on the other. This suggests that when translating from the Indo-European languages into Finnish, the transla-

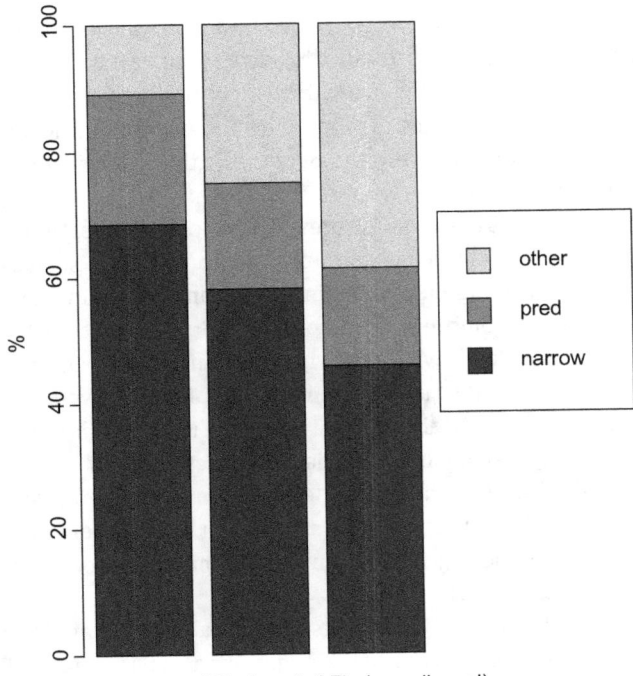

Figure 10: StrDiff in parallel English, parallel Finnish and monolingual Finnish datasets.

tors sometimes change the structural difference, and it seems that typically this happens away from "narrow" and to "other". This is a real translationese effect on the data: not only does coding the data on the basis of English distort the picture of how StrDiff is distributed in the parallel data (as shown in the difference between the first two bars), but the parallel data itself is biased (as shown in the difference between the last two bars).

5 Discussion

Section 4 showed the results of a parallel corpus study and compared them to comparable monolingual data from Finnish. In this section, I will relate the findings to previous research as well as to methodological concerns.

The most important finding of this study is that the strategies for expressing contrastive negation are much more varied than the literature's focus on PA and SN conjunctions would let us believe (e.g. Anscombre and Ducrot 1977; Rudolph

1996; Izutsu 2008). For one thing, even though SN conjunctions are generally discussed as a homogenous group, they actually display a lot of variation even among languages that are closely related genealogically, culturally and areally: *bensì* in Italian or *vaan* in Finnish do not display quite the same behavior as *sondern* in German. This is further support to the hypothesis that constructions are language-specific (Croft 2001).

Another point where the results of this study break with those of the previous studies is the association between corrective conjunctions and additive semantics. Additive constructions are seldom mentioned in studies on SN conjunctions and contrastive negation (e.g. Anscombre and Ducrot 1977; Horn 1985; McCawley 1991), and, conversely, studies on additivity rarely make a connection with corrective conjunctions (e.g. Forker 2016; but for counter-examples, see Svensson 2011; Andorno and De Cesare 2017). Additives were also a locus of much cross-linguistic variation, with Portuguese having a special construction, [*não X como Y*], solely for additivity and with Finnish showing a large amount of constructional competition in this area. This is a natural finding, given that the semantic relation of additivity is arguably more general than other similar relations (see Mauri 2009: 80–83; De Cesare 2017: 1–2).

This study is, to my knowledge at least, the first large-scale cross-linguistic investigation that specifically focuses on contrastive negation in all its formal and functional variety. Many areas of interest were discussed only cursorily or not at all. A particularly interesting area is forms of linking between the contrasted elements that fall outside of conjunction systems. I have largely glossed over discourse markers such as *rather*, *instead* and *on the contrary* (see Lewis 2006; 2011). Such expressions interact with the conjunctions in the constructionalization of contrastive negation by strengthening the corrective interpretation of an emerging conjunction, as in the collocation *but rather* in the development of the English corrective *but* (Rissanen 2008: 352–353); *bensì* in Italian (Giacalone Ramat and Mauri 2011: 661) and *mas sim* in Portuguese are other instances of this. Another gap not addressed here is the role of the negator: for instance in French, the special negator *non* (and *non pas*) specifically appears in contrastive constructions, though it is optional in them. Svensson (2011) finds that French and Swedish differ as to the degree to which the combination of 'not' and 'only' is constructionalized into a fixed unit. Whether this parameter also follows the areal pattern seen here and in other previous research remains to be seen.

Mauri's (2007; 2009: 147–149) typological study suggests that corrective conjunctions are more common in Europe than elsewhere, and the relation is frequently expressed asyndetically. This follows the general pattern by which conjunctions are more typical in languages with a written tradition (Mithun 1988). Interestingly, at least Finnish has been noted to have borrowed the distinction between *mutta* and *vaan* from Swedish or possibly German (Hakulinen 1955: 309). The picture is complicated by the fact that the basic typological divide between languages that make a distinction between PA and SN and those that do not does not follow clear genealogical or areal lines. Even neighboring, genealogically closely related languages such as Swedish and Danish or Spanish and Portuguese use different strategies. On the other hand, the patterns of conjunction use did show some areal tendencies: among the languages studied here, those spoken in central western Europe (Dutch, English, French, German) display similar behavior in how they use corrective conjunctions, be they PA/SN or SN. Languages further away from this nexus (Estonian, Finnish, Italian, Portuguese) displayed more divergence. These findings are largely compatible with Mauri (2007; 2009), who notes that western European languages have similar conjunction systems. In fact, the results of this paper suggest that there are additional similarities to the ones uncovered by Mauri: in her study, German is an outlier among the central western European languages as it makes the distinction between PA and SN conjunctions. However, a closer examination of the usage patterns makes *sondern* seem quite similar to its neighboring PA/SN conjunctions.

All in all, the data resists an interpretation on purely areal or genealogical lines. Further diachronic work may shed light on how the differences and similarities have come about and whether this has something to do with processes of standardization, for instance. An intriguing possibility from this paper's point of view is the possible role played by translations in the spread of contrastive negation strategies. As one of the reviewers points out, especially the additive constructions may be rooted in the Latin [*non solum X sed etiam Y*] 'not only X but also Y' (see also Rudolph 1996: 302).

From a methodological point of view, I hope to have shown that parallel corpora can be profitably used in cross-linguistic studies. Contrastive negation is *prima facie* a bad candidate for a parallel corpus study: on the face of it, all the languages studied here would seem to have rather similar constructional inventories, which would enable translators to just render them verbatim. However, the analysis did uncover differences among the languages, both categorical (e.g. the restriction of Portuguese *como* to additive contexts) and gradient (the dispreference for additive constructions in Finnish). While a parallel corpus study cannot replace in-depth studies into the constructions of individual languages, it does uncover meaningful differences as well as similarities. Moreover, the examination of a comparable set of Finnish data showed that monolingual corpus data may provide useful context for the findings of a parallel corpus study. For some fine-grained semantic distinctions, comparable corpora may be more useful, as Lewis (2006) argues. However, for broader cross-linguistic comparison, the more modest aim of uncovering the strategies used in a given domain does not necessarily require comparable corpus data. The results obtained here support a nuanced view of translations as linguistic data: they are not a "third code" (Frawley 1984) but a natural form of language use.

I hope that future studies extend this one in several respects. First, contrastive negation is still mostly poorly described in languages spoken outside western Europe. There is much room for both more extensive typological work and contrastive linguistic studies on a more restricted set of languages drawing on comparable corpora. Also, the areal patterning in eastern Europe is interesting and deserves to be looked at in a future study. Second, the cross-linguistic tendencies related to genre need to be explored. In this study, I have only looked at one very particular genre, parliamentary proceedings. However, previous research has shown contrastive negation to be highly register-sensitive at least in English (Silvennoinen 2017). As parallel corpus resources improve, genre and register considerations become easier to incorporate in contrastive research. Third, the connections of corrective conjunctions to other functional domains may be of interest. This will potentially help us to describe the various grammaticalization paths of corrective conjunctions, for instance. Thus, not only are contrastive negation construction interesting, but there is also a lot we can still learn about them.

References

Aijmer, Karin. 2008. Parallel and comparable corpora. In Anke Lüdeling & Merja Kytö (eds.), *Corpus linguistics: An international handbook. Volume 1*, 275–292. Berlin: Mouton de Gruyter.

Andorno, Cecilia & Anna-Maria De Cesare. 2017. Mapping additivity through translation: From French *aussi* to Italian *anche* and back in the Europarl-direct corpus. In Anna-Maria De Cesare & Cecilia Andorno (eds.), *Focus on additivity: Adverbial modifiers in Romance, Germanic and Slavic languages*, 157–200. Amsterdam/Philadelphia: John Benjamins. doi:10.1075/pbns.278.06and.

Anscombre, Jean-Claude & Oswald Ducrot. 1977. Deux *mais* en français? *Lingua* 43(1). 23–40. doi:10.1016/0024-3841(77)90046-8.

Bayley, Paul. 2004. Introduction: The whys and wherefores of analysing parliamentary discourse. In Paul Bayley (ed.), *Cross-cultural perspectives on parliamentary discourse*, 1–44. Amsterdam/Philadelphia. doi:10.1075/dapsac.10.01bay.

Berman, Ruth A. & Dan Isaac Slobin. 1994. *Relating events in narrative: A crosslinguistic developmental study*. Hillsdale, NJ & Hove, UK: Lawrence Erlbaum.

Birkelund, Merete. 2009. Pierre n'est pas français mais danois. Une structure polyphonique à part. *Langue française* 164(4). 123–136. doi:10.3917/lf.164.0123.

Carston, Robyn. 1996. Metalinguistic negation and echoic use. *Journal of Pragmatics* 25(3). 309–330.

Croft, William. 2001. *Radical Construction Grammar: Syntactic theory in typological perspective*. Oxford: Oxford University Press. doi:10.1093/acprof:oso/9780198299554.001.0001.

Croft, William. 2016. Comparative concepts and language-specific categories: Theory and practice. *Linguistic Typology* 20(2). 377–393. doi:10.1515/lingty-2016-0012.

Croft, William & Keith T. Poole. 2008. Inferring universals from grammatical variation: Multidimensional scaling for typological analysis. *Theoretical Linguistics* 34(1). 1–37. doi:10.1515/THLI.2008.001.

Cysouw, Michael & Bernhard Wälchli. 2007. Parallel texts: using translational equivalents in linguistic typology. *Sprachtypologie und Universalienforschung: STUF* 60(2). 95–99. doi:10.1524/stuf.2007.60.2.95.

Dascal, Marcelo & Tamar Katriel. 1977. Between semantics and pragmatics: The two types of "but" – Hebrew "aval" and "ela". *Theoretical Linguistics* 4(1–3). 143–172. doi:10.1515/thli.1977.4.1-3.143.

De Cesare, Anna-Maria. 2017. Introduction: On "additivity" as a multidisciplinary research field. In Anna-Maria De Cesare & Cecilia Andorno (eds.), *Focus on additivity: Adverbial modifiers in Romance, Germanic and Slavic languages*, 1–20. Amsterdam/Philadelphia: John Benjamins. doi:10.1075/pbns.278.00dec.

Dik, Simon, Maria E. Hoffmann, Jan R. de Jong, Sie Ing Djiang, Harry Stroomer & Lourens de Vries. 1981. On the typology of focus phenomena. In Teun Hoekstra, Harry van der Hulst & Michael Moortgat (eds.), *Perspectives on Functional Grammar*, 41–74. Dordrecht: Foris Publications.

Fillmore, Charles J., Paul Kay & Mary Catherine O'Connor. 1988. Regularity and idiomaticity in grammatical constructions: The case of *let alone*. *Language* 64(3). 501–538. https://www.jstor.org/stable/414531 (accessed 26 September 2018). doi:10.2307/414531.

Forker, Diana. 2016. Toward a typology for additive markers. *Lingua* 180. 69–100. doi:10.1016/j.lingua.2016.03.008.

Frawley, William. 1984. Prolegomenon to a theory of translation. In William Frawley (ed.), *Translation: Literary, linguistic and philosophical perspectives*, 159–175. London & Toronto: Associated University Presses.

Gast, Volker. 2015. On the use of translation corpora in contrastive linguistics: A case study of impersonalization in English and German. *Languages in Contrast* 15(1). 4–33. doi:10.1075/lic.15.1.02gas.

Gates Jr., Dave L. & Orin Dale Seright. 1967. Negative-contrastive constructions in standard modern English. *American Speech* 42(2). 136–141. doi:10.2307/453965.

Geurts, Bart. 1998. The mechanisms of denial. *Language* 74(2). 274–307. https://www.jstor.org/stable/417868 (accessed 26 September 2018). doi:10.2307/417868.

Giacalone Ramat, Anna & Caterina Mauri. 2011. The grammaticalization of coordinating interclausal connectives. In Bernd Heine & Heiko Narrog (eds.), *The Oxford handbook of grammaticalization*, 656–667. Oxford: Oxford University Press. doi:10.1093/oxfordhb/9780199586783.013.0054.

Glynn, Dylan. 2014. Correspondence analysis: Exploring data and identifying patterns. In Dylan Glynn & Justyna A. Robinson (eds.), *Corpus methods for semantics: Quantitative studies in polysemy and synonymy*, 443–485. Amsterdam/Philadelphia: John Benjamins. doi:10.1075/hcp.43.17gly.

Greenacre, Michael. 2017. *Correspondence analysis in practice*. Third edn. Boca Raton, FL: Taylor & Francis.

Greenberg, Joseph H. 1966. *Language universals: With special reference to feature hierarchies.* Reprinted. Berlin/New York: Mouton de Gruyter.

Gries, Stefan Th. 2009. *Quantitative corpus linguistics with R: A practical introduction.* New York: Routledge.

Hakulinen, Lauri. 1955. Suomen kielen käännöslainoista [On calques in Finnish]. *Virittäjä* 59(4). 305–318. https://journal.fi/virittaja/article/view/33253 (accessed 26 September 2018).

Haspelmath, Martin. 2003. The geometry of grammatical meaning: Semantic maps and cross-linguistic comparison. In Michael Tomasello (ed.), *The new psychology of language: Cognitive and functional approaches to language structure,* volume 2, 211–242. London: Lawrence Erlbaum.

Haspelmath, Martin. 2010. Comparative concepts and descriptive categories in crosslinguistic studies. *Language* 86(3). 663–687. https://www.jstor.org/stable/40961695 (accessed 26 September 2018). doi:10.1353/lan.2010.0021.

Horn, Laurence R. 1985. Metalinguistic negation and pragmatic ambiguity. *Language* 61(1). 121–174. https://www.jstor.org/stable/413423 (accessed 26 September 2018). doi:10.2307/413423.

Horn, Laurence R. 1989. *A natural history of negation.* Chicago: University of Chicago Press.

Huddleston, Rodney & Geoffrey K. Pullum. 2002. *The Cambridge grammar of the English language.* Cambridge: Cambridge University Press.

Izutsu, Mitsuko Narita. 2008. Contrast, concessive, and corrective: Toward a comprehensive study of opposition relations. *Journal of Pragmatics* 40(4). 646–675. doi:10.1016/j.pragma.2007.07.001.

Jasinskaja, Katja. 2010. Corrective contrast in Russian, in contrast. *Oslo Studies in Language* 2(2). 433–466.

Jasinskaja, Katja. 2012. Correction by adversative and additive markers. *Lingua* 122(15). 1899–1918. doi:10.1016/j.lingua.2012.08.015.

Kassambara, Alboukadel & Fabian Mundt. 2017. factoextra: Extract and visualize the results of multivariate data analyses. R package version 1.0.5. https://CRAN.R-project.org/package=factoextra.

Koehn, Philipp. 2005. Europarl: A parallel corpus for statistical machine translation. *MT summit 2005.*

Koenig, Jean-Pierre & Beate Benndorf. 1998. Meaning and context: German *aber* and *sondern.* In Jean-Pierre Koenig (ed.), *Discourse and cognition: Bridging the gap,* 365–386. Stanford: CSLI Publications.

Lambrecht, Knud. 1994. *Information structure and sentence form: Topic, focus, and the mental representations of discourse referents.* Cambridge: Cambridge University Press. doi:10.1017/CBO9780511620607.

Larrivée, Pierre. 2018. Metalinguistic negation from an informational perspective. *Glossa: A journal of general linguistics* 3(1). https://www.glossa-journal.org/articles/10.5334/gjgl.403/# (accessed 26 September 2018).

Lê, Sébastien, Julie Josse & François Husson. 2008. FactoMineR: An R package for multivariate analysis. *Journal of Statistical Software* 25(1). doi:10.18637/jss.v025.i01.

Lehmann, Christian. 1988. Towards a typology of clause linkage. In John Haiman & Sandra A. Thompson (eds.), *Clause combining in grammar and discourse,* 181–225. Amsterdam/Philadelphia: John Benjamins. doi:10.1075/tsl.18.09leh.

Levshina, Natalia. 2015. European analytic causatives as a comparative concept: Evidence from a parallel corpus of film subtitles. *Folia Linguistica* 49(2). 487–520. doi:10.1515/flin-2015-0017.

Levshina, Natalia. 2016a. Why we need a token-based typology: A case study of analytic and lexical causatives in fifteen European languages. *Folia Linguistica* 50(2). 507–542. doi:10.1515/flin-2016-0019.

Levshina, Natalia. 2016b. Verbs of letting in Germanic and Romance languages: A quantitative investigation based on a parallel corpus of film subtitles. *Languages in Contrast* 16(1). 84–117. doi:10.1075/lic.16.1.04lev.

Lewis, Diana M. 2006. Contrastive analysis of adversative relational markers, using comparable corpora. In Karin Aijmer & Anne-Marie Simon-Vanderbergen (eds.), *Pragmatic markers in contrast*, 139–153. Oxford: Elsevier.

Lewis, Diana M. 2011. A discourse-constructional approach to the emergence of discourse markers in English. *Linguistics* 49(2). 415–443. doi:10.1515/ling.2011.013.

Malchukov, Andrej L. 2004. Towards a semantic typology of adversative and contrast marking. *Journal of Semantics* 21(2). 177–198. doi:10.1093/jos/21.2.177.

Mauranen, Anna. 1999. Will "translationese" ruin a contrastive study? *Languages in Contrast* 2(2). 161–185. doi:10.1075/lic.2.2.03mau.

Mauri, Caterina. 2007. Conjunctive, disjunctive and adversative constructions in Europe: Some areal considerations. In Paolo Ramat & Elisa Roma (eds.), *Europe and the Mediterranean as linguistic areas: Convergencies from a historical perspective*, 183–213. Amsterdam & Philadelphia: John Benjamins. doi:10.1075/slcs.88.10mau.

Mauri, Caterina. 2009. *Coordination relations in the languages of Europe and beyond*. Berlin/New York: Mouton de Gruyter.

McCawley, James D. 1991. Contrastive negation and metalinguistic negation. *CLS* 27(2). 189–206.

Miestamo, Matti. 2005. *Standard negation: The negation of declarative verbal main clauses in a typological perspective*. Berlin/New York: Mouton de Gruyter.

Mithun, Marianne. 1988. The grammaticization of coordination. In John Haiman & Sandra A. Thompson (eds.), *Clause combining in grammar and discourse*, 331–359. Amsterdam/Philadelphia: John Benjamins. doi:10.1075/tsl.18.13mit.

Moeschler, Jacques. 2015. Qu'y a-t-il de représentationnel dans la négation métalinguistique ? *Nouveaux cahiers de linguistique française* 32. 11–26.

Nenadic, Oleg & Michael Greenacre. 2007. Correspondence analysis in R, with two- and three-dimensional graphics: The ca package. *Journal of Statistical Software* 20(3). doi:10.18637/jss.v020.i03.

Nuyts, Jan. 2006. Modality: Overview and linguistic issues. In William Frawley (ed.), *The expression of modality*, 1–26. Berlin: Mouton de Gruyter. doi:10.1515/9783110197570.1.

Nuyts, Jan, Pieter Byloo & Janneke Diepeveen. 2010. On deontic modality, directivity, and mood: The case of Dutch *mogen* and *moeten*. *Journal of Pragmatics* 42(1). 16–34. doi:10.1016/j.pragma.2009.05.012.

Palmer, F. R. 2001. *Mood and modality*. 2nd ed. Cambridge: Cambridge University Press. doi:10.1017/CBO9781139167178.

Pitts, Alyson. 2011. Exploring a "pragmatic ambiguity" of negation. *Language* 87(2). 346–368. https://www.jstor.org/stable/23011627 (accessed 26 September 2018). doi:10.1353/lan.2011.0035.

R Core Team. 2016. R: A language and environment for statistical computing. Vienna: R Foundation for Statistical Computing. https://www.R-project.org/.

Rissanen, Matti. 2008. From "quickly" to "fairly": On the history of *rather*. *English Language and Linguistics* 12(2). 345–359. doi:10.1017/S1360674308002657.

Rudolph, Elisabeth. 1996. *Contrast: Adversative and concessive expressions on sentence and text level*. Berlin/New York: Walter de Gruyter.

Silvennoinen, Olli O. 2017. Not only apples but also oranges: Contrastive negation and register. In Turo Hiltunen, Joe McVeigh & Tanja Säily (eds.), *Big and rich data in English corpus linguistics: Methods and explorations*. (Studies in variation, contacts and change in English 19.) Helsinki: VARIENG. http://www.helsinki.fi/varieng/series/volumes/19/silvennoinen/.

Silvennoinen, Olli O. 2018. Constructional schemas in variation: Modelling contrastive negation. *Constructions and Frames* 10(1): 1–37. doi:10.1075/cf.00009.sil.

Stivers, Tanya, N. J. Enfield, Penelope Brown, Christina Englert, Makoto Hayashi, Trine Heinemann, Gertie Hoymann, et al. 2009. Universals and cultural variation in turn-taking in conversation. *Proceedings of the National Academy of Sciences* 106(26). 10587–10592. doi:10.1073/pnas.0903616106.

Svensson, Maria. 2011. Marqueurs corrélatifs en français et en suédois : l'exemple de *non seulement... mais* et *inte bara... utan*. *Revue française de linguistique appliquée* XVI(2). 41–56.

Szmrecsanyi, Benedikt. 2004. On operationalizing syntactic complexity. In Gérard Purnelle, Cédrick Fairon & Anne Dister (eds.), *Le poids des mots. Proceedings of the 7th International Conference on Textual Data Statistical Analysis. Louvain-la-Neuve, March 10–12, 2004, Vol. 2*, 1032–1039. Louvain-la-Neuve: Presses universitaires de Louvain.

Thompson, Sandra A. & William C. Mann. 1987. Antithesis: a study in clause combining and discourse structure. In Ross Steele & Terry Threadgold (eds.), *Language topics: Essays in honour of Michael Halliday. Volume II*, 359–381. Amsterdam/Philadelphia: John Benjamins.

Tiedemann, Jörg. 2012. Parallel data, tools and interfaces in OPUS. *Proceedings of the 8th International Conference on Language Resources and Evaluation (LREC 2012)*, 2214–2218.

Tottie, Gunnel. 1991. *Negation in English speech and writing: A study in variation*. San Diego: Academic Press.

van der Auwera, Johan. 2013. Semantic maps, for synchronic and diachronic typology. In Anna Giacalone Ramat, Caterina Mauri & Piera Molinelli (eds.), *Synchrony and diachrony: A dynamic interface*, 153–176. Amsterdam/Philadelphia: John Benjamins. doi:10.1075/slcs.133.07auw.

van der Auwera, Johan & Kalyanamalini Sahoo. 2015. On comparative concepts and descriptive categories, *such* as they are. *Acta Linguistica Hafniensia* 47(2). 136–173. doi:10.1080/03740463.2015.1115636.

van der Auwera, Johan, Ewa Schalley & Jan Nuyts. 2005. Epistemic possibility in a Slavonic parallel corpus – a pilot study. In Björn Hansen & Petr Karlík (eds.), *Modality in Slavonic languages: New perspectives*, 201–217. Munich: Otto Sagner.

Van linden, An & Jean-Christophe Verstraete. 2011. Revisiting deontic modality and related categories: A conceptual map based on the study of English modal adjectives. *Journal of Pragmatics* 43(1). 150–163. doi:10.1016/j.pragma.2010.07.031.

Van Olmen, Daniël. 2011. *The imperative in English and Dutch: A functional analysis in comparable and parallel corpora*. Antwerp: University of Antwerp doctoral dissertation.

Van Valin, Robert D. Jr. 2005. *Exploring the syntax-semantics interface*. Cambridge: Cambridge University Press. doi:10.1017/CBO9780511610578.

Wälchli, Bernhard & Michael Cysouw. 2012. Lexical typology through similarity semantics: Toward a semantic map of motion verbs. *Linguistics* 50(3). 671–710. doi:10.1515/ling-2012-0021.

Åke Viberg
Contrasting semantic fields across languages

Abstract: This paper will discuss corpus-based methods to study semantic fields from a contrastive perspective using the verbs of cutting and breaking (C&B) in English and Swedish as an example. The choice of the semantic field as the unit of comparison (rather than individual words) brings specific types of research questions into focus such as the pattern of semantic differentiation between members of the field. A second issue is field-specific patterns of polysemy, i.e. whether certain types of semantic extensions are shared between members of the field. Special attention is paid to the choice of data. An earlier typological study by Majid and Bowerman (2007) used data elicited with video clips to get comparable data. The present study is based on a large translation corpus consisting of subtitles to achieve comparability and to identify correspondent items across languages. The use of this corpus raises questions about its representativeness (how representative the corpus is of the compared languages in general) and about authenticity: to what extent various translation effects influence the result. To counterbalance and to assess such problems, samples were drawn from two registers (fiction and news) of monolingual English (BNC) and Swedish (KORP) corpora. The samples had to be restricted in size since they were manually coded. Certain aspects of meaning could also be investigated based on very large corpora with automatically generated word sketches (showing collocational patterns) provided by SketchEngine and KORP.

Keywords: (corpus-based) contrastive study, verb semantics, cut and break, English, Swedish

1 Introduction

The primary aim of this paper is to discuss which research questions are pertinent in the contrastive study of a semantic field and how that affects the choice of data and methods of analysis. The discussion will be founded on a corpus-based study of verbs of cutting and breaking (C&B). The choice of this field is motivated by the fact that there already exist some studies of such verbs based on different

---

Åke Viberg, Uppsala University, Department of linguistics and philology, Uppsala, Sweden

https://doi.org/10.1515/9783110682588-009

approaches to data. Particular attention will be paid to Majid and Bowerman (2007), which is a typological study of 28 diverse languages based on elicitation with video clips illustrating various cutting and breaking events.

The analysis of a semantic field can be done in several steps. The first is to describe the *pattern of differentiation* between the members of the field, i.e. the set of field-internal semantic distinctions. These distinctions can be described with semantic components of some type (depending on the underlying theory). In a contrastive study, certain components turn out to be shared (possibly universal), whereas others are language-specific. Shared components can be lexically and grammatically realized in different ways. For example, *break* can be semantically represented (roughly) as X CAUSES Y to BECOME BROKEN and realized in a simple sentence such as *Peter broke the vase*. In Swedish, the same components are realized as a verb and a particle in *Peter hade* ('had' CAUSE) *sönder* ('asunder' BROKEN) *vasen* ('the vase'). Second, the description should also cover *patterns of polysemy*. Polysemy can be *field-internal*, for example, *break* can also mean BECOME BROKEN (*The vase broke*). Polysemy can also be *field-external*, for example, both *break* and *cut* can be used as verbs of motion (*Mary broke up from camp*, *Mary cut across the field*). It is possible to see that words from a certain field (the source field) have a general tendency to extend into specific target fields. With respect to individual words, a basic assumption is that the meanings are organized as a *meaning potential* that shows the relationships between its various meanings (cf. Viberg 2012, Section 10.1 and references there; see also Allwood 2003). However, the discussion in this paper will focus on the use of the C&B verbs as separation verbs. The full meaning potential of the English verbs *break* and *cut* is so complex that a systematic examination of non-literal meanings must be left for separate articles.

Outline of the paper. Section 2 will give a summary of the extensive typological study of C&B verbs (Majid and Bowerman 2007). Section 3 will present a brief overview of theoretical approaches to the description of C&B verbs, before introducing the corpora on which this study is based in Section 4. The next sections will primarily be concerned with the patterns of differentiation within the field of C&B verbs when they refer to separation in a concrete sense. For simplicity, such meanings will at an early stage of the analysis be referred to as *literal*, whereas other meanings are referred to as *non-literal*. Section 5 looks at the differentiation between verbs of Breaking primarily when they have a literal meaning and ends with a short discussion of their non-literal meanings. Section 6 describes verbs of Tearing relatively briefly. Section 7 is devoted to the patterns of differentiation of verbs of Cutting when they have a literal meaning, whereas Section 8 discusses the relationship between C&B verbs and hand actions. Section 9 gives a brief overview of verbs that incorporate information about parts or pieces in their meaning. The semantic structure of C&B verbs in their literal use is summed up in Section 10. Section 11 discusses the representativeness of the analysis given so far by bringing non-literal meanings into the discussion and also by looking at the distribution of various meanings across registers. Section 12 is devoted to discussion and conclusion.

2 Earlier typological and contrastive studies

In Majid and Bowerman (2007) video clips depicting 61 C&B events were shown to speakers of 28 typologically diverse languages (one to seven consultants per language). This type of elicitation ensures comparability across languages based on non-verbal stimuli that do not cause linguistic interference from another language and is particularly suited to collecting data from languages spoken in preliterate societies, where large corpora are not available and are difficult to compile.

As stated by Majid et al. (2007), it is an open question whether verbs of cutting and breaking form a well-defined field in all languages or overlap with what in English is expressed by verbs with related but distinct meanings such as opening and taking apart. There is such an overlap in early child language as, for example, when a small child says "open" when breaking a leg off a plastic doll. To test that question, the video clips included illustrations of reversible separation such as opening the mouth or taking the lid off a tea pot. Multivariate statistics were used to identify major semantic distinctions and clustering among the verbs used across languages to describe the video clips (see Majid et al. 2008). The distinction between reversible and irreversible separation turned out to be the most basic one. Languages as used by adult speakers tend to use different verbs to express such concepts (see Figure 1). In the following, the term verbs of separation will be reserved for verbs of the irreversible type.

Among the verbs expressing irreversible separation, a second distinction was made between clean (CUT) and messy (BREAK) separation. The separation made with a knife (used in the conventional way) has a predictable locus and results in pieces with a regular form, whereas breaking, for example by smashing a bottle against a stone, results in an unpredictable number of separations and irregular pieces. A third distinction identified verbs of tearing as a separate class, which, like breaking, was characterized by messy separation but applied primarily to flexible objects. Breaking could further be subdivided into *snapping* and *smashing* in some languages and, in addition, *poking a hole* formed a category of its own in many languages.

First distinction				
Reversible	Irreversible			
OPEN	CUT		BREAK	TEAR
Second distinction				
	Clean separation	Messy separation		
	CUT	BREAK		TEAR
Third distinction				
		Rigid object BREAK		Flexible object TEAR

Figure 1: Basic distinctions between C&B verbs (based on Majid et al. 2008).

Four Germanic languages including English and Swedish were analyzed with cluster analysis (Majid et al. 2007). It turned out that English had two major clusters (BREAK vs. CUT), whereas German had three (adding TEAR) and Dutch four (adding a distinction between cutting-with-single-blade and cutting-with-scissors). Swedish had as many as five clusters (adding SNAPPING): "a large breaking cluster (*hugga*), snapping (*bryta*), cutting-with-a-single-blade (*skära*), cutting-with-scissors (*klippa*), and tearing (*slita*)" (Majid et al. 2007: 190). The Swedish and English data of the typological study can be compared to the corpus data that will be presented in this study.

Elicitation with video clips supports an analysis made from a world-to-word (Malt et al. 2010) or onomasiological (Geeraerts 2010) perspective, starting with a conceptual structure and looking at its various lexico-syntactic realizations. For languages where extensive corpora are available, it is possible to collect a large number of examples of words from a word-to-world (or semasiological) perspective. This approach makes it possible to study how the use of verbs to describe C&B events is related to the complete set of uses of such words (i.e. their meaning potential). The two perspectives are also related to basic disagreements about the nature of semantics and to the opposition between externalism and internalism in semantics (see Gross 2016 and Riemer 2016 for overviews).

There are two earlier contrastive studies based on corpora that used a partly different methodology but like the present study (see Section 3) were based on frame semantics. Bouveret and Sweetser (2009) account for the semantic differentiation between the three major French correspondences of *break*: *romper*, *casser* and *briser* and also discuss some of the metaphoric extensions. Fuji, Radetszky, and Sweetser (2013) compare English with Japanese and focus on the semantic differentiation between the C&B verbs when they are used with a concrete meaning.

The typology of C&B verbs has also inspired studies based on methods used within neurolinguistics (Kemmerer 2019, 141–157). In Kemmerer et al. (2008), subject's brains were scanned with functional Magnetic Resonance Imaging (fMRI) while they made discriminations between triads of words and decided that a word such as *hack* was more similar to *chop* than to *carve*. This made it possible to see what areas of the brain were activated by various verbs (see Section 10.1).

3 Theoretical framework of the present study of C&B verbs

When the aim is to account for all occurrences of a word in a set of samples from corpora, it is difficult to find a single theoretical framework into which all observations can be fitted. Nonetheless, it is important to relate the results to a wider framework. Models have strong and weak points and are useful for different purposes, and for that reason, this paper will be relatively eclectic with respect to theoretical models of lexical structure, such as models based on semantic predicates or semantic frames.

The present study represents a further development of two earlier studies of C&B verbs. Viberg (1985) presented an analysis of Swedish C&B verbs based on the type of semantic predicates used in Miller and Johnson-Laird (1976) and suggested that *break* and its Swedish correspondences had a prototypical meaning that combined the notions of separation (conceptualized as "disconnection" in that study) and non-functionality. Separation refers to the material destruction or loss of connectedness between various parts of an object, whereas non-functionality refers to the fact that an object (typically an artefact) cannot be used in the conventional way. In its purest form, this state of affairs is referred to as the second term in the antonymous pair *hel* 'whole' and *trasig* 'broken'. A broken vase is typically both materially disintegrated (partly or completely) and no longer suitable for use. The suggested prototypical core concept of breaking was: notCONNECTED(x) & notPOSSIBLE(USE(w,x,S_w)).

In Viberg (2007a), the analysis of Swedish and English C&B verbs was related to FrameNet, a lexical database founded on frame semantics (Fillmore 1982; see also: Electronic sources). In frame semantics, verbs (and other relational words) evoke frames – schematic structures of recurring situations. Separation corresponds to fragmentation. The frame Cause_to_fragment is defined in the following way: "An AGENT suddenly and often violently separates the WHOLE_PATIENT into two or more smaller PIECES, resulting in the WHOLE_PATIENT no longer existing as such". Table 1 shows an example of the canonical syntactic realization of the frame Cause_to_fragment (freely based on FrameNet).

Table 1: The syntactic realization of the frame Cause_to_fragment.

Frame elements	AGENT	Action	WHOLE	PIECES
Grammatical relations	Subject	Predicate	Object	Adjunct
Phrase structure	NP	V	NP	PP
Example	I	smashed	the toy boat	to flinders

Loss of function is covered by the frame: Render_nonfunctional, which has the definition: "An AGENT affects an ARTIFACT so that it is no longer capable of performing its inherent function", for example: *I* (AGENT) *broke the TV* (ARTIFACT). The frame Cutting focuses on separation: "An Agent cuts a(n) Item into Pieces using an Instrument (which may or may not be expressed)".

A major advantage is that FrameNet has a broad coverage, which makes it possible to relate a certain frame (or semantic field as in this study) to the overall structure of the lexicon. A second advantage is that FrameNet provides a simple and clear picture of the most basic relationships between the conceptual/semantic structure and the syntactic realization. Much remains to be worked out. Conceptually, a verb such as *smash* is defined with respect to the frame elements that are realized as its arguments, whereas the action as such is incompletely analyzed. Problems remain also with respect to the syntactic realization, for example how to fit verbal particles into the analysis in a systematic way (cf. Viberg 2007b).

4 In search of data: A survey of the corpora the study is based on

4.1 General considerations

The choice of data is of primary importance for a contrastive study and needs to be thoroughly justified, but that is not always done. Three problems will be briefly discussed: Equivalence, Authenticity and Representativeness. To begin with, a basic problem for a contrastive (or typological) study is to establish equivalence between elements to be compared. *Equivalence* refers to the problem of identifying correspondent elements across languages. Using a set of video clips represents one way of solving that problem. For a corpus-based contrastive (or typological) study, there are basically two choices, either to use a *translation corpus* and compare original texts with their translations or to use *comparable corpora*, which only contain original texts in two or more languages selected in such a way that they represent the same types of texts. The use of a translation corpus makes it possible to identify correspondences (e.g. all Swedish words that are used as translations of *break*) and to compare the correspondents when they are used in equivalent contexts, whereas a comparable corpus study typically starts from previously established correpondences.

Second, *Authenticity* refers to the problem of using data that represents ordinary language use. The occurrence of various types of translation effects can make translated texts different from original texts. For elicitation with video clips, for instance, it is important to make sure that the illustrated events are culturally meaningful in a comparable way across languages. Finally, *Representativeness* refers to choosing data that in some sense are representative of the languages under study and not restricted to a specific type of texts (or situations). Languages are variable along many dimensions. For instance, the stimuli used in elicitation with video clips and the participants are selected by the researcher(s). It is important to assure that the stimuli cover the most typical events across the compared set of languages. Corpus data in general represent many individual users of a language, but as demonstrated in Section 11, the various uses of a word can vary dramatically depending on the register. For that reason, it is important to include data from different registers.

4.2 Data for the present study

The present study is based on all occurrences of basic English C&B words and their Swedish equivalents in samples from corpora of various types. Swedish C&B verbs (referred to as verbs of disconnection) have earlier been studied in Viberg (1985) based on monolingual Swedish corpora. Data were accessed via micro fiche, which affected the tractability of counts based on systematic samples. Despite that, the picture of the basic structure of the field is the same as what emerges in the present study, but the description of the complete meaning potential of the C&B verbs was more restricted. There is also a contrastive study (Viberg 2007a) based on the *English Swedish Parallel Corpus (ESPC)* compiled by Altenberg and Aijmer (2000).[1] This corpus contains originals and translations in both languages, which makes it possible to use it both as a comparable corpus and as a translation corpus. The ESPC corpus, like the related *English Norwegian Parallel Corpus* (ENPC, Johansson 2007), is well suited for contrastive studies and played

---

[1] See Electronic sources at the end of the References for web addresses to corpora and other web-based material.

an important role for the emergence of corpus-based contrastive studies in the middle of the 1990s (Aijmer et al. 1996). This corpus is particularly useful for the study of relatively frequent phenomena. However, the size of the ESPC is relatively restricted in comparison to the multilingual corpora becoming available today (around 700,000 words of original texts in each language + translations). The translation data of the present study will be based primarily on samples from large corpora of subtitles.

Subtitles appear to provide corpus-data that are relatively close to spoken *everyday* language and thus represent a language variety that is relatively similar to the spoken data in the studies in Majid and Bowerman (2007). A basic finding in psycholinguistic studies is that the frequency of a word correlates highly with word-processing times (e.g. in lexical decision). Keuleers et al. (2010) found that word frequencies based on subtitle corpora explained more of the variance than frequencies based on ordinary written corpora (books, news and even Internet sources) and interpreted this as an indication that subtitles were a better approximation of everyday word use than ordinary written corpora. Another important finding was that contextual diversity, the number of texts in which a word occurs, is more important as a predictor than its raw frequency. The number of texts (films etc.) on which the samples in the present study are based has not been calculated, but the number must be very high, taking into consideration that the average number of words per film is relatively restricted.

Natalia Levshina has pioneered the use of subtitles as a source for contrastive and typological studies (e.g. Levshina 2016). She has also presented a very useful characterization of subtitles as a special register (Levshina 2017). Quantitative analyses based on n-gram frequencies were used to compare samples from American and British English representing two written registers (fiction, news) and two spoken registers (informal conversation, TV and radio broadcasts). In addition, original English subtitles were compared to English subtitles translated from French and other languages. The major conclusion was that subtitles were not fundamentally different from the other varieties of English. In particular, subtitles turned out to be similar to informal spoken conversations. However, there were a number of characteristic differences. The language of subtitles was less vague and narrative and contained fewer discourse markers than informal conversations. On the other hand, subtitles were characterized by more emotional and social interactive expressions such as greetings and politeness formulas. Translated subtitles turned out not to be fundamentally different from original English subtitles, but original subtitles were closer to natural dialogue. Levshina (2017: 336) concludes "if film dialogue is a reflection of real dialogue, subtitles are a reflection of a reflection. At the same time, they are remarkably close to real informal language".

The Open Subtitles organization (OpenSubtitles.org) makes available a very large number of subtitles for movie and TV programs in a wide range of languages. As a part of OPUS (see: http://opus.nlpl.eu/), these texts have been aligned and collected into an extensive parallel corpus with a query system that makes it possible to search for key words in context together with their translations. The corpus is continuously expanding. Subtitles 2016 comprises more than 17 billion words and spans 65 languages (Lison and Tiedemann 2016). The Open Subtitles corpus has served as the major corpus for the present study. Its size made it possible to identify correspondences of the Swedish and English C&B verbs, including many extended and often colloquial uses. Since the corpus is constantly being updated and older versions are not available anymore after some time, different versions have been used, namely Subtitles 2013, 2016 and 2018. The texts from older versions are usually included the most recent version.

A specific problem is that the query program that was used for the present paper did not identify original and translated versions in a simple way. Even if original and translated subtitles are not fundamentally different, various types of translation effects will occur (cf. Viberg 2016a for discussion of translation effects). For that reason, some of the C&B verbs were analyzed in monolingual English and Swedish corpora. This also provided an opportunity to look at register variation. Two registers were compared with Subtitles regarded as a third register: Fiction and News (see Section 11). English data were taken from the British National Corpus (BNC) using SketchEngine and Swedish data from KORP (Borin et al. 2012).

The monolingual corpora offer tools to prepare word sketches. A *word sketch* is "a summary of a word's grammatical and collocational behavior, produced automatically, from a large corpus" (Kilgariff and Tugwell 2002: 125). Such sketches show which words characteristically co-occur with a key word in various syntactic positions, for example, the characteristic subjects, objects and adverbials of a verb and the head of an adjective. The collocates are rank ordered according to salience based on the statistical significance of each combination. Word sketches can be obtained for English and several other languages with SketchEngine. For Swedish, similar sketches can be obtained with KORP (Borin et al. 2012: 476). Such sketches are referred to as word pictures (ordbilder) in KORP, but for simplicity they will be referred to as word sketches, since they are based on the same basic idea even if slightly different probability statistics are used. Exploratory studies based on word sketches will be presented below to complement the description of the meaning patterns of C&B verbs.

5 Breaking and messy separation

5.1 Establishing the major correspondences

Table 2 shows the most frequent translations of *break* (as a verb) in Subtitles 2013. A distinction is made between literal uses referred to as Separation and various Non-literal uses (*break the law/a promise/the silence*). With respect to literal separation, it is meaningful to make a broad distinction between the breaking of a bone in the body (*break an arm/ a leg/ a finger/ the collarbone/ the pelvis*) and the separation of other concrete objects (*break a bottle/ a chair/ a clock*). As can be observed in Table 2, *bryta* is the dominant translation when *break* refers to the breaking of a bone.

Table 2: *Break* and its major Swedish correspondences in Subtitles 2013.

break: Meanings	N	Swedish translations			
		bryta	sönder	trasig	OTHER
Separation					
BreakBONE	75	54	0	0	21
Other separation	176	22	64	26	64
Non-literal	534	124	0	0	410
Total	785	200	64	26	495

Actually, what is referred to as BreakBONE in Table 2 covers two types of BodyHarm depending on the Agentivity. There is a distinction between intentionally inflicting bodily injury, usually on another person (InflictBodyHarm) and accidentally hurting oneself (ExperienceBodyHarm). Example (1) refers to accidentally hurting oneself (ExperienceBodyHarm). Literal translations are given in single quotation marks.

(1)   I **broke** my arm once when I was a kid.
      Jag **bröt** armen en gång som barn.
      'I broke the arm once as child.'

The injured body part appears as an object and usually appears in a definite form in Swedish, whereas the body part is modified by a possessive pronoun referring to the injured person in English. Example (2) refers to intentionally hurting or inflicting bodily injury on a person (InflictBodyHarm).

(2) *If you **break** someone's collarbone, that's a good thing.*
    *Om du **bryter** nyckelbenet på någon.*
    'If you break the collarbone on someone.'

In the subtitles, the second, violent type is much more frequent than the accidental one (a register characteristic, cf. Section 11), but no distinction is made in Table 2, since the same type of separation is involved. In Swedish, the verb *bryta* is the dominant translation when the Whole refers to a bone. No alternative translation is very frequent: *knäcka* 'crack' (4 examples), *krossa* 'crush' (3), *spräcka* 'crack' (2). *Bryta* is not a general equivalent of *break* when it refers to literal separation. The Swedish verb is primarily used when the Whole is a rigid and oblong object and the separation is achieved by bending as in (3).

(3) *I'd give each one of 'em a stick and – one for each one of 'em – then I'd say "you **break** that."*
    */---/- sen sa jag att de skulle **bryta** av den*

Non-literal meanings of *break* are approximately twice as frequent as the literal ones that refer to physical separation.

Table 3 looks at the correspondence between *break* and *bryta* from the opposite direction by starting with the Swedish verb. Non-literal uses are more than twice as frequent as the literal ones. *Break* is more dominant as a correspondence of *bryta* than the opposite way around. This leads to the conclusion that *bryta* has a narrower range of meanings than *break* when it is used with both a literal and a non-literal meaning.

Table 3: *Bryta* and its major English correspondences in Subtitles 2013.

bryta: Meanings	N	English translations	
		break	OTHER
Separation			
BreakBONE	67	57	10
Other separation	35	20	15
Non-Literal	238	128	110
Total	340	205	135

5.2 Verb + *sönder*: an overview

The most frequent translation of *break* when it refers to other types of separation than breaking a bone is the Swedish verbal particle *sönder*. This particle accompanies a verb which can have a very general meaning. In (4), *ha* 'have' refers to a caused event, whereas *gå* 'go' in (5) refers to a pure change.

(4) It's not a party until someone **breaks** the Jacuzzi.
   Ingen fest förrens [sic!] någon **har sönder** jacuzzin.
   '[...] someone has asunder the Jacuzzi.'

(5) When the rudder **breaks** on one of those old tenders there's nothing to do but pray.
   Om rodret **går sönder** på en sån där skorv kan de bara be till Gud.
   'If the rudder goes asunder [...]'

Sönder contrasts with other particles, in particular *av* 'off', which refers to a single locus of the separation *bryta av en pinne* 'break (off) a stick', *skära av ett rep* 'cut off a rope', whereas *sönder* refers to the creation of many pieces: *bryta sönder en pinne* 'break a stick into pieces', *skära sönder ett rep* 'cut a rope into many pieces'. When non-functionality is focused, the degree of separation is irrelevant and an example such as *Peter hade sönder koppen* 'Peter broke the cup' can be used, even if the separation was partial and only resulted in a small crack.

The most basic function of the verb is to signal the distinction between causative, inchoative and stative meanings collectively referred to as the dynamic system. This system is summed up in Table 4 with idealized examples.

Table 4: The dynamic system in Swedish illustrated with idealized examples.

CAUSATIVE	
Peter broke the cup	Peter slog sönder koppen.
	'Peter hit asunder the cup.'
INCHOATIVE	
The cup broke.	Koppen gick sönder.
	'The cup went asunder.'
STATE	
The cup is broken.	Koppen är sönder /trasig.
	'The cup is asunder/rag–ADJ.'
a broken cup	en trasig kopp
	'a rag–ADJ cup'

Not all verbs that are combined with *sönder* have a general meaning. To various degrees, the verbs in addition to the dynamic meaning signal the manner of breaking. To shed light on this, a sample of 1,000 examples of *sönder* was extracted from the large corpus Subtitles 2016. As can be observed in Table 5, *break* corresponds primarily to the two causative combinations *slå* + *sönder* and *ha* + *sönder* and to the inchoative *gå sönder*. The stative *vara* + *sönder* often corresponds to *be broken*. The verbs *riva* and *slita* will be discussed in Section 6 (Tearing). The cases that are not accounted for are indicated at the bottom of Table 5 as OTHER. It refers to alternatives that only occur a few times as well as unclear cases.

Table 5: The major correspondences of Verb + *sönder* in Subtitles 2016.

sönder: Meanings		N	English translations					
CAUSATIVE			break	OTHER (selection)				
Swedish verb	Gloss							
slå	'hit'	165	59	smash	27	bust	14	
ha	'have'	138	101	smash	3	bust	6	
göra	'do'	10	7					
ta	'take'	13	6	take	2			
riva	'tear'	72	1	tear	49	rip	6	
slita	'tear, rip'	67	3	tear	38	rip	11	
skjuta	'shoot'	71	4	shoot	39	blow	14	
skära	'cut'	13	0	cut	7			
Various other verbs		80	5					
INCHOATIVE								
gå	'go'	225	126					
falla	'fall'	23	1	fall	7			
STATIVE								
vara	'be'	57	29 (=be broken)					
OTHER		66						
Total		1000	342					

5.3 The dynamic system

5.3.1 Causative breaking

The most frequent causative verb is *slå* 'hit/strike/beat' (6).

(6) No, I just don't want you to **break** his RV, Dad.
    Nej, jag vill bara att du inte ska **slå sönder** hans husbil, pappa.
    'No, I want only that you not shall hit asunder his housecar, daddy'

In (6), *slå* 'hit' is used in its prototypical meaning, which refers to an intentional hand action causing a forceful impact by contact, when the subject is human. However, *slå sönder* – like *break* – often refers to an accidental event as in (7), but *slå* is not completely generalized, since this verb can only refer to situations where the breaking is caused by forceful impact of some kind.

(7) She won´t trust strangers with her make-up case, ever since a porter dropped it and **broke** three vials of rare Swiss lamb placenta.
    /---/ sen en bärare tappade den och **slog sönder** tre kapslar schweizisk lamm-moderkaka.
    'after a porter dropped it and hit asunder three vials Swiss lambmothercake'

Break is the most frequent correspondent to *slå sönder* but has a more general meaning. *Smash* is a frequent alternative and is a semantically more direct correspondent to *slå sönder*, whose meaning is well captured in the definition of *smash* 1 in the Longman dictionary (Summers 2001): "to break into many small pieces violently or noisily or to make something do this by dropping, throwing or hitting it".

Both in English and Swedish the intentionality of a caused event (whether it was intentional/voluntary or not) must in most cases be inferred pragmatically. The most likely interpretation of (7) is that the porter dropped the make-up case unintentionally, even though this is not expressed explicitly. Other languages can signal the lack of intention grammatically. It is probably no coincidence that several examples in Kittilä's (2005) typological study of involuntary agent constructions contain breaking verbs. The German examples in (8) and (9)[2] have parallels in a number of typologically diverse languages.

---

[2] Both examples are from Kittilä (2005) but presented in a slightly different way.

(8) *Ich [nom] habe den Teller [acc] (absichtlich/unabsichtlich) zerbrochen.*
 'I have broken the plate (voluntarily/involuntarily).'

(9) *Mir [dat] ist der Teller [nom] (*absichtlich / unabsichtlich) zerbrochen.*
 'I accidentally broke the plate (*voluntarily/involuntarily).'

Like English, Swedish can use adverbials to express intentionality, but that option is seldom exploited. Swedish also has an auxiliary-like verb *råka* 'happen to' that signals unintentionality as in (10), but that is an infrequent option.

(10) *Jag **råkade** slå sönder ett fönster. [made-up example]*
 'I **happened** to break a window. /I broke a window **by accident**.'

The way intentionality is expressed in a certain language is important also because it may affect non-verbal thinking. Breaking events play a prominent role among the examples of intentional and accidental actions used as test stimuli in a study of eye-witness memory (Fausey and Boroditsky 2010). Silent video clips showing events such as (a man) *Sits at table, breaks pencil in half* (Intentional) vs. *Sits at table, breaks pencil in half while writing* were shown to speakers of English and Spanish, who took part in a linguistic task (verbal description) and in a non-linguistic memory task. Intentional events were described similarly with sentences mentioning an actor (*The man broke the pencil*). Contrary to that, English speakers tended to describe accidental events in a similar way as intentional events, whereas Spanish speakers tended to use non-agentive expressions with the clitic *se* as in. *Se rompió el florero / The vase broke (itself)/ was broken* (cf. *Jon rompió el florero / John broke the vase*). This linguistic contrast was reflected in a memory task. English speakers tended to remember the actor better than the Spanish speakers when the event was accidental, whereas performance was similar when the event was intentional.

As mentioned, *ha sönder* is a frequent alternative to causative *break* and is neutral with respect to the manner of breaking. The same is true of *ta* 'take' and *göra* 'do/make' in combination with *sönder*, see for example (11).

(11) *Jag slår vad om att jag inte **gör sönder** en enda flaska*
 'I bet you [on] the old phone book I don't **break** a bottle.'

The alternation between *ha* 'have', *göra* 'do/make' and *ta* 'take' as generalized causative verbs in combination with *sönder* actually reflects regional variation in spoken Swedish. As shown by Andersson (2007), who based his study on more than 5,000 answers to a web questionnaire, *göra sönder* is favored in Western

Sweden and *ta sönder* in Southern Sweden, whereas *ha sönder* is characteristic of Middle and Northern Sweden. *Ha sönder* is the dominant alternative in printed publications and must be regarded as the standard form according to Andersson. Rather few examples are found of the non-standard forms in the Subtitles corpus, but it is interesting to note that they are represented as correspondences of *break*.

5.3.2 Inchoative breaking

Break with an inchoative meaning mostly corresponds to *gå sönder*. *Sönder* can also be combined with *falla* 'fall' to express a successive change (a durative inchoative meaning), but in that case it seldom corresponds to *break* (see 12).

(12) Den här byggnaden håller på att falla **sönder**.
 'This building is falling apart.'

There are also a number of simple breaking verbs with an inchoative meaning in Swedish. Their closest correspondences in English can also be used with a causative meaning, for example: *spricka* (causative form: *spräcka*) – *crack*; *brista* – *burst, split*; *rämna* – *burst (wide open)*. The correspondences are only approximate, but a closer analysis must be left for a special study of the verbs of breaking.

5.3.3 Stative expressions

Sönder can be combined also with *vara* 'be' and then the most frequent correspondence is *(be) broken* (see 13). A frequent alternative correspondence is *trasig*, an adjective productively derived with the suffix *-ig* from the noun *trasa* 'rag' (frequently used in the plural *trasor* 'rags'), see (14).

(13) Call and tell them their computer's **broken**.
 Ring och säg att deras dator **är sönder**!

(14) The propellers **are broken** anyway.
 Propellerna **är** ändå **trasiga**.
 'The propellers are anyway ragged.' (rag-ADJ-PLUR)

Since *trasig* is an adjective, it can also be used as an attributive modifier of a noun, for example *en trasig tekokare* corresponding to *a broken teakettle*. This is a function that *sönder* cannot have, but relatively frequently *sönder* appears as the initial element of a compound participle *ett sönderslaget fönster* 'a broken window' (*sönder-* + the past participle of *slå* 'hit'). Broken is the most frequent translation of *trasig*, but participles of a number of different verbs are also used in English as correspondences of *trasig* (see 15).

(15) en trasig strålkastare 'a busted headlight'
     ett trasigt rör   'a cracked pipe'
     en trasig gitarr   'a smashed guitar'
     trasiga kläder   'shredded clothes'

According to the Swedish historical dictionary (SAOB), the use of *trasig* with reference to 'textile material' (my Clothes) is the oldest one (first attested 1618), whereas the extension to other artefacts is more recent (earliest attestation 1810) followed by the extension to abstract domains (see below). The present-day use of *trasig* can be illuminated by a word sketch. As mentioned, the large Swedish collection of corpora KORP makes it possible to produce word sketches (Borin et al. 2012: 476). Table 6a shows the list of the 15 most prominent heads of *trasig* in the corpus Social media, which is very large (more than 8 billion words).[3] It is possible to classify most of the heads into a restricted number of categories as demonstrated in Table 6b. It should be noted that the combinations in Table 6a only account for 9.6% of the occurrences of *trasig* (including predicative uses). It is possible to extend the list. A look at the 100 most prominent heads, which account for 20% (27,948 tokens) of the occurrences of *trasig*, showed many further examples of the same categories.

Table 6: The most prominent heads of the adjective *trasig* 'broken, ragged' in Social media.

a. The 15 most prominent heads		
TOTAL corpus: 8.55 G tokens	Accessed: 2017–12–06	
kläder	clothes	1,924
människa	man, human being	2,515
själ	soul	1,184
jeans	jeans	1,023
sko	shoe	978

---

[3] Note that the corpus is continuously expanding, so the total number of words in the corpus may differ in tables presented below. Note also that the ranking is based on salience according to statistically significant word combinations (Borin et al 2012: 476) and not on the raw frequency.

Table 6 (continued)

kondom	condom	521	
knä	knee	496	
tand	tooth	658	
lampa	lamp	537	
familj	family	814	
barndom	childhood	410	
leksak	toy	438	
dator	computer	621	
bil	car	715	
uppväxt	adolescence	408	
Total above:		13,242	=9.6%
Total of *trasig* in corpus		137,563	

b. Categorization

Category	English gloss
Clothes	clothes, jeans, shoe
Other Artefacts	condom, lamp, toy, computer, car
Body part	knee, tooth
Human feelings and relations	man, soul, family, childhood, adolescence

The categories Clothes and Other artefacts have already been commented on. When *trasig* refers to a body part, it contrasts to the past participle of *bryta*, which is *bruten*. *Trasig* is primarily used with body parts that are not typical "bones". The last category is called "Human feelings and relations" and refers to abstract, negative characteristics of the head nouns. This category is interesting because it refers to concepts that are metaphorically related to the head noun (perhaps basically: POVERTY IS PHYSICAL HARM, see Dodge 2016) but several mappings are involved. The meaning of *trasig* in this use is hard to pin down exactly but expresses compassion and refers to suffering and bad treatment: 'miserable', 'wretched'. It is used as a correspondence to a broad variety of English expressions. Examples (16) to (18) are taken from the Subtitles corpus.

(16) Rip came from **a broken home** which meant he hustled for every dollar he made.
Rip kom från **ett trasigt hem** och måste slåss för varje dollar.
'Rip came from a ragged home and must fight for every dollar.'

(17) I'm such an unholy **mess of a girl**.
   Jag är en förfärligt **trasig flicka**.
   'I'm a terribly ragged girl.'

(18) She told about **the squalor and filth** into which she and her brother were born and how they grew up like animals.
   Hon berättade om **det trasiga, fattiga liv** hon och hennes bror levt.
   'She told about the ragged, poor life she and her brother (had) lived.'

The choice between *bruten* and *trasig* is summed up in Table 7.

Table 7: Describing the state of being separated in Swedish and English (literal uses).

Type of Whole	Swedish		English	
	Predicative	Attributive	Predicative	Attributive
BONE OBLONG OBJECT	vara + bruten	bruten + N	be + broken	broken + N
ARTEFACT	vara + sönder	trasig + N	Various participles	
CLOTHES (flexible)	vara trasig			

5.4 Aspects of the meaning potentials of *break* and *bryta*

For reasons of space, it will only be possible to outline the meaning potentials of *break* and *bryta*. English *break* has a very wide range of non-literal meanings, whereas the non-literal meanings of Swedish *bryta* are more restricted and to a great extent correspond to a subset of the non-literal meanings of *break*. Word sketches will be used to capture those similarities but the characterization of the many language-specific (with respect to Swedish, at least) uses of *break* must be left for a separate paper.

A word sketch obtainable with KORP (Borin et al. 2012) sheds additional light on the use of *bryta* in Swedish. As is often the case, the top-ranked subjects represent specialized or idiom-like meanings. Five of the fifteen highest-ranked subjects refer to disastrous events that are said to "break out" (Swed. *bryta ut*), when they start (*helvete* 'hell', *krig* 'war', *världskrig* 'world war', *sjukdom* 'illness', *förkylning* 'cold'). There are only five subjects among the 50 top-ranked subjects that are human, for example: *tjuv* 'thief', which often appears in the expression *bryta sig in* 'break in (and steal)', and *domare* 'referee', in expressions like 'break the match'. The top-ranked object is *ben* 'leg; bone'. It is followed by *kontakt* 'contact' and *mönster* 'pattern', which have a general meaning and cover several more specific extended meanings of *bryta* at an abstract level. Among the rest of the top-ranked objects, it is possible in many cases to find examples with close English equivalents. The 50 top-ranked objects fall into the categories shown in Table 8. Most of the objects referred to as Other belong to various abstract categories. (There are also a few unclear cases.)

Table 8: Major categories of the 50 top-ranked objects of *bryta* in Social media.

TOTAL corpus 10.17 tokens			Accessed: 2018-11-16
Category	Tokens	Types	
Body part	37,156	12	
Other concrete objects	5,345	3	
Agreement	13,126	5	
Law	11,948	6	
Social relationship	25,311	6	
Pattern	28,467	8	
Other	17,012	10	
Total above	138,365	50	15.60% of all *bryta*
Total of *bryta* in corpus	886,772		87.2 tokens per million words

Body parts reach a high frequency both in terms of types and tokens. (cf. Break-Bone in Table 3). They represent a productive type of object. The few concrete objects that fit into the event type 'Other separation' mostly appear in specialized uses such as *bryta isen* 'break the ice', which is mostly used in an extended sense (as in English).

Table 9 shows some of the major categories of objects of *break* based on the BNC and the word sketch provided by SketchEngine. The 50 most frequent objects were inspected. (A ranking based on raw frequencies was chosen.) Together these objects represent a little more than 50% of all objects of *break* (8,886).

As can be observed, body parts (BONES) form a salient aspect also of the uses of *break*. The three abstract categories in Table 9 have close correspondences in Swedish. Agreement refers to examples such as *break one's word*, *break a promise* (Swed. *bryta ett löfte*). Expressions such as *to break the law* (Law) have direct correspondences in Swedish except that the construction is different. In Swedish,

Table 9: Some of the major categories of objects of *break* in BNC (SketchEngine).

Category	Number of:	
	Tokens	Types
Body part	1,543	13
Other concrete objects	574	8
Agreement	243	4
Law	581	3
Social relationship	44	1
Total above	2,985	29
Total other objects	1,551	21
Total	4,536	50

PPs with the preposition *mot* 'against' are used: *bryta mot lagen* lit. 'break against the law'. Many types of Social relationships can also be broken both in English and Swedish, for example *break off an engagement*, Swed. *bryta en förlovning*. The word sketches only make it possible to illuminate some aspects of the meaning potentials of *bryta* and *break* but show rather clearly that the majority of the uses of *bryta* correspond to some use of *break*.

6 Tearing: Separation by pulling apart

TEARING refers to messy separation and applies primarily to flexible objects (Majid et al. 2008). The English verb *tear* is interesting because, like the Swedish basic C&B verbs, it refers to manner: separate by pulling. Unlike *break* and *cut*, which primarily refer to the result, respectively MESSY and CLEAN separation, *tear* has a prominent manner component. OED refers to pulling in the definition of the primary sense of tear "To pull asunder by force (a body or substance, now esp. one of thin and flexible consistence, as cloth or paper)".

Table 10 shows the most frequent translations of *tear* in a sample from Subtitles 2011 using SketchEngine. Two Swedish verbs *riva* and *slita* together account for around 50% of the translations. In addition, there is a large number of verbs that are only used a few times (seven times or less in the sample). *Tear* is polysemous, but the meanings that do not refer to literal separation will not be discussed in this paper.

Table 10: *Tear* and its major Swedish correspondences in Subtitles 2011.

Meaning	Whole	N	Swedish translations	
			riva	slita
BodyHarm	Human	84	6	51
Separation	Flexible object	28	23	1
Demolition	Building	41	20	3
Removal		24	5	14
Other		158	18	26
Total		335	72	95

In the Subtitles, *tear* is extremely frequently used as a separation verb with reference to violent types of body harm. The dominant correspondence in such uses is *slita*, which basically refers to very forceful and violent pulling (often resulting in separation, cf. *rip*). Like in example (19), BodyHarm is often referred to in threats and in general the distinction between literal and non-literal meaning is fuzzy.

(19)   Release him or I swear I'll **tear** you to pieces!
       Släpp honom, annars lovar jag att **slita** dig i bitar!

When *tear* is used to refer to pulling apart an object made of flexible material such as paper or cloth (TEARING), its closest Swedish semantic correspondent is *riva*, see (20) and (21).

(20)   Why did you have to **tear up** that letter?
       Varför **rev** du **sönder** brevet?

(21)   I had to **tear** my trouser leg.
       Jag fick **riva sönder** byxbenet.
       'I got (=had to) tear asunder the trouserleg.'

Both *tear* and *riva* are frequently used to refer to the complete separation of a building. In this meaning, *tear* is often combined with the particle *down*, whereas *riva* takes the building as a direct object, usually without any particle (see 22). An alternative to *tear down* is *demolish* as in (23), but that option is not very frequent as a translation of *riva* in the subtitles (see Table 11).

Table 11: *Riva* and its major English correspondences in Subtitles 2011.

riva			English translations					
			tear	rip	scratch	demolish	grate	claw
Meaning	*Whole*	N						
BodyHarm	Human	24	10	5	3	0	0	0
Separation	Flexible object	45	25	12	0	0	0	0
Demolition	Building	94	40	0	0	7	0	0
Cavity	Skin	29	1	0	21	0	0	2
Grating	carrots, cheese	4	0	0	0	0	2	0
Removal		19	6	6	0	0	0	0
Other		74	26	11	1	0	0	0
Total		289	108	34	25	7	2	2

(22) No. They **tore down** Seattle's first Pony Express office to build it.
Nej, de **rev** Ponnyexpressens första kontor i Seattle för att bygga det.

(23) The forestry company will **demolish** the farm and plant trees instead.
Skogsbolaget kommer att **riva** gården och plantera skog här.

The Swedish verb *riva* has several uses where it refers to pulling along a surface and corresponds to other English verbs than *tear*. One such use refers to the pulling of various types of food such as carrots or cheese along a grater as in (24).

(24) Sam **grated** the cheese himself.
Sam har själv **rivit** osten.

Another such use of *riva* is when the separation is caused by pulling something sharp (typically nails or claws) along a surface (typically the skin if the object is human). This creates a cavity such as a wound, a scratch or a mark. The most general English correspondence in this case is *scratch* as in (25).

(25) My cat **scratched** me.
Min katt har **rivit** mig.

A more specific correspondence is '(to) claw', which most directly corresponds to Swedish *klösa* (related to *klo* '(a) claw'). Unlike *scratch*, *riva* is not used when the contact is so weak that no cavity is created. A frequent Swedish correspondence is *klia*, which typically refers to scratching used to alleviate itching, see (26).

(26) (Nothing) is worse than having an itch you can never **scratch**.
Inget är värre än en klåda som man inte kan **klia** på.

Table 12 sums up the most important uses of *riva* as a separation verb.

Table 12: The Swedish verb *riva* used as a separation verb.

MANNER	WHOLE	English V	Swedish V
separate by pulling apart	FLEXIBLE OBJECT (paper, cloth)	tear	
separate completely (by pulling down)	BUILDING	tear/pull down, demolish	riva
separate by pulling along grater	FOOD (carrots, cheese)	grate	
separate (and hurt) by pulling nails or claws along surface	SKIN, other SURFACE	claw	klösa
		scratch	
pull nails along skin to alleviate itching	SKIN		klia

Both *tear* and its closest Swedish correspondences can refer to removal. In (27), separation is prominent and the meaning can be paraphrased 'to remove by separation'. Removal is profiled and separation is reduced to a manner component. In examples of this type, the object refers to parts (or pieces) and not to the whole as in the examples above where separation is focused, for example *I tore my shirt (into pieces)*.

(27) By the time we got to the scene, coyotes had **torn off** some of the major body parts.
När vi kom hade prärievargar **slitit av** några stora kroppsdelar.

Tear can also refer to removal by pulling carried out in a forceful and violent manner as in (28) without necessarily indicating (irreversible) separation. Separation is not excluded and many examples are vague in this respect.

(28) She tried to **tear off** all his clothes.
Hon försökte **slita av** honom kläderna.

Summing up, TEARING in the sense of "messy separation of a flexible object" is expressed by *tear* in English and *riva* in Swedish. *Slita* and *rip*, which refer to more violent actions, can also be used, but have not been analyzed in detail. The core component of *riva* is PULLING (manner of motion), which is shared by most of its uses. A possible exception is the reference to the demolition of a building, even though the English correspondences *tear down* and *pull down* in this case must be regarded as extensions based on this concept.

7 The verbs of cutting

7.1 Establishing the major correspondences

Table 13 shows the most frequent translations of the verb *cut* in Subtitles 2013. Like *break*, *cut* is frequently used to describe BodyHarm in the Subtitles. In the majority of cases, reference is made to intentional infliction of bodily injury on another person (InflictBodyHarm) and extreme violence is often involved as in (29).

(29) *After he **cut** her throat, he stabbed her in the chest… **cut** open her stomach… and, uh, took out her intestines.*
*Efter att han **skar** halsen av henne, så högg han henne i bröstet… **skar** upp hennes mage… och, ja, tog ut hennes inälvor.*
'[…] cut the throat off her […] cut up her stomach […]'

Like *break*, *cut* can also be used to refer to events when people hurt themselves unintentionally (ExperienceBodyHarm), see (30).

(30) *It's blood from when I **cut my hand** making it for you.*
*Det är blod från när jag **skar mig** då jag täljde den åt dig.*
'[…] when I cut myself […]'

BodyHarm is a special type of separation, which is represented separately since it is characteristic of the subtitles. When *cut* refers to other types of physical separation, the action is usually intentional, when the subject is human, see example (31).

(31) *I'm good at **cutting** things off.*
*Jag är bra på att **skära av** saker.*

As shown in Table 13, the English verb *cut* has several frequent Swedish correspondences, when it is used literally. In particular, there are four Swedish verbs that all refer to cutting something using an instrument with a sharp edge. They

Table 13: Major Swedish correspondences of *cut* in Subtitles 2013.

cut: Meanings	N	Swedish translations				
		skära	klippa	hugga	kapa	OTHER
BodyHarm	123	80	1	14	0	28
Other Separation	109	34	31	5	12	27
Non-Literal	217	5	4	1	0	207
Total	449	119	36	20	12	262

all contrast semantically and can in general not be substituted for one another. As a first approximation, *skära* refers to cutting with a knife, *klippa* to cutting with scissors and *hugga* to cutting with an axe, whereas *kapa* is neutral with respect to instrument. *Cut* has many non-literal uses but Swedish *skära* and the other correspondences seldom correspond to *cut* when it is used non-literally.

The other way around, Table 14 shows the major correspondences of *skära* in Subtitles 2013. The verb *cut* dominates strongly as a correspondence of *skära*. The alternatives can all be regarded as specific semantic alternatives to *cut*. Table 14 also shows that *skära* is seldom used with a non-literal meaning.

Table 14: Major English correspondences of *skära* in Subtitles 2013.

skära: Meanings	N	English translations				
		cut	slice	slit	slash	OTHER
BodyHarm	98	67	4	3	2	22
Other Separation	41	28	4	1	0	8
Non-Literal	14	3	0	0	0	11
Total	153	98	8	4	2	41

The proportion of non-literal uses is low also for *klippa* as shown in Table 15.[4] Like *skära*, *klippa* has *cut* as the dominant correspondence. Certain objects of *klippa* are conspicuously recurrent, in particular 'hair', which is represented separately in Table 15. It is notable that Swedish often uses the reflexive *klippa sig*, even when the agent is different from the subject of *klippa*: *Lisa klippte sig* (lit. Lisa

---

[4] Since *klippa* has lower frequency than *skära*, the larger corpus Subtitles 2016 was used instead of Subtitles 2013.

Table 15: Major English correspondences of *klippa* in Subtitles 2016.

klippa: Meanings	N	English translations			
		cut	get a haircut	mow	shear	OTHER
BodyHarm	7	5	0	0	0	2
cut hair	40	21	8	0	0	11
Other Separation	53	33	0	7	3	10
Non-Literal	13	5	0	0	0	8
Total	113	64	8	7	3	31

'cut herself') corresponds to *Lisa cut her hair, Lisa got a haircut*. Another frequent object refers to 'grass': *klippa gräset/ gräsmattan*; *cut the grass/ the lawn* (lit. 'the grass mat'). The most frequent correspondence is actually *mow the lawn*. In Swedish, *klippa gräset* presupposes that a lawn mower is used. If a scythe is used, the traditional expression is *slå gräset* lit. 'strike the grass', typically without any explicit mentioning of the instrument. Another special case is when *klippa* refers to the cutting of wool off sheep, which is referred to by *shear* in English.

The verb *hugga* has three major correspondences in the Subtitles corpus (see Table 16): *cut, chop* and *stab*. Intuitively, the most salient meaning is 'chop wood, to cut wood with an axe', but *hugga* has a number of other uses that share the reference to striking a sharp instrument forcefully against something in order to cut it. *Hugga* can be used also with reference to cutting stone with a chisel and a mallet. The manner of motion is the central meaning component and is present also in uses that do not involve cutting, for example to grab something swiftly with force (see Section 8.1). In the subtitles, *hugga* usually corresponds to *cut* or *chop* when *hugga* refers to the infliction of body harm and the instrument is an ax or a sword. The frequent use of *stab* as a correspondence appears to be characteristic of the subtitles and refers to the forceful thrusting of a sharp and pointed

Table 16: Major English correspondences of *hugga* in Subtitles 2016.

hugga: Meanings	N	English translations					
Literal		cut	chop	stab	bite	slash	OTHER
BodyHarm	115	25	18	36	0	5	31
Other Separation	53	15	11	5	2	1	19
Non-Literal	22	1	0	0	1	0	20
Total	190	41	29	41	3	6	70

instrument (typically a knife) into someone's body. With respect to Other Separation, both *chop* and *cut* are used as correspondences of recurring combinations such as *hugga ved* 'chop wood' and *hugga ner träd* 'cut down trees'.

7.2 How should the contrast between Swedish and English be interpreted?

What distinguishes Swedish from English is that the choice between *skära*, *klippa* and *hugga* is obligatory in most contexts. There is no verb with a general meaning that corresponds to *cut*. This does not mean that the number of lexical distinctions that can be made is restricted in English. A large number of more specific verbs are represented in WordNet (see Electronic sources), an electronic lexical database that represents the conceptual structure of the lexicon in terms of semantic relations such as synonymy, antonymy and hyponymy. For verbs, the special relation troponomy has been introduced. Troponyms of a verb have a more specific meaning than the superordinate verb and have added a manner component (a kind of "manner hyponymy", for example. *look – stare/gloat/glance* etc.). The verb *cut* has 53 direct troponyms, which in many cases have troponyms as well. In total, *cut* has 119 troponyms. Figure 2 shows a selection consisting of the troponyms that involve an instrument. At the top, the closest superordinate concept of *cut* is shown in terms of the set of synonyms (*synset*) that can express this concept.

```
separate, disunite, divide, part (force, take, or pull apart)
              "He separated the fighting children"; "Moses parted the Red Sea"
   cut (separate with or as if with an instrument) "cut the rope"
      saw (cut with a saw) "saw wood for the fireplace"
         whipsaw (saw with a whipsaw)
      scythe (cut with a scythe) "scythe grass or grain"
         cradle (cut grain with a cradle scythe)
      chop, hack (cut with a hacking tool)
         axe, axe (chop or split with an axe) "axe wood"
      tomahawk (cut with a tomahawk)
      sabre, saber (cut or injure with a saber)
      shear (cut or cut through with shears) "shear the wool off the lamb"
      pink (cut in a zigzag pattern with pinking shears, in sewing)
```

Figure 2: A selection of troponyms of *cut* in WordNet.

Instruments can be semantically incorporated in Swedish as well, but among the verbs in Figure 2, only *saw* (Swed. *såga*) and *hack* (Swed. *hacka*) have a Swedish correspondence. In principle, these verbs are not subordinate to *skära* or any other Swedish cutting verb. If a saw is used, *cut* must be translated by *såga* in the following example from Subtitles 2016: *They wanted to cut down her tree – De ville såga ner trädet*. As demonstrated in Table 17, all of the Swedish verbs of cutting semantically incorporate a manner component. When a certain verb is used, a specific instrument is mostly understood without being mentioned, but the choice of verb is often determined by the way the instrument is used. *Skära* is typically associated with separation with a knife but that requires that the knife is moved along the object. If someone is stabbed with a knife, *hugga* must be used. Both *hugga* and *klippa* have a prominent semantic motion component (see Section 8) that is part of the core meaning. Even *såga* 'saw' presupposes that the saw is moved in a certain way, and this can give rise to extended meanings such as the following one where *såga* refers to the movement of the bow across the strings of a violin: *Jag såg musikerna entusiastiskt såga sig genom första satsen*. (KORP: Novels II) 'I saw the musicians enthusiastically saw their way through the first movement' (own translation). Uses of this type are infrequent with *såga* but are relatively frequent with *hugga* and *klippa*.

Table 17: Major verbs of cutting in Swedish.

Swedish verb	MANNER	BLADED INSTRUMENT					
		knife	scissors	axe	saw	scythe	tongs
skära	Move along surface	X					
klippa	Move two blades towards one another		X				X
hugga	Forceful swinging motion	X		X			
slå 'strike'	Swinging motion					X	
knipsa	Pinching						X
såga	Motion back and forth	(X)			X		
kapa	Cut crosswise	X	X	X	X	?	X

The verb *kapa* can imply the use of many different instruments (depending on the context), but it cannot be regarded as semantically superordinate to the other verbs of cutting since *kapa* usually implies that something is cut crosswise and with precision. *Kapa* has a relatively low frequency in general registers and is primarily used in certain technical contexts, for example when something is cut into pieces of a specific length.

Table 17 mentions only instruments of a traditional type. Today, technologically more advanced instruments are used such as lawn mowers (rather than scythes) and chainsaws. In manufacturing, cutting can be done with an air jet, a waterjet, heat or laser. It appears that *skära* is extended to cover many of these cases but that has not been studied systematically. The traditional cutting instruments are the most relevant ones for a typological comparison and most extensions of the cutting verbs are based on traditional (sometimes even obsolete) uses.

The most important difference between *cut* and the basic Swedish cutting verbs is that *cut* simply refers to separation with a bladed instrument, whereas the Swedish verbs distinguish between different types of instruments and incorporate a manner component. *Skära* in many respects is the most direct correspondence to *cut*, but unlike that verb, *skära* cannot be used as a superordinate of the other cutting verbs as demonstrated in Figure 3. Arguably, *dela* '(to) divide' (*del* '(a) part' +-*a* Infinitive) can serve as a superordinate term for C&B verbs in Swedish.

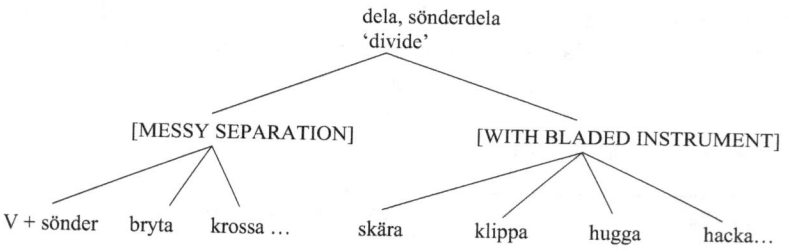

Figure 3: Schematic tree showing the hierarchical structure of Swedish C&B verbs.

The differentiation between verbs of cutting is culturally very variable and it is easy to find examples of rich differentiation between such verbs in non-European languages. Brown's (1925) dictionary of Setswana lists, in addition to *sega* 'cut with a knife' and *rèma* 'chop, hew', around 40 verbs under *cut*, some of which are very culture-specific and require a long phrase as translation, for example *setlhèla* 'cut off a piece of meat, while holding it in the mouth', *gabèla* 'cut up pumpkin for cooking' and *ragola* 'cut by putting knife under and jerking'.

C&B verbs incorporate several types of meaning. Section 8 will give two examples how Manner is a central component of the meaning. The incorporation of information about various parts and pieces will then be looked at in Section 9.

8 Hand actions and C&B verbs

The core meaning of *cut* can roughly be paraphrased 'to cause the separation of an object by using a bladed instrument'. The large number of non-literal meanings of *cut* (the pattern of polysemy) can be described as elaborations of this core. As was shown in Section 6, the verbs of tearing can be used as motion verbs and refer to pulling without resulting in separation. Certain verbs, which have a core meaning that belongs to another field, are used as C&B verbs only in very restricted contexts. A clear example of that is Swedish *slå* 'hit/strike' that refers to cutting only when it has an object that refers to grass and closely related concepts. *Slå hö* (lit. 'hit hey') refers to the cutting of hey with a scythe. In actual practice there is a continuum and in several cases it is an open question whether a verb is a C&B verb or only is used as such a verb in restricted contexts. The major hypothesis that will be tested in this section is that the Swedish verbs *hugga* and *klippa* refer to special forms of hand actions that result in separation. Several semantic fields contain verbs describing physical actions (i.e. goal-directed bodily action sequences carried out by humans). Hand actions such as putting and throwing or giving (handing) and taking (removing) as well as hitting are prominent examples. Viberg (2016b) argues that a large part of the extensions of Swedish *slå* 'hit' are best understood as semantic shifts from a prototype representing *slå* as a hand action.

In addition, Sections 8.1 and 8.2 provide examples how the patterns found in the Subtitles can be compared to data from monolingual corpora. All occurrences of *hugga* and *klippa* in the corpus Novels II in KORP were analyzed. A second data source was word sketches based on the complete Social media corpus in KORP.

8.1 The meaning potential of *hugga*

Table 18 presents an overview of the most frequent meanings of *hugga* in Swedish fiction (all occurrences of *hugga* in Novels II).

Table 18: Major meanings of *hugga* in Swedish fiction (Novels II).

	Body Harm	Separation	Bite	Grasp	Effort	Pain/ Emotion	Verbal	Other	Total *hugga*
Freq.	15	67	10	28	5	16	5	21	167
%	9	40	6	17	3	10	3	13	

As expected, Body Harm is less frequent than in Subtitles and (other) Separation is the most prominent meaning. However, *hugga* is basically a physical action verb that refers to a forceful, swinging motion of the arm and hand. That is the motivation for the frequent use of *hugga* as a correspondence of *cut* when *cut* refers to the stabbing with a knife in the Subtitles. Relatively frequently, *hugga* refers to the forceful grabbing of something. In general, *hugga* in this meaning is combined with the bare noun *tag* (related to *ta* 'take'), a bare noun that is used as a stressed particle followed by *i* 'in' in the phrase *hugga tag i* (cf. 'grab hold of') as in *Jag högg tag i hans arm* 'I grabbed his arm'. With reference to certain animals, *hugga* refers to biting in a sudden and forceful manner (see 32).

(32) *Vi måste **hugga** som en orm – snabbt.* (Subtit 2016)
  We must **strike** as the serpent, fast and sure.

Hugga + *i* 'in' can also be generalized and refer to effortful physical action of an unspecified type as in *Nu hugger vi i.* 'Lets' get going', but that is not a very frequent use.

One special use that is characteristic of Swedish cutting verbs in general is the reference to Pain and painful Emotion. This use has parallels in many other languages as documented in Reznikova et al. (2012), a typological study of pain predicates based on data from more than 20 diverse languages. One of the major sources of pain predicates were verbs referring to Destruction/Deformation: CUT, PRICK, STAB. When *hugga* refers to pain it is often combined with the particle *till*[5] and appears in an impersonal construction with the formal subject *det* 'it' as in (33).

(33) *Det **högg till** i hjärtat när jag hörde att Bobby var död.* (Sub 2016)
  'It hewed to in the heart [...]'
  'Almost had a heart attack when I heard about Bobby.'

There are also a few examples of *hugga* in combination with the particle *till* used as a Verbal communication verb as in: *"I Cardiff", högg hon till med*, '"In Cardiff", she guessed'. In such examples, *hugga* refers to an utterance produced erratically and on the spur of the moment without any deeper reflection and appears to be motivated by the association of *hugga* with a sudden action.

Word sketches based on the use of *hugga* in Social media shed some further light on the semantics of the verb. The highest ranked subject is *hund* 'dog', followed by *gädda* 'pike', which is associated with the meaning BITE. The pike is known to give a forceful pull on the fishing rod when it bites. The most prominent objects are categorized in Table 19.

---

[5] The basic meaning of *till* as a preposition is 'to' but here it is used as a stressed particle with a momentary (semelfactive) meaning. *Hugga* has basically a frequentative meaning. Etymologically it is formed via reduplication.

Table 19: Categorization of the 50 top-ranked objects of *hugga* in Social media.

Category	Types	Tokens	Examples
PARTICLE	1	2,923	hold (Swedish: *tag*)
TREE/WOOD	8	6,455	firewood, tree, fir, birch, Christmas tree, forest
HUMAN	10	3,529	friend, victim, police, wife
BODYPART	9	5,430	head, hand, arm, throat, leg, tooth
TOOL	3	1,512	knife, spoon, axe
Total above	31	19,849	
OTHER	19	7,749	
Total *hugga* in corpus		165,049	

One of the most frequent objects is *tag*, the bare noun that is used as a stressed particle in the phrase *hugga tag i* 'grab forcefully' reflects the use of *hugga* as a hand action. Word sketches identify objects that are associated with specific meanings of the verb. Tree/Wood points to what is intuitively one of the most characteristic uses of *hugga* as a separation verb. The most frequent individual noun is *ved* 'firewood', primarily used in bare form directly after the verb: *hugga ved* 'cut/chop wood'. Human objects appear to refer primarily to victims of inflicted body harm. However, some objects are characteristic of several meanings of the verb. Body parts appear as objects, when *hugga* refers to BodyHarm in the same constructions as appear in Subtitles, but examples that refer to PAIN are also frequent (see example 33). 'Tooth', which has been categorized as a body part, is used as an instrument in expressions such as *hugga tänderna i en grillad kyckling* lit. 'cut one's teeth into (i.e. start eating) a grilled chicken'. This can be extended as in *hugga tänderna i en klassisk deckare* lit. 'cut one's teeth into (i.e. start reading) a classical detective story'. Knife and axe are typical tools associated with *hugga*. The unexpected tool *sked* 'spoon' is used primarily with reference to events in which children are pounding the spoon in the table or forcefully grabbing the spoon (*hugga efter skeden* 'hew after/try to grab the spoon'). Examples of this type are prominent because Social media includes a large corpus Family life (a discussion forum).

Summing up, cutting wood with an axe is a prominent meaning of *hugga* as a separation verb, but BodyHarm, which is characteristic of Subtitles, is relatively often referred to also in Social Media. Basically *hugga* is a hand-action verb and the reference to a forceful movement of the arm and hand (and an instrument held in the hand) is a core component of the meaning shared by all meanings except the abstract ones referring to pain and verbal communication. The latter only share the association with forcefulness and suddenness.

8.2 The meaning potential of *klippa*

Separation is the dominant meaning of *klippa* in Swedish fiction as can be observed in Table 20.

Table 20: Major meanings of *klippa* in Swedish fiction (Novels II).

	Body Harm	Other Separation	Motion (ear, eye)	Hitting 'throw a punch'	Verbal com.	Other	Total *klippa*
Frequency	2	110	16	14	11	44	197
%	1	56	8	7	6	22	

Like *hugga*, *klippa* can be used to refer to body movements but that is restricted to eyes (i.e. eyelids,) and ears (of animals such as horses and rabbits): *kaninen klippte med öronen* 'the rabbit twitched its ears'. *Klippa* in combination with the particle *till* can also be used as a verb of Hitting: *Peter klippte till Harry* 'Peter dealt Harry a blow'. This is clearly a hand action, but it is not completely clear how the movement involved in this action it is related to the movement when a pair of scissors is used. *Klippa* can also be used as a Verbal Communication verb and refers to an abrupt interruption that ends the conversation as in (34).

(34) *Jag försökte fråga honom om hans egen uppväxt, men han **klippte** genast av min fråga och sade att det inte var mycket att orda om.* (NovelsII)
'[...] he cut off my question.'
'I tried to ask him about his own youth, but he **cut me short** and said that that was not much to talk about.' [Own translation]

Word sketches give a good picture of the uses of *klippa*. Table 21 shows a categorization of the 50 top-ranked objects in Social media. Practically all of them are concrete. Conformity with the Subtitles corpus is good with respect to the two most frequent categories of objects, Body parts and Plants. Looking at individual nouns, both cutting the hair and cutting grass/the lawn (*mow*) were singled out separately in Table 15 that shows the major translations of *klippa* in Subtitles 2016.

Body parts are frequent objects of *klippa* as well as of *hugga*, but are represented by different sets. Those of *hugga* are primarily associated with BodyHarm, whereas those of *klippa* are associated with caring of the body (hairdressing, manicure).[6]

---

[6] Examples with the umbilical cord are exceptions. Like in English, the expression *klippa navelsträngen* 'cut the umbilical cord' is used with a literal as well as a non-literal meaning ('become independent').

Table 21: Categorization of the 50 top-ranked objects of *klippa* in Social media.

Category	Types	Tokens	Examples
BODY PART	9	33,304	hair, fringe, nail, toe nail, umbilical cord
PLANTS	5	21,451	grass, lawn, bush, hedge, twig
CLOTH	1	439	cloth
CARD	2	3,542	punch card, credit card
LINE (CORD)	3	6,777	tape, cord, cable
PIECE/CAVITY	5	3,228	piece, patch, slip, top; hole
TEXT	2	1,103	text, quotation
FILM	2	2,076	film, scene
ABSTRACT	1	1,934	contact
Total (above)	31	73,854	= 15.70% of the total number of *klippa*
OTHER	19	23,535	
Total of *klippa* in the corpus		470,315	Accessed: 2018–02–22

Plants as objects are associated with horticulture. One characteristic that cuts across many of the categories is practically motivated. A pair of scissors is particularly useful to cut flexible material such as hair, cloth, paper and lines in a concrete sense (cord, string, rope). All of these are relatively thin and either have an oblong or a flat and thin shape. However, the choice of verb is not directly controlled by the type of object. The method of cutting is decisive. If you cut off a twig with a pair of gardening shears, you must use *klippa*, but if you use a knife you must use *skära* (or *hugga*, if the knife is used to chop off the twig).

A special case that needs to be identified as such is when the object (Whole) refers to film or text, for example *Jag klipper ur artiklarna* 'I cut out the articles'. In this example, the Whole is understood and refers to the paper containing the articles, but the meaning has often been extended to cover modern techniques of editing (by computer) where the Swedish correspondence *klippa* is no longer motivated by the use of a pair of scissors (e.g. the cut command in a word processing program is called *klipp ut* 'cut out [with a pair of scissors]'). The only abstract example is *klippa kontakten* 'cut the contact'. This use is related to several metaphors that are based on the notion of *cutting bonds* or ties with reference to various abstract domains (see 35).

(35) Ni **klipper av** de sista **banden** till tryggheten. (Sub 2016)
You're **cutting** the last **bonds** which bind you to safety.

Summing up, separation with a two-bladed instrument is the core component of *klippa*. The cutting with a pair of scissors, which can be regarded as the prototype, involves a hand action and the use of other tools such as tongs and shears require similar motions. Even if *klippa* can be used to refer to other types of body movements such uses are not very frequent. Separation is a more prominent part of the meaning potential than it is of *hugga*.

9 Verbs incorporating information about parts and pieces

Cutting and breaking typically result in the creation of various kinds of pieces that are associated with different types of verbs. In addition, reference to a certain kind of pieces is semantically incorporated into many verbs, in particular verbs of cutting as shown in Table 22. In general, English and Swedish are similar with respect to these kinds of verbs. For that reason, this table will be commented on rather briefly.

Table 22: Verbs incorporating various types of parts or pieces.

Focus on separated parts		Focus on created pieces		Creation of hole /cavity	
English	Swedish	English	Swedish	English	Swedish
limb	kvista	slice	skiva	scratch	riva2
bark	barka	dice	tärna	scratch	rispa
(un)scale	fjälla	fillet	filea	scratch	repa
bone	bena	shred	strimla	claw	klösa
peel	skala	crumble	smula	notch	skåra
skin	flå	piece	klyfta	hole	håla
skin	skinna	splinter	flisa		

Unlike breaking, which typically results in the creation of irregular pieces such as shards or splinters, cutting typically results in regular pieces such as slices, cubes and dices. This type of pieces can be incorporated into verb roots as in *to slice a loaf of bread, to dice a cucumber*. These verbs are mostly associated with food preparation. Pieces are typically created as a result of cutting and breaking and differ from parts which can usually be perceptually distinguished in an intact whole. In addition to that, parts often fulfill a specific function. Parts can often be reversibly separated from the whole (cf. *take apart – reassemble, open – close*). There is, however, a special variety of separation verbs that refer to the irreversible separation of a part from its whole, for example *to peel an orange, to bone a fish*. In this case, there is no creation involved since the part is in existence both before and after the separation event. A specific type of part that is created by various types of separation is a cavity such as a hole, a cut, a crack or a scratch as in *You scratched my car!* (cf. Section 6).

10 Summing up the differentiation pattern of the C&B verbs

This section will sum up the semantic differentiation pattern of the C&B verbs (i.e. the field-internal semantic contrasts). The results of the present study can be compared to the typological study discussed in Section 2. Majid et al (2007: 190) identify five clusters in Swedish: "a large breaking cluster (*hugga*), snapping (*bryta*), cutting-with-a-single-blade (*skära*), cutting-with-scissors (*klippa*), and tearing (*slita*)". The major difference with the present study is that the breaking cluster is identified with *hugga*. It should rather be identified with Verb + *sönder*, whereas *hugga* represents a third type of cutting verb. With these adjustments, the major distinctions presented in Figure 1, based on Majid et al. (2007), provide a good typological framework into which Swedish and English can be fitted. English with few basic distinctions and Swedish with many basic distinctions are situated at different ends if the number of distinctions are ordered in a scale.

10.1 Toward a more fine-grained semantic analysis

The contrastive analysis of English and Swedish has made it possible to identify a number of fine-grained distinctions which are summed up in Table 23 and related to the frame elements of FrameNet (cf. Table 1).

All of the semantic features can be incorporated into the verb in various combinations. Minimally the features of Action are specified in the verb. This applies to verbs in general. In English, the action is usually intentional when *cut* is used as in *Peter cut the rope*, whereas *break* tends to be non-intentional, in particular when the object is an artifact as in *Peter broke the cup*. In both examples, the verb is causative, whereas it is inchoative in *The cup broke*. In Swedish, the use of Verb + *sönder* makes it possible to signal the dynamic system analytically.

Table 23: Major semantic distinctions between C&B verbs.

Frame elements	Major semantic features
ACTION	
AGENTIVITY	Intentional/Non-intentional
DYNAMIC SYSTEM	Causative/Inchoative/Stative
RESULT	Clean/Messy separation; Damage; Creation
WHOLE	Rigid/Flexible; Compact/Flat/Oblong
PIECES	Regular/Irregular; Flat/Oblong
INSTRUMENT	One-bladed: Knife/Axe/Saw; Two-bladed: Scissors/Tongs
MANNER OF MOTION	Bending/Pulling/Hitting/Dropping

The Result of the Action can be referred to as clean or messy separation, which is physically based. The result can also be functionally evaluated in terms of human usefulness as Damage (*a broken cup*) or as Creation. In the latter case, CUTTING can be regarded as the manner component of a verb of Creation 'produce by cutting' as in *Peter* [Agent] *carved a moose* [Product] *out of wood* [Material]. Functions of these two types have not been discussed, but C&B verbs are closely related to verbs of damage (*ruin, destroy*) and there are separation verbs such as *grind* that basically refer to production (*grind flour*).

How the choice of C&B verb is influenced by features of the Whole (typically realized as a grammatical object) has been a recurrent theme and has been discussed in particular in connection with the word sketches. Table 23 refers to some general features. It should be added, that there are examples of languages with classificatory verbs where such features are explicitly marked on the verb (see comments on Klamath, an Amerindian language spoken in Oregon, in Viberg 2007a: 28–29, based on Barker 1963). The characterization of Pieces also focuses on general features. There is a close relationship between Regular and Irregular pieces and Clean and Messy separation. In addition, there are many verbs that refer to very specific types of pieces as shown in Section 9. To a large extent, such distinctions are based on Shape. With respect to Instrument, a major distinction is made between one- and two-bladed instruments. In English, *cut* refers to the use of a bladed instrument in general, whereas the Swedish verbs of cutting obligatorily make a distinction between various types of instrument. In addition, there is large number of verbs in both languages that refer to specific tools such as *saw* and *hack*.

As discussed in connection with the Swedish verbs of cutting, Instrument is closely related to the Manner of motion, in particular different types of hand actions. A major difference between English and Swedish is that *cut* and *break* refer primarily to the result (CLEAN and MESSY separation), whereas Manner of motion is an obligatory component of the most basic Swedish C&B verbs. The extent to which a verb is mainly used as a separation verb or can also be used to refer to hand actions that do not result in separation varies along a continuum. *Bryta* refers to separation by bending. This verb is only marginally used to refer to bending without (irreversible) separation in the expressions *bryta servetter* 'fold napkins' and *bryta ett gevär* 'broach a rifle'. At the other end of the continuum, the hand action is the core component of *hugga* 'hew, chop', a verb that relatively often is used without referring to separation. The English verb *tear* and its Swedish correspondence *riva* basically refer to separation by pulling but can also refer to removal of a whole object from a location by pulling without causing separation.

Many of the features in Table 23 have parallels in the neurolinguistic study by Kemmerer et al. (2008) referred to in Section 2. The study was carried out within the framework of Simulation theory which holds that the interpretation of words results in partial activation of the same sensorimotor areas in the brain as when the referents are directly experienced and, more specifically, that action verbs activate similar areas as the corresponding actions. The findings supported the theory and identified five components of Cutting verbs: ACTION, MOTION, CONTACT, CHANGE OF STATE and TOOL USE. In particular, the use of different tools (cf. Instrument, above) is characteristic of Cutting verbs. Worth special attention is also the information (Kemmerer 2019, 152) that the verbs of cutting activated an area (the fusiform cortex) representing the shape of entities (cf. Pieces, above)

10.2 From conceptual realization to syntactic realization

The features that are characteristic of the frame elements displayed in Table 23 can be realized in the verb and/or in elements outside the verb as shown schematically in Table 24, a modified version of Table 1 in Section 3. The basic idea is that features associated with one of the frame elements in Table 23 can be incorporated into the meaning of the verb. Incorporation fills the same function as conflation in Talmy's (1985) model of the motion situation. Components that have been incorporated into the verb are shown in capitals in the appropriate column.

To account for Swedish constructions of the type V + *sönder* a special slot has been provided for particles. Particles are, of course, used also in English but are not as prominent as in Swedish in the expression of messy separation with *sönder*. The English particle *off* and the Swedish particle *av* are more similar.

Table 24: Syntactic realization of C&B verbs in English and Swedish (schematic).

AGENT	Action	RESULT	WHOLE	PIECES	INSTRUMENT	MANNER
Subject	Predicate		Object	Adjunct	Adjunct	Adjunct
NP	Verb	Particle	NP	PP	PP	PP
Peter	slog	sönder	flaskan			HITTING
Peter	broke	MESSY	the bottle			
Ann	cut	CLEAN	the bread	into slices	with a knife	
Ann	sliced		the bread	SLICE		
Ann	sawed		the log		SAW	

These particles basically refer to one, complete separation that tends to be clean. However, the meanings are rather complex and require a separate study.

11 The representativeness of the data

The patterns of polysemy of *cut* and *break* are so complex that a systematic account of the non-literal meanings will be accounted for in separate studies. In their use as separation verbs, the C&B verbs refer to common everyday phenomena but they are also used in more abstract domains, which affects their use across various registers. To study this variation and to pass a judgment of the representativeness of the data used in this study, samples from the Subtitles corpus were compared with samples from monolingual corpora representing different registers. A random sample of 500 occurrences of the verb *cut* was drawn from Fiction (imaginary prose) and from News in the British National Corpus (with SketchEngine). For Swedish, data were obtained about *skära* from KORP (Borin et al. 2012). Fiction is represented by the complete set of occurrences of *skära* in Novels II (from 1981–82) and News by the complete set of occurrences in DN 1987 (a leading daily newspaper). The distribution of the meanings of *cut* and *skära* across registers is shown in Table 25, where all the occurrences of the verbs are accounted for. Meanings are identified at a coarse level as the semantic field to which the meaning belongs.

The null hypothesis assuming complete independence between verbs, registers, and meanings was rejected at a statistically significant level in a loglinear model ($\chi^2 = 1223$, df = 32, $p < 0.001$). Since frequencies have not been normalized, the frequencies cannot be directly compared. It is only possible to compare the proportions of various meanings across registers (see Diagram 1 and 2).

Table 25: The use of the verbs *cut* and *skära* across registers.

	English *cut*			Swedish *skära*		
	Fiction	News	Subt13	Fiction	News	Subt13
Total	498	448	449	291	255	153
BodyHarm	49	16	123	36	13	98
Other Separation	147	47	107	134	88	41
Motion	31	10	12	5	6	0
Reduction	14	230	14	7	101	4
Verbal	63	0	25	0	0	0
Sensation	3	0	3	26	3	2
OTHER	191	145	165	83	44	8

The total for Fiction and News does not equal 500 since the samples contained several occurrences of the noun *cut* that have been excluded. Such errors were particularly frequent in the News subcorpus.

Diagram 1. Proportions (%) of various meanings of English *cut* across registers

	FICTION	NEWS	SUBTITLES
BodyHarm	10%	4%	27%
Other separation	37%	14%	24%
Motion	6%	2%	3%
Reduction	3%	54%	3%
Verbal	13%	0%	0%
Sensation	1%	0%	0%
Other	31%	26%	45%

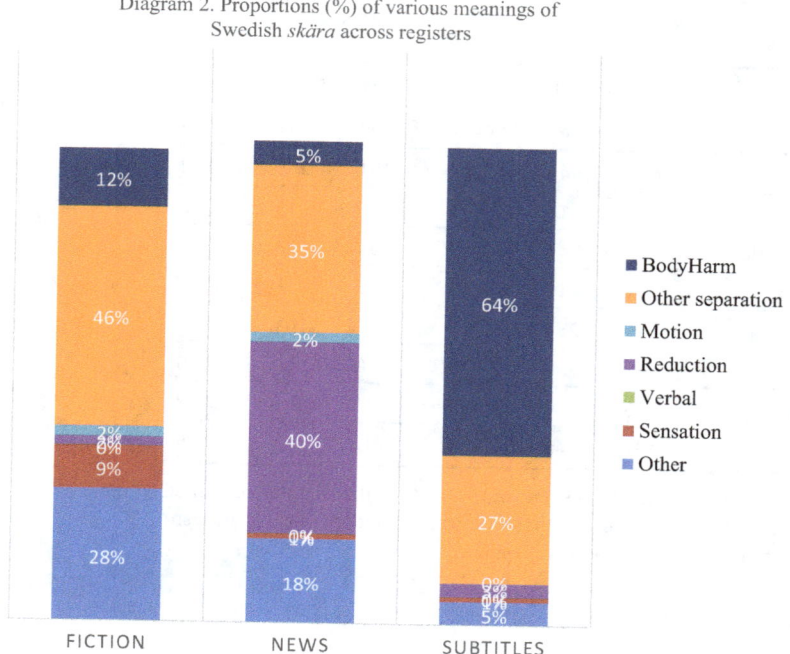

Diagram 2. Proportions (%) of various meanings of Swedish *skära* across registers

Separation, which is divided into BodyHarm and other Separation, accounts for 40% or more of the occurrences in all registers except English News. With that exception, no other semantic field reaches a similar high proportion. (*Other* covers several fields that have not been identified.) Even though the comparison confirms that BodyHarm is characteristic of the Subtitles in both languages, other Separation stands for around 25% of the examples in both English and Swedish, which means that literal meanings are fairly well represented in the Subtitles.

Non-literal meanings are very unevenly distributed across registers. Reduction stands out in News and covers 54% of the occurrences of *cut* and 40% of *skära* in this register. The term refers to a reduction of amounts that can in principle be counted, such as *cut the deficit, cut the workforce*. The frequency of Reduction is low both in Fiction and in the Subtitles. Some further examples are given of meanings that are characteristic of a specific register. Verbal communication is characteristic of English Fiction, where *cut* can be used to introduce a direct report such as: *"We haven't fixed a date yet," she cut in hastily*. Direct reports are in general characteristic of Fiction. *Skära* is not used with this meaning, but *klippa av* (see example 34, above) can be used to refer to an abrupt ending of a conversation. Extensions into the field Motion are more frequent in English than in Swedish, when the verb refers to motion by a human subject in concrete space:

Ann cut across the field. The frequency of this meaning is only moderately high even in English but *cut* appears in many more constructions of that type than Swedish *skära*. Sensation is characteristic of Swedish fiction but does not reach a very high frequency. Often reference is made specifically to physical or emotional Pain as in *det skär i hjärtat* [it cuts in the heart] 'it makes your heart ache'. Meanings that have not been specifically coded are referred to as Other. That category is much more frequent in English than in Swedish and reflects the fact that *cut* has a much wider range of extended meanings than *skära*. The variability of the non-literal meanings is crucial for the description of the full meaning potential of the C&B verbs. In particular, the description of field-external polysemy will require data from several registers.

12 Conclusion and discussion

As stated in the introduction, the primary aim of this paper has been to discuss which research questions are pertinent in the study of a semantic field and how that affects the choice of data and methods of analysis. The first research question, which concerns the patterns of differentiation between the C&B verbs, has been accounted for fairly systematically and summed up in a schematic model of basic semantic distinctions (Table 23) that also makes predictions about possible C&B verbs. The two basic verbs *cut* and *break* in English refer to the result CLEAN and MESSY separation. To choose the correct verb in Swedish requires making further distinctions, such as the indication of different instruments and different hand actions. *Bryta* refers to 'break by bending' and other types of breaking are primarily referred to by the particle *sönder* 'asunder', which can be combined with a large number of manner verbs, even if a few verbs dominate (*ha* '(causative) have' and generalized *slå* 'hit'). The best examples of the three major correspondences of *cut* refer to a bladed instrument: *skära* (KNIFE), *klippa* (SCISSORS) and *hugga* (AX), but even these verbs are associated with different hand actions. The forceful hand action is what *hugga* with an ax, *hugga* with a sword and *hugga* with a knife ('stab') have in common. Tearing, on the other hand, involves a hand action both in English and Swedish ('separate by pulling apart').

The second research question, which concerns the patterns of polysemy and the full meaning potential of the verbs belonging to the field, has only been discussed in broad outline since the meaning potentials of *cut* and *break* are so complex that separate studies are required. When the extension is field-external, C&B serves as a source field and the extended meaning belongs to a target field. Common target fields are Motion, Verbal Communication and Sensation (in particular Pain). At a more fine-grained level, contrasting meanings of C&B verbs within a target field are described.

We will turn now to the three basic problems with data identified in Section 4.1. *Equivalence*, the problem of identifying correspondences across languages, was solved in this study by using a translation corpus. Video elicitation as in Majid and Bowerman (2007) is a good alternative to obtain data that are comparable across languages. Similarly, video elicitation is a very useful complement to learner corpora in the study of second-language learners with first languages that contrast with respect to the basic semantic distinctions made in a specific semantic field (see Viberg 1998 for Swedish verbs of putting and Viberg 1996 for the Swedish C&B verbs *skära*, *klippa* and *riva*).

Authenticity meets with problems due to translation effects. Translated subtitles differ in certain respects from original texts (see Section 4.2). Clear mistranslation also occurs. Video elicitation solves the problem with translation effects. In the present study, monolingual corpora were used to counterbalance the influence of possible translation effects.

Representativeness can often be achieved by using corpora as a data source but certain types of corpora are still scarce. As demonstrated in Section 11, the various uses of a word can vary dramatically depending on the register. Large translation corpora today exist only for a restricted number of registers, which makes it essential to use monolingual comparative corpora as a complement. However, many uses of C&B verbs are characteristic of everyday spoken language. This introduces a problem since corpora of authentic conversation are often lacking in large enough quantities in many languages such as Swedish, for which large written corpora are available. Film subtitles partly fill the need for such data since they represent language written to be spoken and often are colloquial in style. However, elicitation with video clips has the advantage that genuinely spoken language data are produced. On the other hand, the selection of video clips is done by the researcher(s). It is difficult to assure that the stimuli cover the most typical events across the compared set of languages. When studying languages for which large corpora are available, corpus data represent many individual users and are based on texts that originally were produced for purposes independent of the research questions. Another limitation of video elicitation is that many non-literal meanings are difficult to illustrate in a video, if that is required. The coverage of the full meaning potential requires very large data sets for frequent verbs such as *cut* and *break* with many meanings and functions. In the ongoing study of the patterns of polysemy, it has turned out that subtitles contain many examples of colloquial uses of *cut* + Particle (e.g. *cut out*, *cut down*) which can take on a rich variety of meanings.

Manual coding of the complete set of concordance lines in samples from various corpora was combined with automatic searches that produced word sketches. Manual coding is time-consuming and can only be carried out on limited samples, but the accuracy is high since each occurrence of an item is interpreted in its specific context. Word sketches can be carried out on very large (multi-billion) corpora. In this study, word sketches have primarily been used to identify characteristic types of objects, since there is a close relationship between the literal meaning of a C&B verb and the type of object. The top-ranked subjects are often good for identifying extended and abstract meanings since such meanings tend to form idiom-like combinations (see Section 5.4 on *break* and *bryta*) but do not always give a good picture of the most productive types of combinations. Data of this type are particularly useful for the analysis of the patterns of polysemy. More information can be gained from word sketches of the most frequent words than has been done in this study but that must be left for separate studies.

Acknowledgement: I would like to thank Marc Tang for help with the loglinear testing in Section 11 and Jörg Tiedemann for help with the Subtitles corpora and the editors and two anonymous reviewers for valuable comments on the paper as a whole.

References

Aijmer, Karin, Bengt Altenberg & Mats Johansson (eds.). 1996. *Languages in contrast. Papers from a symposium on text-based cross-linguistic studies*. [Lund Studies in English 88] Lund: Lund University Press.

Allwood, Jens. 2003. Meaning potential and context. Some consequences for the analysis of variation in meaning. In Hubert Cuyckens, René Dirven & John A. Taylor (eds.), *Cognitive approaches to lexical semantics*, 29–65. Berlin: Mouton de Gruyter.

Altenberg, Bengt & Karin Aijmer. 2000. The English-Swedish Parallel Corpus: A resource for contrastive research and translation studies. In Christian Mair & Marianne Hundt (eds.), *Corpus linguistics and linguistic theory*, 15–23. Amsterdam & Atlanta, GA: Rodopi.

Andersson, Lars-Gunnar. 2007. Göra, ha eller ta sönder [Do, have or take asunder]. In *Språkets roll och räckvidd. Festskrift till Staffan Hellberg den 18 februari 2007*, 25–34. Department of Swedish, Gothenburg University.

Barker, M. A. R. 1963. *Klamath dictionary*. Berkeley & Los Angelses: University of California Press.

Borin, Lars, Magnus Forsberg & Johan Roxendal. 2012. Korp – the corpus infrastructure of Språkbanken. http://www.lrec-conf.org/proceedings/lrec2012/pdf/248_Paper.pdf. (accessed 13 November 2018).

Bouveret, Myriam & Eve Sweetser. 2009. Multi-frame semantics, metaphoric extensions and grammar. In *Proceedings of the 35th Annual Berkeley Linguistics Society*, 49–60. University of California, Berkeley.

Brown, J. Tom 1925. Setswana-English dictionary. Reprinted 1982. Johannesburg: Pula Press.
Dodge, Ellen K. 2016. A deep semantic corpus-based approach to metaphor analysis. A case study of metaphoric conceptualizations of poverty. *Constructions and Frames* 8(2). 256–294.
Fausey, Caitlin M. & Lera Boroditsky. 2011. Who dunnit? Cross-linguistic differences in eye-witness memory. *Psychonomic bulletin & review* 18. 150–157.
Fillmore, Charles J. 1982. Frame Semantics. In The Linguistic Society of Korea (ed.), *Linguistics in the Morning Calm*, 111–138. Seoul: Hanshin Publishing.
Fujii, Seiko, Paula Radetzky & Eve Sweetser. 2013. Separation verbs and multi-frame semantics. In Mike Borkent, Barbara Dancygier & Jennifer Hinnell (eds.), *Language and the creative mind*, 137–153. Stanford, CA: CSLI Publications.
Geeraerts, Dirk. 2010. *Theories of lexical semantics*. Oxford: Oxford University Press.
Gross, Steven. 2016. (Descriptive) Externalism in semantics. In Nick Riemer (ed.), *The Routledge handbook of semantics*, 13–29. London & New York: Routledge.
Johansson, Stig. 2007. *Seeing through multilingual corpora*. Amsterdam & Philadelphia: John Benjamins.
Kemmerer, David. 2019. *Concepts in the brain. The view from cross-linguistic diversity*. Oxford, Oxford University Press.
Kemmerer, David, Javier Gonzalez-Castillo, Thomas Talavage, Stephanie Patterson & Cynthia Wiley. 2008. Neuroanatomical distribution of five semantic components of verbs: Evidence from fMRI. *Brain & Language 107*, 16–43.
Keuleers, Emmanuel, Marc Brysbaert & Boris New. 2010. SUBTLEX-NL: A new measure for Dutch word frequency based on film subtitles. *Behavior Research Methods* 42(3). 643–650.
Kilgariff, Adam & David Tugwell. 2002. Sketching words. In Marie Hélène Corréard (ed.), *Lexicography and natural language processing. A festschrift in honour of B.T.S. Atkins*, 125–137. Göteborg: EURALEX.
Kittilä, Seppo. 2005. Remarks on involuntary agent constructions. *Word* 56(3). 381–419.
Lakoff, George & Mark Johnson. 1980. *Metaphors we live by*. Chicago: University of Chicago Press.
Levshina, Natalia. 2016. Verbs of letting in Germanic and Romance languages: a quantitative investigation based on a parallel corpus of film subtitles. *Languages in Contrast* 16(1). 84–117.
Levshina, Natalia. 2017. Online film subtitles as a corpus: an n-gram approach. *Corpora* 12(3). 311–338.
Lison, Pierre & Jörg Tiedemann. 2016. OpenSubtitles2016: extracting large parallel corpora from movie and TV subtitles. In Nicoletta Calzolari, Khalid Choukri, Thierry Declerck, Sara Goggi, Marko Grobelnik, Bente Maegaard, Joseph Mariani, Hélène Mazo, Asunción Moreno, Jan Odijk & Stelios Piperidis (eds.), *Proceedings of the 10th International Conference on Language Resources and Evaluation (LREC 2016)*, 923–929. Paris: European Language Resources Association.
Majid, Asifa, James S. Boster & Melissa Bowerman. 2008. The cross-linguistic categorization of everyday events: A study of cutting and breaking. *Cognition* 109. 235–250.
Majid, Asifa & Melissa Bowerman (eds.). 2007. Cutting and breaking events: A crosslinguistic perspective. [Special issue]. *Cognitive Linguistics* 18(2).
Majid, Asifa, Melissa Bowerman, Miriam van Staden & James S. Boster. 2007. The semantic categories of cutting and breaking events: A crosslinguistic perspective. *Cognitive Linguistics* 18(2). 133–152.

Majid, Asifa, Marianne Gullberg, Miriam van Staden & Melissa Bowerman. 2007. How similar are semantic categories in closely related languages? A comparison of cutting and breaking in four Germanic languages. *Cognitive Linguistics* 18(2). 179–194.
Malt, Barbara C., Silvia Gennari & Mutsumi Imai. 2010. Lexicalization patterns and the world-to-words mapping. In Barbara C. Malt & Phillip Wollf (eds.), *Words and the mind. How words capture human experience*, 29–57. New York & Oxford: Oxford University Press.
Miller, George A. & Philip Johnson-Laird. 1976. *Language and perception*. Cambridge, MA: Harvard University Press.
Reznikova, Tatiana, Ekaterina Rakhilina & Anastasia Bonch-Osmolovskaya. 2012. Towards a typology of pain predicates. *Linguistics* 50(3). 421–465.
Riemer, Nick. 2016. Internalist semantics: meaning, conceptualization and expression. In Nick Riemer (ed.), *The Routledge handbook of semantics*, 30–47. London & New York: Routledge.
Summers, Della (ed.). 2001. *Longman dictionary of contemporary English*. 3rd ed. Harlow: Pearson.
Talmy, Leonard. 1985. Lexicalization patterns: semantic structure in lexical forms. In Timothy Shopen (ed.), *Language typology and syntactic description. III. Grammatical categories and the lexicon*, 57–149. Cambridge: Cambridge University Press.
Viberg, Åke. 1985. Hel och trasig. En skiss av några verbal semantiska fält i svenskan. [Whole and broken. A sketch of some semantic fields in Swedish]. In *Svenskans beskrivning* 15. 529–554.
Viberg, Åke. 1996. The study of lexical patterns in L2 oral production. In Kari Sajavaara & Cortney Fairweather (eds.), *Approaches to second language acquisition*, 87–107. (Proceedings from EUROSLA 2 in Jyväskylä June 1992.) [Jyväskylä Cross-Language Studies 17]. Jyväskylä University, Finland.
Viberg, Åke. 1998. Crosslinguistic perspectives on lexical acquisition: the case of language-specific semantic differentiation. In Kirsten Haastrup & Åke Viberg (eds.), *Perspectives on lexical acquisition in a second language*, 175–208. [Travaux de l'institut de linguistique de Lund 38]. Lund: Lund University Press.
Viberg, Åke. 2007a. Whole and broken. Breaking and cutting in Swedish from a crosslinguistic perspective. In Elisabeth Ahlsén, Peter Juel Henrichsen, Richard Hirsch, Joakim Nivre, Åsa Abelin, Sven Strömqvist, Shirley Nicholson (eds.), *Communication – action – meaning. A Festschrift to Jens Allwood*, 17–42. Gothenburg University: Department of Linguistics.
Viberg, Åke. 2007b. Wordnets, framenets and corpus-based contrastive lexicology. In Pierre Nugues & Richard Johansson (eds.), *FRAME 2007: Building frame semantics resources for Scandinavian and Baltic languages*, 1–10. Department of Computer Science, Lund University.
Viberg, Åke. 2012. Language-specific meanings in contrast. A corpus-based contrastive study of Swedish *få* 'get'. *Linguistics* 50(6). 1413–1461.
Viberg, Åke. 2016a: What happens in translation? A comparison of original and translated texts containing verbs meaning SIT, STAND and LIE in the English-Swedish Parallel Corpus (ESPC). *Nordic Journal of English Studies (NJES)* 15(3). 102–148. http://ojs.ub.gu.se/ojs/index.php/njes (accessed March 2019)
Viberg, Åke. 2016b. Polysemy in action: The Swedish verb *slå* 'hit, strike, beat' in a crosslinguistic perspective. In Päivi Juvonen & Maria Koptjevskaja-Tamm (eds.), *Semantic shifts*, 177–222. Berlin: Mouton de Gruyter.

Electronic sources

BYU-BNC. British National Corpus: http://corpus.byu.edu/bnc/
ESPC. *The English Swedish Parallel Corpus*. http://www.englund.lu.se/content/view/66/127/
Film subtitles: http://opus.lingfil.uu.se/ http://www.opensubtitles.org
FrameNet: http://www.icsi.berkeley.edu/~framenet/
KORP. http://spraakbanken.gu.se
OED. Oxford English Dictionary. http://www.oed.com/
SAOB. Svenska Akademiens Ordbok. [The Dictionary of the Swedish Academy]
    https://www.saob.se/
Sketch Engine: http://sketchengine.co.uk

www.ingramcontent.com/pod-product-compliance
Lightning Source LLC
Chambersburg PA
CBHW070753230426
43665CB00017B/2335